PRAISE FOR *BANANAS, BEACHES AND BASES*

"This is the work of a well-traveled feminist mulling over the inequalities of the postmodern world. In a lively overview of tourism, the food industry, army bases, nationalism, diplomacy, global factories, and domestic work, Enloe persuasively argues that gender is key to the workings of international relations."

—Aihwa Ong, University of California, Berkeley

"This new edition of *Bananas, Beaches and Bases* demonstrates beyond all doubt the enduring brilliance of Cynthia Enloe's fastidious documenting of women's lives as they shape and are shaped by the power-play of international politics. In sharpening and freshening feminist curiosity in the contemporary period, this edition reminds us of both the stubborn tenacity of gendered inequality as it is etched into everyday life and, in more optimistic terms, the potentially transformative capacity with which women's lives inhere. A gritty yet erudite text illuminating the international topography of the current-day global gender regime that is of interest to fresh eyes as well as readers looking to get a handle on patriarchy's mutability."

—Paul Higate, Reader in Gender and Security at the School for Sociology, Politics and International Studies, the University of Bristol and editor of *Military Masculinities: Identity and the State*

"This book is a rare gem. International relations will never look the same again. Through *Bananas, Beaches and Bases* and the many lives women live, Cynthia Enloe most persuasively shows that global politics is not where it is supposed to be. This updated edition of this classic is very welcome indeed."

—Jef Huysmans, Professor of Security Studies, The Open University (UK)

"Cynthia Enloe's unparalleled skill in making the everyday lives of women visible in and relevant to international politics is on full display as she employs her feminist curiosity to challenge the boundaries of the "international." Listening carefully and not afraid to admit surprise, Enloe weaves a tapestry of stories that reveal the workings of power from the personal to the political and back. Her sustained and deeply political engagement with women from all walks of life— all over the world—makes us genuinely smarter about global politics. You will not be able to put this book down."

 —Annick T. R. Wibben, author of *Feminist Security Studies: A Narrative Approach*

"With *Bananas, Beaches and Bases*, Cynthia Enloe sparked an immense paradigm shift and produced multiple wildfires of feminist scholarship, from international relations to political economy to feminist theory. Now another generation of students, activists, and scholars can be made "smarter" with this new edition of this essential text."

 —Ethel Brooks, professor of Women's and Gender Studies and Sociology, Rutgers University

"Cynthia Enloe is unequaled in her ability to make feminist sense of international politics. This groundbreaking book illustrates the inadequacies of analytic frames that do not take the workings of gendered power seriously, arguing persuasively that the most complex and comprehensive understandings of international politics must be fueled by feminist curiosity. A compelling, lucid, and engaging book—a must for all our bookshelves."

—Chandra Talpade Mohanty, Author of Feminism *Without Borders: Decolonizing Theory, Practicing Solidarity*

Bananas, Beaches and Bases

Bananas, Beaches and Bases

Making Feminist Sense of
International Politics

Cynthia Enloe

Second Edition
Completely Revised and Updated

UNIVERSITY OF CALIFORNIA PRESS
Berkeley Los Angeles London

University of California Press, one of the most distin-
guished university presses in the United States, enriches
lives around the world by advancing scholarship in the
humanities, social sciences, and natural sciences. Its
activities are supported by the UC Press Foundation and
by philanthropic contributions from individuals and
institutions. For more information, visit www.ucpress.edu.

University of California Press
Berkeley and Los Angeles, California

University of California Press, Ltd.
London, England

Library of Congress Cataloging-in-Publication Data

Enloe, Cynthia H., 1938–
    Bananas, beaches and bases: making feminist sense of
international politics/Cynthia Enloe.
—Second edition, Completely Revised and Updated.
        pages   cm
    Includes bibliographical references and index.
    ISBN 978-0-520-27999-5 (paperback)
    ISBN 978-0-520-95728-2 (ebook)
        1. Women—Political activity.   2. International
relations.   3. Feminist theory.   I. Title.
    HQ1236.E55 2014
    320.082—dc23

                                        2014009218

Manufactured in the United States of America

23   22   21   20   19   18   17   16   15   14
10   9   8   7   6   5   4   3   2   1

In keeping with a commitment to support environmen-
tally responsible and sustainable printing practices, UC
Press has printed this book on Natures Natural, a fiber
that contains 30% post-consumer waste and meets the
minimum requirements of ANSI/NISO z39.48–1992 (R 1997)
(*Permanence of Paper*).

For Joni

CONTENTS

ILLUSTRATIONS

PREFACE TO THE SECOND EDITION

There were exposed plumbing pipes overhead. It all seemed very precarious. If any of them sprung a leak, water would wash away the history of British women's political activism. This was the Fawcett Library in London in the years before it became what it now is, the Women's Library, wonderfully housed at the London School of Economics. But it was the below-the-pipes (and below-the-pavement) atmosphere that gave me the sense that I was on the edge, uncovering a layer of international political life that had been kept out of sight. Well, not out of sight of feminist historians. They had already begun to do their own excavations, bringing Mary Wollstonecraft, Josephine Butler, Mary Seacole, and the Pankhursts up to the surface for all of us to see, to think about afresh.

But I was an unenlightened political scientist. For me, getting down on my knees to read Butler's descriptions of nineteenth-century military prostitution, filed in boxes sitting under those water pipes, was thrilling. Thanks to the archivists at the Fawcett Library—and their energetic counterparts at the Thomas Cook travel library and the Schlesinger Library on the History of Women in America, at Radcliffe Institute, Harvard University—international politics would never look the same to me again.

In recent decades, hardworking and irreverent researchers, teachers, and writers—women and men—have revealed that making diverse women visible exposes the actual workings of international politics. Women as Chinese businessmen's mistresses, women sewing clothes for Tommy Hilfiger and washing pesticides off Chiquita's bananas, women married to CIA operatives, women working in discos around military bases, women auditioning for the Miss World contest, women scrubbing floors in Saudi Arabia, and women lobbying delegates in the corridors of the UN—they observe, they cope, they calculate, they strategize, and sometimes they organize. Here is what I've learned from taking these women seriously: if we pay sustained attention to each and all of these unheadlined women, we will become smarter about this world, smarter than a lot of mainstream "experts."

Smarter. I've thought a lot about what it means to become smarter. I don't think it means simply to become more clever, more facile, more hip. It sometimes means to become more cautious. It certainly means to become more nuanced in one's explanations. And *nuanced* does not mean vague. It means capable of describing with clarity the multiple relationships at work and their consequences.

To become smarter in the feminist sense of *smarter,* one therefore has to constantly stretch one's gender curiosity. Asking "Where are the women?" won't necessarily reap instant or superficial rewards. In fact, one might feel as though one is risking one's status as a serious person when asking where the women are—and why they are there, who is benefiting from their being there, and what they think about being there. One's mentor, editor, or boss may make it clear that he or she considers spending one's time pursuing these gender questions a waste.

Becoming smarter in this feminist sense will not make us more comfortable. We are likely to start wondering about our own complicity in the makings of this world's dysfunctions, its inequalities, its abuses and injustices. For we are not simply readers and questioners standing above or outside what we are exploring. We are living in this world. Even if we don't think of ourselves as members of an elite (although if we are able to read this page, we are indeed among the world's privileged), our ideas and actions are helping shape this world. We have our own relationships to all the women whose lives we are trying to understand. That should stoke the fires of our feminist curiosity, but it should also make us uneasy.

In making women visible, I've discovered, one turns a bright light on men-as-men. It has been feminist-informed investigations of international politics that have yielded the most valuable insights into the complex politics of masculinities. That is plural. But the meanings assigned to different ways for a boy or a man to demonstrate his manliness are not merely multiple; they usually are unequal and often rivals to each other. Disparaging certain kinds of femininities is common fodder in these rankings and contests. This is a key motivation for anyone exploring the international politics of masculinities to adopt an explicitly feminist curiosity.

All the women and men who have tried to make us genuinely smarter about international politics have revealed that what is "international" is far broader than mainstream experts assume, and that what is "political" reaches well beyond the public square. Sometimes taking these two new understandings on board has made my head spin. But it also has energized me.

Redrawing the map of international politics has made the investigations into, and the conversations about, those politics a lot more lively. For me, that has been one of the genuine joys of being part of this collaborative, transnational feminist exploratory journey. Many more people, certainly a lot more women, are now in the conversation. They are adding their own stories, experiences, puzzles, and findings to that conversation. The windows and doors have been thrown wide open.

Well, they should be.

Having the good luck to be able to track the international politics of women's lives and of ideas about masculinities and femininities over several decades has reinforced a hunch I had early on: *patriarchy is ingeniously adaptable.*

I remember when I first began to hear the French phrase "Plus les choses changent, plus elles deviennent les memes"— which was usually shortened by the speakers to merely "plus ça change …," as if the sophisticated listener should be able to fill in the rest. "The more things change, the more they stay the same." Usually it was uttered with a sigh and a shrug (a "Gallic shrug," even if the speaker wasn't French). The people who said it seemed to the young, insecure me to be so worldly, so all-knowing. They had been around. They rarely admitted surprise. They seemed so smart. But as I spent more time digging away in feminist archives and taking part in conversations with women activists from Turkey, Iceland, Canada, Korea, Okinawa, Norway, Britain, and the United States, I came to be suspicious when I heard that world-weary phrase. It began to sound lazy rather than smart. It started to sound merely like a reason for not being curious, for not paying close attention.

So when I say that one thing that doing this latest digging has led me to conclude is that patriarchy is remarkably adaptable, I do not want to imply that it's the "same old, same old." Quite the contrary. Making patriarchy sustainable has, I think, taken a lot of thinking and maneuvering by those who have a vested interest in privileging particular forms of masculinity to appear "modern" and even "cutting edge" while simultaneously keeping most women in their subordinate places. They have not used only intimidation and outright coercion—though certainly some of those who feel endangered by challenges to patriarchy have wielded both. They have also used updated language ("our sons and daughters in uniform"), the arts of tokenism (two women in a cabinet of twenty), and the practices of cooptation (consumers offered low-cost clothes so they will lose interest in Bangladeshi factory women's working conditions). To investigate how any patriarchal system's beneficiaries try to sustain that system of gendered meanings and gendered practices requires not smug world-weariness. It calls for renewed energy, refueled collaborations. Oh, and a readiness to be surprised.

I hope readers will put a bookmark where the back notes in this book begin and flip regularly to them. For the harried, distracted reader, it is easy to imagine that notes are just the technical trappings of an academic book. But they're more, much more than that. People who write books put a lot of work into their notes, and not just to prove they are true-blue academics. They hope their readers—you—will follow up on their noted leads. I see notes as bread crumbs, added to help curious readers do their own tracking. Starting with these noted sources, readers can launch their own investigations into American soldiers' uses of brothels in postinvasion France, into the difficult choices that migrant domestic workers are making, into where women are in today's global trade in fruit.

Notes also are an extended thank-you. I am indebted to every one of the researchers and writers whose perceptive works I've cited here.

This book was begun at a heady moment in feminist publishing and bookselling. While I was writing the original version, I was browsing and buying books and journals—those revealing women's ideas and experiences—on the shelves of feminist bookstores. The fact that so many larger presses and larger booksellers today publish and offer feminist-informed books and magazines is due to the pioneering work of feminist publishers and feminist booksellers, who broke new ground in those exciting years. Today I still am a fan and almost daily customer of my local independent bookstore, Porter Square Books. To its book-loving staff, thank you.

One of the lasting legacies of those years has been the ever-expanding circle of feminist thinkers, students, and researchers in the far-reaching Feminist Theory and Gender Studies section of the International Studies Association. When we see each other, we trade hunches and findings; we encourage each other in our continuing investigations into the workings of patriarchy in all its guises. And we laugh. Whoever imagines that "feminists don't have a sense of humor" clearly has never hung out with feminist researchers.

During recent months I have garnered fresh insights that inform this book from Ximena Bunster, Sohaila Abdulali, Madeleine Rees, Nadine Peuchguirbal, Ray Achison, Sarah Taylor, Marie Butler, Abigail Ruane, Ann Tickner, Sandra Harding, Ayse Gul Altinay, Cynthia Cockburn, Carol Cohn, Jeff Ballinger, Elora Chowdhury, Gai Liewkeat, Wenona Giles, Ethel Brooks, Gwyn Kirk, Tess Ewing, David Vine, Insook Kwon, Terrell Carver, Gyoung Sun Jang, Sandra McEvoy, Katherine

Moon, Catherine Lutz, Lois Wasserspring, Lepa Mladjenovic, Aaron Belkin, Ruri Ito, Ailbhe Smyth, Rela Mazali, Sandra Whitworth, Victoria Basham, Pat Ould, Vanessa Ruget, Annadis Rudolfsdottir, Vron Ware, Nhung Dinh, Mikaela Luttrell-Rowland, Teresia Teaiwa, Fumika Sato, Kimberly Khanhauser, and Aleen Grabow. A steady stream of juicy press clippings has come my way from my British friends Debbie Licorish and Bob Benewick. At Clark University, my good colleagues Valerie Sperling, Kristen Williams, Anita Fabos, and Denise Bebbington, dedicated teachers all, have generously nudged me to keep exploring the gendered politics of contemporary international affairs with students.

Julie Clayton has, as ever, been a miracle worker, tracking down hard-to-find photographs and doing such a skilled job in formatting the entire manuscript.

The first publisher of *Bananas* was Pandora Press, a small, innovative feminist British publisher. I was, I confess, nervous when I learned that the American publisher most interested in copublishing it would be a major university press. I thought to myself: Oh, but then activist women and profeminist men will never see the book. I was wrong. I was missing a crucial development: feminists were rising into the ranks of influential editors inside many university presses. Naomi Schneider, now executive editor at the University of California Press, has been a believer in *Bananas*, making sure that it would be available to a wide and diverse range of interested readers. It was Naomi who convinced me to look anew at all the topics and questions here, to undertake this thorough updating and revision. Only Naomi could have persuaded me. Also on the skilled publishing team that has turned this newly updated manuscript into the handsome book you are holding are Kate Warne, Claudia Smelser,

Christopher Lura, Elena McAnespie, and Bonita Hurd. I am indebted to each of them.

None of us research and write books in a vacuum. I'm not a writer who heads for the mythical cabin-in-the-woods. All during this digging and composing, I've been seeing friends, sharing my puzzles, absorbing their ideas. You know who you are. You are the best. Thanks.

Joni Seager has been across the hall here in our Cambridge apartment writing about Rachel Carson's classic, still-salient *Silent Spring* at the same time that I've been writing about today's activists, world-traveling tourists, and domestic workers. Every day we've called out to each other: "You won't believe this!" Joni was here when I first began to wonder what I would uncover if I started peeling back the gendered international politics of bananas. We're still here together, still digging, still exclaiming, still laughing.

PREFACE TO THE FIRST EDITION

I began this book thinking about Pocahontas and ended it mulling over the life of Carmen Miranda. Pocahontas is buried in World's End cemetery, England. Carmen Miranda has a museum dedicated to her in Rio. Neither is the usual starting point for thoughts about contemporary international politics, but each woman made me think in new ways about just how international politics works.

Pocahontas was a Powhatan Indian, the daughter of a tribal chief who acted as an intermediary between her own people and colonizing Englishmen; she later married one of these English settlers and traveled to London, as if confirming that the colonial enterprise was indeed a civilizing mission. She never returned to her New World homeland, however, for she died of civilization's coal dust in her lungs.

Carmen Miranda lived three centuries later, but her life has remarkable parallels with her Indian foresister's. She was a Brazilian grocer's daughter who became a Hollywood star and the symbol of an American president's Latin American policy.

She died prematurely of a heart attack, perhaps brought on by the frenzied pace of life in the fast lane of America's pop culture.

These women were not the sorts of international actors I had been taught to take seriously when trying to make sense of world affairs. But the more I thought about Pocahontas and Carmen Miranda, the more I began to suspect that I had been missing an entire dimension of international politics—I got an inkling of how relations between governments depend not only on capital and weaponry but also on the control of women as symbols, consumers, workers, and emotional comforters. I also began to see that brand names like Benetton and Chiquita Banana are more than merely vehicles for making international politics relevant to the already harried book-buyer. These logos, and the processes by which they have been created, marketed, and assigned meaning, expose another neglected international *political* relationship. Here I consider women-as-consumers in both industrialized and Third World countries, as global political actors. Furthermore, as tourism demonstrates, companies and their government allies are marketing things not usually thought of as "consumer goods": tropical beaches, women's sexuality, the services of flight attendants.

The chapters that follow are just a beginning. Other feminists are also seeking a better explanation of why international politics operate in the ways they do. Some of the most exciting work is being done by Third World feminist theorists, such as Swasti Mitter, Chandra Mohanty, and Peggy Antrobus. As the notes make clear, I am especially indebted to these pioneers. Those whom Adrienne Rich has referred to as "the women in the back rows of politics" are about to be given the serious attention they have long deserved. All of us, as a result, are likely to become much smarter and more realistic about what kinds of power have constructed the international political system as we know it. From these revelations may come fresh proposals for making relations between countries less violent, more just, and ultimately more rewarding for women as well as men.

The idea for this book grew out of conversations with Philippa Brewster, friend and director of Pandora Press—conversations which ranged from feminist musings about polyester fashions and film stars to puzzling over the international politics of feminist publishing. One thing became more and more clear as this sometimes daunting project evolved: it makes a big difference to work with feminist editors. Candida Lacey, the editor for this book, has been of inestimable help in keeping it focused, never forgetting the audience, always remembering the wider world beyond the author's study or the editor's office. We have wrinkled our brows together over the stickier analytical points, and we have laughed out loud over some of the more bizarre discoveries.

It is probably a bit insane to take on the topics covered in this book. It has only been possible to make the attempt because I have had the wise and generous support of insightful friends and colleagues. First and foremost has been Joni Seager, coauthor of the groundbreaking feminist atlas, *Women in the World*. There was much less chance of my slipping into parochial assumptions with her as a constant sounding board, reading every chapter, passing on gems of information that a mere political scientist would never have seen. Others who have read chapters and given me valuable suggestions—and caveats—include Margaret Bluman, Laura Zimmerman, Serena Hilsinger, Ximena Bunster, and Margaret Lazarus. Superb copyediting has been done by Daphne Tagg. Margaret Bluman, my agent for this book, has also encouraged me to think that the questions posed were important ones for women committed to genuine social change.

A political scientist is often a bit intimidated by historians and archivists. But as I pursued my hunches about the light that Pocahontas and Carmen Miranda might shed on international politics, I knew I had to tread on historians' ground. No one made me feel more at home in this adventure than David Doughan, librarian of the Fawcett Library, that treasure house of surprising information about British and imperial women's history. Ann Englehart and Barbara Haber both encouraged me to make full use of the splendid resources of Radcliffe College's Schlesinger Library. Edmund Swinglehurst, of the Thomas Cook Archives in London, opened up the world of tourism history. In addition to my own digging, I was aided by the research skills of my brother, David Enloe, as well as Lauran Schultz, Shari Geistfeld, and Deb Dunn.

Among the many others who shared their special knowledge with me were Beryl Smedley, Gay Murphy, Mary Ann White, Pam Moffat, Nien Ling Lieu, Susan Parsons, Saralee Hamilton, Jacqui Alexander, Georgina Ashworth, Sr. Soledad Perpinan, Raquel Tiglao, Theresa Capellan, Elizabeth Odour, Lucy Laliberte, Wendy Mishkin, Peter Armitage, Cortez Enloe, Philippe Bourgois, Lois Wasserspring, Ann Holder, Saundra Studevant, Carolyn Becraft, Elaine Salo, Elaine Burns, Mary McGinn, Sandina Robbins, Nira Yuval Davis, Christine White, Sidney Mintz, Linda Richter, Rachel Kurian, Laurel Bossen, Beth Schwartz, Peg Strobel, Janice Hill, Julie Wheelwright, Antoinette Burton, Sally Davis, Patrick Miller, Anita Nesiah, Joanne Liddle, and Eva Isaksson.

Over the three years during which this book has taken shape I have had my share of misgivings. Generous friends not only have put up with my occasionally odd preoccupation, but have reminded me of the point of pursuing feminist puzzles. So I am, as ever, indebted to each of them for their daily acts of friendship, especially Joni Seager, Gilda Bruckman, Judy Wachs, Serena Hilsinger, and Lois Brynes.

CHAPTER ONE

Gender Makes the World Go Round

Where Are the Women?

Perhaps you have never imagined what it would feel like if you were a woman fleeing your home with your young children, escaping a violent conflict between government troops and rebel soldiers, crossing a national border, pitching a tent in a muddy refugee camp, and then being treated by aid staff workers as though you and the children you are supporting were indistinguishable, "womenandchildren."

Maybe, if any of your aunts or grandmothers have told you stories about having worked as domestic servants, you can more easily picture what your daily life would be like if you had left your home country to take a live-in job caring for someone else's little children or their aging parents. You can almost imagine the emotions you would feel if you were to Skype across time zones to your own children every week, but you cannot be sure how you would react when your employer insisted upon taking possession of your passport.

It probably feels like a stretch to see yourself working in a disco outside a foreign military base. It is hard to think about

Figure 1. Egyptian women protesting sexual harassment hold up signs in Arabic and English, Cairo, 2013. Photo: OPantiSH.

how you would try to preserve some modicum of dignity for yourself in the narrow space left between the sexualized expectations of your foreign male soldier-clients and the demands of the local disco owner who takes most of your earnings.

While you might daydream about becoming a senior foreign policy expert in your country's diplomatic corps, you may deliberately shy away from thinking about whether you will be able to sustain a relationship with a partner while you pursue this ambition. You try not to think about whether your partner will be willing to cope with both diplomacy's social demands and the pressures you together will endure living in a proverbial media fishbowl.

If you keep up with the world news, you may be able to put yourself in the shoes of a women's rights activist in Cairo, but how would you decide whether to paint your protest sign only in Arabic or to add an English translation of your political message just so that CNN and Reuters viewers around the world can see that your revolutionary agenda includes not only toppling the current oppressive regime but also pursuing specifically feminist goals?

As hard as this will be, it will take all of this imagining—and more—if you are going to make reliable sense of international politics. Stretching your imagination, though, will not be enough. Making feminist sense of international politics requires that you exercise genuine curiosity about each of these women's lives—and the lives of women you have yet to think about. And that curiosity will have to fuel energetic detective work, careful digging into the complex experiences and ideas of domestic workers, hotel chambermaids, women's rights activists, women diplomats, women married to diplomats, women who are the mistresses of male elites, women sewing-machine operators, women who have become sex workers, women soldiers, women forced to become refugees, and women working on agribusiness plantations.

That is, making useful sense—feminist sense—of international politics requires us to follow diverse women to places that are usually dismissed by conventional foreign affairs experts as merely "private," "domestic," "local," or "trivial." As we will discover, however, a disco can become an arena for international politics. So can someone else's kitchen or your own closet.

And so can a secretary's desk. Consider, for instance, women who work as secretaries in foreign affairs ministries. They are treated by most political commentators as if they were no more interesting than the standard-issue furniture. But women as secretaries have played interesting roles in international events as significant as the controversial Iran-Contra Affair, which exposed the clandestine American military intervention in Nicaragua in the 1980s, and as the secret Israel-Palestine peace negotiations in Oslo in the 1990s. Who pays attention to women as clerical workers when, allegedly, it is elite men (and a handful of elite women) who determine the fates of nations? Feminist researchers do. They challenge the conventional presumption that paying attention to women as secretaries tells us nothing about the dynamics of high-level politics. Feminist-informed investigators pay attention to low-status secretarial women because they have learned that paying attention to (listening to, taking seriously the observations of) women in these scarcely noticed jobs can pull back the curtain on the political workings in lofty state affairs. Devoting attention to women who are government secretaries, for instance, exposes the far-reaching political consequences of feminized loyalty, feminized secrecy, feminized record-keeping, feminized routine, masculinized status, and masculinized control.[1]

Thanks to innovative research by feminist-informed scholars, we know to look for secretaries throughout international politics. For instance, we recently have learned that in the 1920s and 1930s, some enterprising women—German, British, Dutch—pursued jobs in the newly launched League of Nations, the international organization founded in the wake of horrific World War I to remake interstate relations. These women were breaking new ground not only by becoming the first international civil servants but also by, as women, pursuing their own careers far from home. Working as secretaries and also as librarians, these women were the ones who ensured that the League of Nations documents would be produced and archived professionally. Because of these staff women's efforts, we now can launch our provocative reassessments of the League as a site not only for preventing war but also for promoting international social justice. These women did not think of themselves as furniture.[2]

Some women, of course, have not been treated as furniture. Among those women who have become visible in the recent era's international political arena are Hillary Clinton, Mary Robinson, Angela Merkel, Christine Lagarde, Michelle Bachelet, Ellen Johnson Sirleaf, and Shirin Ebadi.[3] Each of these prominent women has her own gendered stories to tell (or, perhaps, to deliberately not tell). But a feminist-informed investigation makes it clear that there are far more women engaged in international politics than the conventional headlines imply. Millions of women are international actors, and most of them are not Shirin Ebadi or Hillary Clinton.

To make reliable sense of today's (and yesterday's) dynamic international politics calls both for acquiring new skills and for redirecting skills one already possesses. That is, making feminist sense of international politics necessitates gaining skills that feel quite new and redirecting skills that one has exercised before, but which one assumed could shed no light on wars, economic crises, global injustices, and elite negotiations. Investigating the workings of masculinities and femininities as they each shape complex international political life—that is, conducting a gender-curious investigation—will require a lively curiosity, genuine humility, a full tool kit, and candid reflection on potential misuses of those old and new research tools.[4]

Most of all, one has to become interested in the actual lives—and thoughts—of complicatedly diverse women. One need not necessarily admire every woman whose life one finds interesting. Feminist attentiveness to all sorts of women is not derived from hero worship. Some women, of course, will turn out to be insightful, innovative, and even courageous. Upon closer examination, other women will prove to be complicit, intolerant, or self-serving. The motivation to take all women's lives seriously lies deeper than admiration. Asking "Where are the women?" is motivated by a determination to discover exactly how this world works. One's feminist-informed digging is fueled by a desire to reveal the ideas, relationships, and policies those (usually unequal) gendered workings rely upon.

For example, a British woman decides to cancel her plans for a winter holiday in Egypt. She thinks Egypt is "exotic," the warm weather would be welcome, and cruising down the Nile sounds exciting; but she is nervous about political upheaval in the wake of the overthrow of Egypt's previous regime. So instead she books her winter vacation in Jamaica. In making her tourism plans, she is playing her part in creating the current international political system. She is further deepening Egypt's financial debt while helping a Caribbean government earn badly needed foreign currency. And no matter which country she chooses for her personal pleasure, she is transforming "chambermaid" into a major globalized job category.

Or consider an American elementary school teacher who designs a lesson plan to feature the Native American "princess" Pocahontas. Many of the children will have watched the Disney animated movie. Now, the teacher hopes, she can show children how this seventeenth-century Native American woman saved the Englishman John Smith from execution at Jamestown, Virginia, later converted to Christianity, married an English planter, and helped clear the way for the English colonization of America. (The teacher might also include in her lesson plan the fact that Pocahontas's 1614 marriage to John Rolfe was the first recorded interracial marriage in what was to become the United Sates.) Her young students might come away from their teacher's well-intentioned lesson having absorbed the myth that local women are easily charmed by their own people's foreign occupiers.

The lives of Hollywood actresses can take on new international import when viewed through a feminist analytical lens. For example, in the 1930s, Hollywood moguls turned the innovative Brazilian singer Carmen Miranda into an American movie star. Then they put Miranda to work bolstering President Franklin Roosevelt's efforts to promote friendlier relations between the United States and Latin America. Soon after, an international banana company made her image into their logo, creating a new, intimate relationship between American housewives and a multinational plantation company. Today, however, Carmen Miranda has become an archetype of a certain over-the-top Latinized femininity. Men and women dress up with fantastic fruit-adorned hats and put their Carmen Miranda look-alike images up on YouTube and their Facebook pages.

Or consider the implications of a gendered encounter between a foreign male soldier and an impoverished, local woman today: an American—or Australian or Canadian or Ugandan—male soldier on an international peacekeeping or humanitarian mission responds to his comrades' homophobic innuendos by finally going along with them to a local brothel in order to prove that he is "one of the boys." Though he may think of himself as simply bolstering his own manly credentials, his attempts to compensate for his insecure masculine identity help shape power relations between his country's military and the society it is supposed to be protecting. He is also reinforcing one of the crucial bulwarks of today's militarized international political relations: heterosexualized masculinity.

The woman tourist and the chambermaid; the schoolteacher and her students; the film star, her studio owners, the banana company executives, the American housewife, and contemporary YouTube enthusiasts; the male soldier, the brothel owner, and the woman working as a prostitute—all are dancing an intricate international minuet. Those who look closely at the gendered causes and the gendered consequences of that minuet are conducting a feminist investigation of today's international political system.

These "dancers," however, are not in a position to call the tune. Yet even a woman who is victimized is not mindless. It is crucial to this feminist-informed investigation into unequal international relations that we not create a false (and lazy) dichotomy between the allegedly "mindless victim" and the allegedly "empowered actor." Women who are pushed to the far margin of any power system continue to assess and strategize even with the minimal resources they have available; sometimes they move beyond private strategizing to collective organizing. Nonetheless, acknowledging the severely restricted agency exercised by women pushed to the margins is not to deny that some international actors wield a lot more influence and garner far more rewards than do others. Thus, to investigate the gendered workings of international politics we will have to make power visible—power in all its myriad forms. This exploration can be uncomfortable.

WHERE DOES POWER OPERATE?

To do a gender investigation fueled by a *feminist* curiosity requires asking not only about the meanings of masculinity and femininity but also about how those meanings determine where women are and what they think about being there. Conducting a feminist gender analysis requires investigating *power:* what forms does power take? Who wields it? How are some gendered wieldings of power camouflaged so they do not even look like power?

A feminist gender analysis calls for continuing to ask even more questions about the genderings of power: Who gains what from wielding a particular form of gender-infused power? What do challenges to those wieldings of that form of power look like? When do those challenges succeed? When are they stymied?

Most of us, understandably, would prefer to think that the appeal of a company's marketing logo is cultural, not political. We would like to imagine that going on holiday to Jamaica rather than Egypt is merely a social, even aesthetic, matter, not a political choice. Many women and men would also prefer to think of sexual relationships as existing in the intimate realm of personal desire and attraction, immune to political manipulation. Yet corporate executives choose certain logos over others to appeal to consumers' stereotypes of racialized femininities. Government officials market their women's alleged beauty or their deferential service in order to earn needed tourism revenues. To foster certain bases of "social order," elected legislators craft particular laws to punish certain sexual attractions while rewarding others. Power, taste, attraction, and desire are not mutually exclusive.

If one fails to pay close attention to women—all sorts of women—one will miss who wields power and for what ends. That is one of the core lessons of feminist international investigation.

Power operates across borders. Think about the power dynamics of marriage. Whose marriage to whom is recognized by which governments for which purposes? To answer this multifaceted question, one has to pay attention to power. One has to investigate who has the power to rule that a male citizen can marry a woman or a man of another country and thereby confer his own citizenship status on his new spouse, whereas a woman who marries a person from another country cannot. Those with access to political power use that power to control marriage because marital relationships between people of the same or opposite sex affect transnational immigrations and access to the privileges of state-bestowed citizenship. Marriage is political. Marriage is international.

The politics of marriage can become even more intensely international as a result of gendered pressures from outside: colonial rule, new international norms of human rights, transnational religious evangelizing, and membership in new interstate unions whose standards have to be met. A family's wedding album rarely shows what power was wielded nationally or internationally and by whom in that ceremony. One has to dig deeper, even when the digging makes one uneasy.

One of the most important intellectual benefits that comes from paying serious attention to where women are in today's international politics—and investigating how they got *there* and what they *think* about being there—is that it exposes *how much more political power is operating than most non-gender-curious commentators would have us believe.*

This assertion—that many commentators underestimate power—may seem odd, since so many gender-*in*curious commentators appear to project an aura of power themselves, as if their having insights into the alleged realities of power bestows on them a mantle of power. Yet it is these same expert commentators who gravely underestimate both the amount and the kinds of power it has taken to create and to perpetuate the international political system we all are living in today. It is not incidental that the majority of the people invited to serve as expert foreign affairs commentators are male. For instance, one study revealed that, although white men constitute only 31 percent of today's total U.S. population, they made up 62 percent of all the expert guests on the three most influential American evening cable news channels.[5]

The flaw at the core of these mainstream, seemingly "sophisticated" commentaries is how much they take for granted, how much they treat as inevitable, and thus how much about the workings of power they fail to question—that is, how many types of power, and how many wieldings and wielders of power, they miss.

Too often gender incurious commentators attribute women's roles in international affairs to tradition, cultural preferences, and timeless norms, as if each of these existed outside the realms where power is wielded, as if they were beyond the reach of decisions and efforts to enforce those decisions. What sacrifices a woman as a mother should make, what priorities a woman as a wife should embrace, what sexualized approaches in public a woman should consider innocent or flattering, what victim identity a refugee woman should adopt, what boundaries in friendships with other women a woman should police, what dutiful-daughter model a girl should admire—in reality, all of these are shaped by the exercise of power by people who believe that their own local and international interests depend on women and girls internalizing these particular feminized expectations. If women internalize these expectations, they will not see the politics behind them. Political commentators who do not question these internalizations will accept the camouflaged operations of power as if there were no power at work at all. That is dangerous.

Women's collective resistance to any one of these feminized expectations can realign both local and international systems of power. As we will see, even stymied or only partially successful resistance by women can expose both who wields power to sustain the gendered status quo and what those power-wielders fear they will lose if women's resistance succeeds. This is why every suffrage movement in every country—the United States, Britain, Brazil, Mexico, China, Egypt, Kuwait—has raised such intense political alarm. Today, likewise, every effort by immigrant domestic workers to unionize—and every attempt by women garment and electronics workers to go out on strike, every move by women banana workers to be heard inside a male-led labor union, every campaign by an "out" lesbian to gain elective office, every demand by women married to soldiers and diplomats to pursue their own careers—not only has the potential to upset the gendered norms and roles on which the current global system has come to rely but also exposes where power operates to sustain the gendered status quo, as well as who benefits from that current gendered status quo.

Thus, if one is interested in gaining a reliable sense of national and international politics, one should be curious about all sorts of women's resistance, whether or not that resistance succeeds.

As one learns to look at the world through gender-curious feminist eyes, one learns to ask whether anything that passes for natural, inevitable, inherent, traditional, or biological has been *made*. One asks how all sorts of things have been made—the receding glacier, the low-cost sweatshirt, the heavily weaponized police force, the masculinized peace negotiation, the romantic marriage, the all-male Joint Chiefs of Staff. Asking how something has been made implies that it has been made by someone with a certain kind of power. Suddenly there are clues to trace; there is blame, credit, and responsibility to apportion, not just at the start but at each point along the way.

That is, a feminist, gender-curious approach to international politics offers a lot more topics to investigate because it makes visible the full workings of myriad forms of power.

WHO TAKES SERIOUSLY THE IDEAS OF TRANSNATIONAL FEMINISTS?

Despite the remarkable activist engagement that has generated today's multistranded transnational women's movement, many journalists (and the editors who assign their stories), foreign-policy experts, and policy decision makers remain oddly confident in their dismissal of feminist ideas.

Among the most loosely organized, social-media-energized, recent transnational women's movements have been Girl Rising, Slut Walks, Femen, and Vagina Monologues, with its accompanying V Day. Each tends to be fluid and not to depend on paid staffs or brick-and-mortar headquarters. The activists in each adapt their actions and messages to suit local needs and conditions. The organizations' distinguishing features are Internet savvy, feminist creativity, and convention-defying public performance.[6]

Simultaneously, a host of more explicitly organized transnational feminist groups and networks challenge the conventional workings of international politics today. Here is an admittedly incomplete list:

- Women Living Under Muslim Laws
- International Network of Women in Black
- Women's Global Network for Reproductive Rights
- International Women's Health Coalition
- Our Bodies Ourselves Global Network
- Equality Now

Figure 2. Anna Hutsol, cofounder of the topless direct-action feminist group Femen, and her mother in their Ukrainian home village, 2013, prior to physical attacks aimed at Hutsol and other Femen activists. Photo: Dmitry Kostyukov/The New York Times/Redux.

- International Action Network on Small Arms Women's Network
- Women's Initiatives for Gender Justice
- International Domestic Workers Network
- International Gay and Lesbian Human Rights Commission
- Women's International League for Peace and Freedom
- NGO Working Group on Women, Peace and Security
- Women in Conflict Zones Network

The Women's International League for Peace and Freedom was founded a century ago by transnational feminist peace activists in the midst of World War I.[7] Many groups on this partial list, by contrast, have been created in the years since the 1990s. New transnational networks and coalitions are on the brink of being launched today. Each network has its own gendered international political history. Their feminist activists do not always agree. Their members debate each other over what is causing what, which goal should be prioritized, which international power-holder should be the focus of protests or lobbying. They debate with each other over which compromises can be swallowed and which cannot. But the activists working in these organized groups also have come to share much in common: each is headed by women leaders; each, simultaneously, fosters autonomy among its grassroots activists; each urges women to take part in not only local but also international politics; each builds alliances with other all-women groups and with mixed men's and women's networks; each depends on donors, interns, and volunteers; each monitors trends and decisions in a particular arena of international politics; each posts data and analyses on its own website, usually in several languages; each uses its own gender-conscious investigations and analyses as a basis for crafting strategic campaigns to challenge both the oppression women experience and the practices that privilege certain men and certain masculinities; each aims its political campaigns not only at governments but also at the media, international agencies, and corporations.[8]

Why do most of us not hear the names of these organizations regularly on the nightly news or on the main Internet news sites? Editors, mainstream experts, and some academic scholars employ several strategies to dismiss the analytical (that is, explanatory) value of these groups' insights and impacts. One common rationale for ignoring the work of these transnational feminist networks is to dismiss them as representing only a "special interest." By contrast, the international expert is, so he (occasionally she) claims, interested in "the Big Picture." That is, the common assumption is that one-half of the world's population is equivalent to, say, logging companies or soccer clubs; thus, the thinking goes, their actions do not shed light on the world but simply are intended to advance their own limited self-interests.

A second rationale for not taking seriously the ideas and actions of these contemporary globalized women's advocacy groups—ideas and actions that should be thoughtfully weighed, not automatically accepted—is that the arenas of politics that these feminist activists do expose are presumably merely domestic or private, as opposed to, for instance, the allegedly "significant" public arenas of military security or government debt. In other words, the conventional failure to take seriously the thinking behind transnational women's advocacy is itself rooted in unrealistically narrow understandings of "security," "stability," "crisis," and "development." All four concepts are of utmost concern to those worried about the international Big Picture. Each of these four concerns—security, stability, crisis, and development—is routinely imagined to be divorced from (unaffected by) women's unpaid and underpaid labor, women's rights within marriage, the denial of girls' education, women's reproductive health, and sexualized and other forms of male violence against women, as well as the masculinization of militaries, police forces, and political parties. The conventional Big Picture, it would appear, is being painted on a shrunken canvas.

Third, these feminist transnational groups' analyses and actions can be ignored—their reports never cited, their staff members never invited to speak as experts, their leaders or activists never turned to for interviews—on the questionable grounds that their campaigns are lost causes. Behind this justification is the notion that challenging entrenched masculinized privileges and practices in today's international affairs is hopeless, therefore naive, therefore not worthy of serious attention. Further underpinning this final argument are the stunningly ahistorical assertions that (a) any advancements that women have gained have come not as a result of women's political theorizing and organizing but because women have been given these advancements by enlightened men in power, and (b) we collectively have "always" understood such useful political concepts as "reproductive rights," "sexual harassment," "systematic wartime rape," and "the glass ceiling." This latter assertion overlooks the fact that each of these revelatory concepts was hammered out and offered to the rest of us by particular activists at particular moments in recent political history.

All three of these spoken or unspoken rationales, and the assumptions they rely upon, are themselves integral to how international politics operates today. All three assertions that deny the significance and analytical value of transnational feminist organizing *are* the very stuff of international politics.

The very rarity of professional international political commentators taking seriously either women's experiences of international politics or women's gender analyses of international politics is, therefore, itself a political phenomenon that needs to be taken seriously. What so many non-feminist-informed international commentators *ignore* has been explored by the burgeoning academic field of gender and international relations. That is, paying close attention to—and explaining the causes and consequences of—what is so frequently ignored can be fruitful indeed.[9]

At the same time, we can be more curious about who does not pay attention to women's experiences—of war, marriage, trade, travel, revolution, and plantation and factory work. Who reaps rewards when women's experiences of these international affairs are treated as if they were inconsequential, mere "human interest" stories? That is, one becomes an international political investigator when one seeks to figure out who is rewarded if they treat women's experiences and women's gender analyses as if either were mere embellishments, almost entertainment, as if neither sheds meaningful light on the causes of the unfolding global events. Rewards are political.

Consider one common journalistic trivializing device: using a photograph or a bit of video footage of women to illustrate a news story—women shown grieving seems especially alluring to editors—but then interviewing only men for the main content of the journalistic account. Most coverage of international affairs is crafted with the presumption that only men—diverse men, rival men—have anything useful to say about what we all are trying to make sense of. Feminists routinely count how many men and how many women are interviewed in any political news story. A ratio of six to one or seven to zero is common.[10]

Since 2000, new social media have been used by many women, especially young women, to break through the masculinity-privileging walls of mainstream, established media. Women have become skilled bloggers, users of Twitter, Tumblr, YouTube, and Facebook. In addition, some feminist journalists have created alternative, independent international outlets, most prominent being the online international news service Women's eNews, which commissions local women journalists to cover stories about women's politics that the bigger media companies ignore.[11]

These recent media innovations are not the first time that women have tried to fashion alternative media in order to make

Figure 3. Mary Phillips, a Scottish suffragette, selling the British suffragist newspaper *The Vote,* 1907. Photo: Museum of London.

visible women's political issues, women's critical analyses, and women's political activism. Suffragists in the early 1900s set up their own printing presses and publishing houses to put out independent broadsides, pamphlets, and newspapers to let their fellow citizens know why women campaigners were demanding voting rights for women on the same terms as for men.

Then, in the 1980s and 1990s, scores of new magazines, publishing houses, archives, and bookstores were established by feminists in India, Mexico, Britain, the United States, Canada, Italy, Germany, Netherlands, Switzerland, Spain, Australia, South Africa, Japan, South Korea, Sweden, Pakistan, and Turkey in order to provide media outlets for literally thousands of women who were writing feminist-informed histories, novels, poetry, memoirs, political theory, health guides, investigatory journalism, and cinema reviews. Other women started women's radio programs and documentary film distribution companies. Many of the women involved in these media politics were aware of women in other countries doing the same; they read and distributed each other's publications, visited each other's bookstores, and traded encouragement and practical advice across national boundaries.[12]

As influential as these past and present local and international feminist media innovations were—and still are—in offering alternative information and perspectives, they did not and still do not have sufficient resources (for instance, for news bureaus in Beijing, Cairo, Nairobi, London, Tokyo, and Rio de Janeiro). Nor can they match the cultural and political influence wielded by large well-capitalized or state-sponsored media companies—textbook publishers, network and cable television companies, national radio stations and newspapers, Internet companies, and major film studios. These large media companies have become deliberately international in their aspirations. They are not monolithic, but together they can determine what is considered "international," what is defined as "political," what is deemed "significant," and who is anointed an "expert."[13]

Thus it is important to investigate, despite their differences, these influential media companies' common dismissal of unorganized and organized women as insignificant and to weigh carefully the risks that such dismissals carry. Each dismissal hobbles us when we try to explain why international politics takes the path it does.

WHAT WE MISS: TWO BRIEF CASE STUDIES

First case: the transatlantic antislavery movement. Despite the emergence of feminist historians, it is easy to portray the transatlantic antislavery movement of the early and mid-1800s as an all-male movement. The slave trade—and the profitable exports of cotton, tobacco, and sugar that the slave trade enabled—was a globalized business. Challenging that trade would drastically alter the international politics of the time. That is accepted. But it is the American male antislavery activists Frederick Douglass, John Brown, and William Lloyd Garrison, and their British ally the abolitionist William Wilberforce, who continue to be publicly celebrated. Thanks only to the work of African American feminist historians have the political contributions of abolitionist Sojourner Truth been recognized.[14] Overlooked by all but feminist historians have been the lesser-known British and American women antislavery activists, women who created mass movements in the early and mid-1800s. Not only did they strategize and campaign (e.g., British antislavery women provided the backbone for the sugar boycott and introduced mass petitioning), but these women activists, black and white, also overcame their lack of voting rights, their exclusion from the halls of governments, and the obstacles to travel and communication (letters from London took more than two weeks to reach Boston's antislavery hub) to create an effective transatlantic alliance, one of the world's first transnational women's movements.[15]

What do we miss if today we persist in portraying this important early international political movement as an all-male affair? First, we grossly underestimate how much racialized gendered power it took for proslavery advocates to sustain the slave trade and systems of slave labor for as long as they did. If those with vested interests in maintaining slavery had faced only male opponents, without the energy, political innovations, and knowledge of domestic consumption that women abolitionists contributed, they might have been able to sustain the exploitive racist system longer or at lower political cost.

Second, if we continue to ignore the distinct ideas and actions of the British and American women abolitionists, we will underestimate the internal tensions that marked the transatlantic antislavery movement itself: to sustain their movement over decades and in the face of formidable opposition, male and female antislavery activists not only had to reconcile their differing ideas about race, property, freedom, and the meaning of humanity, but they also had to work out among themselves their contentious differences over femininity, masculinity, respectability, and marriage (e.g., was marriage itself, in its then-current form, as some women abolitionists came to believe, just a more polite form of slavery?).[16]

Finally, if we persist in taking seriously only the male antislavery campaigners in the international movement to abolish the slave trade and slave labor, then we are bound to miss one of the most significant consequences of that political movement: the mobilization in the late 1800s and early 1900s of campaigns to end the political systems of male-only suffrage. The suffrage movement, despite its contradictions and shortcomings, became one of the world's most radically democratizing movements. And it was globalized.[17]

Yet investigations of the international gender politics of both abolitionism and women's suffrage campaigning are virtually absent from most university courses purporting to train students in the skills they will need to make reliable sense of democratization, political mobilization, and international politics.

Second case: the international Arms Trade Treaty. It took eight years. Money had to be raised. Gender-disaggregated data had to be collected. Women had to be interviewed. Interviews had to be translated. Consciousnesses had to be raised. Meetings had to be organized. Visas and plane tickets to New York had to be obtained. Different priorities and understandings had to be aired and reconciled. Alliances had to be forged, then tended and reforged.[18] But on April 2, 2013, by a majority vote (154 in favor, 3 against, 23 abstaining), member states of the United Nations General Assembly adopted the world's first-ever international Arms Trade Treaty. For the first time, governments and companies exporting small arms—rifles, pistols, grenade launchers, and the parts and ammunition for these weapons—would be bound by international law to explicitly assess whether those arms would be used in the importing country for purposes that violated international human rights. This was new.

Buried in its thirteen pages of formal diplomatic language was a transnational feminist success: article 7, paragraph 4. It reads, "The exporting State Party, in making this assessment [of the potential 'negative consequences' of permitting the export of small arms], shall take into account the risk of the conventional arms covered under Article 2 (1) of the items covered under Article 3 or Article 4 being used to commit or facilitate serious acts of gender-based violence or serious acts of violence against women and children."[19]

Eight years and multinational attentiveness and transnational lobbying by scores of women produced this crucial phrase: *gender-based violence.* And not only that. The hotly contested phrase—*gender-based violence*—was placed here, in this section of the Arms Trade Treaty that made it binding (not simply advisory) on the ATT's government signatories.

Including "gender-based violence" as a criterion for government officials when they assessed the legality of exporting any small arms from their own countries' gun manufacturers was a criterion strenuously resisted by certain influential organizations and by officials from powerful governments.

The alliance that developed the reasoning for "gender-based violence" as an assessment criterion was feminist-led and transnational. At its core were three organizations: the Women's International League for Peace and Freedom (WILPF), especially its international staffs in Geneva and in New York, across the street from the UN; the International Action Network on Small Arms (IANSA), Women's Network; and Global Action to Prevent War and Armed Conflict. Together, these three organizations had activist affiliates around the world. While their combined lobbying to persuade governments' UN delegates to support the inclusion of the words *gender-based violence* in the ATT and to "make it binding" is a story yet to be fully told in all its twists and turns, a crucial part of that story was these activists listening to women, asking where women are in today's international politics of guns.

Most of the non-feminist-informed activists who pushed for the Arms Trade Treaty focused their attention on export figures, import figures, patterns of armed conflict, and gun-exporting governments' and their weapons manufacturers' complicity in enabling those damaging armed conflicts. It was their analyses, too, that informed most mainstream news coverage. What the women of IANSA, WILPF, and Global Action did was distinct: they looked deeper into armed conflicts to chart the gendered dynamics of guns, both gun violence's causes and its consequences. IANSA's women activists in Mali, Congo, Brazil, the Philippines, and other countries that had experienced years of violence played a crucial role. They asked, "Where are the women?" And "Where are the guns?" They interviewed women about where guns were in their own daily lives. They revealed how politicized conflict became gendered conflict. They exposed the causal connections between group armed violence and violence perpetrated inside homes and families. And they demonstrated how those guns when not even fired could infuse relationships between women and men with fear and intimidation. Listening to women's diverse experiences of living with guns in their communities and their homes, they painted a Big Picture: the massive international exports of guns sustained gender-based violence as a pillar of international and national patriarchy.

The Vatican was a crucial player in the UN Arms Trade Treaty negotiations. The Vatican has "observer status" at the UN (as does the Palestinian delegation). This status gives the Vatican's delegates access to crucial discussions among voting state delegations, where its opinions and interpretations often carry significant weight. In each UN treaty negotiation process, the state participants decide whether or not observers will be allowed to cast votes on the final proposed document. In the Arms Trade Treaty process, observers were not allowed to vote. But throughout the multistage negotiations, the Vatican's delegates were omnipresent and influential. Its delegates helped to create what feminists called the "unholy alliance" between the UN delegates of the Vatican, Russia, Syria, and Iran. The Vatican led the resistance to including the phrase *gender-based violence* in the Arms Trade Treaty. Over the years, the Vatican's delegates have treated social constructions of male and female as anathema. Thus no "gender." They pressed, instead, for the more patriarchal phrase *violence against women and children*. Furthermore, the Vatican pushed to have *violence against women and children* inserted only in the treaty's opening preamble. That is, they were comfortable with including *violence against women and children* in the final treaty as a motivating reason for creating this new interstate agreement, but were opposed to it being made a binding criterion that governments would be obligated to use when they assessed their own gun exports.

The Vatican was not alone. By itself, its role is never decisive. Numbers of governments and lobbying groups were willing to allow the conventional phrase *violence against women and children* to be inserted and to have it listed merely as one reason among many for limiting the international trade in small arms. What they did not accept was the insertion of the more politically salient analytical phrase *gender-based violence,* or for that to become a formal criterion imposed on governments when they assessed the legality of exporting weaponry.

Ideas matter. Words matter. Placement matters. The strategists of WILPF and IANSA's Women's Network and Global Action, women such as Ray Acheson and Maria Butler, went from state delegation to state delegation to explain why neither the phrase *violence against women and children* nor its placement solely in the nonbinding preamble were sufficient—that is, why neither matched the realities of women's lives. Eventually, more than one hundred state delegations publicly backed the inclusion of the term *gender-based violence* and its placement in the section that would make it a binding criterion in each exporting government's assessment process. The UN delegates of Iceland and Lichten-stein, though representing small countries, were especially help-ful in supporting WILPF's and IANSA's feminist campaigners.

The wide governmental support that the feminists ulti-mately gained was the outcome of scores of women activists spending hours explaining, first, that "women and children" should not be lumped together and treated as mere victims. Second, feminist activists working the corridors of the UN explained to delegates that when violence is described as "gendered" it makes the workings of masculinities and the politics of misogyny visible in the international politics of gun exporting. Third, they explained to scores of delegates that, to be meaningful, the treaty had to legally obligate exporting governments to explicitly determine whether any small arms were likely to be used in the importing country to perpetrate widespread gender-based violence.

The intricately crafted final version of the Arms Trade Treaty was passed by the General Assembly on April 2, 2013 (with the delegates of Syria, Iran, and North Korea casting the three "no" votes). Its passage was the result of many actors, many efforts, many forms of analysis. But if one does not ask, "Where were the women?" one will miss who tried to dilute the ATT and why. If one ignores the thinking and the activism of the WILPF and IANSA women, one also will miss the innovative feminist thinking that causally linked international gun political economies to the political economies of sexualized wartime violence, domestic violence, and the processes of intimidation that severely limit women's economic and political participation. Moreover, one will miss the feminist-informed listening, data collection, analysis, and strategizing that transformed a groundbreaking international agreement between governments into an instrument for furthering women's rights.

The Arms Trade Treaty's gendered politics had taken years to create, but in April 2013 those gendered politics had just begun. To become operational, the ATT would have to be ratified by individual governments. In each country there would be multiple bases for support and for rejection of the treaty. Who in each country would balk at making "gender-based violence" a binding criterion? Who would argue that its inclusion was one of the positive strengths of the ATT? Charting each of these ratifying debates, country by country, will shine a light on the genderings of the international political economies of rifles, pistols, and grenade launchers. Then there will be still further chapters in the gendered ATT story: in those countries that ratify the ATT (that is, which sign on to its binding obligations), who will officials turn to for expert advice when they have to assess whether the guns they are about to export will be used to inflict widespread gender-based violence? The women of IANSA?[20]

WHERE ARE THE MEN?

Most of the time we scarcely notice that many governments still look like men's clubs, with the occasional woman allowed in the door. We see a photo of members of Russia's cabinet, Wall Street's inner circle, the Chinese Politboro, or Europe's central bankers, and it is easy to miss the fact that all the people in these photographs are men. One of the most useful functions that the British prime minister Margaret Thatcher served during the 1980s was to break through our gender numbness. Thatcher herself was not an advocate for women, but when she stood at a 1987 meeting in Venice alongside France's Mitterand, Japan's Nakasone, the United States' Reagan, and the other heads of government, we suddenly noticed that everyone else was male. Twenty-five years later, Angela Merkel, the German chancellor, provided a similar gender-consciousness-raising function when she stood for a photograph with the other heads of government in the Group of Eight, the world's economic powers. One woman in a photo makes it harder for us to ignore that the men are *men*.

Figure 4. Group of Seven summit meeting, including Margaret Thatcher, Venice, 1987. Photo: Daniel Simon/Frank Spooner Pictures, London.

Once we start looking at men as men, we are more likely to become curious about masculinities—what it means to be manly—and about the contests over diverse, unequally ranked sorts of masculinity.

It is widely asserted today that we live in a "dangerous world." It was commonly stated during the four decades of the Cold War, when the threats posed by nuclear weapons were used by both the United States and the Soviet Union to raise the stakes of international rivalries. The notion that we live in a dangerous world gained new saliency after the attacks on New York's towering World Trade Center in September 2001. Since 2001, countless American politicians have based their calls for rolling back citizens' privacy rights, curtailing due process legal protections, giving surveillance agencies free rein, equipping local police

Figure 5. Leaders of the Group of Eight industrialized nations, including Angela Merkel, joined by European Commission and European conflict officials, summit meeting, Northern Ireland, 2013. Photo: Matt Cardy/Getty Images News.

forces with heavier weaponry, casting new immigrants as potential threats, launching weaponized drones, and turning a blind eye toward the antidemocratic actions of U.S. international allies by justifying each move as a contributor to the "war on terror."

Among its many questionable consequences, the absorption of the idea that we live in a dangerous world serves to reinforce the primacy of particular forms of masculinity while subordinating most women and femininity itself. Men living in a dangerous world are commonly imagined to be the natural protectors. Women living in a dangerous world allegedly are those who need protection. Those relegated to the category of the protected are commonly thought to be safe "at home" and, thus, incapable of realistically assessing the dangers "out there."

Notions of masculinity are not identical across generations or across cultural boundaries. That is why one needs to explore the workings and rankings of masculinities in particular places at particular times—and then track them over generations.[21] Comparison may reveal striking similarities but also expose significant differences. A masculinized rivalry is one in which diverse masculinities are unequally ranked and contested: there is a contest over which expression of manliness is deemed most "modern," which most "rational," which the "toughest," which the "softest," which the "weaker." In such rivalries, women are marginalized unless (withstanding ridicule as "unfeminine") they can convincingly cloak themselves in a particular masculinized style of speech and action. Thus a common British assessment of Britain's first and only woman prime minister: "Margaret Thatcher was the toughest man in the room."

While political contests over masculinity marginalize all but a very few women, such contests always put femininity into play. In a patriarchal society—a society whose relationships and inequalities are shaped by the privileging of particular masculinities and by women's subordination to and dependence on men—anything that is feminized can be disparaged. Consequently, rival men are prone to try to tar each other with the allegedly damning brush of femininity. The intent is to rob the opposing man of his purchase on such allegedly manly attributes as strength, courage, and rationality.[22] This masculinized wielding of femininity happens not only on the playground and in local elections but also in international nuclear politics.[23]

Furthermore, this femininity-wielding masculinized contest between men shapes not only the international politics of war and national security but also the international politics of domestic servants, sex workers, wives, women factory workers, and women plantation workers. This contest determines what is considered mere "women's work" and thus unfit for any manly man. What presumptions about a manly man's access to any woman's sexuality fuels sexual harassment of women on and off the job?

In conventional commentaries, men who wield influence in international politics are analyzed in terms of their national, ethnic, and racial identities; their positions in organizations; their class origins; their paid work; and sometimes their sexual preferences. Rarely, though, are men analyzed as *men,* people who have been taught, since childhood, how to be manly, how not to be a "girl," how to size up the trustworthiness or competence of other men by assessing their manliness. If international commentators do find masculinity interesting, it is typically when they try to make sense of "great men"—Napoleon Bonaparte, Abraham Lincoln, Mao Zedong, Nelson Mandela—not when they seek to understand the actions of male factory owners, male midlevel officials, male banana workers, or male tourists. It is a lack of feminist curiosity that makes comfortably invisible such men's efforts to be seen by other men as masculine in doing their jobs, exercising influence, nurturing alliances, or seeking relief from stress. In so doing, such a lack of feminist curiosity also makes dangerously invisible these men's attempts (sometimes thwarted) to use diverse women in their daily pursuits of precarious masculine status.

BEYOND THE GLOBAL VICTIM

Some men and women active in campaigns to influence their country's foreign policy—on the right, as well as the left—have called on women to become more educated about international issues, to learn more about "what's going on in the world." Women are told, "You have to take more interest in international affairs because it affects how you live." The gist of the argument is that women need to devote precious time and energy to learning about events outside their own country because, as women, they are the *objects* of those events. For instance, a woman working for a software company in Ireland is told she should learn more about the European Union because what the EU commissioners decide in Brussels is going to help determine her wages and maybe even the hazards she faces on the job. An American woman similarly will be encouraged to learn about the ongoing fighting in Syria because political contests in the Middle East will affect her children's chances of a safe future.

There are two things striking about this conventional line of argument. First, those who are trying to persuade women to "become informed" are not inviting women to reinterpret international politics by drawing on their own experiences as women. If the explanations of how the EU and Middle East politics work do not already include any concepts of femininity, masculinity, or patriarchy, they are unlikely to do so after more women start listening to the recognized gender-incurious international experts. Because these persuaders are not curious about what paying close attention to women's complex experiences could contribute to an understanding of international politics, many women, especially those whose energies are already stretched to the limit, may be understandably wary of spending precious time reading about fighting in Syria or decisions made in Brussels.

When the common women-need-to-learn-more-about-foreign-affairs approach is articulated by gender-incurious activists (women or men), women are usually portrayed as the objects, even victims, of the international political system. Women should learn about capitalist globalization, or the Middle East's Arab Spring, or the workings of the United Nations, or climate change because each has an impact on them. In this worldview, women are forever being acted *upon*. They are the victims of garment factory disasters; they are the targets of sexual assaults in wartime; they are the trafficked, the low paid, the objectified. Rarely are women seen as the explainers or the reshapers of the world. Rarely are they made visible as *thinkers* and *actors*.

If women are asked to join an international campaign—for peace, for refugees, against war, for religious evangelism, against hunger—but are not allowed to define the problem and its causes, it looks to many locally engaged women like abstract do-gooding with minimal connection to the battles they are waging for a decent life in their households and in their own communities.

A lot of books about international politics leave their readers with a sense that "it's all so complex, decided by people who don't know or care that I exist." The spread of capitalist economics, even in countries whose officials call themselves socialists, can feel as inevitable as the tides (which, we are learning, are actually not inevitable). Governments' capacities to wound people, to destroy environments and dreams, are constantly expanding through their uses of science and bureaucracy. International relationships fostered by these governments and their allies use our labor and our imaginations, but it seems beyond our reach to alter them. These relationships seem to have created a world that can turn tacos and sushi into bland fast foods, destroy rain forests, melt arctic ice, globalize pornography, and socialize men from dozens of cultures into a common new culture of high-risk banking. One closes most books on "international security" or "international political economy" with a sigh.

They purport to explain how it works, but they offer knowledge that makes one feel as though it is more rewarding to concentrate on problems closer to home.

Most important, many of these analyses of international affairs leave one with the impression that "home" has little to do with international politics. When home is imagined to be a feminized place—a place where womanly women and feminine girls should feel most comfortable, and where manly men and real boys should stop in now and then for refueling—then this consequence of many mainstream explanations can send the roots of masculinized international politics down even more deeply.

There is an alternative incentive for delving into international politics. That is, seeing oneself in it, not just being acted upon by it. To do this, however, requires remapping the boundaries of the "international" and the "political": it requires seeing how one's own family dynamics, consumer behaviors, travel choices, relationships with others, and ways of thinking about the world actually help shape that world. We are not just acted upon; we are actors. Though, even recognizing that one is not part of any elite, acknowledging oneself as an international actor can be unnerving. One discovers that one is often complicit in creating the very world that one finds so dismaying.

The world is something that has been—and is being—made every day. And ideas about and practices of both femininity and masculinity, combined with attempts to control women, are central to that world-making. So are challenges to those conventions and resistance to those attempts. It is not always easy to see those attempts and, thus, to resist them. Policy makers may find it more "manly" (even if some of the policy makers themselves now are women) to think of themselves as dealing in guns and money, rather than in notions of femininity, marriage, and sexuality. So they—and most of their critics as well—try to hide and deny their reliance on women as feminized workers, as respectable and loyal wives, as "civilizing influences," as sex objects, as obedient daughters, as unpaid farmers, as coffee-serving campaigners, and as spending consumers and tourists. If we can expose their dependence on feminizing women, we can show that this world is also dependent on artificial notions of masculinity.

As a result, this seemingly overwhelming world system may begin to look more fragile and open to radical change than we have been led to imagine.

Thus this book is only a beginning. It draws on the theoretical and organizational work of women in Britain in the 1890s, Algeria in the 1950s, the Philippines in the 1980s, Chile in the 1990s, and Egypt in the beginning of the twenty-first century. Most of the conclusions here are tentative. What readers themselves write in the margins of these pages as they test the descriptions and explanations against their own experiences of the internationalized politics of femininity and masculinity will be at least as valuable in creating a different world as what appears here in deceptively solid print.

CHAPTER TWO

Lady Travelers, Beauty Queens, Stewardesses, and Chambermaids

The International Gendered Politics of Tourism

Americans traveling to France to walk World War II battlefields. British yoga devotees flying to Bali for a retreat. Russians traveling to Turkey for a beach holiday. Gay men and lesbians vacationing in Thailand, attracted by the country's welcoming culture. Japanese traveling to Hawaii for hula lessons. Men of assorted nationalities traveling to private game reserves to shoot endangered animals. Tourism nowadays attracts millions of travelers destined for an ever-widening array of destinations. By 2013, at the same time that China was becoming one of the most popular destinations for foreign tourists, Chinese travelers themselves had become the world's most numerous overseas tourists, outrunning (and outspending) Germans and Americans.[1]

Almost anyplace can be transformed into a tourist attraction: ancient ruins; sandy beaches; a mosque, temple, church, or synagogue; a beloved author's house; the site of a famous assassination; a gorillas' habitat; a desert, coral reef, or volcano. That is, when a place becomes a tourist site, people will pay money to be taken to see it and to be sheltered and fed while they are looking. More and more countries depend on tourism for major portions of their export earnings. Countries such as Jamaica, Bahamas, Samoa, Fiji, and Rwanda garner an astounding (or dismaying) 40 percent of their export earnings from tourism. Nepal, Croatia, Egypt, Tanzania, and Morocco are among the countries that have come to depend on the tourism business for at least 20 percent of their export earnings.[2] An estimated 1.8 billion tourists traveled worldwide in 2012, creating 7 percent of all jobs globally and generating revenues amounting to at least 5 percent of the global gross domestic product.[3]

Tourism has become big business. Travel for pleasure has become a crucial process in world affairs, generating income and profits for governments and private companies, creating both well-paying careers and exploitive jobs, and enticing millions of people to visit places far from their homes. People who become tourists form ideas (some new, some simply reconfirmed) about the people they meet, the food they taste, and the ways of doing things they experience. People who service those tourists form their own ideas about the travelers, how demanding or respectful they are, and how much they flaunt or downplay their wealth. Tourism creates affections, desires, resentments, admiration, friendship, and contempt.

It is all too easy to discuss international tourism as if it were ungendered. One could talk about "tourism" and "hotel corporations" as if women and men played identical roles in each. One could refer to countries' balance of payments and the environmental risks that accompany irresponsible resort development and massive influxes of tourists as if ideas about masculinity and about femininity did not influence either. Each of these does matter. But none of them can be fully understood without investigating the distinctive ways men and women relate to—that is, shape and are affected by—each aspect of tourism.

Tourism as a concept is gendered. Tourists as people are gendered. Tourism-promoting policies are gendered. Profit-seeking tourism companies and the ever-increasing numbers of people who work for them are gendered. And all five are political. All five involve the workings of power. That is, the industry, the people in it, and the people it is supposed to serve shape—and are shaped by—ideas about and practices of diverse masculinities and femininities. Those ideas and practices affect who has power and who is affected by how power is wielded. Asking "Where are the women?"—as tourists, as those who service tourists, as those promoting tourism, and as those imagined by tourists—reveals how significant gendered international politics are in tourism.

As tourism's investigators, however, we are not floating above history. We are asking this feminist question, "Where are the women?" at a particular moment in the ongoing gendered history of international politics. It is a time when more women than ever are traveling voluntarily for both business and pleasure. This is also a historical moment when more women than ever in scores of countries depend on paid employment in tourism, but one when women working in tourism are earning, on average, 10 percent to 15 percent less than men employed in tourism.[4] As a result, this is a historical moment when transnational feminist activists are exerting effective pressure on international agencies—the World Bank, the UN World Tourism Organization, the International Labor Organization—to pay serious attention to women's rights and women's opportunities when they devise their tourism policies. Simultaneously, at this moment in the world's gendered history, more women politicians are moving into positions of influence in tourism-policy-making: one in five of the world's ministers of tourism is a woman, a higher proportion than among the ministers of any other branch of government. Most of those women tourism ministers are in African governments.[5]

FOOTLOOSE AND GENDERED

Tourism has its own international political history, one that reaches back to the Roman empire. In many societies being feminine has been defined as sticking close to home. Masculinity, by contrast, has been the passport for travel. A principal difference between women and men in countless societies has been men's cultural license to travel away from a place thought of as "home." As feminist geographers have revealed, a woman who voluntarily travels away from the ideological protection of home and without the physical protection of an acceptable male escort is likely to be tainted with unrespectability.[6]

Voluntarily is a crucial condition. For centuries, women of diverse societies have been forced to travel—as enslaved or indentured workers, as refugees, as sex slaves, as disempowered members of patriarchal families. Those women's travels did not threaten patriarchal systems of power. Indeed, those women's enforced travels often strengthened existing oppressive masculinized gender systems.

For a woman to travel for her own pleasure or benefit is something quite different. She is a woman exerting her physical autonomy. This defies the not uncommon laws that require a woman to have her father's, son's, uncle's, or husband's permission to travel.[7] We think of the Saudi Arabian government's denial of women's right to drive as extreme. It is indeed extreme (and currently is being challenged by Saudi women activists), but it is an extreme point on a more conventional spectrum that welds acceptable femininity to relative physical immobility. Think corsets. Think high heels. Think drivers licenses: in 2010, while 80 percent of all British adult men had drivers licenses, only 66 percent of British women had driver's licenses. That latter proportion had grown dramatically over the previous four decades owing in large measure to the insistence by the British women's movement that women have the right to autonomy.[8] Some women, though, may unwittingly reinforce the patriarchal link between unrespectable womanhood and geographical mobility with their own gestures of defiance. A bumper sticker that appeared in the 1980s on women's well-traveled vans: "Good girls go to Heaven. Bad girls go everywhere." This slogan is liberatory only if *bad* is defined as "in defiance of patriarchy."

By contrast, a man is deemed less than manly until he breaks away from home and strikes out geographically on his own. Some men leave the farm and travel to the city or mining town to look for work. Other men go off on road trips with buddies or set off hitchhiking with a knapsack and a good pair of boots. Still other men answer the call to "join the navy and see the world."

"I cut off my hair and dressed me in a suit of my husband's having had the precaution to quilt the waistcoat to preserve my breasts from hurt which were not large enough to betray my sex and putting on the wig and hat I had prepared I went out and brought me a silver hilted sword and some Holland shirts."[9] So Christian Davies set off in the 1690s to enlist in the British army. If she could not travel as a woman, she would disguise herself as a man. The stories of Christian and women like her are not unmixed tales of feminist rebellion, however. While some of the women ran away to sea or enlisted as drummer boys to escape suffocating patriarchal village life, others claimed they were simply acting as loyal wives or sweethearts, following their men. If a woman was exposed—while being treated for a battle wound or giving birth—the punishment she received frequently depended on which of these two interpretations was believed by the men who pulled away her disguise.

Vita Sackville-West came from a privileged background, but she emulated her working-class sisters and resorted to male disguise. After World War I, demobilized male veterans were a common sight in Europe. In 1920 Vita dressed as a man and ran away to Paris impulsively with her woman lover. In this masculine camouflage she felt liberated:

> The evenings were ours. I have never told a soul of what I did. I hesitate to write it here, but I must.... I dressed as a boy. It was easy, because I could put a khaki bandage round my head, which in those days was so common that it attracted no attention at all. I browned my face and hands. It must have been successful, because no one looked at me at all curiously or suspiciously.... I looked like a rather untidy young man, a sort of undergraduate, of about nineteen. I shall never forget the evenings when we walked back slowly to our flat through the streets of Paris. I, personally, had never felt so free in my life.[10]

More recently, women have been lured into joining the military—without a disguise—by thoughts of leaving home. Getting away from home, not killing an enemy, was what Peggy Perri, just out of nursing school, had in mind when she and her best friend decided to enlist in the U.S. Army nursing corps in 1967, in the early years of the U.S. war in Vietnam. "Pat and I were both living at home and we were both miserable. I was living at my mother's house. I was unhappy, really unhappy," Peggy recalled. "Pat and I had become nurses with the expectation that we could go anywhere and work. We wanted to go somewhere, and we wanted to do something really different."[11]

Peggy was not a classic "good girl." She chewed gum and liked parties. But she did not want to surrender her status as a respectable young woman. "We needed to know that there was going to be some kind of structure to hold us up. The military sure promised that.... I was infatuated by the idea of going to Vietnam.... I really didn't know where I wanted to go. I wanted to go everywhere in the world." She soon got her wish. "I remember we got our orders; my mother took me shopping in every major department store. Pat and I both bought new sets of luggage, Pat's was hot pink!... It was January and we would go to all the 'cruise' shops looking for light-weight clothing. I wanted everyone to think I was going on a cruise."

The most famous of the women who set out to travel farther than convention allowed without disguise are now referred to as the "Victorian lady travelers." Most of them came from the white middle classes of North America and western Europe. Not for them the parlor, village well, or dinner party. They set out on foreign travels that were supposed to be the preserve of men. They defied the strictures of femininity by choosing parts of the world that whites in the late nineteenth and early twentieth century considered "uncharted," "uncivilized." Not for them the then-chic tourist destinations of Italy and Greece. These Victorian lady travelers wanted *adventure*. And they were not content to wait until adventure came to them. They would go in search of it. That meant traveling to lands just then being occupied by imperial armies, religious missionaries, and capitalist traders. They crossed deserts, paddled up rivers, and climbed mountains.

In their own day these women were viewed with suspicion by their compatriots because they dared to travel such long distances with so little proper (that is, white) male protection. Often their male escorts were local male guides, such as the Mongolian male guide who taught Mildred Cable and Francesca French how to walk by starlight across the Gobi Desert: "At first I stumbled and hurt my feet among the stones.... Then I realized that he had used his daylight powers of sense to train the more subtle instinct which served him in the dark, and gradually I too learnt the art of training and trusting my instincts until I also felt secure in the clear darkness, which is the only darkness that the desert knows." Between 1926 and 1941, the two women crossed the Gobi five times.[12]

Even if their husbands accompanied them, as missionaries or scientists, the Victorian women travelers insisted upon the separateness of their own experiences. The fact that most of them were white and chose to travel into societies whose populations were not, added to the aura of unconventional daring surrounding their journeys. Space and race, when combined, have different implications for women and men, even of the same social class.[13]

Mary Kingsley, Isabella Bird, Alexandra David-Neel, Nina Mazuchelli, Annie Bullock Workman, Nina Benson Hubbard—these were among the most prominent women of the nineteenth and early twentieth centuries who took for themselves the identities of "adventurer" and "explorer." Both labels were thoroughly masculinized. Masculinity and exploration had been as tightly woven together as masculinity and soldiering. These audacious women challenged that ideological assumption, but they have left us with a bundle of contradictions. While they defied, apparently self-consciously, the ban on travel to remote areas by "proper" women, in some respects they seem conventional. Some of them rejected female suffrage. Some refused to fully acknowledge how far their own insistence on the right to adventure undermined not only Victorian notions of femininity but also the bond being forged between Western masculinity and Western imperialism.

Mary Kingsley is one of the most intriguing and best known of the lady travelers. Mary's father was an explorer, her brother an adventurer. Born in 1862, Mary grew up as the twin movements of women's domestication and imperial expansion were flowering in Victoria's England. She seemed destined to nurse her invalid mother and keep the home fires burning for her globe-trotting brother. But Mary had other ideas, and in 1892 she set out on the first of several expeditions to Africa. She traveled with African male porters and guides, but without a white male escort, as she headed into the West African interior. For it was in the continent's interior where "real" adventures were thought to happen. In subsequent years she befriended European male traders plying their business along the coasts and up the rivers of Africa. Her detailed knowledge of African societies' ritual fetishes was even acknowledged by the men of the prestigious British Museum.[14]

Mary Kingsley also became one of the most popular speakers on the lively lecture circuit. She drew enthusiastic audiences from all over England to hear about her travels to Africa and her descriptions of lives lived in the newly penetrated areas of Victoria's empire. Many women travelers helped finance their travels by giving public lectures. The lecture circuit may have provided a crucial setting in which the women who stayed at home could become engaged in the British empire. By listening to Mary Kingsley describe colonial policies and their consequences for local peoples, these women could vicariously take part in British officials' debates over how best to incorporate African and Asian peoples into that empire.

The women lecture-goers are as politically interesting as Mary Kingsley herself. Together, lecturer and audience helped to fashion a British culture of imperialism. The stay-at-home listeners would develop a sense of imperial pride as they heard another woman describe her travels among their empire's allegedly more exotic peoples. And they could expand their knowledge of the world without risking loss of that feminine respectability which enabled them to feel superior to colonized women. Their imperial curiosity, in turn, helped Mary Kingsley finance her gender-convention-defying travels.

A century later, in the 1980s, librarians at the American Museum of Natural History in New York mounted an exhibition honoring some of the American women who had made contributions to scientific exploration. "Ladies of the Field: The Museum's Unsung Explorers" was designed to make visible Delia Akeley, Dina Brodsky, and other women explorers whose contributions to science had been neglected because the women had been dismissed as amateurs or as mere wives-of-explorers. The exhibition consisted of just three small glass cases in the anteroom of the Rare Book Library. As two women visitors peered through the glass to read faded diaries and letters, they could hear the shouts of schoolchildren racing through millennia of dinosaurs not far away. Here there were no curious crowds. They were the only visitors. Something about finding themselves before this modest exhibit prompted the strangers to exchange a few words. As they looked at a photo of Delia Akeley

Figure 6. Delia Akeley on expedition in Africa for the American Museum of Natural History. Photo: Carl Akeley/American Museum of Natural History, New York.

standing proudly between giant tusks she had just collected for the museum, one woman said, "A friend of mine had wanted to be an explorer, but she resigned herself to being a librarian."[15]

Historians often think it worth noting when the "first white woman" arrived, as if that arrival transformed a place. The coming of a white woman destined it to be drawn into the international system. If a white woman traveler reached a place, could the white wife or the white female tourist be far behind?

FEMININITY, PROGRESS, AND
WORLD'S FAIRS

The idea that the world is out there for the taking by ordinary citizens as well as adventurers emerged alongside the growth of tourism as an industry. Long before Disney opened its Epcot world theme park in Florida in 1982, world's fairs, together with museums and travel lectures, nourished this idea.

Without leaving her own country, the world's-fair-goer could experience remote corners of the world, choosing to "visit" the Philippines, Alaska, Japan, or Hawaii. It is estimated that in the United States alone, close to 1 million people visited world's fairs between 1876 and 1916.[16] World's fairs were designed to be more than popular entertainments; they were intended by their planners to help the public imagine an industrializing, colonizing global enterprise.

At the heart of all world's fairs was the idea of progress, global progress. It could be best celebrated, fair investors believed, by graphically comparing "uncivilized" with "civilized" cultures. Between the two extremes, fair designers placed African American and Native American cultures—those apparently already on the progressive track to civilization. They constructed elaborate scenes that they imagined visitors would find exotic. They imported women and men from as far away as Samoa and the Philippines to demonstrate their point. They called on the budding profession of anthropology to order their ideas and ensure authenticity. In the end, fair designers created living postcards, clichés of cultures apparently at opposite ends of the modernity scale.

The imported native peoples in their exotic environment were as crucial to the celebration of progress as were exhibits of the latest feats of technological invention. Walking between a re-created simple Samoan village and a powerful, shiny loco-motive gave fairgoers an exhilarating sense of inevitable prog-ress. By implication, it was America—or France or Britain—that was leading the way in the march of globalized progress. To convey this, the cultures most deeply affected by the colonial experience were placed farthest along the fair's road of progress. Eventually, or so the world's-fair scenario suggested, the alleg-edly primitive peoples of the world would be led into the light of civilization by imperial trusteeship. The world's fair expressed an elaborate international political cosmology.

However, it was a gendered America, a gendered Britain, a gendered France that was imagined as leading the procession and formulating the heartening comparisons. A reporter for the *Omaha Bee* captured this spirit when describing the 1898 Trans-Mississippi and International Exposition: "To see these ever for-midable and hereditary enemies of the white man encamped together in a frame of architectural splendor erected by cour-age, manhood, and sterling integrity, will impress upon the growing sons and daughters a lesson which will bear fruit in years hence when the yet unsettled and uncultured possessions of the United States shall have become jewels upon the Star Spangled Banner."[17]

The year was 1898. The U.S. government was extending its imperial reach. American men were exerting their manliness by defeating Spanish, Cuban, Puerto Rican, and Filipino men. Their manly endeavors proved that industrialization and the rise of urban middle-class lifestyles were not, as some had feared, weakening white American manhood. Within several decades Americans would no longer have to be satisfied with fair exhibits of Cuban and Puerto Rican dancers or Philippine villagers. Those countries would have built tourist hotels, beach resorts, and casinos to lure American pleasure-seekers—all due, it was imagined, to worldwide progress generated by a civilizing sort of American masculinity.

The world's fairs of this energetic era preached that white men's manliness fueled the civilizing imperial mission, and that, in turn, pursuing the imperial mission revitalized the nation's masculinity. At the same time, world's fairs were designed to show that civilized women's domestication was proof of the manly mission's worthiness.

Thus femininity as well as masculinity structured the comparisons and the lessons visitors were to derive from the world's fairs. Women became the viewers and the viewed. White women were meant to come away from the fair feeling grateful for the benefits of civilization they enjoyed. They were not expected to measure progress from savagery to civilization in terms of voting rights or economic independence; instead they were expected to adopt a scale that positioned women's domesticated respectability at one end, and women's hard manual labor at the other. White men, for their part, were expected to look at "savage" men's treatment of their overworked women and congratulate themselves on their own civilized roles as protectors and breadwinners. Without the Samoan, Filipino, and other colonized women, neither male nor female fairgoers would have been able to feel so confident about their own places in this emergent world.

Some American women saw the world's fair as a perfect venue for showing women's special contributions to the nation's progress. America's Centennial Exhibition in 1876 featured a Women's Pavilion, which celebrated the new concept of domestic science, as well as arts and crafts by women from around the world. Progress, technology, and feminine domestic space were combined in a revised version of gendered civilization. In 1893 there was to be a great fair at Chicago to commemorate the four-hundredth anniversary of Columbus's discovery of America. Susan B. Anthony, the suffragist, led a drive to ensure that women would not be excluded from the planning as they had been in designing the 1876 exhibition. The all-male U.S. Congress responded to women's lobbying by mandating the appointment of a Board of Lady Managers to participate in the design of the 1893 Columbian Exposition. The board commissioned a Women's Building. It was among the fair's largest and most impressive, designed by a woman architect, twenty-three-year-old Sophia Hayden. But the Women's Building and its exhibits did not challenge the underlying message of the fair. The white women who took charge of this ambitious project still believed their mission was to demonstrate that American women were leading the world in improving the domestic condition of women. The Women's Building was filled with exhibits of the latest household technology that would lighten women's load. Nor did these women, as unconventional as they were in other ways, challenge the racial hierarchy that was implicitly condoned by the fair. The Board of Lady Managers, chaired by a wealthy Chicago socialite, rejected the proposal that a Black woman be appointed to any influential post.[18]

PACKAGE TOURS AND THE RESPECTABLE WOMAN

Tourism is as much ideology as it is physical movement. It is a bundle of ideas about industrial, bureaucratic life.[19] It is a set of presumptions about womanhood, manhood, education, and pleasure.[20]

In the worldview of tourism, certain women have been set up as the quintessence of the exotic. They are unfamiliar, they are beautiful, they are natural. The women who populate the masculinized tourism fantasy do not push vacuum cleaners or grocery carts, they do not attend parent-teacher meetings, they do not keep track of the household budget. They do not pass critical judgment on men. With these fantasized women, the male tourist feels he has entered a region where he can shed civilization's constraints, where he is freed from standards of behavior imposed by respectable women back home. But, by the mid-nineteenth century, more of these men's daughters were on the move.

Thomas Cook perhaps deserves credit for making the world safe for the respectable woman tourist. On an English summer's day in 1841, walking to a temperance meeting, Thomas Cook had the idea of chartering a train for the next meeting so that participants could board a single train, pay a reduced rate, and while traveling to their meeting be treated to "hams, loaves and tea" interspersed with exhortations against the evils of drink. Some 570 people signed up for that first trip.[21]

Initially, Thomas Cook was concerned primarily with working men like himself. He wanted to provide them with a diversion that did not involve liquor. Only later did Cook come to realize that package tours might attract working men and their wives and children and, eventually, women traveling without a male member of the family. By the 1850s, Britain's more adventurous middle-class women were beginning to earn their own incomes and think about traveling for pleasure, if not to West Africa, then at least to Germany. They still needed to safeguard their respectability in order to stay marriageable and so were looking for a chaperoned tour led by an honorable man. Thomas

Cook, temperance advocate, offered precisely such a service. He only realized the business potential of respectable travel for women in 1855, after receiving a letter from four sisters—Matilda, Elizabeth, Lucilla, and Marion Lincolne of Suffolk. The Lincolne sisters came from a large, middle-class temperance family. All of them had worked for wages when they were in their twenties and had income to spend on pleasure. They wanted to see firsthand the beauties of the Rhine and the fabled cities of the Continent:

> How could ladies alone and unprotected, go 600 or 700 miles away from home? However, after many pros and cons, the idea gradually grew on us and we found ourselves consulting guides, hunting in guide-books, reading descriptions, making notes, and corresponding with Mr. Cook.... Tis true, we encountered some opposition—one friend declaring that it was improper for ladies to go alone—the gentleman thinking we were far too independent.... But somehow or other one interview with Mr. Cook removed all our hesitation and we forthwith placed ourselves under his care....
>
> Many of our friends thought us too independent and adventurous to leave the shores of old England, and thus plunge into foreign lands not beneath Victoria's sway with no protecting relative, but we can only say that we hope this will not be our last Excursion of the kind. We would venture anywhere with such a guide and guardian as Mr. Cook.[22]

Cook was so struck by Matilda and her sisters' letter that he began to run excerpts in his advertisements, making appeals directly to women. By 1907, the company's magazine, *The Traveller's Gazette*, featured on its cover a vigorous young woman bestriding the globe.

Today, a century later, the Thomas Cook Group operates in seventeen countries, serving 23 million travelers per year, generating annual sales of $14.8 billion.[23] It has inspired scores of

Vol. LVII. Established 1851   **FEBRUARY, 1907.**   GRATUITOUS COPY

THE TRAVELLER'S GAZETTE.

An Illustrated Journal Devoted to Travel

Published Monthly
by
THO.ˢ COOK & SON
CHIEF OFFICE.
LUDGATE CIRCUS, LONDON. E.C.

NOTICE TO TRAVELLERS.—Cook's interpreters in uniform meet the Principal Trains and Steamers at the chief cities and parts of Europe and the East, to render assistance in all holders of Cook's Tickets.

Figure 7. Cover of one of Thomas Cook's early travel brochures, 1907. Thomas Cook Archives, London.

competitors. The package-tour holiday is a profitable commodity for some of the international economy's most successful companies. They attract travelers not only from Britain and the United States but also from Japan, China, and South Korea. They take tourists who feel daunted by traveling to unfamiliar parts of the globe on archeological tours in Armenia, monastery tours in China, synagogue tours in Cuba, wildlife tours in Tanzania and Kenya, biking tours in Italy, and Inca archeological tours in Peru. Their operators offer what enterprising Thomas Cook offered: protection, knowledge, convenience, and access. Each tour is shaped and reshaped by the ongoing workings of masculinity and femininity.

Outside the train station in Leicester, England, one can find Thomas Cook's statue. He is portrayed standing with a well-worn valise and rolled umbrella at his feet, his pocket watch in his left hand, waiting for his first tourists.

THE TOURISM FORMULA FOR DEVELOPMENT

From its beginnings, commercialized tourism has been a powerful motor for global integration. Even more than other forms of investment, it has symbolized a country's entrance into the world community. Foreign-owned mines, military outposts, and museum explorations previously drew "remote" societies into the international system, usually on unequal terms. Tourism entails a more politically potent kind of intimacy—because a tourist is not expected to be very adventurous or daring, to learn a foreign language, or to adapt to any but the most superficial local customs. For the male tourist, making sense of the strange local currency and learning when to tip and when not is about all that is demanded. The female tourist, however, must also absorb minimal knowledge about when to wear what length sleeves and skirts and when to cover her hair. Whole websites now are devoted to offering guidance to women tourists on proper feminine attire in specific countries. When one searches for the equivalent guidance for the male tourist, one is taken back to the site offering women advice.

When a government announces its plans to promote tourism as one of its major industries, the implication is that its officials are willing to meet the expectations of those foreigners who want political stability, safety, and congeniality when they travel. A government that decides to rely on money from tourism to reach its development goals is a government that has decided to be internationally compliant enough that even a woman traveling on her own will be made to feel at home there. As women travelers have become crucial for a country's tourism success, that guarantee has taken on even more political and economic significance.

When mass tourism began to overtake elite travel following World War II, most pleasure travel occurred within and between North America and western Europe. In the mid-1970s, a mere 8 percent of all tourists were North Americans and Europeans traveling on holiday to developing countries. A decade later, 17 percent were.[24] Middle-class Canadians who, a decade earlier, thought of going across the border to Cape Cod or Florida in search of holiday warmth were as likely to head for the Bahamas or Cuba. During these same recent years, their French counterparts were more apt to make Tunisia or Morocco rather than Nice their holiday destination. Similarly, Scandinavians now were choosing Sri Lanka or Goa instead of the Costa del Sol.

By the early twenty-first century, most Caribbean governments had made tourism central to their development strategies. These were deliberate political decisions that they made to lessen their countries' dependence on raw commodities and on the large sugar and banana multinational corporations, companies intimately associated with their nations' colonial pasts. However, this tourism-based development strategy has carried a risk: any climate-change-driven increase in the number and severity of the region's hurricanes, and any alteration of major airlines' routes and fares, could jeopardize even the most carefully thought-out local Caribbean development plan.

Similarly, the developing country Egypt was thrown into a tailspin when its 2011–13 Arab Spring political uprising scared off thousands of European and North American tourists. Given that tourism revenues had generated 11 percent of the country's gross domestic product, and that tourism companies employed 18 million Egyptians, this amounted to an economic crisis.[25] Thus it came as a particular blow when the Geneva-based World Economic Forum issued its 2013 report on international tourism ranking Egypt as "the least safe and secure of 140 tourist destinations."[26] It did not help that much of the international reporting about Egyptian politics featured stories of local and foreign women's experiences of sexual harassment in public spaces.

Perhaps the most cautionary tale comes from India. As many women—not just European and North American women but also Japanese, Korean, Chinese and Latin American women—have successfully pushed for the right to be geographically mobile, and as more women have earned enough from working paid jobs to have discretionary money to spend, any government's tourism-dependent development strategy could be undermined if the country gained an international reputation as a place unsafe for women. It is the international character of the reputation that is politically significant for the tourism strategists. In Egypt, as well as India, local women activists for a decade had been naming and challenging local men's sexual harassment and sexual assaults; and they had been critiquing their police and politicians for trivializing women's experiences of physical insecurity. This local feminist activism on behalf of local women's rights and security, however, scarcely made global headlines. It was when sexual harassment and sexual assaults appeared to jeopardize foreign women tourists' safety that the media and officials started to pay attention.[27]

The five-man gang rape and murder of a twenty-three-year-old Indian woman medical student on a New Delhi rogue bus in December 2012 sparked a historic Indian public outcry. This was not the first sexual assault on an Indian woman by a gang of Indian men, but it touched a raw nerve. Thousands of Indian men joined women in the streets to demand that the Indian police begin to take seriously sexual harassment, stalking, and assaults on Indian women. Indian feminist activists, who had been working to stop violence against women—and the ideas fueling that violence—for years, suddenly were called for interviews by mainstream Indian and international media journalists. An op-ed essay by an Indian feminist writer telling of her survival of rape thirty years earlier was featured in the *New York Times*. The writer, Sohaila Abdulali, insisted that the commonly held notion that an Indian woman's honor depended on her sexual purity was not only patriarchal, but it also silenced women targeted for assault and thwarted efforts to hold male perpetrators accountable. It was, Abdulali said, a patriarchally distorted notion perpetuated not only by mothers, fathers, and neighbors but also by police officers, judges, and politicians—a notion that needed to be directly challenged. Frequently, sexual assaults were hidden away in family closets as if they were stories of feminized and familial shame. Rather, Abdulali insisted, sexual assaults should be reported to police, should be treated by everyone as the crimes they were. Accused assailants should be investigated and vigorously prosecuted in open courts of law. Abdulali titled her op-ed essay "I Was Wounded; My Honor Wasn't."

Within hours, it went globally viral, adding to the energy of the Indian women's campaign.[28]

In the weeks following the 2012 gang rape, Indian feminists kept up the pressure on their government. An authoritative panel of three senior Indian judicial officials, the Verma Committee, issued a report in late January 2013 blaming the police and the judicial system for routinely failing to take violence against women seriously. New groups of Indian men organized to transform their own and other men's attitudes toward women.[29]

The international media attention provoked by Indians' protests pushed the government to pass laws that otherwise might never have gotten out of parliament. It energized Indian feminists and enabled the forging of new political alliances. But it also made a lot of women outside of India rethink their travel plans. During the first three months of 2013—when international media were headlining the Delhi rape and the subsequent protests—the number of foreign tourists dropped by 25 percent compared to those same months a year before. The number of female tourists dropped even more sharply, by 35 percent. Indian tourism officials tried to dismiss the numbers, saying that tourism had not been affected by the rape or the protests.[30]

These tourism figures revealed that Indian officials were disaggregating their tourism figures by gender. Not all countries do. Despite officials' attempts to dismiss any suggestion that violence against women—foreign or Indian—was making a dent in India's large tourism industry, these officials, together with private tourism companies operating in India, went into action to reassure foreign women. Tourism and women travelers' contributions to tourism had become too important to Indian development planners to allow them to be jeopardized. Tourism accounted for 6 percent of the India's gross national product and

10 percent of its organized employment, amounting to 20 million jobs, with an estimated additional 70 million Indians working in the large informal sector dependent on tourism.[31] The Thomas Cook company was one of the first to act, launching new women-only tours of India and offering its women travelers free cell phones equipped with emergency numbers for hospitals and police stations. New Delhi's luxury hotel the Imperial created "single lady corridors" for its female guests, staffed by women employees, while the Tourism Ministry set up a multilingual toll-free help line that would be answered only by women staff.[32]

It was not clear, however, whether India's male-dominated political and business elites would continue to take Indian feminists' analyses, and violence against Indian women, seriously once the international media turned its attention elsewhere and the threat to tourism receded.

BEAUTY PAGEANTS AND TOURISM

The Miss World Pageant is owned by its founder, the British businessman Eric Morley, and his family. The Miss Universe Pageant is owned by American billionaire Donald Trump.[33] Although both competitions are unabashedly profit-seeking enterprises, many tourism boosters have come to see placing local women in both of these two globalized competitions as a way to enhance their own country's development goals. Tourism's beauty-pageant supporters believe that having one of their country's women crowned the "most beautiful woman in the world" will generate positive attention, especially to their otherwise overlooked countries, and that it will attract more visitors. A young woman who chooses to compete has her own ambitions; but she will be tightly managed, especially at the contests' national and international levels. By that point, many people will have become invested in her diet, her complexion, her wardrobe, her personality, and her expressed values. Furthermore, a patriarchal version of nationalist pride in the country's beautiful women can pour fuel onto these international beauty competitions.[34] Some local nationalists have agreed; others have loudly protested that such competitions denigrate "their" women. India's conservative Hindu nationalists have objected, and South Sudanese living in the United States were divided when a Miss South Sudan beauty contest was launched in 2007.[35] The Venezuelan government has been one of the most assiduous in recruiting, training, and managing local young women for international beauty competitions.[36]

Iceland was only two generations away from being a poor country, dependent on fishing and sheepherding, with an inhospitable climate, a sparse population, and a language that no one else could speak. Then in the 1980s, Iceland's aggressively probusiness, male-dominant ruling Independence Party promoted not only deregulated banking and thermal energy production but also tourism to accelerate Iceland's development. Competing in international beauty contests was imagined by this ruling masculinized elite as a good fit with their neoliberal development package.[37]

Many Icelanders seemed to enjoy and take pride in the revived Miss Iceland events. Annadis Rudolfsdottir, an Icelandic feminist and researcher, found in her interviews that many women and men watched the finals on television and liked what they saw. And there was a generalized pride expressed when a Miss Iceland was elected Miss World in both 1985 and 1988.[38] One consequence was that Icelandic young women now were commercially cast as allures for North American and European male tourists. This implied a masculinized, sexualized tourist scenario: European men could fly to Iceland for cheap fares, drink the summer-sun-filled nights away in Reykjavik bars, and pick up readily available beautiful Icelandic young women. Icelandair, the state airline, joined in the effort, advertising "One night stands."

The local organizers of the Miss Iceland competition had decided to focus their efforts on winning the Miss World Pageant, rather than Miss Universe, because Miss World's international organizers cultivated a feminine image that was more virginal, less overtly sexy than the Miss Universe competition. That fit with the Icelandic organizers' conscious decision to tie Miss Iceland—and the overwhelmingly blonde young women recruited to compete—to a version of Icelandic nationalism that celebrated the country's environmental purity. The famed Blue Lagoon became a perfect backdrop for the ceremony, and ice from one of the country's glaciers was served to invited guests. The women competing for the title of Miss Iceland, Annadis Rudolfsdottir found, not only would have to be outwardly beautiful (guaranteed by putting them on strict diets) but also would have to "radiate with a glow of inner beauty," just like Iceland's thermal waters.[39]

Iceland's feminists decided that humor was the best strategy for ridiculing the presumptions undergirding the Miss Iceland competition. They crowned a cow outside a Reykjavik hotel and held a mock public auction of women. Gradually, early in the twenty-first century, Icelanders' interest in the contests waned, even though a Miss Iceland was crowned Miss World again in 2005. Then in 2013, after the probusiness Independence Party, with its ally the new rural-based Progressive Party, defeated the Socialist-Green governing alliance to win a parliamentary majority, the organizers sought to revive interest in the Miss Iceland competition. Local feminists responded. Propelled by social media, they swamped the contest with their own candidates. One hundred Icelandic feminists—including the researcher Annadis Rudolfsdottir and a feminist member of parliament, Sigridur Ingibjorg—nominated themselves for Miss Iceland.[40]

STEWARDESSES AND CHAMBERMAIDS

The men who were the early airline owners and managers took their labor cues from the longer established railroad and ocean-liner companies. It was the latter companies who first honed a racial and gendered division of labor designed to maximize profits while constructing an aura of safety and leisure for their paying passengers. Initially, ocean-liner crews were male, ranked by class and race. Still today, white male officers exude both competence and romance for passengers. The Indonesian, Filipino, and other men of color serving in the dining rooms and belowdecks reflect for passengers (an overwhelming majority of whom are white and heterosexually married) a comforting global hierarchy while permitting the company to pay lower wages. In the mid-twentieth century, women crew members multiplied when company executives began to realize that their women passengers preferred to be waited on by women. Elaine Lang and Evelyn Huston were among the handful of British women who signed up to work on the *Empress of Scotland* in the 1930s, a time when shore jobs were hard to find. They worked as stewardesses, rising gradually in rank but finding it impossible to break into the ship's all-male officer corps. Their best hope was to service first-class rather than steerage-class passengers:

"Work and bed, work and bed, that's all it was." Today hundreds of women are hired to work as service personnel in the burgeoning cruise-ship industry. A racialized gendered division of labor continues to keep the ever-larger cruise ships and the multi-million-dollar cruise industry afloat.[41]

When the men who founded the first airline companies initially considered pilots, they thought only of men, despite women being among the first generation of airplane pilots. Blanche Scott is credited with being the first white woman pilot, while Bessie Coleman is recorded as the first African American woman pilot, though she had to go to France to get access to flight training. Although the first woman who earned a pilot's license, Harriet Quimby, did so as early as 1911, and there were an estimated seven hundred women pilots by 1935, it was not until 1973 that a scheduled U.S. airline hired its first woman pilot, Emily Howell.[42]

The airlines' male managers only gradually adopted feminized ideas about who should be hired to work in the airplane cabins, servicing passengers. In 1930 the owner of the Boeing Air Transport (later to become United Airlines) began to think that it was asking too much for male copilots to do double duty as cabin service personnel. Rejecting the model of the African American male porter made popular by American railroad companies, Boeing Air Transport's manager initially thought that his flying customers would be most comfortable if they were serviced in the cabin by Filipino male stewards, adopting the racialized gendered imperial labor model chosen by the U.S. Navy, which routinely recruited Filipino men to work as personal stewards for its white navy officers. He changed his mind—and his gendered labor model—only when he was approached by Ellen Church, herself a nurse and a trained pilot. Church realized that the men who ran the fledgling airlines were unlikely to overcome their own sexist presumptions and hire a woman as a pilot, so she proposed that women trained as nurses—white women—would be most capable of serving as airline cabin crew members. They were skilled professionals and their presence in the cabin would reassure passengers, many of whom were only then overcoming their flying nervousness. The first eight women "stewardesses" took off with Boeing Air Transport in 1930. The feminization of the airlines' cabin crews was rapid. By 1937, America's airlines had in their employ 105 male stewards and 286 stewardesses. After World War II, with the rapid rise of international mass tourism, the masculinized cockpit crews were complemented by thoroughly feminized cabin crews.[43]

Pan American Airlines' founder and ambitious leader, Juan Trippe, adopted the same gender model but slightly altered its racialized pattern. Trippe became convinced that the only way Pan Am could project its image as the tourist industry's post–World War II dominant global carrier—and in the process deflect the emerging competition in Asia by the rapidly growing Japan Airlines—was to hire Asian American women to work as stewardesses on Pan Am's transpacific flights. In 1955, therefore, Pan Am hired its first group of what it called its nisei stewardesses. *Nisei* is the term typically applied to U.S.-born Japanese Americans. Most, though not all, of the Pan Am women were Japanese American women raised in Hawaii. Nonetheless, all the Asian American women Trippe hired were labeled "nisei" because, in the minds of most Americans during the 1950s, the term was identified with the patriotic Japanese American men who fought in the U.S. Army's famous 442nd Regimental Combat Team during World War II. Nisei, wartime heroism, and Pan Am's global tourist business would be merged with feminized airline cabin service.[44]

Despite its contrivance by male executives to profit deeply masculinized businesses, this feminization of airline cabin crews was not perceived as simply oppressive by most of the women hired to be flight attendants during the 1950s to 1970s. Many of these women saw their employment as comfortably meshed with respectable femininity and as opening doors for paid careers and global travel. Two changes, however, radicalized many women working as flight attendants: the deterioration of their in-flight working conditions and the growing numbers of male executives who attempted to sexualize stewardesses and their services for the sake of corporate mass marketing. During this era Singapore Airlines, a government company, ran a centerfold advertisement that featured an Asian woman of somewhat vague ethnicity. She could have been Chinese, Indian, or Malay. She stood in a misty, impressionistic setting, looking out at the reader demurely, holding a single water lily. There was no information about the airline's fare rates or safety record, just this message in delicate print: "Singapore Girl ... You're a great way to fly." On long-distance flights in the 1980s, when the majority of passengers were presumed to be male, Sri Lanka's airline, also government-owned, declared, "When your business is business ... our business is pleasure."[45]

Faced with these changes, many women flight attendants decided to organize. In 1972, two women working as flight attendants for a U.S. airline organized Stewardesses for Women's Rights to challenge the sexist presumptions and stereotypes held by both their corporate employers and their sexually harassing male passengers. Openly identifying with the wider women's movement of the 1970s, the activists in Stewardesses for Women's Rights took as their motto: "Fly me? Go fly yourself!" The women of this organization helped women flight attendants win equal pay, the right to continue working as flight attendants after they married, protection against sexist uniform requirements (no more hot pants, no more thigh-high leather boots), and guarantees that they would be treated as the safety professionals they were.[46]

Yet today, four decades later, as airlines have become even more globally competitive, company executives have worked to roll back those gains, requiring attendants to take on extra tasks and cutting the number of attendants per flight. In response, women and men employed as flight attendants—who are now of a greater racial, ethnic, and age diversity—are speaking out against their working conditions. As one woman flight attendant recently wrote to a journalist who seemed unaware of her deteriorating working conditions: "I am one of those flight attendants going to Dallas picking up trash, holding five cans and reminding everyone who didn't listen to the announcement to put their seat belts on and turn off their electronic devices.... So before you write that we are all complainers, come walk a mile in my shoes with a full 737 with only three of us working."[47]

GLOBALIZED CHAMBERMAIDS

After tourists land at their destination, they expect to be freed from humdrum domestic tasks. To be a tourist means to have someone else making your bed.

Thus chambermaids—along with waitresses, cooks, and security guards—are as crucial to the international tourism industry as miners and banana, rubber, and sugar workers were to colonial industries. Still, a chambermaid seems different. Even a low-paid, overworked male employee on a banana or sugar plantation has a machete, a symbol of strength, a sign that his work is manly. Many nationalist movements have rallied around the image of the exploited male plantation worker; he has represented the denial of national sovereignty.

Nationalist leaders who have become alarmed at the tourism-dependent policies fostered by foreign bankers and adopted their own governments have been reluctant to rally around the symbol of the oppressed chambermaid. Men in nationalist movements may find it easier to be roused to anger by the vision of a machete-swinging man transformed into a tray-carrying waiter in a resort for white patrons—he is a man who has had his masculine pride stolen from him. Caribbean nationalists in the region's diverse island societies have complained that their respective governments' protourism policies have turned each of these societies into a "nation of busboys." To them, "nation of chambermaids" does not have the same mobilizing ring. After all, a woman who has traded work as an unpaid agricultural worker for work as a low-paid hotel cleaner has not lost any of her femininity; she has simply confirmed it.[48]

Tourism is what economists call a "labor-intensive" industry—that is, it has a high ratio of human labor to capital investment and machinery. People who come to a place as tourists expect a lot of service. As in other labor-intensive industries—in garment manufacture, health care and child care, food processing, and electronics assembly—owners make money and governments earn tax revenues to the extent that they can keep down the cost of the wages and benefits allocated to the relatively large numbers of workers they must hire.

Since the early nineteenth century, employers have tried to minimize the cost of employing workers in labor-intensive industries by defining most jobs as "unskilled" or "low-skilled"—jobs, in other words, that workers, allegedly, know how to do naturally.

Women in most societies are presumed to be naturally capable cleaners, washers, cooks, and servers. Since tourism companies need precisely those jobs done, they can keep their labor costs low—and their profits high—if they can define those jobs as naturally women's work. By the early 1980s, in the Caribbean, when newly independent countries such as Barbados and Jamaica were making tourism central to their development plans, 75 percent of tourism workers were women.[49] Ideologies of femininity had become crucial to Caribbean governments' tourism politics.

Caribbean countries were not alone. In the late 1980s, China's post-Mao-era officials, newly eager to attract foreign industry and foreign currency, were approving the construction of new hotels within coastal zones set aside for electronics, garments, and other export factories and helping managers to hire workers. Shenzhen's new Bamboo Garden Hotel employed 360 employees; 80 percent were women.[50] At the same time, in the Philippines, both the authoritarian Marcos regime and its successor, the democratizing Aquino regime, relied on tourism to earn badly needed foreign exchange. The Manila Garden Hotel employed 500 workers, 300 of whom were women. But the democratic popular mobilization that brought down Ferdinand Marcos in 1986 also energized Filipino hotel workers, many of whom joined the Philippines' National Union of Workers in Hotel, Restaurant and Allied Industries. Women within the Filipino union created their own Women's Council. Beth Valenzuela, a single mother working in the hotel's food department, was one of the Manila Garden Hotel's active women unionists. She told a Filipino reporter that she hoped to make the Women's Council a place where issues of particular importance to women hotel workers could be studied and discussed. The council also would train women union members in public speaking and decision making, skills that in the past "have been jealously guarded by the men as their exclusive preserve."[51]

Both the International Labor Organization and the UN World Tourism Organization recently have been pressed by transnational feminists to be more gender-conscious in their tracking of labor conditions in today's booming international tourism industry. In turn, UN Women, the agency of the UN mandated to monitor and advocate women's rights in all political and economic sectors, has begun to pay attention to tourism. The ILO has revealed that in the first decade of the twenty-first century, while women made up 55.5 percent of all workers at all levels in the fast-growing hotels, catering, and tourism sector worldwide, women constituted as much as 70 percent of workers in this sector in certain geographic regions. Women today can be found working as hotel managers, travel agency owners, and pilots. Latin America today has the highest proportion of women employers in tourism. In Nicaragua's and Panama's tourism sectors, more than 70 percent of employers are women. Nonetheless, most women working in tourism are concentrated in the sectors that are the lowest paid and most vulnerable to off-season dismissals.[52]

Globally, in 2012, of all people in the tourism industry employed as servers, cleaners, travel salespersons, and tour guides—that is, those on the lowest rungs of the industry's ladder—90 percent were women. The highest percentages of men in the industry were employed as gardeners, bartenders, porters, and maintenance and construction workers; they were not at the peak of influence, but they were better compensated than their female counterparts. Researchers for UN Women have reported on the myriad ways that sexist stereotyping has prevented most women employed in the expanding tourism industry from gaining the development and empowerment benefits that tourism potentially could distribute. Particularly exploited in the tourism industry are women who perform unpaid labor in family-owned tourism businesses. Overall, both the current global tourism industry and the governments dependent on tourism revenues remain reliant on sex segregation and gendered pay inequity.[53]

Three areas of the global tourism industry that appear most promising for women's genuine empowerment are artisan crafts production, food production, and all-women local tours. For example, a group of eleven Ecuadoran women living on Santa Cruz Island organized a bakery specifically to supply bread to the cruise companies that were carrying thousands of tourists annually to see wildlife on the Galapagos Islands. To succeed, the women reported, they not only had to perfect their bread-making and develop business skills but also had to persuade two groups of men of their endeavor's worth: their resistant husbands and the skeptical men running the cruise companies. Their success with both groups produced increasing economic security for the women and, the women said, gave them an increased sense that they could control their own lives.[54]

A second example comes from the foothills of the Himalayas. Three Nepali sisters, Lucky, Dicky, and Nicky Chhetri, decided there was nothing natural about Nepali men dominating the fast-growing local trekking business. They got training and licensing as authorized Himalayan trekking guides and then set up a program to train other Nepali women in the skills of trek guiding. They created all-women tours for foreign women, naming their enterprise Three Sisters Adventure Trekking. By 2010, 10 percent of all trekking guides in Nepal were Nepali women. As Lucky Chhetri told a UN Women researcher: "We have demonstrated that women are mentally, physically and emotionally as strong as men."[55]

Figure 8. The Nepali women who founded the Three Sisters Adventure Trekking company, engaged in ice-climbing training in Chulu West, 2009. Photo: Darek Zaluski, Poland.

Still, as important as these women-run artisan and small business ventures are, especially for rural women, they open only small windows of opportunity for a limited number of women; they do not fundamentally alter the gendered politics of the massive globalized tourist industry. They scarcely transform the industry's politics. Moreover, even women who succeed in launching craft, food, and guiding cooperatives can have a difficult time keeping control over them. Too often, especially if they are successful, middlemen move in to siphon off their profits.[56]

SEX TOURISM IN INTERNATIONAL POLITICS

Early in the twenty-first century, Thailand's tourism authorities were actively selling Thailand as a gay- and lesbian-friendly tourist destination. One British gay travel company estimated that in 2012 Thailand reaped $1.6 billion in tourism revenues from gay and lesbian tourists. And in surveys, Thailand outranked the United States and Argentina in popularity among the world's gay and lesbian tourists.[57] But just two decades earlier, Thailand was best known for its heterosexual sex tourist appeal to men.

Pat Bong is a neighborhood of Bangkok that for decades has catered to foreign men. In the late 1980s, Thailand had become a major destination for international tourists, and tourism had become central to the Thai government's development strategy. Thailand's male officials were, at best, ambivalent about sex tourism and, thus, about the rights of Thai women and girls. At the time, there were four hundred thousand more women than men living in Bangkok, and male tourists outnumbered female tourists by three to one. Pat Bong's urban landscape made the census figures come alive. Although the government passed a Prostitution Prohibition Act in 1960, six years later it undercut that ban by passing an Entertainment Places Act, which opened enough loopholes to encourage coffee shop and restaurant owners to add prostitution to their menus. In the early 1980s, it was estimated that Bangkok had 119 massage parlors, 119 barbershop-cum-massage parlors and teahouses, 97 nightclubs, 248 disguised brothels, and 394 disco-restaurants, all of which sold sexualized companionship to male customers. Some of the women who worked as prostitutes in these Bangkok establishments had migrated from the countryside, where agricultural development projects had left them on the margins; other women already were second- and even third-generation sex workers, increasingly cut off from the rest of Thai society. In this decade, a woman working in a Bangkok massage parlor could earn an average of 5,000 baht per month; wages in nonentertainment jobs open to women—in the garment industry, as domestic servants, and as agricultural workers—averaged a paltry 840 baht per month.[58] Marriage to a foreign man frequently appeared to a woman to be the only avenue out of Pat Bong, but it too could prove illusory. For example, one woman reported that she "had lived with an English man working as a technician on an oil rig. But he left her and went back to England. She said she was not working when she was with him, but returned to her job after some months since he failed to send her money and it was impossible for her to keep such an expensive flat. 'What else can I do? After all, these men are good business.'"[59]

Sex tourism is not an anomaly; it is one strand of the many-stranded, gendered tourism industry. While economists in industrialized societies presume that the "service economy," with its explosion of feminized job categories, follows a decline in manufacturing, policy makers in many developing countries have been encouraged by international advisers to develop service sectors *before* manufacturing industries mature. Bar hostesses before automobile workers, not after.[60]

At this point, it is important to draw some distinctions. Sex tourism and sex trafficking are different, though intertwined, phenomena. They do share crucial features: both are gendered; both are patriarchal; both are political; both are commercialized; both are international. Sex tourism is the process of encouraging overwhelmingly male tourists—from North America, western Europe, the Middle East, Russia, and East and Southeast Asia—to travel from one country to another to gain access to women's sexual services. Racialized, sexualized enticements are created (using the Internet to great effect), fantasies of masculinity are wielded, flights are scheduled, hotels are booked, certain women are commodified and made available, police are bribed. Profits are made. All of these activities have been listed here in the unhelpful passive tense. That dilutes their political content. Each one of these sex tourism activities is done by someone. By whom? To study sex tourism calls for naming who does what at each step along the way. Sex tourism—and all the men and women who make sex tourism possible—continues to shape the economic, political, and cultural relationships between countries. In particular, taking the workings of sex tourism seriously shines a bright light on the ways in which both masculinized sexual anxieties and efforts to assuage those anxieties shape relationships between countries today.

The people in the business of sex tourism know that a "tourist" can take multiple forms. Often the male travelers whom sex tourism agents think of as a potential market are not men dressed in shorts, holding maps, and carrying cameras strapped around their necks. Rather, they are men on business trips, men on diplomatic assignments, men deployed on international military operations. When these men seek after-hours recreation, they become a potential clientele for sex tourism businesses. Many of these male customers do not ask whether the women and girls (and occasionally boys) offered to them for a fee are performing these sexualized services of their own free will. Such curiosity might take the pleasure out of the sexualized experience.[61]

This brings us to sex trafficking. When investigating the workings of sex tourism—men traveling for sex to India, to Kenya, to Cambodia, to Ukraine, to the Dominican Republic, to Cuba, and to the new sites being opened by sex tourism entrepreneurs each year—one has to ask: "How voluntary, deceived, intimidated, or coerced are the women who work in this particular sexualized commerce?" Answering that question takes careful, detailed research. The answer cannot be assumed a priori.[62] Because any woman's freedom to refuse work in a sexualized massage parlor or to walk away from being prostituted in a disco or coffee shop cannot be assumed, many feminists use the common term *sex worker* with great care. *Sex worker* has been adopted by many commentators to show respect for the woman who is performing commercialized sex with paying male customers. But it is a term that implies labor autonomy. By contrast, *sex slave* and *trafficked woman* are terms developed by feminists in the 1990s to capture the realities of forced (whether paid or unpaid) sexual servicing. Any girl or woman who has been trafficked or turned into a sex slave has not lost her dignity as a human being; rather, her essential dignity has been severely violated by those who have devised her enslavement and by those who gain satisfaction or profits from her enslavement. Alternatively, a phrase such as *woman in prostitution* leaves usefully pending the exact nature of any woman's sexualized servicing of men until one has investigated the precise conditions under which the woman is living.

When exploring the workings of sex tourism—and the roles played by sex traffickers in sustaining sex tourism—at any time in any place, it is useful to discover three things: (a) under what conditions any woman or girl first entered prostitution, (b) under what conditions she is daily living her life in prostitution, and (c) the actual opportunities she has to leave prostitution if she chooses. If the forced movement of girls and women from one region to another (e.g., northeast Thailand to Bangkok) or from one country to another (e.g., Nepali women and girls to New Delhi, or Russian women to New York, Amsterdam, or Seoul) is revealed, then one has to uncover the traffickers' allies.

Those alliances will be gendered. To move people against their will (or deceptively, without their full understanding) across national borders today requires complex alliances. Research into the current interplay of sex tourism and sex trafficking, therefore, calls for developing sophisticated feminist investigatory skills. One has to be able to investigate the discreet yet interlocking gendered workings of deceit, greed, indebtedness, coercion, intimidation, shame, isolation, and fear.[63]

In the last thirty years, feminists working transnationally have pressed governments and international agencies of the United Nations to track sex tourists and the companies facilitating sex tourism, as well as the patterns of sex trafficking. As a result of this feminist data-collecting activism, one can today look at a map of the world to see sex tourists' and sex traffickers' travels. The lines of coerced travel displayed in the feminist-informed *Penguin Atlas of Women in the World* are myriad, criss-crossing the globe.[64] Especially prominent among the destination countries (countries to which sex-trafficked women are forcibly sent) are Thailand, Saudi Arabia, South Africa, and the United States. In 2006 alone, an estimated fifty thousand women were trafficked just into the United States.[65]

The countries in which women are most likely to be snared in the traffickers' nets are of three sorts. The first sort is those countries that have gone through recent economic crises and whose governments, in the name of "austerity," have shredded their public-safety nets, leaving women desperate for work and most likely to believe traffickers' false promises of decently paid employment in another country. The second is those countries that have been hit by catastrophic natural disasters and whose governments are ill equipped or unwilling to provide security for the thousands of women and men, girls and boys, physically displaced and separated from their families. The third sort is those countries (and regions of countries) that have endured militarized violence which has uprooted people, forcing them to flee and become refugees. What this means for anyone trying to carefully sort out the relationships between sex tourism and sex trafficking in any given time and place is that investigating those dynamic connections will require a curiosity about how women and girls (each) experience economic crisis, natural disaster, or armed conflict.[66]

The AIDS epidemic, starting in the early 1980s and, despite scientific and medical advances, continuing today, increased the appeal of young girls for many male sex tourists. These men imagined that having sex with a child made them less vulnerable to HIV/AIDS. In international politics, it has been somewhat easier to mobilize government officials—especially those in ministries of tourism, offices of immigration, and border police, as well as local police—to confront child-sex trafficking than to tackle the sex trafficking of adult women. It has been easier to persuade diverse governments that a ten-year-old girl could not willingly be so far from her home and voluntarily having sex with an adult man.

A problematic alliance of American congressional liberals and conservatives passed an anti-sex-trafficking law in 2000 that enabled women and men who escaped from forced labor or forced sex work to be issued temporary U.S. visas; it also required the State Department to conduct an annual international assessment of which governments were taking effective steps to reduce all forms of human trafficking, including sex trafficking, and which governments were failing to take such steps.

The State Department's 2013 assessment, the *Trafficking in Persons Report,* concluded that trafficking—for exploitive labor in factories, cotton and tomato fields, brothels, and private homes—was widespread internationally and that it was victimizing girls, women, boys, and men. What most media turned into headlines was the State Department's worldwide three-tiered rankings of governments according to their genuine efforts to prevent and reduce trafficking, as well as to their efforts to protect the rights of those who were being trafficked. Among the seventeen governments that the State Department's researchers found to be most negligent (ranking in "Tier 3") were Algeria, Central African Republic, China, Congo (DRC), Cuba, Equatorial Africa, Eritrea, Guinea-Bissau, Iran, Libya, Mauritania, North Korea, Papua New Guinea, Russia, Sudan, Syria, and Uzbekistan.[67]

This three-tiered ranking, however, was only of government officials' unequal efforts. It did not reflect where women, girls, men, and boys were being deceived or forced into sexualized or unsexualized labor; nor did it rank countries that served as traffickers' transit points and as final destinations. Thus the State Department's awarding of "Tier 1" rankings to, for instance, Colombia, France, Israel, Italy, Norway, South Korea, and the United States did not mean those societies were free of sex trafficking or the sex tourism that trafficking enables.

One achievement in international political-institution-building has been the establishment within the UN system, inside the Office of the High Commissioner for Human Rights, of a Special Rapporteur on the sale of children, child prostitution and child pornography. Reporting to the UN Human Rights Council in Geneva in 2013, Special Rapporteur Najat Maalla M'jid noted that poor children were the most vulnerable to trafficking. Abusers—customers and traffickers—sought out children on beaches, in karaoke bars, and in hotels—that is, in places where tourists were concentrated. She also reported that traffickers were increasingly using the Internet to make contact with the children, through online chat rooms, either directly or through their intermediaries. She estimated that child sex trafficking had become a $20 billion a year business.[68] As feminist activists and UN monitors note, that $20 billion is the estimate for only the sex trafficking in children, not the revenues flowing from the trafficking of adult women.[69]

CONCLUSION

Tourism is not just about escaping work and drizzle; it is about power, increasingly internationalized power. That conventional political commentators do not discuss tourism as seriously as oil or weaponry may tell us more about those commentators' own ideological constructions of "seriousness" than it does about the politics of tourism.

Government and corporate officials have come to depend on international travel-for-pleasure in several ways. First, over the last sixty years they have come to see tourism as an industry that can help diversify local economies made vulnerable because of their reliance on one or two raw export products. Thus tourism is embedded in the inequalities of international trade but is often tied to the politics of particular products such as sugar, bananas, tea, and copper. Second, officials have looked to tourism to provide them with foreign currency, a necessity in the ever more globalized economies of both poor and rich countries. Third, tourism development has been looked upon as a spur to more general social development; the "trickle down" of modern skills, new technology, and improved public services is imagined to follow in the wake of foreign tourists. Fourth, many government officials have used the expansion of tourism to secure the political loyalty of local elites. For instance, facilitating certain hotel licenses or zoning exemptions may win a politician more strategic allies today than providing patronage in the form of a mere civil-service appointment. Finally, many officials have hoped that tourism would raise their own nation's international visibility and even its prestige. As contradictory as it may at first seem, international tourism promotion can be imagined to bolster nationalist pride.

Many of these hopes have been dashed. Yet tourism continues to be promoted by bankers, development planners, and private investors as a means of making the international system less unequal, more financially sound, and more politically stable. A lot is riding on sun, surf, ruins, service, and souvenirs.

To get a grip on the realities of international tourism's politics, one has to hone one's gender-analytical investigatory skills. Take a tourism-dependent hotel—perhaps a large hotel owned by the world's biggest hotel company, the InterContinental Hotels Group (Hilton and Marriott rank as the world's number two and three hotel companies), or a hotel owned by a smaller regional company that attracts foreign travelers. Try doing a feminist gendered political analysis of just that hotel, from top to bottom. The "top" might be located in a government ministry or in a corporate boardroom far from where the hotel's female housekeepers are being pressured to use toxic cleaning materials and to lift the ever-heavier mattresses. Don't leave out the hotel's guests.

To start: Where are the women? Where are the men? Then track who is making which decisions for whom. Make visible how the workings of racialized ideas about femininities and masculinities are shaping the myriad relationships within the hotel. Tell the stories of any employees who have attempted to alter any of these unequal relationships. What have been the consequences of these efforts for each group in the hotel? When you are tracking the hotel's guests, be sure to make visible those elite men who use this hotel for their masculinized business meetings or for their sexual assignations.

Now make your feminist gender analysis of this hotel sensitive to the historical moment in which you have conducted it. What buildup of tourism in this country or this town has led to today's hotel business? Find out if this hotel had a similar or perhaps different pattern of gendered divisions of labor and guests ten years ago. Finally, spell out the implications of your findings for the gendered tourism politics of this hotel company, of women workers, of international relations.

Without ideas about masculinity and femininity—and the enforcement of both—in the societies of departure and the societies of destination, it would be impossible to sustain the tourism industry and its political agendas in their current form. It is not simply that ideas about pleasure, travel, escape, bed-making, and sexuality have affected women in rich and poor countries. The very structure of international tourism has *needed* patriarchy to survive and thrive. Men's capacity to control women's sense of their security and self-worth has been central to the evolution of tourism politics. It is for this reason that actions by women—as tourists, airline flight attendants, hotel housekeepers, union organizers, women in prostitution, data collectors, wives of businessmen, and organizers of alternative tours for women—should be seen as political, internationally political.

CHAPTER THREE

Nationalism and Masculinity

*The Nationalist Story Is Not Over—and It Is
Not a Simple Story*

In the depths of the post-banking-crash recession, Catalonians took to the streets in Barcelona. Women and men of all ages, unemployed young people, public workers who still had jobs but who had seen their wages cut, and older people whose pensions were in jeopardy, all joined in the Catalan chanting and singing. All of Spain was suffering from the economic crisis that had begun with the international banking failures of 2008, but the people who came out to march through downtown Barcelona on this sunny May evening organized as Catalans, a proud regional ethnic group within Spain's multiethnic society. Among the demonstrators' most prominent banners were those that blamed what they called "the Troika" for their woes: the European Union's Commission, the European Central Bank, and the German government, headed by Chancellor Angela Merkel, the latter because the Germans had been the most assertive of the EU's member states in insisting that Spain (as well as Ireland, Greece, and Portugal) engage in deep public-spending cuts to rebalance their budgets. The economic crisis was affecting the lives of all Spaniards, but for many of these marchers it had reignited an intense sense of their own Catalan national identity. The elected officials of Catalonia promised to give their region's citizens a chance to vote in an upcoming referendum on Catalonian independence.

To the north, politicians of the ruling Scottish National Party were pressing London to allow Scottish citizens to vote for Scotland's independence from the United Kingdom. Scottish National Party leaders assured Scots than an independent Scotland would keep its membership in the thirty-five-member European Union, though EU officials in Brussels warned that an independent Scotland would have to apply for EU membership. That uncertainty gave some Scottish proindependence voters pause.

Across the Atlantic, Quebec voters had twice in recent years voted to remain a province within a multiethnic Canada. But the winning margins had been narrow, and it seemed likely that, before long, Quebec nationalists would press for another referendum on Quebec independence.

In Africa, after years of bloody fighting, South Sudan had broken away from Sudan to become one of the world's newest recognized sovereign states.

Back in Europe, Yugoslavia had fragmented into ethnically defined small nation-states as the result of a violent, multisided 1992–95 civil war. Czechoslovakia had broken in two, becoming the Czech Republic and Slovakia. The Soviet Union had broken apart in the early 1990s without a war, leaving a still-ethnically diverse but Russian-dominated state of Russia, now with a score of ethnically defined (though not ethnically homogeneous) new states on its borders, among them Latvia, Estonia, and Lithuania on the Baltic Sea, plus Ukraine and Belarus on its European borders, and Kazakhstan, Kyrgyzstan, and Tajikistan along its western Asian frontiers. Moscow was waging a brutal war to keep the ethnically distinct region of Chechnya within the Russian domain.

Cartographers were being kept busy.

Nationalism, which burst onto the international political scene in the mid-1800s, had generated the political power to splinter empires: the Ottoman, the Hapsburg, the Russian, the British, the French, the Dutch, the Spanish, the Portuguese, the Danish, the Japanese, and the American. The Americans of thirteen northern colonies, and the Latin Americans to their south, were the first to wield nationalist ideas to effectively challenge Spanish, Portuguese, and British imperial rule. World War I, a war so horrible that it was (optimistically) imagined to be "the war to end all wars," seemed to give even more potent validation to nationalist ideas. Meeting at Versailles in 1919, the victors left their own multinational, multiethnic empires intact but carved up the losing Ottoman and Hapsburg imperial domains into what the male elite carvers thought were peoples with the right to "national sovereignty." It took the combination of World War II, popular anticolonial movements, and a succession of violent armed conflicts to compel the remaining imperial rulers to recognize the rights of national sovereignty belonging to most of the peoples they ruled.

But the Serbs, Croatians, Lithuanians, Slovaks, Catalans, Quebequois, and Scots—as well as the Okinawans; Tibetans; Chechens; Uyghurs; the Kurds living in Iraq, Turkey, Syria, and Iran; and the Tamil minority in Sri Lanka—have made it clear that the story of nationalism is far from over, and that it remains a complicated story with narratives still hotly contested.

Moreover, in the twenty-first century, nationalist energies have made themselves felt internationally not only in ethnically based separatist movements but also through the foreign policies of powerful central governments. Russian nationalists have been determined to suppress the ethnic Chechen rebellion and have narrowly defined the "true" Russian nation in order to suppress Russian gays and lesbians. The Chinese political leadership has spoken in the language of nationalism while not only continuing to deepen China's rule of Tibet and to claim Taiwan but also extending China's claim of sovereignty over the oil-rich South China Sea. The Turkish political elite has wielded nationalism while seeking to deny that modern Turkey is a multiethnic state. Japan's nationalists have expressed new confidence and wielded new electoral influence, partly in response to the Chinese government's regional assertiveness. American officials have continued to assert U.S. rule over a host of island societies in the Caribbean and South Pacific, from Puerto Rico to American Samoa and Guam, while also using various forms of nationalist rhetoric to justify conducting wars and drone strikes far from established U.S. borders.[1]

Popular movements have harnessed nationalist sentiments and images to cast a harsh light on the homogenizing effects of globalization. Starbucks opened more outlets worldwide; Hollywood concocted what studio directors thought of as action-packed "global films"; multilateral agreements were hammered out between governments to enable Walmart and other corporate behemoths to chase smaller, local companies out of the marketplace; large fishing companies decimated fish stocks off the shores of Canada and Iceland. Each manifestation of globalized commerce has seemed to threaten not just rival businesses but the very essence of national identity.[2]

All of these stories, past, present, and those hinting the future, are typically told as if gender were irrelevant. What matters, so these conventional narratives go, is which people think of themselves as Scottish—or Icelandic, Catalan, Chechen, or Okinawan—and what they do with the feelings this nurtures. The storytellers often craft their tales—of humiliation, mobilization, struggle, victory, and defeat—as if nationalism were experienced identically by women and men, and as if women and men played identical roles in defining and critiquing nationalist goals. What follows from these questionable notions is the further assumption—also typically unexamined—that nationalist movements are created and spin out their consequences without taking into account ideas about masculinity and femininity.

It turns out that these three assumptions are an unreliable basis for making sense of the world we are living in.

Women have had distinctly uneasy relationships with nationalism. On the one hand, thousands of women have discovered in nationalist movements a new public persona and an opening for new political participation. Seeing themselves as, and being seen by others as, members of a nation have given these women an identity larger than that defined by domesticated motherhood or marriage. On the other hand, even when they have been energized by nationalism, many women have discovered that, in practice, as women, they often have been treated by male nationalist leaders and intellectuals chiefly as symbols—patriarchally sculpted symbols—of the nation. Women have served as symbols of the nation violated, the nation suffering, the nation reproducing itself, the nation at its purest. Being reduced to a symbol has meant that women have not been treated as genuine participants (with their own ideas, goals, and skills) in the nationalist movements organized to end colonialism, ethnic domination, racism, and globalized capitalist exploitation.[3]

Moreover, because a nation is framed as an "us," it puts a premium on belonging. It has a strong potential to be exclusivist, even xenophobic. Women active in ethnic minority communities, especially in new immigrant communities, are wary of nationalism's exclusivist tendencies. Afro-Caribbean Scots, Algerian Catalonians, Haitian Quebecois, Korean Japanese, Polish Irish, Iraqi Americans, Turkish Germans, Moroccan French, Kurdish Turks—members of each of these communities have cause to worry when nationalism begins to dominate the public conversation. For many feminists today, approaching nationalism with extreme caution is necessary because, they have concluded, building alliances between women's advocates in all of their country's ethnic and racial communities is crucial for a vibrant, sustainable women's movement.

As feminist ideas and feminist organizing have grown more influential internationally in the late twentieth century and the early twenty-first century, more women have spoken out against being turned by nationalist leaders into mere symbols of the nation. They have made more demands for gender equality inside the nationalist movements that have sought their support. Not all of these feminist-inspired demands have been welcomed. As a result, women's political relationships with nationalist movements have been complex and often fraught. Stories of those complexities have often been silenced—in history books, in national holiday celebrations, in national museum exhibitions. After all, a writer, an events organizer, a curator who adds gendered complexity to the story of any nationalist movement might deprive that movement—and the very idea of "the nation"—of some of its luster.

Any commentator, nevertheless, who remains incurious about women's experiences, ideas, and actions, consequently, will draw a picture of nationalism and of any given nationalist movement that is simplistic. Drawing simplistic portraits of nationalist movements will produce a canvas that makes international politics look simpler than it is.

WOMEN, COLONIALISM, AND ANTICOLONIALISM

Colonialism was good for the postcard business. Colonial administrators, soldiers, settlers, and tourists were looking for ways to send home images of the societies they were ruling, images that were appealing and yet which made it clear that these alien societies needed the allegedly civilizing governance only whites could bestow. The colonial postcard images were frequently eroticized and surprisingly standardized—a Zulu woman from southern Africa and a Maori woman from New Zealand were asked to assume similar poses for the British imperialists' "grapher."

French colonialists, too, mailed home postcard pictures, choosing images of Arab women in their North African colonies. Some were veiled, others were not. Some were obviously posed in a photographer's studio, others apparently caught on film unawares.[4] Many of these postcards convey a sexual message. "Aicha and Zorah" is the caption for a photo of two young Algerian women, unveiled and looking straight at the photographer—and thus at the buyer and eventual recipient of the postcard. The two women are sitting on a window ledge behind an ornate iron grille. Another card, captioned "Moorish woman"— as if representing all Arab women—shows a woman wearing neither a veil nor a robe to cover her breasts. She too is leaning against a window grille, looking through it from the inside, available, though almost beyond reach.

Figure 9. "The Beauty of Kraal, Zululand": a Zulu woman pictured on a colonial postcard from South Africa; photo taken in the early 1900s.

Figure 10. "Kia-Ora: Greetings from Maoriland": a Maori woman pictured on a British colonial postcard from New Zealand, circa 1930.

Malek Alloula was the collector of these French colonial postcards. He was an Algerian nationalist. The ephemera of colonialist culture, these postcards captured for him the imperial concepts of masculine adventure and the "exotic" that were as crucial to French colonial domination as the Foreign Legion. European "Orientalism" nurtured an appreciative fascination with these cultures while justifying European rule in the name of "civilization." The image of the tantalizingly veiled Muslim woman was a cornerstone of this Orientalist ideology and of the imperial structure it supported.[5]

Malek Alloula used these images to explore his own identity as a male nationalist: for a man, to be conquered is to have *his* women turned into fodder for imperialist postcards. Becoming a nationalist requires a man to resist the foreigner's use and abuse of *his* women.

But what of the women themselves? Aicha and Zora must have had their own thoughts about being posed unveiled and behind bars—just as did the Maori and Zulu women who posed for the British photographers. Perhaps they later saw the postcard on sale near a hotel. Maybe they were flattered; maybe they were humiliated. How were they persuaded to sit for the photographer in the first place? Were they paid? Who got the money? Malek Alloula and other male nationalists seem remarkably *in*curious about the abused women's own thoughts—about the meaning they might have assigned to foreign conquest.

Colonized women have served as sex objects for foreign men. Some have married foreign men and thus facilitated alliances between foreign governments and companies and conquered peoples.[6] Others have worked as cooks and nannies for the wives of those foreign men. In simply trying to earn an income, they may have unintentionally bolstered white women's sense of moral superiority by accepting their religious and social instruction. Simultaneously, many women living under colonial rule have sustained men in their communities when their masculine self-respect has been battered by colonists' contempt and condescension. Women have planted maize, yams, and rice in small plots to support families so that their husbands could be recruited to work miles away in foreign-owned mines or plantations. Women as symbols, women as workers, and women as nurturers have been crucial to the entire colonial undertaking.[7]

Thanks to feminist historians, we now are learning more about the complex ideas and strategies of women who lived under colonial rule. For instance, some Korean urban women living under Japanese rule in the second and third decades of the twentieth century carved out new identities for themselves as modern New Women. They even traveled to Tokyo to study and to work with Japan's first generation of outspoken feminist writers and artists. These Korean women were not pawns of the colonial rulers, but they did reject what some Korean nationalist men imagined were the ideals of Korean traditional feminine purity. Trying to craft a life as an autonomous woman in an era of colonial rule at a time when nationalist sentiments are politically salient can be risky. There may appear to be almost no cultural space in which to stand, speak, or breathe freely. Who these Korean New Women were, what they stood for, how they should be remembered, whether they should be thought of as "loyalists" or "traitors," are still questions hotly debated among today's South Korean feminists and nationalists.[8]

For Korean feminists these gendered historical investigations of nationalism have increasing significance today, as Koreans continue to determine what they think about the presence in their country of large U.S. military bases, as they build up their own national military, as South Korea's immersion in the global political economy becomes ever deeper, as the prospects of reunification with North Korea wax and wane, and as growing numbers of Koreans who travel abroad as tourists, students, and business executives migrate, creating a large Korean diaspora in the United States.[9]

And what about those women who worked for, or found their own reasons to work with, the Nazi occupiers of France, or the Soviet occupiers of East Germany, or the American occupiers of Iraq? What criteria are being used today, and by whom, to determine whether any of these women should be seen now as French, German, or Iraqi patriots or pariahs? It is the very saliency of women—and ideas about femininity—during years of foreign occupation and in an ongoing nationalist project that continues to make the writing of feminist history so politically fraught, and necessary.

Nationalist movements rarely have taken women's experiences as the starting point for an understanding of how a people becomes colonized or how it throws off the shackles of that material and psychological domination. Rather, nationalism typically has sprung from masculinized memory, masculinized humiliation, and masculinized hope.

"Not only are we prevented from speaking for women but also [not allowed] to think, and even to dream about a different fate. We are deprived of our dreams, because we are made to believe that leading the life we lead is the only way to be a good Algerian."[10] The speaker, Algerian feminist Marie-Aimée Hélie-Lucas, was describing the conditions under which her postcolonial nationalist government—an independent government she had fought to establish—could rationalize its new legislation to restrict women's social and political participation, despite women's active part in their country's anticolonial war. She was quick, however, to warn her feminist listeners gathered in Helsinki at an international meeting: "Probably most of the women present at this Symposium take for granted that they belong to a country, a nation, which does not have to prove its existence; it allows for transcending the concept of nation, and criticizing it. It has not been allowed for us[;] ... it is not for so many people in still colonized countries, or countries facing imperialism at war.... [Under these conditions it is] much more difficult to come to criticize the nation, and even the State which pretends it represents the Nation."[11]

Marie Aimée Hélie-Lucas went on to cofound Women Living Under Muslim Laws, one of today's most valuable sources of transnational feminist information.[12] Perhaps not surprisingly, Women Living Under Muslim Laws, which now is a broad transnational network of feminists in countries as diverse as Egypt, Sudan, Bosnia, Tunisia, Pakistan, and Malaysia, has been sharply critical of any nationalist discourse used to deny women's rights or to limit women's public organizing.

A "nation" is an idea, a powerful idea. At the core of this idea is the image of a collection of people who have come to believe that they have been shaped by a common past and are destined to share a common future. That belief is usually (though not inevitably) nurtured by a common language and a sense of otherness, of being distinct from groups around them. Nationalism is a package of interwoven ideas and values, one of which is a commitment to fostering those beliefs and promoting those policies that permit the nation to stay cohesive and control its own destiny. Colonial rule has provided especially fertile ground for nationalist ideas because it has given an otherwise disparate people such a potent shared experience of foreign domination.

The experience of foreign domination can trump differences among people of diverse classes, varied skin tones, different regional affiliations, and perhaps even different religions and ethnicities.

The nation has the potential for unfurling a big umbrella. In this generous vision, multiethnicity, religious tolerance (sometimes linked to a secular state), and regional diversity are consciously embraced, seen not as threatening the nation but rather as the distinguishing hallmarks of the big-umbrella nation. Tito of Yugoslavia attempted to institutionalize this form of nation; so did Gandhi and the Baathist parties of Iraq and Syria; so too did Pierre Trudeau of Canada and Nelson Mandela of South Africa. Some of these big-umbrella nationalists have pursued democratic politics, while others have slipped into militarized authoritarianism to enforce their vision. Many people, nonetheless, who have embraced nationalism have been suspicious of the big-umbrella vision of the nation. Instead, they have opted for a "purer" nation, a tightly "wrapped umbrella" sort of nation. In this alternative, narrower vision, national strength is believed to flow from social and cultural homogeneity. Which vision—the big umbrella or the wrapped umbrella—of nationalism any woman supports or simply has to cope with in her life will have an effect on her personal and political choices.

In practice, one of the major differences between the open- and shut-umbrella versions of the nation is the official attitude toward intermarriage. Does the nationalist government make it easy or difficult for a woman of the dominant (or ruling) community to marry a man from outside her community? If a woman marries a man of a different religion, race, or linguistic heritage, is she seen as strengthening the nation or betraying it? An example: as the multiethnic, religiously pluralistic Iraq fashioned by the Baathists (and then ruled by Saddam Hussein, the country's final Baathist leader, using ever more authoritarian methods) violently fell apart in the 1990s and the beginning of the twenty-first century, the number of multiethnic and multisect marriages dramatically declined, becoming less and less popularly acceptable. For some Iraqis this decline was taken as a sign of how much they had lost as a result of authoritarian rule, the United States–led military invasion, and the emergence of a postwar sectarian regime. As intermarriage was increasingly deprecated, it felt to these Iraqis as if they had lost the big-umbrella nation they had known and valued.[13]

One becomes a nationalist, of either the big-umbrella or wrapped-umbrella variety, when one begins to recognize shared public pasts and futures with people one does not know personally, people beyond one's family and town. But it is not women's past experiences, present realities, and strategies for the future that are made the basis of the dominant understandings of nationalism they are urged to support. Yet, as Algerian feminists have warned, it is risky for a woman to criticize a movement that claims to represent her own nation or a regime that exercises authority in the name of that nation. Living as a nationalist feminist is one of the most difficult political projects in today's world.

GENDERED COLONIALISM

Many women from imperial countries have served their own governments by teaching in state and mission schools. A young white American woman recalled the thrill she felt when she sailed to Manila as one of the first teachers to help establish American rule over the Philippines in 1901. Pattie Paxton was recruited by the U.S. Army. As she sailed out of San Francisco

Bay, American soldiers were still engaged in a campaign to quash Filipino anticolonial insurgents who had fought their former Spanish rulers in the name of nationalism.

Pattie Paxton hardly fits the conventional picture of an imperialist. She had just graduated from college, a rare achievement for a young American woman at the turn of the twentieth century. A classmate had told her of "the interesting flora in the Philippine Islands, of orchids, of pleasant Nipa houses, and the best behaved children he had ever seen" while assuring Pattie that the army would never send teachers to "dangerous spots." Paxton recalled later that she saw herself "playing my small part in this great adventure" and seeing "the world at the expense of Uncle Sam." Her mind was made up when she learned that her college friend Stella was going as well, and that they could make the voyage together. Aboard ship they met other unmarried young women teachers, as well as men just out of the University of California. The women met in one of the staterooms "to read and gossip" and joined the young men to "spend pleasant evenings on deck singing, chiefly college songs."[14]

Few American women raised their voices to protest at the sailing. Susan B. Anthony, despite her leadership of the emergent American suffrage movement, found she had few followers when she protested to President McKinley in 1900 that the annexation of Hawaii and colonial expansion in the Caribbean and the Pacific did little more than extend American-style subjugation of women. Indeed, opposing Anthony's critiques, some suffragists in the United States and Europe even argued that their *service* to their respective empires was proof of their reliability as voters.[15]

After several weeks in Manila and Iloilo, during which they lived like tourists and provided a seemingly innocent change for the American soldiers, Pattie and Stella were sent to the provincial town of Bacolod, headquarters of the American Sixth Infantry. In Bacolod, prominent Filipino families, who for generations had accommodated Spanish colonizers, were trying to accommodate the country's newest foreign occupiers. Sabina, the landowner with whom Pattie and Stella were lodged, did her best to introduce the two young women to her relatives and friends. Then, at last, the two American women received their first teaching assignments. They were sent to a village in the Negros mountains where Filipino anti-imperialist *insurrectos* were still active. Pattie and Stella did not seem perturbed; this was the adventure they had longed for. They wasted no time in setting about transforming the village's two existing schools, one for boys and one for girls. Each reflected the earlier Spanish colonists' approach to learning: religious texts and recitation in unison. "Upon such a foundation," Paxton recalls, "we were to build American schools, and in that foundation we recognized at least three strong blocks: a disciplined group, an eagerness to learn, a desire to excel. In addition," she remembers gratefully, "we found the teachers keen to learn our language and our methods of teaching."

Paxton spent four years teaching in the Philippines. Some of her most frustrating moments came when she could not persuade local Filipino officials to encourage little girls to attend school. She was plagued, too, by a lack of proper materials. But she made do, taught vocabulary and numbers, learned local songs, and helped her students make handicrafts. And life was not all work. There were picnics and holiday celebrations to attend with the American soldiers.

Pattie Paxton was not overtly racist. She was disgusted by an American colonel's "white man's burden" dinner speech and by his wife's arrogance. Nonetheless, Paxton and the other young women who came to the Philippines to teach in those heady days of American colonial rule helped to establish the values and institutions that would become the objects of an intense Filipino nationalist controversy eight decades later. Corazon Aquino became president of the Philippines in 1986 on a wave of democratizing nationalism, but she herself was a graduate of an American college. Like many other Filipinos today, she remained torn between nationalist pride and an admiration for American values, the legacy of Pattie, Stella, and other women who saw adventure in working in the service of colonialism.

European and American women taught more than just letters and numbers in their governments' colonies; they also taught notions of respectability. They traveled to colonized societies as settlers, explorers, and missionaries. They served colonial administrations without pay as the wives of soldiers, planters, missionaries, and administrators. European and American women volunteered to work as nurses, governesses, and teachers. The masculinized colonial governments expected women in all these roles to set standards of ladylike behavior. The Victorian code of feminine respectability, it was thought, would set a positive example for the local colonized women. Colonial male administrators also hoped that such a code would maintain the proper distance between the small numbers of white women and the large numbers of local men. Sexual liaisons between colonial men and local women usually were winked at; affairs between colonial women and local men were deemed threats to imperial order.[16]

Ladylike behavior was a mainstay of imperialist civilization. Like sanitation and Christianity, this version of feminine respectability was meant to convince both the colonizing and the colonized peoples that foreign conquest was right and necessary.[17] Ladylike behavior also was intended to have an uplifting effect on the colonizing men: it would encourage them to act according to those Victorian standards of manliness thought crucial for colonial order. Part of that empire-building masculinity was protection of the respectable lady. She stood for the civilizing mission that, in turn, justified the colonization of benighted peoples.

"Among rude people the women are generally degraded, among civilized people they are exalted," wrote James Mill, one of the most popular promoters of British colonialism in the nineteenth century.[18] British colonial officers blamed the existing ideologies of masculinity in the colonized societies for women's degradation; if men's sense of manliness was such that it did not include reverence toward women, then they could not expect to be allowed to govern their own societies. Thus, for instance, in India, British commentators created the idea of the "effeminate" Bengali male, only to berate him because he wasn't manly enough to recognize his obligation to protect and revere women.[19] British officials passed legislation in India improving women's inheritance rights (1874, 1929, 1937), prohibiting widow-burning (1829), and allowing widow remarriage (1856), all in the name of advancing civilization. At the same time, Victorian values allowed these British officials to enact laws that imposed prison sentences on wives who refused to fulfill their sexual obligations to their husbands and imposed a system of prostitution that provided Indian women to sexually service British soldiers stationed in India. The riddle of two such contradictory sets of colonial policies unravels if one sees British masculinized imperialism not as a crusade to abolish male domination of

Figure 11. Area set aside for European women at the marriage of a maharaja's daughter in colonial India, 1932. Photo: Harold Lepenperg/ Acme Cards, London.

women but as a crusade to establish European masculinized rule over the men in Asian and African societies.[20]

In the early twentieth century, masculinity—its importance to the nation and the threats to its healthy survival—was a topic of a lively, if nervous, political debate in several imperial countries. The Boer War, following in the wake of the Crimean War, shook Britons' confidence that their men were masculine enough to maintain the empire. Robert Baden-Powell founded the Boy Scouts in 1908 to combat venereal disease, intermarriage of the races, and declining birthrates, all of which were believed to endanger the maintenance of Britain's international power. Baden-Powell and other British imperialists saw sportsmanship, combined with respect for the respectable woman, as the bedrock of British imperial success. Although Boy Scout branches

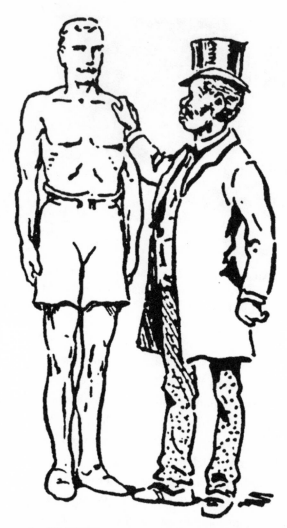

A WHITE MAN AND A MAN.

Figure 12. "A white Man and a man." From *Rovering to Success: A Book of Life-Sport for Young Men,* by Robert Baden-Powell; illustration drawn by the author. London: Herbert Jenkins, 1922.

were eventually established throughout the world, Baden-Powell's original intention was to restore manly self-control in white boys: in their hands lay the future of the empire. To make certain that his followers did not mistake his intentions, Baden-Powell contrasted the images of "a white man" and "a man." The latter was pictured in Baden-Powell's guides as short and black, wearing a top hat and a rumpled coat. This was not what a Boy Scout aspired to become. He wanted to emulate the "white man" standing next to this figure: tall, muscular, eyes straight ahead, body at attention.[21]

The "white man" towered over the black man not only because he had learned how to fight tooth decay, walk without slouching, and properly carry his rucksack but also because he had learned the importance of revering women, especially mothers and "the right girl." The surest way for a young man to find the "right girl" was to marry a Girl Guide. All of this required the same kind of skillful maneuvering that a Boy Scout learned to employ when paddling his canoe through the rapids:

> You will, I hope, have gathered from what I have said about this Rock, "Woman," that it has its dangers for the woman as well as for the man. But it has also its very bright side if you only maneuver your canoe aright.
>
> The paddle to use for this job is chivalry.[22]

NATIONALISM AND THE VEIL

During the Arab Spring's popular uprisings of 2011–13 in the Middle East, women came out into public spaces wearing diverse attire to demonstrate against authoritarian rulers and for democratization. Women protestors in Bahrain created a women-only encampment in the middle of the city to demand that their country's monarchy adopt political reforms. Most of Bahrain's women protestors were attired in long black robes, their heads covered. Their apparently monochromatic traditional attire did not hamper them from developing new political ideas or implementing fresh forms of public activism. In 2011–12, joining male protestors in Cairo's Tahrir Square, by contrast, Egyptian women—demonstrating first against the rule of Hosni Mubarak and then against the post-Mubarak elected government's uses of sexual harassment to dampen women's public political activism—were notable for their diverse attire: some were in headscarves, some had their hair exposed. In 2013, in Taksim Square, the heart of Istanbul's most secular multiethnic urban neighborhood, Turkish women turned out in the thousands, along with Turkish men, to protest the autocratic decision of Prime Minister Recep Tayyip Erdogan government to uproot trees to make way for a new shopping mall and a faux Ottoman military barracks. Many of the protesting Turkish women were bareheaded, but some were wearing headscarves.

Many of these politically active women across the Middle East were consciously defining new gendered nations, national communities in which secular women and religiously observant women would see each other as mutually respectful allies, where a woman's choice of dressing one way or another would not be used as a criterion for including her or excluding her from the nation.[23]

No practice has been more heatedly debated among nationalists than the veil: should a Muslim woman demonstrate her commitment to the nationalist cause by wearing a veil or headscarf—or by throwing off the veil and letting her hair flow freely? Men and women in Algeria, Egypt, Iraq, Iran, Iran, Turkey, Indonesia, and Malaysia have lined up on both sides of this con-

Figure 13. Bahrain women at their own demonstration site calling on the monarchy to democratize, Bahrain, 2012. Photo: Reuters.

troversy. Male nationalist elites have wielded the feminized headscarf and veil to achieve their own political ends. At one end of the patriarchal nationalist spectrum, Iran's revolutionary male elite made women's wearing of head-covering, hair-hiding scarves and long chadors integral to their campaign to reform the gendered meaning of the Iranian nation after the fall of the Shah Mohammad Reza Pahlavi in 1979. The nation's honor was seen as dependent on women's honor, as expressed in women covering their hair, presumably because the sight of it was too tempting for Iranian men.

At the other end of the same patriarchal nationalist spectrum, Turkey's most persistently influential nationalist, Kemal Ataturk, banned both men's popular red fez and women's headscarves in the 1920s in the name of modernizing and secularizing post-Ottoman Turkey.[24] If Turkey could no longer rule a sprawling empire, it would have to rely on a more homogenous, modernized national community. Banning the headscarf and "giving" women the right to vote were cemented together in the Ataturk version of postimperial modernizing nationalism. His own wife could not wear a headscarf, and, according to Ataturk's dictate, neither could the wives of any of his military officers. Turkish girls who continued (voluntarily or under pressure from their parents) to wear headscarves could not attend state universities, nor could they be hired in the government's civil service or be elected to parliament. It was this gendered form of Turkish nationalism that the early-twenty-first century Islamicist government of Prime Minister Erdogan was challenging by promoting the wearing of the headscarf among Turkish women, allowing—for the first time since the 1920s—those young women wearing headscarves entrance into state universities. When the women protestors converged on Istanbul's Taksim Square in 2013, they were forging political democratizing alliances between bare-headed and head-covered women, they were implicitly rejecting both the Ataturk and the Erdogan masculinist formulas for gendered nationalism.[25]

Earlier, European colonial officials and men and women from the colonizing societies also exercised moral and coercive pressure to tilt the argument one way or the other, usually toward rejecting the veil. The more that colonialists promoted the anti-veil movement in the name of their own Western civilizing mission, the harder it became for Muslim women in colonized (or neocolonized) countries to control the argument. For if colonial male administrators and progressive European women took prominent public stances against women wearing headscarves or the veil, and if they did so without an authentic alliance with local women, as was usually the case, they ensured that rejection of the veil would be taken as compliance with colonial rule. In Algeria, French administrators saw removing the veil from women as part of France's "civilizing mission." Egyptian feminists in the 1920s and 1930s had more success in controlling the debate, but they too risked being tarred with the antinationalist brush when they stepped out in public unveiled. The privileged status of those antiveil women who came from the local upper classes, as many did, only partly protected them from ridicule.[26] As women mobilized to join the Arab Spring uprising of 2011–2013, they began to take a fresh interest in Egyptian women's debates of the 1920s and 1930s. There were gendered political lessons to be drawn—and applied—so that women would not again experience the sequence of political participation in a nationalist movement followed by a postrevolutionary marginalization.[27]

European women in Egypt during the colonial period usually expressed strong opinions about the headscarf and the veil. They saw both of these as emblematic of Muslim women's suppressive seclusion and linked it to the harem. Many of the European women who wrote about the veil did so not primarily out of genuine curiosity about the lives and thoughts of Egyptian women but because it allowed them to feel sanguine about their own condition as European women: "By thinking of themselves as all powerful and free *vis-à-vis* Egyptian women, Western women could," as Mervat Hatem points out, "avoid confronting their own powerlessness and gender oppression at home."[28] All too often, those European women who traveled to Egypt and stayed on as teachers and governesses, and sometimes as wives of Egyptian men, were notably reluctant to explain why they felt so much freer in the "Orient."

Men in many communities appear to assign ideological weight to the outward attire and sexual purity of women in the community because they see women as (1) the community's—or the nation's—most valuable *possessions,* (2) the principal *vehicles* for transmitting the whole nation's values from one generation to the next, (3) *bearers* of the community's future generations—or, crudely, nationalist wombs, (4) the members of the community most *vulnerable* to defilement and exploitation by oppressive alien rulers, and (5) those most susceptible to *assimilation* and co-option by insidious outsiders. All five of these presumptions have made women's behavior important in the eyes of nationalist men. But these ideas have not necessarily ensured that women themselves would be taken seriously as active creators of the nation's newly assertive politics. Nor have these ideas guaranteed that male privilege would be effectively challenged in the new independent state derived from that nation.[29]

PATRIARCHY INSIDE THE NATIONALIST MOVEMENT

Women in Jaffna, Sri Lanka, formed a study group in the late 1980s in the midst of what they could not know would turn into a twenty-five-year-long civil war. Their goal was to analyze exactly how their oppression as women was causally related to their oppression as Tamils in a Singhalese-dominated Sri Lankan state. Some women had become politically conscious because the Tamil nationalist movement made them aware that their status as Tamils affected their chances of educational and economic opportunities in Sri Lanka. It was only after this initial politicization through nationalism that they became aware that women and men were being made to play quite different roles in the escalating violence between Tamil guerillas, the government's military, and the occupying Indian army. The changes wrought by ethnic mobilization and spiraling violence prompted these Tamil women to come together in a study group. There was no guarantee, however, that their examination of women's conditions in Tamil and Sri Lankan societies would make them feel more comfortable with the nationalist movement as the movement evolved and became ever more militarized. Their discussions even had the potential of prompting some of the women to see feminists in the Singhalese community as potential allies.[30] That, in turn, could have threatened their status as trusted women within the increasingly besieged Tamil community.

Today, in the aftermath of the government military's devastating defeat of the Tamil guerrillas and its violent retaking of the country's northern region, Sri Lankan Tamil women have become sharply critical of the militarism and misogyny they have witnessed on all sides of the long conflict. Beyond that, new groups of activist Sri Lankan women, such as the Association of War Affected Women, have pressed both the government and international organizations to recognize the importance of women's full participation in the current postwar nation-rebuilding efforts, efforts that will shape women's relationships to men, to politics, and to economics for decades to come. Experience has made many of these feminist activists wary of the militarization that so often accompanies nationalism.[31]

Women in many communities who have tried to assert their sense of national identity have discovered that coming into an emergent nationalist movement *through* the accepted feminine role of bearer of the community's memory and children is empowering. Being praised by men in the nationalist movement for bearing more children and raising them to become loyal nationalists does not always feel like being patronized or marginalized; it can feel confidence-enhancing. However, a woman who begins to go out of her home in the evening to attend nationalist meetings in the name of securing a better future for her children still may meet strong resistance from her husband. He may accuse her of neglecting her domestic duties, of having a sexual liaison, of making him look a fool in the eyes of other men, who may taunt him for not being able to control his wife. He never imagined that supporting the nationalist movement would entail losing control of his wife. He may even beat her to limit her new nationalist activities.

Such experiences have raised domestic violence to the status of a political issue for women in some nationalist movements. When they first became involved in nationalist activities, they may not have imagined that critiques of foreign rule, foreign bases, foreign investment, or local authoritarian rule would lead to critiques of relations between husbands and wives. In fact, many women became involved *as* good wives and good mothers. Only later did they conclude that they would have to overcome male resistance in their homes and neighborhoods if they were to participate fully in the movement. A Filipino nationalist who was active in resisting her government's alliances with foreign bankers, corporations, and militaries describes taking a new step in nationalist organizing:

> We have a forum, we call it the women's soirée, where we invite women who are involved in the movement and also encourage them to bring their husbands.... One evening our topic was "Feminism and Marriage—Do They Mix?" We went into a discussion of the family and some even questioned the value of the family because of the oppression of females that emanates from the family.

Then some of the men started airing their grievances, such as that since their wives joined this movement they are no longer attending to the needs of the children.... It was a very healthy exchange, and it was a very different kind of dialog because it was a group dialogs not just between husbands and wives.[32]

Women active in nationalist movements in the Philippines, Ireland, South Africa, Canada, Sri Lanka, South Korea, Mexico, and Nicaragua began to analyze how femininity, masculinity, marriage, "home," and the international system were integrally tied to one another.[33] In doing so they were far ahead of those women in industrialized countries who scarcely glimpsed the political connections. The process that ties these potent ideas together is not just globalized consumer advertising and the arms trade; it is domestic relations between women and men. If women, they argued, are kept in marginalized roles as domestic caregivers—by men who are lovers or by fathers or husbands—then the chances of halting foreign-financed invasion, ending an unfair military-bases treaty, or holding accountable a multinational corporate employer will be slim. In this sense foreign base commanders and capitalist entrepreneurs may depend on domestic violence and the constraints it enforces on women's public activism as much as they do on alliances with men in the local elite.[34]

On the other hand, it can be very difficult for women to raise these sorts of "women's issues" inside a nationalist movement that is under siege, precisely because they are actually issues about men's power. The more imminent and coercive the threat posed by an adversary's power—a foreign force or the local government's police—the more successful men in the community are likely to be in persuading activist women to keep quiet, to swallow their grievances, to suppress their analyses. When any nationalist movement becomes militarized, either on its leaders' initiative or in reaction to external intimidation, male privilege in the community is likely to become even more entrenched.

When, on top of this silencing, foreign governments become involved to defend an ethnic group from attack by an alien-backed power and thereby legitimize their involvement, local male privilege gains a foreign ally. This is what happened in 1980s Afghanistan. Two decades before the most recent United States–led military actions in Afghanistan, the U.S. government and its allies framed the war in Afghanistan as a classic Cold War narrative: the Soviet Union had invaded a neighboring country, propping up a puppet regime that lacked a popular base; the antiregime insurgents represented the real nation, and their brave resistance deserved the Free World's moral and military support. This story became murky, however, when one looked at the situation from the vantage point of Afghan women. The cause for which the insurgent mujahideen fought was a traditional-rural-clan way of life that is unambiguously patriarchal. One of the policies the Soviet-backed government in Kabul pursued that so alienated male clan leaders was the expansion of economic and educational opportunities for Afghanistan's women. While there is little evidence that the Soviet-backed Kabul regime enjoyed wide public legitimacy, outside observers report that its tenure proved beneficial to those mainly urban women who were able to take advantage of the government's policy. Women conveniently slipped off the policy stage when U.S. officials designed their Cold War response to the civil war in Afghanistan.[35]

Given this experience, it was little wonder that in the twenty-first century, as U.S. military allies withdrew their troops and

Washington set its own troop-withdrawal timetable, Afghan women's advocates, such as those in the Afghan Women's Network, were suspicious. Women's rights, they predicted, again would be reduced to a mere bargaining chip on the negotiation table when men on all sides sat down to sort out among themselves the political future of the country.[36]

Military mobilization, it is true, may make it necessary for men to permit women to acquire new skills and take on new responsibilities. But simultaneously, militarization puts a premium on communal unity in the name of national survival, a priority that can silence women critical of patriarchal practices and attitudes; in so doing, nationalist militarization, even while it calls on women to make contributions, can privilege men.

Militarization during the first intifada of the 1980s has provided young Palestinian men with new opportunities to prove their manhood, often in defiance not only of Israeli men's authority but also of what many perceive as their fathers' outworn authority. On the other hand, "women are bearing the brunt of the *intifadah*," as one Palestinian told a reporter in 1988. The Israeli government's use of soldiers to enforce strict curfews and to arrest an estimated six thousand Palestinian men raised women's household chores to the stature of national imperatives: "They have to watch the money, make all the family chores, bake their own bread, grow vegetables, take care of chickens and goats. These traditional roles are more important now." Najwa Jardali, a Palestinian woman long active in a movement to provide day care and health clinics for women in the occupied territories, warned Western women not to imagine that day care was simply a women's issue. With militarization, it became a national concern: "Most Western feminists wouldn't regard kindergarten as important[,] ... but for us it's very important. The military government doesn't allow us kindergartens in schools, and day care enables women to get involved in other activities." Proof of day care centers' national importance was the Israeli military's efforts to harass the women teachers and close them down.[37]

The popular image of the Palestinian nation until then had been the young male street fighter of the Palestine Liberation Organization. With his checkered scarf, and a rock in hand, defiant and alert, he stood for an entire nation. Palestinian women remained in the shadows. They were reduced to being the protected, or the unprotected. But in 1988 Palestinian women began holding their own marches in the occupied territories to protest against the Israeli government's "Iron Fist" policy. They defied heavily armed soldiers with chants of "We are people, we are women. Never are we subdued. Never do we feel self-pity." The community's leadership committee, the Unified National Command of the Intifada, began addressing women's as well as men's concerns in its bulletins. The nature of Israeli military policy compelled Palestinians to develop a new way of organizing, one reliant less on outside help and more on small neighborhood committees, less susceptible to police and military disruption. In this type of organization, especially with so many men and boys jailed after the more visible stone-throwing confrontations, women began to come into their own as political actors. Women on the neighborhood committees went from house to house recruiting more members and collecting money and food for the besieged, asking people knowledgeable about health care to provide health services, and urging participation in demonstrations.[38] Would such militarizing pressures lead to an enduring reordering of femininity and masculinity within the Palestinian nation?

THE OTHER NOSTALGIA

The common practice of sweeping nationalist debates about masculinized power, and about women's relations with men, under the nation's historical rug has bestowed inordinate power on future nationalist male leaders: they can claim that they are inheritors of an unambiguous legacy of communal solidarity. In reality, they may be inheritors of a patriarchal victory won within the community a generation ago. The history of any nationalist movement is almost always a history filled with gendered debate. If a decade or a century later it looks as though there was no confusion, no argument about women's relations to men in the ruling community and to men in their own ethnic community, that is probably evidence only that the nostalgic patriarchal narrative of the nation's history has won for the time being.

And the impact of winning—or of being defeated—can be tricky to calculate at the time if the nation is fragile and outside threats are formidable. For example, Hue-Tam Ho-Tai, a Vietnamese feminist historian, describes one of those seemingly minor incidents in which the patriarchal side of the nationalist debate inched a step further toward victory.[39] In the 1920s there was a vital women's movement in French-ruled Vietnam. It raised issues of literacy, marriage conditions, and public participation challenging some of the most entrenched ideas of Vietnamese Confucian culture. Male intellectuals within the early nationalist movement also began speaking out against patriarchal values and practices that, they said, deprived the Vietnamese nation of women's talents and energies, both of which were needed to throw off French colonialism.[40] Vietnamese women were encouraged by male and female nationalists to learn to read and write. The Trung sisters, who had led the Vietnamese against Chinese colonialists in the first century A.D., were heralded as models for contemporary Vietnamese. Women began to join the Indochinese Communist Party and other nationalist groups. In the process, earlier women's groups became overshadowed by mixed nationalist organizations. Fighting for women's rights increasingly came to be seen as part of creating a Vietnamese sense of nationhood vital enough to challenge French colonial rule, a rule that grew harsher as the nationalist movement spread. During the 1930s there seemed to be little tension between advocating women's rights and joining the struggle for national rights: each bolstered the other; both questioned the capacity of Vietnam's traditional Confucian culture to protect the nation from foreign domination.

Then some women activists began to examine relations between men and women inside the nationalist movement. At a Communist Party conference in the 1930s, women delegates were told by nationalist leaders to omit mention of problems between husbands and wives in their public report. Raising such questions on the floor, they were warned, would only generate hostile feelings within the nationalist movement at a time when it was already threatened by arrests by French police. The women excised those sections from their report. Problems were deemed legitimate only if they were seen as obstacles to nationalist unity; a suggested problem was generally dismissed if it made men in the nation anxious.

To make sense of the decline of the French empire, we have to understand how women saw the choices they faced at each precarious step in the creation of an effective Vietnamese nationalist movement. Many Vietnamese women did find strength and meaning through participation in the nationalist struggles during the next four decades of war.[41] Later women may not have had the same choices. But every time women succumb to the pressure to hold their tongues about problems they are having with men in a nationalist organization, nationalism becomes that much more masculinized. Vietnamese women have been almost invisible in the senior ranks of the unified country's party and government: in 1979, five years after the expulsion of American troops, women constituted a mere 17 percent of the Vietnamese Communist Party's membership; a decade after the nationalist victory, the Politburo of the party, the most powerful decision-making body, was an all-male enclave. Women have even lost some of the influence they acquired in village and collective farm councils during the war.[42]

Women in early-twenty-first-century Vietnam began to challenge this masculinization of public life. It was a moment when Vietnam's international relationships were expanding: Vietnam had become a popular foreign tourist destination, large global corporations such as Nike had contracted Vietnamese factories to produce goods for export, and many Vietnamese were growing nervous about China's territorial expansionism. Furthermore, witnessing a widening gap between rich and poor, more Vietnamese citizens were openly criticizing the arrogance and corruption of their own elite. This also was a time when Vietnamese feminist academics were building wider networks with women's studies researchers in other countries.[43] It did not go unnoticed by Vietnamese feminists that, in 2013, only two of the sixteen members appointed by the male leadership to the Politboro were women. Thus it could prove difficult for Vietnamese women's advocates to push forward if they could not retrace the steps of the nationalist movement back to the points at which women's relations with men were shoved off the nationalist agenda.

Nationalism places a high value on anything indigenous. Thus Sri Lankan feminist scholar Kumari Jayawardena explains that "those who want to continue to keep the women of our countries in a position of subordination find it convenient to dismiss feminism as a foreign ideology."[44] Sometimes this dismissal is combined with a homophobic attack. Feminists pressing their own nationalist movements to rethink the roles of women in politics, to reassess the effects of militant violence on women and men in the community, have been labeled lesbians by critics. In the wartime years of 1992–95, Serbian nationalist supporters of the invasion of Bosnia by Yugoslavia's then-president Slobodan Milosevic similarly taunted Serbia's antimilitarism feminists in Women in Black with homophobic slurs. Calling women lesbians is designed to dismiss the feminists as tainted by alien ideas, as if heterosexuality were the sole indigenous practice in the local community, and to marginalize feminist ideas as stemming from degenerate women.[45]

Nationalist feminists have crafted critiques that raise important questions about the relationships between precolonial and colonial culture. If their nation was free of patriarchy before the imposition of foreign colonial rule, then the task would be relatively simple: by joining with men to roll back foreign domination and restore precolonial values, they could restore equality between women and men inside the community. *If*, however, women discovered that patriarchal values and practices predated colonial rule, and if, subsequently, these values and practices were exploited and exacerbated by colonialists, then regaining control of that society would not liberate women. In Turkey, the Philippines, Korea, and Vietnam, women's advocates have become wary of nationalist spokespeople who glorify the precolonial past. They have become uncomfortable when women warriors and queens are offered as proof that women had genuine influence over land and sexuality in the past. And yet they have to conduct these historical explorations carefully, knowing that outsiders might use their findings to discredit the nationalism they want to transform.[46]

CONCLUSION

Nationalism has provided millions of women with spaces in which to be international actors. To learn that one's own culture is full of intellectual and artistic riches, to learn that outsiders depend on coercion, not innate superiority, when wielding their influence, to recognize bonds of community where before there were only barriers of class, region, and party, to discover that one is valued outside the realms of home and kin—all this has been empowering for thousands of women as well as men. National consciousness has induced many women to feel confident enough to take part in public organizing and public debate for the first time in their lives. Furthermore, nationalism, more than many other ideologies, has a vision that includes women, for no nation can survive unless its culture is transmitted and its children are born and nurtured, two activities that nationalists deem essential.

Nationalism, by definition, is a set of ideas that sharpens distinctions between "us" and "them." It provides, moreover, analytical tools for explaining how inequities have been created between "us" and "them." A woman who becomes politicized through nationalism is more likely to see a man from her community as sharing a common destiny than she is to see women from another community as having a shared future, especially if those women, no matter what their politics, come from a community that has treated her own with derision.

But many of the nationalisms that have rearranged the pattern of world politics over the last two centuries have been patriarchal nationalisms. Their spokespeople—historians, novelists, poets, artists, generals, political organizers—have presumed that all the forces marginalizing or oppressing women have been generated by the dynamics of colonialism, neocolonialism, or capitalist globalization, and hence that the precolonial, preglobalized society was one in which women enjoyed respect and security. Following this nonfeminist analysis, simply restoring the nation's independence will ensure women's liberation. Many nationalists have assumed, too, that the significance of the community's women being raped or vulgarly photographed by foreign men is that the honor of the community's men has been assaulted—although some women survivors of wartime rape, such as those in Bangladesh, have been silenced for years because of the stigma attached even by male nationalists to rape victims.[47] And frequently nationalists have urged women to take active roles in nationalist movements but have confined them to the roles of ego-stroking girlfriend, stoic wife, or nurturing mother.

Repeatedly, male nationalist organizers of diverse cultures have elevated unity of the community to such political primacy that any questioning of relations between women and men inside the movement or the community could be labeled as divisive, even traitorous. Women who have called for more genuine equality between the sexes—in the movement, in the workplace, in the home—have been told that now is not the time, the nation is too fragile, the enemy is too near. Women must be patient, they must wait until the nationalist goals are achieved; *then, and only then,* can relations between women and men be addressed. "Not now, later," is the masculine advice that rings in the ears of many nationalist women.

"Not now, later," is weighted with implications. It is advice predicated on the belief that the most dire problems facing the nascent national community are problems that can be explained and solved without reference to power relations between women and men. That is, the causes and effects of foreign investments and indebtedness can be understood without taking women's experiences seriously; foreign military bases and agribusiness-induced landlessness can be challenged without coming to grips with how each has relied on women's labor and silence; and the subtle allure of cultural globalization can be dissected without reference to masculine pride and desire. Each of these presumptions seems politically shallow.

In addition, the "not now, later," advice implies that what happens during the nationalist campaign will not make it harder in the future to transform the conditions that marginalize women and privilege men. It also rests on the prediction that political institutions born out of a nationalist victory will be at least as open to women's analysis and demands as the institutions created within the nationalist movement. Both of these assumptions are questionable.

The very experiences of a nationalist campaign—whether at the polls in Quebec, Scotland, and Catalonia; on the streets of Seoul, Istanbul, Belgrade, Haifa, and Jaffna; or in the hills of Vietnam and Algeria—frequently harden masculine political privilege. That cementing occurs if men are allowed to take most of the policy-making roles in the movement, as well as if they are more likely to be arrested, gain the status of heroes in jail, and learn public skills, all of which will enable them to claim positions of authority after the campaign is won. If women are confined to playing the nationalist wife, nurse, porter, girlfriend, or mother—albeit making crucial contributions to a successful nationalist campaign—they are unlikely to have either the political skills or the communal prestige presumed to be requisites for exercising community-wide authority at a later time. The notion of what "the nation" was in its finest hour—when it was most unified, most altruistic—will be of a community in which women sacrificed their desires for the sake of the male-led collective. Risky though it may indeed be for a nationalist movement to confront current inequities between its women and men in the midst of its mobilizing era, doing so is more likely to produce lasting change than waiting until the mythical "later."

There is a long history of nationalist women challenging masculine privilege in the midst of popular mobilization. Erasing those women's efforts from the nationalist chronicles makes it harder for contemporary women to claim that their critical attitudes are indigenous and hence legitimate. Thus nationalist feminists today in countries such as Vietnam, Palestine, Turkey, Bangladesh, India, Egypt, Syria, Sri Lanka, and Jamaica have invested energy in recapturing local women's nationalist history. As Honor Ford Smith of the Jamaican feminist theater group Sistren has recalled,

> What we knew was that a spate of tongue-in-cheek newspaper and television reports had projected white feminists in Europe and North America as "women's libbers," hysterical perverts....
> We did not know of the struggles of women for education and political rights between 1898 and 1944. We did not know the names of the early black feminists.[48]

Challenges have been hardest to mount when women within a movement have lacked the chance to talk with each other in confidence about their own experiences and how they shape their priorities. Women in an oppressed or colonized national community are usually not from a single social class, and thus they have not experienced relations with the foreign power or the co-opted ruling elite in the same ways. Nor do all women within a national community have identical sexual experiences with men—or with other women. Women who have not had the space to discuss their differences and anxieties together have been less able to withstand nationalist men's homophobic or xenophobic charges.

Women's efforts to redefine the nation in the midst of a nationalist campaign have been thwarted when potentially supportive women outside the community have failed to understand how important it is to women within the community not to be forced to choose between their nationalist and their feminist aspirations. As stressful as it is to live as a feminist nationalist, to surrender one's national identity may mean absorption into an international women's movement led by middle-class women from affluent societies. This is the caveat issued by Delia Aguilar, a Filipino nationalist feminist: "When feminist solidarity networks are today proposed and extended globally, without a firm sense of identity—national, racial and class—we are likely to yield to feminist models designed by and for white, middle-class women in the industrial West and uncritically adopt these as our own."[49]

Given the scores of nationalist movements that have managed to topple empires, create new states, and unsettle existing states, it is surprising that the international political system has not been more radically altered than it has. But a nationalist movement informed by masculinist memory, imbued with masculinist pride, and holding a patriarchal vision of the new nation-state is likely to produce just one more actor in an untransformed international arena. A dozen new patriarchal nation-states may make the international bargaining table a bit more crowded, but this will not change the international game being played at that table.

It is worth imagining, therefore, what would happen to international politics if more nationalist movements were informed by women's multilayered experiences of oppression. If more nation-states grew out of feminist nationalists' ideas and experiences, then community identities within the international political system might be tempered by cross-national identities. Resolutions of interstate conflicts would be more sustainable, because the significance of women to those conflicts would be considered directly. They would not be dismissed as too trivial to be the topic of serious state-to-state negotiation.

CHAPTER FOUR

Base Women

Where are the women on and around a military base? How did they get there? Who benefits from their being where they are? And what does each woman think about where she is on or near the base?

Start with a base laundress. She is most likely a civilian hired directly by the base command or indirectly by a private defense contractor. She might be the same nationality as most of the soldiers whose uniforms and sheets she is washing. Or she might be from the local community, but with quite a different nationality. She could even be from a distant country, a place from which the private contractor prefers to recruit its female workers. While working in the base's large laundry, she develops her own thoughts about what the military personnel on this base are doing with their deadly weaponry, but is careful not to express her political thoughts out loud. She may value her job, which is enabling her to support her children or to send money home to her parents. Or she may find the job exploitive but feel as though neither the officers in the base chain of command nor her

profit-preoccupied contractor will listen to her. She knows there
are other women on the base—women soldiers, pilots, or sailors;
wives of male officers and enlisted men; and women who come
onto the base secretly to have paid sex with some of the men. But
she does not think of any of these women as her natural allies.[1]

A military base is a complicated microworld dependent on
diverse women: (a) women who live on the base, (b) women who
work on the base but go home at night, (c) women who live outside the fence but are integral to what goes on inside the fence
and to what military men and women do when they leave the
base for recreation, and (d) women who may live far from a base
but who are in almost daily contact with men on the base via the
Internet. Paying attention to all these women makes one smarter
about the international politics of military bases.

The United States today has more military bases outside its
own borders than any other country.[2] One of the reasons so
many people in other countries think the United States qualifies
as an "empire" is its global network of military bases.[3] Furthermore, the specification "outside its own borders" overlooks the
American military bases on island territories controlled by the
United States, territories whose residents do not have their own
voting members in Congress and who do not have the right to
vote in American presidential elections. These islands are places
that other people might call colonies. Get out your atlas or spin
your globe to find Guam. The Pacific island of Guam is rapidly
becoming one of the most militarized places on the planet,
owing to the U.S. military's twenty-first-century buildup there.
But the fact that most mainland Americans would be hard-
pressed to find Guam on a map and have given scant thought to
the women and men living on Guam only underscores the gendered international political reality of most military bases: their

operations rely on particular dynamics between women and men, and yet most of those operations are defined as "off limits" to civilian scrutiny.[4]

The late twentieth century set a high-water mark in the spread of overseas military bases. The Soviet Union had scores of bases in East Germany, in Poland, and throughout its Baltic and western Asian regions. France and Britain maintained bases in their colonies and former colonies. The United States exercised control over many of the Pacific and Caribbean territories it had colonized at the end of the nineteenth century, as well as over those it captured from Japan at the end of World War II, most notably Okinawa. Simultaneously, its Cold War rivalry with the Soviet Union became the justification for the American military to multiply its bases—with the support of Congress—in Iceland, western Europe, Central America, Turkey, South Korea, the Philippines, and Japan.

Twenty-five years later, in the early twenty-first century, the Soviet Union is no more, and most of its Baltic and eastern European bases have been shut down. However, today the Russian military has agreements with the government of Syria and with some of the former Soviet states to maintain its military bases on their territories: for instance, the large Russian naval base at Sevastopol, Ukraine, as well as Russian bases in Kyrgyzstan and Tajikistan. The French government has lost its empire but still maintains military bases in several of its African former colonies, such as Gabon and Senegal, and has opened a new base in Mali. The British empire has shrunk to a mere shadow of its Victorian size, and a cost-conscious British government has continued to close many of its overseas bases. The British military's training base in Belize closed in 2010, while its bases in Germany are due to completely shut down by 2019.[5]

Occasionally, a shrinking empire simply has passed along its old bases to a new global power. Thus, in 2001, the Americans took over—and expanded—Camp Lemonnier, a former French military base in Djibouti, on the Horn of Africa.[6] In the next decade, justified by what Washington officials called their "war on terror," the Defense Department created AFRICOM, a new military command structure (headquartered in Italy) for its operations in Africa: in Kenya, the Central African Republic, South Sudan, and Ethiopia.[7] One of its newest bases is a drone base in Niger.[8] Some of these U.S. bases in Africa are elaborate and large, others are tent cities. Each base depends on a formal agreement with the host country's current government, though some of those governments are politically weak; allowing the U.S. military to operate on their soil can jeopardize an already wobbly government's local legitimacy.

Similarly, the Pentagon took over and expanded a former British imperial base in the Indian Ocean territory of Diego Garcia, compelling its local residents to abandon their homes.[9] In the Persian Gulf, the U.S. military has bases in Bahrain, Saudi Arabia, and Qatar. Keeping friendly relationships with the autocratic monarchies of these three countries has meant that American officials have expressed only lukewarm support for Arab Spring sentiments and prodemocracy movements in these countries.

Every one of these bases has been and continues to be gendered. There are both women and men in uniform on most of these bases. There are contractors: mostly male contract workers on the small bases, but women contract workers, as well, on the larger bases. Each of the men and women—civilian and military—deployed to each base has relationships that extend beyond that base, intensified by the Internet, which affect how that man or woman thinks about what he or she is doing there. Even bases deliberately located far from local towns send out sociocultural ripples, shaping local people's gendered understandings of the nation, modernity, security, and citizenship. That is, the workings and impacts of each base have been shaped by ideas and practices of masculinities and femininities, and by particular relationships (intended and unintended) between diverse women and men. Each base's commander and his (almost always *his*) superiors back home in the capital— Washington, Moscow, London, Paris—have crafted rules meant to bolster certain ideas about valued manliness and proper womanhood and to control scores of daily interactions between women and men.

Any base—no matter whether it is the base of a foreign military or a local military—is militarized not just because it houses soldiers; it is *militarized* insofar as most decisions are judged by a principal criterion: how well does this proposed rule or practice serve that military's priorities—not environmental priorities, not civilian democratic priorities, not racial justice priorities, not national development priorities, and not women's rights priorities. Every militarized ritual, rule, and arrangement has as its primary goal the effective operation of that country's military, including the smooth operation of the facility on which its soldiers, sailors, and pilots are based.

A military base does not need to be thoroughly militarized. Potentially, any base can be held accountable by civilian authorities for meeting other, nonmilitary goals. But that requires those civilians in office—and those in voting booths—to resist the appeals of militarized values, militarized civilian jobs, and militarized money. Many civilians do not. Insofar as civilian officials and civilian voters become militarized, they will come to see the military base's priorities as serving their own interests.[10]

Consequently, each of the basing policies designed to sustain a militarized base calls for a feminist enquiry. That, in turn, calls for exploring what are each policy's gendered intents and its gendered consequences:

- housing policies
- curfew policies
- civilian hiring policies
- commercial policies
- prostitution policies
- sexually-transmitted-diseases policies
- marriage policies
- sexuality policies
- race policies

That is only a partial list of military policy decisions intended in part to shape masculinities and femininities and to choreograph the interactions between women and men on and around any military base. There are more:

- environmental policies
- policing policies
- judicial policies
- sexual assault policies
- health care policies
- recreation policies
- alcohol policies
- morale policies

- child care policies
- domestic violence policies
- chaplaincy policies
- divorce policies

The combined list is long because managing a military base requires the management of myriad gendered, racialized, ranked, and nationalized relationships. Each of these military policies ensures that different groups of women are where they are supposed to be in the ideal universe of military effectiveness. Yet women on and around any military base cannot be treated as if they are homogeneous. Policies intended to control women have had to be fine-tuned to take account of their diversity, as seen through the eyes of commanders and civilian officials. The categories of women associated with military bases are complex and overlapping: young, single, white, Asian, Black, Latino (in the U.S. military's categorizing), older, married to officers, married to enlisted men, single parents, married parents, paid, unpaid, officers, enlisted, civilian, nursing, uniformed, on-base, off-base, deemed respectable, deemed not respectable. Some base policies have been intended to ensure that dissimilar women are unlikely to make common cause. Those policies frequently have been successful.

Nevertheless, military bases' gendered policies have not been fixed, either geographically or historically. Military officials (uniformed and civilian) have altered their gendered ways of doing things as ideas about each group of women have changed and as ideas about soldiering, about masculinities, and about delicate interstate alliances also have changed. Government officials and commanders have redesigned or simply tweaked their policies, too, as they have tried to adapt when some women have radically altered their understandings of themselves, their rights, their interests, and their political capacities. Can ex-wives of generals today be dismissively shrugged off as easily as they could be by militaries thirty years ago? Can a base commander continue to assume that women working in discos around his base will never make common cause with the country's middle-class feminist activists?

In this sense, no military base has been stable in its gendered politics, even those whose fenced and walled boundaries seem to have remained stubbornly fixed over decades. To engage in a feminist analysis of any military base anyplace in the world means watching it through a gendered lens over time. Look for the persistent convictions. Look for the new meanings. Look for the confusions.[11]

RACE AND SEX ON THE UNSINKABLE AIRCRAFT CARRIER

Most bases have managed to slip into the daily lives of the nearby community. A military base, even one controlled by sol-diers of another country, can become politically invisible if its ways of doing business and seeing the world insinuate them-selves into a community's job market, schools, consumer tastes, housing patterns, children's games, adults' friendships, gossip, and senses of pride and security.

On any given day, therefore, only a handful of the scores of bases scattered around the world are the objects of dispute. Most have draped themselves in the camouflage of normalcy. Real estate agents, town officials, charity volunteers, bartenders, schoolchildren, local police, local journalists, religious clergy, building contractors, business owners, crime syndicates, tourism companies—all accept the base, its soldiers, and, if a large base, their civilian spouses and children as unremarkable givens. They may even see them as valuable, as good for their own well-being. When the Pentagon decided to expand its Camp Lemonnier base in Djibouti, six hundred local civilian workers, mostly men, were hired for jobs in base construction and other expansion services.[12]

Likewise, rumors of a base closing—in Iraq, Afghanistan, Germany, or Belize—can be the cause for local nationalist celebration. Yet, simultaneously, the expected closing can send shivers of economic alarm through a civilian community whose members have come to depend for their own economic well-being on base jobs and soldiers' spending. Thus, for instance, in Ecuador in 2008, when a nationalist popular movement and a newly elected nationalist president, Rafael Correa, compelled the U.S. Air Force to close its base at Manta, there were complicated local reactions. Some residents were thrilled, seeing the foreign-base closure as a victory for both demilitarization and Ecuadorian sovereignty; but other Ecuadorians worried about whether the economic gains and the sense of security they had perceived as flowing from the base's 450 personnel, and from the American spending, would be so easily replaced.[13] That is, when any base is being closed, one needs to be curious about who among the local population—by political inclination, by economic class, and by gender—will feel vindicated and who will be anxious.

The normalcy that sustains a military base in a local community rests on finely tuned ideas about masculinity and femininity. If the fit between local and foreign men, and local and foreign women breaks down, the base may lose its protective camouflage of normalcy. It may become the target of nationalist resentment that could subvert the very structure of an international military alliance. On the other hand, when a base does not seem to provoke controversy is a time when gender politics are at work to keep the waters calm. That is, controversy—set off by a sexual assault, discovery of polluted water, escalating noise—can pull back the camouflage curtain to reveal gendered base dynamics that are usually invisible. However, one does not have to wait until a controversy breaks out to explore those base dynamics.[14] One can conduct a feminist-informed gender analysis of a base when routine reigns. Normalcy is always interesting to a feminist investigator.

"A friendly, unquestioning, geographically convenient but expendable launching point for the projections of U.S. military power" is what many British people believed their country had become in the 1980s.[15] They felt as though their country, once a global power, had become less a sovereign nation than a land-based "aircraft carrier" for Americans' Cold War armed forces. Between 1948, when American forces returned to postwar Britain, and 1986, the U.S. military created some 130 bases and facilities in England, Scotland, Wales, and Northern Ireland. They did this with the British government's—often secret—acquiescence.[16] Some of these installations were mere offices, hardly noticeable to the casual passerby. Others, like those at Greenham Common, Molesworth, Mildenhall, and Holy Loch, were full-fledged communities with elaborate facilities, heavy weaponry, and large workforces.

Most of the larger bases in Britain had their roots in the American installations that had been established during World War II. These were easier to reestablish during the Cold War precisely because they had become a familiar part of British life in the early 1940s. But even during World War II, local acceptance could not be taken for granted. Policy makers had to fashion racialized and gendered policies that would make the introduction of thousands of foreign soldiers palatable to local civilians, but do it in a way that would not offend the voters back home. In 1940s Britain this meant ensuring that British and American men could work together as allies, not sexual rivals.

During World War II, a potentially explosive topic of policy debate among British and American officers was how to manage the relations between African American male soldiers and white British women.[17] During the course of the war, 130,000 Black American soldiers were stationed in Britain. Though they represented only a fraction of all the American troops based there, they became the focus of intense controversy—in village pubs, the press, Parliament, and war rooms. When the first soldiers arrived in 1942, the American military was a segregated institution. However, Blacks had become a political force to be reckoned with in America; the Democratic administration of Franklin Roosevelt had entered office indebted to thousands of Black voters in northern cities who had transferred their electoral support from the Republican to the Democratic Party.

British society in 1942 was overwhelmingly (though not totally) white, imbued with a sense of imperial superiority over the Asian and African peoples it still ruled. British armed forces had fought World War I, and were fighting World War II, with regiments mobilized in India, Africa, and the West Indies.[18] When white male British officials during World War I sought to choreograph race and gender to wage that earlier war, they had thought sexually; they had worked hard to manipulate prostitution policies to wage what was then called the Great War.[19] Two decades later, during the early 1940s, both the British and the American, male-led governments were ready with racial formulas when they sat down to talk about how to ensure that African American men stationed in Britain would relate to white British women in ways that would enhance the joint war effort.

White British women, however, had their own ideas. When they dated Black American soldiers, they made comparisons between African American and white British manhood. British women often found the former to be more polite, better company, and perhaps more "exotic." By 1943, some white British women were giving birth to children fathered by African American GIs. Some were choosing to marry their Black American boyfriends. Certain male members of Winston Churchill's cabinet became alarmed at what they considered a dangerous trend.

Top-level discussions already had begun in 1942. Three possible solutions were suggested in the all-white, all-male Cabinet sessions: (1) stop the U.S. government from sending any Black male soldiers to Britain, (2) if that were impossible, confine African American soldiers to certain coastal bases in Britain, or (3) if all else failed, press the American armed forces to send more African American women soldiers and Red Cross volunteers to Britain so that Black male soldiers would not have to look to white British women for companionship.[20]

None of these proposals proved feasible. The Allies' war effort depended too much on optimum use of human resources to keep over a hundred thousand American troops out of Britain or holed up in coastal towns. Furthermore, the postwar experience following World War I, when many British whites turned against West Indian Black men who had served as maritime workers in the port of Liverpool, suggested that coastal quarantining was no insurance against racial hostility. Finally, the American government refused to send thousands of African American women to Britain. Leaders of the NAACP (National

Figures 14 and 15. African American soldiers and their dates in one of London's "colored" clubs, probably the Bouillabaisse on New Compton Street, 1943. Photos: The Hulton Picture Company.

Association for the Advancement of Colored People) made it clear to the Roosevelt administration that they did not see such a plan as respectful of Black womanhood: Black women were volunteering for the U.S. Army to be soldiers, not sexual companions. Furthermore, some Britons did not think that the plan was wise; white British men might start dating the Black American women. In the end, only eight hundred African American military women were sent to Britain, and those not until 1945; they were members of the historic 6888th Central Postal Directory Battalion.[21]

At the same time that British and American officials were hammering out complicated policies for racialized gendered relationships in wartime Britain, other male officials of the same allies were devising policies that would allow the British government to enlist West Indian Afro-Caribbean and Indian women into the British military without their deployment upsetting the entrenched racial segregation that organized work and social life in Washington, D.C.[22]

Back in Britain, attempts to prevent white British women from dating Black soldiers took the more diffuse forms of official and unofficial warnings directed at local white women. British women who went out with African American men stationed at nearby bases were warned that they were more likely to get VD. Women who dated Black soldiers were branded as "loose" or even traitorous to Britain. Whenever some infraction of disciplinary rules involved an African American soldier, the press was likely to specify his race. British parents who allowed their daughters to date Black GIs were portrayed by local British papers as "irresponsible."

During the early years of the war, there was a widespread suspicion, expressed in British newspapers and by members of

Parliament, that Black American soldiers were more likely than white GIs to be charged for sexual offenses such as rape and to receive harsher sentences if convicted. By 1945, while Blacks (the great majority of them male) constituted only 8 percent of all U.S. troops stationed in Europe, they represented 21 percent of all American servicemen convicted of crimes. When the criminal convictions are broken down by category, the discrepancies are even more startling: Black soldiers were 42 percent of those convicted of sex crimes.[23] Nonetheless, in August 1942, Britain's Parliament passed the United States of America (Visiting Forces) Act, which gave the American authorities the right to try American soldiers for offenses committed on British soil. It was one step toward permitting the Americans to maintain their kind of racial-sexual system despite the unusual circumstances of wartime.

Many white Americans were afraid that if sexual relations between Black men and white women were allowed in wartime Britain, sexual segregation would be harder to maintain in postwar America. Governmental and press persuasion was hardly overwhelming in its success, however. A Mass Observation survey, a British wartime public opinion poll, conducted in August 1943 revealed that only one in seven of the Britons questioned disapproved of marriages between Blacks and whites; 25 percent told interviewers that they had become more friendly toward Black people partly because of meeting African American soldiers.[24] Yet by the end of the war, and especially after the first babies had been born of white British women and Black soldiers, it took considerable social courage for a young white British woman to go out to a local pub with a Black soldier.

American military commanders were not passive in these racialized gendered wartime debates. General Dwight Eisenhower, senior U.S. commander in Europe, tolerated white-Black dating because he believed that the U.S.-British alliance would be harmed if American white officers tried to impose their segregationist "Jim Crow" conventions on the British. Other American male officers, however, thought that clashes between white and African American soldiers in Bristol and Leicester were due to white male soldiers' justifiable resentment of Black troops "using up" the limited pool of local white women. Some American officers were also firmly opposed to "mixed" marriages and used their authority to prohibit men under their command from marrying British women. By the end of World War II, at least sixty thousand British women had filed applications with U.S. officials to emigrate to America as war brides.[25] Very few of those whose prospective husbands were Black were accepted by authorities. There appeared to be a "gentleman's agreement" between British and American middle-level white male officials to forbid marriages between Black GIs and white British women. The Black soldier intent on marriage would be transferred and given a serious talking-to by his superior; the woman was counseled by an American military officer or a British welfare officer.[26]

Whom male soldiers meet and whom they marry while stationed on overseas bases has continued to be an issue in the minds of U.S. military strategists. Their concern derives largely from a distrust of the motives of the local women. American male soldiers seeking to marry Korean, Japanese, Vietnamese, Thai, Okinawan, Filipino, and German women have been routinely discouraged, if not by commanders, then by military chaplains. Those women who have, nonetheless, married American male soldiers and become U.S. military wives have found that, on top of coping with the pressures and rules that shape the lives of all military wives, they have to cope with both American white citizens' responses to them and their own U.S.-based diaspora's often less than welcoming responses. In both cases, the responses are based on a common assumption that these women must have met their military husbands while working in a disco or massage parlor near an American overseas base.[27]

Marriage, in other words, has been made integral to international security politics chiefly by those military strategists—uniformed and civilian, American, Canadian, British, Russian, Turkish, Japanese—who have become convinced that only a certain sort of militarized marriage, with a certain sort of wife, can ensure their country's military's smooth operation. Not taking seriously marriage politics—and the power wielded on its behalf—leaves one unable to fully comprehend international politics. Taking seriously the international politics of militarized marriages requires, in turn, a genuine curiosity about the lives and ideas of the diverse women married to male soldiers.

THE MILITARY WIVES "PROBLEM"

By the late 1960s, the American military base at Effingham had become an integral part of the social and economic life of nearby Long Crendon, a modest English village in Essex. The expansion of the base in the 1950s had wrought subtle but fundamental changes in townspeople's lives. The Americans started to hire local men and women and soon became one of the region's principal employers. More American soldiers arrived, bringing with them more wives and children. And with the families came American-style consumption: "air transports began to fly in to Effingham laden with deep-freezers, washing machines, pressure- and microwave cookers, hi-fi equipment, Hoovers, electric organs and even Persian carpets."[28] Some of the appliances made their way on to the flourishing local secondhand market. Still, the ideological spillover from the American model of family life was contained by the married soldiers' preference for staying on the base, where the U.S. Defense Department provided everything to make them feel as though they had never left home.

This continued to be the model of base construction through the 1990s, as American overseas bases multiplied during the Cold War: the suburb with family houses, grass to mow, men employed as soldiers and civilian women as unpaid housewives.[29] Betty Friedan, the feminist who wrote the devastating critique of American white suburban women's entrapment, would have recognized the Pentagon's gendered community model immediately.[30]

The American military strategists' Cold War and post–Cold War thinking was this: keeping married soldiers happy on a foreign base required keeping soldiers' wives happy or, if not happy, at least silently resigned. For a century both British and American military commanders had been weighing the advantages and disadvantages of allowing their soldiers to marry. It was a sometimes confusing calculus. On the one hand, they calculated, marriage raised the moral tenor of their male troops and cut down on their drunkenness, indebtedness, and venereal disease. On the other militarized hand, marriage might divide a soldier's loyalty, making him slower to mobilize, while burdening the armed forces with responsibilities for maintaining housing, health care, and family harmony. The military marriage debate remains unsettled today not only in the United States but also in other countries whose governments depend on married male soldiers to carry out their national security and foreign policies and on the women their male soldiers have married to conform to the model of the Good Military Wife.[31]

Despite commanders' ambivalence, the rising post–World War II need to accommodate male soldiers' wives and children altered the nature of a military base. No longer could a soldier's wife be as easily marginalized as she had been in earlier centuries, dismissed as merely a low-class "camp follower" living on the edge of military operations, cooking her husband's food, and doing his laundry in return for meager rations. There were too many of them now. And they were "respectable" women. For the British, Canadian, and American armed forces, which today have to recruit—and *keep*—large numbers of expensively trained male volunteers without the aid of compulsory male conscription, civilian wives' dissatisfaction with military life can produce worrisome manpower shortages. A dissatisfied wife will urge her husband not to reenlist. The washing machines and electric organs flown into the U.S. base at Effingham in the 1960s were early evidence of the American army's attempt to satisfy not only male soldiers but also their wives.

By 2010, there were seven hundred thousand civilian American women married to active-duty U.S. male military personnel. Some lived on overseas bases. Many lived on or near U.S. domestic bases. By the early twenty-first century, the U.S. military had become the most married force in the country's history: 58.7 percent of active-duty military personnel were married. The army had the highest proportion of married personnel; the marines the lowest. Of all heterosexual spouses of U.S. active-duty personnel, only 6.3 percent were men; 93.7 percent were women.[32] As the Pentagon tried to adapt to life after the ending (in 2011) of the "Don't ask, don't tell" ban on openly gay and lesbian military personnel, it also had to adapt, base by base, to having more civilian married partners in same sex marriages demand access to the same benefits enjoyed by heterosexual spouses of military personnel.[33]

Many women married to male soldiers have been content with the privileges that have come with living on a military base: low-cost housing, shopping discounts, access to medical care, a sense of shared values, and, for many African American military wives, less overt racism than experienced in society beyond the base. Many women married to American male soldiers also saw themselves as models of self-sacrificing feminized patriotism, enduring regimens, constant moves, virtual single parenting, long spousal separations, and wartime fears for their husbands' safety. Some of the women deployed with their husbands to the larger U.S. overseas bases—for instance, in Britain, Germany, South Korea, and Japan—have also taken on the role of informal American ambassador, trying to represent what they saw to be the best of American values while living abroad. Their efforts have been open to varied interpretations in their host countries, appreciated by some local people but appearing to others to be just an updated feminized version of an older imperialism.[34]

For those women who gained a sense of political purpose, community, security, and comfort from living as military wives on bases, there was a price to be paid: adherence to the military's gendered presumptions about proper femininity, good marriages, and ranked propriety. Central to this package has been the official presumption that a civilian wife would merge her loyalty to her soldier-husband with her uncritical loyalty to his employer, the government: the military's adversary was to be her adversary; her husband's rank would determine her friendships and her children's friendships. Living up to the military's model of the Good Military Wife also meant giving up aspirations for a career of one's own and, especially if one was married to an officer and was invested in his rise through the ranks, doing hours of unpaid volunteer work. Military wives' unpaid labor has been the glue that has made many a base a working "community." Such feminized, wifely volunteer work takes an even more prominent role when a woman follows her husband to an overseas base, because the opportunities abroad for a military wife to gain paid employment and pursue her own professional career have been particularly slim.[35]

Military base commanders and their civilian superiors—from the early years of the Cold War through the U.S.-led wars in Afghanistan and Iraq—have counted on most women to see the satisfactions that come from being an unpaid, loyal military wife as outweighing the frustrations.[36]

It came, therefore, as an unwelcome surprise when, in the 1980s, a group of politically experienced wives and ex-wives of American male military officers began to organize and speak out about what they saw as the unfairness of the Pentagon's gendered political marriage system. They found sympathizers in Congress, especially Representative Patricia Schroeder, a Democrat from Denver. These military wives steered clear of any discussions of the U.S. government's foreign policies; they talked about spousal benefits and divorce rules.

Among the early activists were older women who had fulfilled the model military wife role, many for up to twenty years, doing the unpaid work on countless bases that would be considered a plus when their officer-husbands came up for promotion. These women found that when their husbands filed for divorce in order to marry a usually younger woman, they would lose not only their marriages but also their housing, health benefits, and store discounts. Officials in the Pentagon had ruled that their divorcing husbands did not have to count these base benefits when calculating alimony. Initially, according to Carolyn Becraft, one of the politically active wives, the divorced women focused their anger on the young women who were marrying their officer-husbands. But as they got together to analyze their situations and to frame their political message, they realized that it was not the new wives who were their problem. It was the Pentagon officials. Those officials, these women concluded, cared more about their male officers' economic security than about civilian military wives' economic security. The result of their lobbying was a congressionally mandated change in the benefits accorded by the Pentagon to military spouses and ex-spouses.[37]

Soon after, in the ongoing gendered political marital history of the U.S. military, women doing volunteer work on American bases around the United States and abroad began to speak out publicly about domestic violence, about male soldier-husbands beating their military wives. Although few of these women called themselves feminists, many were fully aware of the emergent battered women's movement in the United States. They had absorbed the lesson that wife abuse was not something any woman had to be ashamed about or had to silently endure. However, a military base turned out to be a very difficult environment in which to turn violence of this sort into a legitimate issue.[38] First, most base commanders—and their Washington superiors—did not want to hear about it. They had other priorities. They expected military wives to cope. Second, these same officials frequently imagined that male soldiers were just acting out of stress, and stress was what soldiering was all about. Third, airing the realities of domestic violence on a base tarnished the reputation of that base, which would hurt the base commander's chances for his next promotion. Finally, and importantly, allowing domestic violence within their soldiers' homes to become a public issue was likely to raise the always thorny question of the culture of violence nurtured in the military as a whole. That certainly was not a question that senior officers wanted explored in the wider public arena.

Trying to break the silence shrouding violence against women is always a challenge. Breaking the culture of gendered silence on a military base was harder still. Feminized silence, it became clear, was a pillar of U.S. national security.

Despite the formidable obstacles, women working with military wives succeeded, by the 1990s, in getting congressional armed service committee members, especially women in Congress, to pressure the Defense Department to acknowledge the incidences of domestic violence in male soldiers' households. On the other hand, as activists would discover when, a decade later, they would try to get senior military officials to face up to their complicity in the epidemic of sexual violence perpetrated by male soldiers on their uniformed female comrades, the military's prioritizing of male soldiers' value and their complementary reliance on women's silence remains stubbornly entrenched.

Today, thousands of women married to male soldiers live in the United States on or near one of the Defense Department's many domestic bases. Some of the largest: Camp Pendleton, California; Fort Campbell, Kentucky; Fort Lewis-McChord, Washington; Fort Hood, Texas; Naval Air Station, Virginia; Fort Bragg, North Carolina; Fort Carson, Colorado. Each of these bases is as gendered as every U.S. base in South Korea, Turkey, Japan, Guam, Djibouti, and Germany. The women who live on or near these domestic bases in the roles of military wives often feel pressured to stay silent about the hardships that have been part of the government waging its extended wars in Iraq and Afghanistan, where bases were not created to accommodate spouses and children. Many of these women take part in wives' associations, but their activities frequently are shaped by the cautionary influence of the women married to the base's senior officers and by the expectations of base commanders, who make it clear that a wives' association's chief job is to help military wives cope; it is not to alter the way the base is run.

Among the American military wives living on or near domestic bases in the current political era who have spoken out publicly, despite these pressures, have been those women whose military husbands have returned from Afghanistan and Iraq severely wounded, physically and mentally. These civilian women have become a vocal presence on many domestic military bases, demanding from base commanders transparency, attention, resources, and candor. In breaking the silence expected of military wives, these women not only have made clearer the actual costs of these two wars but also have exposed the unfairness of camouflaging those costs by shifting them onto the shoulders of soldiers' civilian family members.[39]

During the post-9/11 administration of President George W. Bush, a new concept in American overseas basing was developed, "the lily pad." Lily pad bases would be low-impact bases, overseas bases that still would require formal agreements with local host governments, but would have a smaller social and cultural "footprint."[40] No suburban housing, no lawns, no bowling allies, no golf courses, no discos outside the gates. And no wives.

For many local people living around American bases overseas, the lily pad formula might seem a welcome change. Bases would come with less heavy sociocultural baggage. There would be no questionable entertainment districts appealing to off-duty male soldiers outside the fence of a lily pad. Fewer American armored vehicles would race through a civilian town's busy streets. But the Pentagon's motivations appear to have less to do with sensitivity to local concerns than with shedding the feminized dimensions of the big Cold War bases. Lily pads simultaneously offer smaller targets for local antibases protests. One consequence of the Pentagon's adoption of the lily pad basing strategy for the thousands of women married to American soldiers is that more of their husbands will be deployed far from home more of the time. Military wives who have experienced virtual single motherhood are due to experience more of it.

One source of political weakness hobbling those military wives seeking to change the sexist policies governing life on military bases has been the division between women as military wives, women as civilian base workers, women as military personnel, and women drawn into prostitution around military bases. The four groups of women, whom male military elites see as distinct, often share the same compartmentalized imagining of themselves. Women soldiers who launched their twenty-first-century campaign to make sexual assaults against women soldiers a national issue could have learned a lot by turning to activist military wives and to women in military prostitution for analysis and strategic advice.

IS A MILITARY BASE SECURE FOR WOMEN SOLDIERS?

Any military base—local or overseas—is a place where certain forms of masculinity are nurtured and rewarded, other forms disparaged or punished. Drill sergeants are often the chief molders and enforcers of the desired militarized masculinity—that is, a mode of acting out one's manhood that makes soldiering, especially combat soldiering, real or fantasized, a principal criterion against which to judge one's behavior and attitudes.

This particular mode often accords primacy to toughness, skilled use of violence, presumption of an enemy, male camaraderie, submerging one's emotions, and discipline (being disciplined and demanding it of others). Beyond drill sergeants, many different actors on a base play their parts in shaping and encouraging certain militarized masculine attitudes and behaviors: chaplains, psychiatrists, commanders, midlevel officers, even wives. Off-base actors also can celebrate certain forms of manliness while ridiculing others: fathers, legislators, media commentators, entertainers.

Nor is the privileged form of militarized masculinity universal. The nurtured and rewarded form of militarized masculinity can vary from country to country, with some country's militarized masculine norm being crafted to serve international peacekeeping, others to fit into humanitarian missions, while still others are intended to enhance combat roles. We know today that we need to investigate these differences, as well as commonalities, between, for instance, the diverse masculinities that are privileged and celebrated in the Irish, Japanese, Nigerian, Chinese, Swedish, British, United States, South Korean, Brazilian, Israeli, Bangladeshi, Fijian, and Canadian militaries. Each of these militarized masculine norms is wielded in particular domestic and foreign operations.[41]

A military woman has a personal stake in charting and making sense of which mode of masculinity is made the favored norm on the base to which she is assigned, whether in Texas or Bahrain. Knowing this could make her life rewarding and secure; not knowing it could put her career and her physical safety at risk.

Military women are virtually always a minority of all the uniformed personnel on any of their country's military bases, sometimes a very small minority. With many governments adjusting to the end of the Cold War by ending male conscription (what Americans call "the draft"), defense strategists and their legislative allies have had to devise ways to increase the numbers of women recruited into their government forces without jeopardizing the military's valuable image as a place where a man can prove his manliness. In 2013, among the militaries with the highest percentages of women in their ranks are those of Ukraine, Latvia, New Zealand, Canada, Australia, Israel, South Africa, and the United States. To understand each military—those with high proportions of women and those with the lowest proportions (such as the Russian, Japanese, Chinese, and Turkish)—one needs to explore not only how uniformed women experience pride, patriotism, and camaraderie but also how uniformed women experience sexual harassment and sexual assault.

In the United States, women have grown from just 2 percent of the active-duty military—during the U.S. war in Vietnam, in the 1970s—to 14.5 percent by the time of American troop withdrawal from Iraq in 2011. The branch with the highest percentage of active-duty women (thus the branch most reliant on women to fulfill its mission) is the air force, with 19 percent. The branch with the lowest percentage (and the one most resistant to women's participation) is the marines, with just 6.8 percent.

The gendered politics of any military can play out rather differently for uniformed women belonging to different social classes, ethnic groups, or racial groups. Among women in the current American military, the numbers of African American women have stood out: while African American women were just 12 percent of all the country's women, in 2011, they constituted 17.2 percent of all women who were active-duty military officers and 29.6 percent of all women in the military's active-duty enlisted ranks. Looking more closely, especially at differences among military branches, one notes that in that same year a stunning 39.1 percent of all women in the active-duty enlisted ranks of the army were African American women. That was more than three times their proportion of all women in the country's civilian population.[42]

By contrast, Hispanic women, who were approximately 15 percent of all women in the U.S. population, appeared more likely to choose a different branch when they volunteered for the U.S. military. Hispanic women's proportion of all active-duty women, which has been steadily rising since 1990 as a result of the Pentagon's deliberate recruiting campaigns, reached its peak in the enlisted ranks of the marines: 19.6 percent. Asian and Pacific Islander American women accounted for only 4 percent of the total U.S. female population in 2011, but they constituted 20 percent of all women in the navy's enlisted ranks.[43]

Owing to three decades of lobbying by American women in the military—especially women officers such as navy pilot Rosemary Mariner, working in collaboration with women members of the House of Representatives and Senate—the Defense Department has gradually, usually begrudgingly, opened more and more types of military jobs to women.[44] American civilian feminists often have been ambivalent about investing their limited resources in challenging sexism inside the military because they have prioritized antiwar campaigns and worried that elevating women soldiers to "first-class citizenship" status would send the roots of already potent militarism even deeper into their country's cultural soil. Nonetheless, since 1990, barrier after barrier to women's military training and deployment has been dismantled; the latest change was the 2013 lifting of the Pentagon's ban on women in combat roles. The U.S. military did not lead the way. Militaries of the Netherlands, Canada, Australia, and New Zealand were out in front of the United States in ending their sexist bans on military women in the jobs that the Pentagon classifies (and, changing its mind, then reclassifies) as "combat." Exactly how the opening of combat roles to women will be implemented in practice in the United States is a story yet to be told. Changing the formal rules of any institution is only the beginning of its gendered transformation and, by itself, is no guarantee that the institutional culture will become significantly less patriarchal.

At the same time that organizational sexist barriers have been lowered, there has been an upsurge in reported sexual assaults by U.S. military men on military women and on military men. Some feminist analysts have wondered aloud whether the increased reporting of violence against women inside the U.S. military has been at least in part a result of the increase in the proportions of women and their inching up the ranks and moving into the military's most masculinized occupations. As in other spheres of many societies, some men have acted out their resentment of women's advancements in arenas that until recently had been securely masculinized, by attacking women as "intruders." Other feminists have warned that the recent upsurge in reporting should be treated quite separately from the actual incidences of sexual assault. They warn that many women soldiers in past eras have endured rape and attempted rape in silence, never thinking it was safe or useful to speak about those assaults for the record. In any area of international politics, paying close attention to silences is a crucial investigatory strategy.

Violence against women, a central issue for women's advocates since the 1970s, was a topic that even feminist peace activists, wary of working for women's military equality, felt unambiguous about when it occurred inside the military. This was not a question of merely militarized careers or promotions. Thus, by 2013 a national campaign organized by women activists brought together military women, civilian feminists, journalists, documentary filmmakers, and women in Congress to challenge the Defense Department and the entire chain of command.[45] Together, they shone their spotlight on the military academies and on particular military bases (for instance, Lackland Air Force Base in San Antonio, Texas). They forced the Veteran's Administration, a large federal institution whose officials for generations had collectively thought of their services as being intended only for male veterans, to vastly broaden their self-perception. In the middle of the wars in Iraq and Afghanistan, to respond to the rising number of women veterans they were seeing as patients struggling with the aftereffects of sexual assault, the VA's health professionals scrambled to develop a new medical concept. They decided to call it "military sexual trauma." The VA then created special clinics around the country to provide care specifically for women veterans who were suffering from military sexual trauma, a subset of post–traumatic stress disorder. Military sexual trauma was brought on, according to these medical professionals, by having been raped by a fellow male soldier.[46]

As the politics of American intramilitary sexual violence quickly intensified, the Defense Department was pressed to issue a report on both the incidence of reported sexual assaults and the survey results estimating the incidence of actual assaults. It estimated that reported sexual assaults were just the tip of the iceberg, that during just the fiscal year 2011 (that is, October 1, 2010, through September 30, 2011), nineteen thousand military personnel had been sexually assaulted by their American military colleagues. During FY 2012, that number jumped to twenty-six thousand. The majority of those American military personnel said that they had been assaulted by military men, often their superiors. Men made up 85 percent of the total active-duty personnel during this era. Women, though only 15 percent of the U.S. active-duty forces, were disproportionately assaulted. Women in the military were thus much more likely than men to be targeted by military men for attack. Most of the women and men who were subjected to sexual assaults did not report those assaults. Male victims told reporters that it was women coming forward to speak out about rapes that had given them the courage to overcome their years of secret shame and publicly tell their own stories.[47]

On and off the record, military women told of being sexually assaulted when going to the latrines at night, when sleeping in their own barracks, when meeting with a superior officer in his office. Controversy soon swirled around the very notion, long cherished by American military officers, that the military's hierarchy itself—not civilian criminal justice authorities—is best equipped to investigate, prosecute, try, and punish its own personnel. Yet in practice, the sanctity of the "chain of command" had erected another, less visible wall around any already-fenced-off military base. It was a double fence that many women survivors of military rape felt had jeopardized their safety.

Rebekah Havrilla, a former army sergeant, told the Senate Armed Services Committee in March 2013 that she had been raped by her male superior while she was deployed in Afghanistan in 2007. She did not report him: "I chose not to do a report of any kind because I had no faith in my chain of command." Instead, Sargeant Havrilla had sought counsel from the army chaplain on her base. His response to her: "The rape was God's will." He urged her to go to church.[48]

Two related questions frequently have gone unexplored during the debate over what to do to effectively prevent and prosecute sexual violence inside the American military. First, what, if any, are the causal linkages between, on the one hand, sexual violence perpetrated by men on women inside the military and, on the other, sexual violence perpetrated by U.S. military men against civilian women living around U.S. military bases at home and abroad? Second, how exactly do diverse men inside the military absorb the masculinized idea that women are property to be used by men in ways that allegedly confirm their own manhood and simultaneously preserve the masculinized atmosphere in certain institutional spaces?

The two questions are analytically related: answering either question will help to answer the other. Failure to ask—and try to answer—these two related feminist analytical questions has meant that the politics of masculinity has been swept under the militarized rug. It also has meant that American military women rarely have tried to make common cause with women in other countries who have endured abuse as a consequence of U.S. soldiers being based abroad. Most often, sexual violence inside the military has been treated merely as a domestic issue. In reality, it has been a dynamic of international politics.

PROSTITUTION, WOMEN IN PROSTITUTION, AND THE INTERNATIONAL GENDERED POLITICS OF NATIONAL SECURITY

Military men's sexualized relations with women—and other men's attempts to control those relations—have been a major thread running through international politics for at least the last two centuries. These sexualized relations include befriending, dating, marrying, purchasing sex, and coercing sex. The lines separating these five different sorts of relations often are blurred, yet at other times they are drawn in bold ink. What is odd is that this multistranded topic so rarely is explored by mainstream investigators of international politics and only makes headlines when it erupts into "scandal." Topics treated merely as scandals, however, rarely alter conventional understandings of what is "international" and what counts as "politics."

Military bases and women in prostitution have been assumed to go together, to be a "natural" twosome and thus unworthy of political investigation. In fact, it has taken calculated policies to sustain that alleged fit: policies to shape men's sexuality, to ensure battle readiness, to regulate businesses, to structure women's economic opportunities, to influence military wives, to socialize women soldiers, and to design systems of policing, entertainment, and public health. It is striking that these policies have been so successfully made invisible around most bases, especially bases within the United States.[49]

By the late nineteenth century the British government had troops deployed around the globe to sustain its empire.[50] These troops were not as likely to seek sexual liaisons with working-class white women as with colonized women of color—Chinese women in Hong Kong, Indian women in India, Egyptian women in Egypt. British officials had been thwarted in their efforts to control white working-class women's relationships with British military men in Britain. In the 1860s, in the wake of the disastrous Crimean War and at the behest of Britain's generals and admirals, the men in Parliament, in the name of protecting male soldiers and sailors, had passed the Contagious Diseases Acts. These militarized laws, a form of national security policy, mobilized Britain's civilian local policemen to arrest working-class women in army base towns and naval port towns whom those policemen suspected of being prostitutes. In practice, that was any working-class woman out at night on her own. The suspected women were compelled to undergo vaginal exams with the crudest of instruments. It was the Anti–Contagious Diseases Acts Campaign, led by British feminists of the Ladies National League, that (despite women being denied voting rights) effectively lobbied for twenty years to persuade the all-male Parliament of the unfairness of the Contagious Diseases Acts and to repeal them.[51]

British military officials were determined, however, not to lose control over Britain's colonial women. First, they refashioned marriage policies for soldiers, considering whether to allow British soldiers to marry Indian women: would such marriages harm or enhance military readiness and white settler morale? Some officials believed that if British soldiers were allowed to marry Indian women, they might be less likely to frequent prostitutes and thus, presumably, be less likely to pick up venereal diseases. On the other hand, these men reasoned, such a policy of encouraging interracial marriage might jeopardize British men's sense of their own racial superiority. Second, colonial officials continued to enforce the equivalent of Contagious Diseases Acts outside Britain even after they had been repealed at home in the 1880s. These laws, called the Cantonment Acts, permitted colonial police authorities to conduct compulsory vaginal examinations on civilian women around imperial military bases for the sake of allowing British soldiers overseas to have sexual relations with colonial women without fear of contracting venereal disease.

In 1888, Josephine Butler, founder of Britain's politically effective Ladies National League, launched an international campaign calling for the abolition of the Cantonment Acts. Her new journal, *The Dawn,* criticized British male authorities' double standard: controlling women's allegedly immoral sexual behavior for the sake of protecting male soldiers' allegedly necessary sexual pleasures.[52] Butler's movement was more feminist in its analysis than in its organization. Her chief abolitionist allies appear to have been British men and educated men in the colonized societies. Colonial women—a study in 1891 found that 90 percent of military prostitutes were impoverished local widows—were seen by most prostitution abolitionists as victims, though rarely as organizational allies with their own political ideas and resources.[53]

Anti–Cantonment Acts campaigners were transnational activists, but they saw these policies from an imperial perspective: if such regulations were allowed to persist in India, they would provide lessons for military authorities in other British colonies and even in the colonies of rival imperial powers, such as the Netherlands, who also needed to station soldiers abroad, provide them with sexual access to colonial women, and yet ensure that the soldiers were physically fit enough to carry out their military duties for the empire. A letter written in 1888 to Butler by one of her Dutch campaigning correspondents in Indonesia (then under Dutch colonial rule) charts the international flow of militaries' prostitution strategies:

> One of the official gentlemen quietly remarked that they thought of introducing the Anglo-Indian system of having separate tents inhabited by the licensed women in the camps. At present at a fixed hour in the evening the doors of the Barracks are opened in order to admit a certain number of these poor victims. I can scarcely record all that we have learned. Life in the Barracks is *morally horrible....*

The fact stated here shows that the bad example set by the English government in India is infecting Java, and no doubt other Colonies of other nations, thus doubling and trebling our motives for urging the Abolition of the hideous Indian Ordinances and Cantonment Acts.[54]

By 1895, Butler and her campaigners had persuaded the British government to repeal the Cantonment Acts. Nevertheless, her informants in the colonies reported that, despite the repeal, forced physical examinations of local women did not stop. *The Dawn* published letters from British military officers who expressed the widespread official view that such practices remained necessary. They were allegedly necessary for individual British soldiers (not for Indian soldiers; they seemed to have a strikingly lower incidence of VD, which puzzled their British commanders) and for the very well-being of the British empire. To this argument Josephine Butler editorially retorted, "We had not realized that the women of a conquered race, in the character of official prostitutes, constituted one of the bulwarks of our great Empire!"[55]

In the twentieth century, governments of France, Japan, British, Russia, the United States, and Canada each attempted to enforce military and civilian practices that would sexually control women for the sake of sustaining their military's legitimacy while ensuring their male soldiers' morale and health.[56] The Japanese imperial army's policy of forcing Korean, Filipino, Taiwanese, Malaysian, and Indonesian women into sexual service in their military's "comfort stations," for the sake of allegedly bolstering male soldiers' morale, is perhaps the most famous forced prostitution system designed to wage World War II.[57]

It was this World War II system that gave rise to the concept of "sexual slavery," a concept developed in the 1990s by Korean feminists. They argued, successfully, that such militarized forced prostitution should be understood as a war crime. The "sexual slavery" concept soon after became crucial to those transnational feminists who worked to shed light on the specific sorts of sexual militarized abuse of women that had become integral to waging the 1990s wars both in the former Yugoslavia and in Rwanda. That is, a woman who is forcibly made a "wife" of a warring soldier to be subjected to his repeated sexual violations is not a wife; she is not a prostitute. She is the victim of sexual slavery. These same feminist political and legal activists continued to campaign, persuading governments that "sexual slavery" should be internationally recognized as a prosecutable and punishable war crime. It was their conceptualizing and persuading that led to "sexual slavery" being explicitly listed among the war crimes prosecutable in The Hague before the newly established International War Crimes Court.

The infamous Japanese imperial "comfort women" system, however, was certainly not the only prostitution system used to wage World War II and to create its immediate postwar political systems of occupation.[58] Yet only now, six decades after the end of what Americans still call "the Good War," are we beginning to understand the full scope of the American officials' efforts to make prostitution, and women in prostitution, work for the war effort and for the establishment of the postwar occupation. Recognizing American officials' World War II prostitution policies should not dilute the condemnation of the Japanese imperial army's "comfort women" system. Rather, it should foster a sharp feminist-informed, cross-national, comparative investigation of the sexual politics designed to wage any war.

American officials' World War II efforts to create racialized military prostitution systems included going to great lengths to set up brothels for African American male soldiers separate from those designated for white male soldiers—along wartime Hawaii's famed Hotel Street, around the America occupying forces' bases in postwar Germany, in postwar Korea, and in postwar Japan.[59] Similarly, feminist historian Mary Louise Roberts has uncovered evidence that in postinvasion Normandy, France, American male soldiers and their superiors created self-serving stereotypes of an oversexed French nation and, with it, a racially segregated brothel system. Chief among its damaging political consequences: sexualized conditions of insecurity for many postwar French women, women whom the American men were supposedly there to liberate.[60] That is, the American military occupation era of the mid- to late 1940s, officially defined by Washington as a time of liberation and democratization, was in fact a time of energetic American racialized prostitution-policy-making.

The immediate post–World War II era did not mark the end of the U.S. military's prostitution system. Korean, Okinawan, and Filipina feminist researcher-activists have been teaching us about how racialized prostitution was a constant throughout the American military's conduct of the Korean War, the Vietnam War, and its globally diffuse post-9/11 "war on terror."[61] One of the most stubbornly entrenched beliefs held by many military male commanders has been that military-tolerated, organized prostitution protects "respectable" women. Takazato Suzuyo and her fellow activists who created the feminist group Okinawa Women Act Against Military Violence have spent years documenting American military personnel's violence against civilian women and girls in an attempt to dispel this self-serving military myth.[62]

CLOSING SUBIC: THE SUCCESS OF AN
ANTIBASES MOVEMENT

Tues. 5—Rained all day
Wed. 6—Rained part of day. Got pay check.
Thurs. 7—Rained all day.[63]

Thus wrote Jessie Anglum, wife of an American army officer, in her diary. She did not enjoy her stay in the Philippines. The year was 1901. The American army had been sent by President McKinley to quash a defiant Filipino insurgency. Filipino nationalists first fought the islands' Spanish colonizers and then resisted the Americans' plans to impose their own colonizing rule. Anglum played her own small part in putting down the Filipino insurgency. She was one of the first American military wives to take the long voyage to join her husband in the Philippines. Once off the ship, she was put up in a Manila hotel. As the monsoon rains poured steadily outside the shutters, she was bored. Her husband spent most of his days on maneuvers against the insurgents. She went for occasional carriage rides and had tea with the few other American women then in Manila. But she did not want to be in the Philippines. She had sailed to Asia only out of wifely duty. She counted the days until her husband's tour was over. And she was happy when she could repack her trunks and sail back home.

There were no elaborate American bases when Jessie Anglum endured her damp hotel stay. But in the century following her arrival, the U.S. government made up for that deficiency. By the 1980s, the now-independent Philippines hosted a score of U.S. military facilities. Subic Bay Naval Base and Clark Air Force Base, both situated on the main island of Luzon, were the largest and were deemed by Pentagon strategists to be among the most crucial for American global defense. The two bases served as launching pads for the U.S. war in Vietnam and as a bulwark against Soviet power during the Cold War. Subic and Clark were designed to operate in coordination with U.S. Pacific bases in Hawaii, Guam, South Korea, and Okinawa.

The Pentagon's pan-Pacific vision provided an incentive in the 1990s for women activists in these five Pacific regions to create new political bonds with each other. Meeting at the UN women's conference in Beijing in 1995, they began to trade information, experiences, and strategies. They pieced together a portrait of how civilian women experienced the impacts of the U.S. military bases: prostitution, violence, police harassment, and environmental degradation. In meetings held over the next two decades, these antibases women-activists forged friendships and analyses—of security, of militarization, of insecurity, of peace, of violence, of patriarchy. Among the groups whose members met each other were Gabriela: Alliance of Filipino Women, Okinawa Women Act Against Military Violence, the Asia-Japan Women's Resource Center, and the transnational feminist network Women for Genuine Security.[64] Their members made one of their principal objectives the educating of American mainland citizens about the impacts their government's bases were having on women who must live with those bases. Given how little attention most mainland Americans pay either to overseas military bases or to Pacific island territories and Asian allies, this was a challenge.

During the years of the Cold War and the Vietnam War, Subic Bay Naval Base was the largest of these Pacific U.S. bases. It dominated the Philippines town of Olongapo. The mayor of Olongapo made the Subic Bay base commander one of his chief reference points when he made town policies. The U.S. Navy base was home for many of the 15,000 American military personnel and their families stationed in the Philippines. When an aircraft carrier docked, another 18,000 men poured into town. The base relied on civilian Filipino labor to keep it running. Workers were paid at lower rates than workers on American bases in South Korea or Japan, but for many Filipino men and women these base jobs provided a livelihood. By 1985, the U.S. military had become the second-largest employer in the Philippines, hiring over 40,000 Filipinos: 20,581 full-time workers, 14,249 contract workers, 5,064 domestic workers, and 1,746 concessionaries.[65]

The social problem generated by the U.S. bases that attracted most Filipino feminists' and nationalists' attention was prostitution. Many Filipinos became convinced that U.S. military bases were responsible for creating or exacerbating conditions that promoted prostitution. Prostitution, violence against women, militarism (American and Filipino varieties), and the compromising of Philippines national sovereignty all seemed woven together. The arrival of AIDS in the Philippines in 1987 escalated nationalists' sense that the American-Philippines bases government-to-government agreement—called the Status of Forces Agreement (often colloquially referred to by its acronym, SOFA)—jeopardized, rather than strengthened, Filipinos' national security.

During the 1980s, especially as the Filipino prodemocracy movement gathered nationwide momentum, local Filipino women activists, including activist Catholic nuns, documented the living conditions of women around the large U.S. bases and provided spaces where women in prostitution could seek non-judgmental support. The activist researchers estimated that 6,000 to 9,000 women worked in the bases-dependent entertainment businesses, a number that could jump to 20,000 when an American aircraft carrier came into port and thousands of male sailors were granted leave. They recorded that most women in the sexualized clubs and massage parlors came to Olongapo from poor rural regions of the Philippines. They reported on the "ladies drinks" system used by bar owners to press women employees to persuade off-duty military men to buy more alcohol while purchasing expensive fruit drinks for the women. They explained the "bar fine" system, by which male customers paid the bar owner money for permission to take a woman outside the club to have sex.

These activist researchers also paid attention to the children born of American military fathers and Filipino civilian mothers. Of the approximately 30,000 children who were born of Filipino mothers and American fathers each year during the 1970s and 1980s, these activist researchers found, some 10,000 were thought to have become street children, many of them working as prostitutes servicing American male pedophiles. Unlike children born of American fathers and Vietnamese mothers during the U.S. war in Vietnam—when prostitution was rampant—the U.S. Congress did not grant these Filipino-American children visas to immigrate to the United States under its special post–Vietnam War "family reintegration" plan.[66]

The Filipino researchers also documented the American base commanders' policy that required Filipino public health clinics to set up VD and AIDS examinations for women in the surrounding entertainment businesses. Women who did not go through the exams, or who did not pass the exams, were denied their entertainment-worker licenses. American military men did not have to undergo such exams to get their off-base passes and mix with local Filipino women. The official presumption was that Filipino women infected American military men, never the other way round.[67]

Figure 16. Filipino women working as entertainers around the U.S. Navy's Subic Bay base line up for compulsory VD and HIV/AIDS examinations, 1988. While the base was in operation, all such entertainers were required to undergo these examinations twice a month. Photo: Sandra Sturdevant.

A complex Filipino antibases movement succeeded in persuading the Philippines Senate to vote against renewing the bilateral Status of Forces Agreement with the United States. In 1992, Subic Bay Naval Base and Clark Air Force Base were closed.

Twenty years later, however, Filipino feminists in groups such as Gabriela were reporting that militarized prostitution was on the rise again, as was American military men's abuse of local women. Even without its sprawling Subic Bay and Clark permanent bases, the U.S. Defense Department, in coordination with officials in Manila, was building up the American military presence in the Philippines. The justification no longer was the Soviet threat and the Cold War. Now the justification was expansionist China and the "global war on terror." Subic Bay was being refitted by a private American defense contractor to handle the visits of more American navy ships. More American soldiers were being deployed to the Philippines on what were termed "training" assignments. New Washington-Manila military agreements called these deployments "temporary rotations." This formula meant that both sides in the government-to-government agreement could avoid admitting that the Pentagon was establishing new bases in the Philippines, an admission that would stir up local controversy.[68]

Prostitution has never been timeless. It is not the static "oldest profession." Women in prostitution, women working against the prostitution industry, men profiting from prostitution, men patronizing women in prostitution, and men who make military policies to mold prostitution to suit their militaries' needs—each of these five groups of actors lives in history. Each of them, no matter how seemingly powerless some of them are, help to reshape the local and international politics of prostitution and, thus, the ideas about and practices of masculinity as they underpin military bases.

Consequently, today one must stay alert to changes. One must become curious, for instance, about the women from both the Philippines and the former Soviet Union who voluntarily or unwillingly leave their countries to become the majority of women servicing American military men in and around the U.S.

bases in South Korea, Guam, and Okinawa.[69] One also has to monitor how local feminists interact with nationalists in any movement to limit or close a foreign base: are the women in prostitution turned by nonfeminist nationalists into mere symbols of "national humiliation," or are these women invited to be active partners in any antibases campaign? Are feminists pressed to sublimate their demands for the good of what nonfeminist nationalists think of as the nation?

Similarly, one must delve into the sexual politics that are integral to those American overseas bases in which military men are prohibited from "fraternizing"—that is, from having social relations with local civilian women. Nonfraternization is the Pentagon's rule for many soldiers and sailors based on American bases, in, for instance, Afghanistan, Djibouti, Bahrain, and Niger. Where are the women, the civilian women, the uniformed women?

CONCLUSION

The closings of the Subic Bay and Clark bases in the Philippines have not been the only occasions when a local popular movement has persuaded a national government to end its basing agreement with the United States. Antibases movements have succeeded in Manta, Ecuador, and in Vieques, Puerto Rico.[70] The gendered politics inside each of these successful antibases movements has been distinct. In each of them, women as activists have been crucial to the mobilization and to the meanings adopted in opposition to the U.S. base. But not every antibases movement has made feminist understandings of sexism central to its strategies and its goals. In each of these movements, as well as those in South Korea and Okinawa—the latter two have not succeeded in persuading their governments to end their Status of Forces Agreement treaties with the United States—feminist local antibases activists have had to work constantly to ensure that nationalist ideas do not trump feminist ideas. Exploring these dynamics within any country's antibases debate helps to clarify the complex workings of gendered ideas shaping the international politics of military alliances.

Perhaps the antibases popular movement in which feminist ideas—about masculinized politics and about alternative measures of security—have become most central has been the Greenham Common women's peace camp in southern England during the last years of the Cold War.[71] From 1981 to 1989, a British women's peace encampment grew at Greenham Common, outside the fence protecting the U.S. Air Force base. The women who decided to camp outside the base at Greenham sparked a national debate among Britons over both the unequal alliance between the United States and Britain and the meaning of security—and security for whom—in the nuclear age. Still today, one can meet British women for whom "Greenham" was the turning point in their political lives. They will describe in detail camping in the cold winter mud, singing when arraigned in court, debating with each other for hours the meanings of peace and patriarchy—and family, motherhood, and sexuality. They will retell the story of propping up ladders to climb over the base fence on New Year's night in 1983 to dance atop the Americans' nuclear missile silo and getting out without being caught.

The women who camped at Greenham also will recall the pain of hearing police and some local people call them "dykes" and "whores." Then they will tell of the excitement when thousands of women from all over Britain and Ireland came to Greenham to form a nine-mile human chain around the entire

Figure 17. Women peace campaigners dance on a cruise missile silo inside the U.S. Air Force base at Greenham Common, England, 1983. Photo: Raissa Page/Format.

perimeter of the American base. An Irish woman who traveled from Dublin to join the Greenham chain remembered: "We joined hands and began to sing ... to say: we will meet your violence with a loving embrace, for it is the surest way to defuse it. How strong I felt when I joined my voice to the waves of voices shouting 'Freedom' and when the echoes from so far away drifted across the base."[72]

Journalist Beatrix Campbell interviewed one British woman who thought of herself as a member of the Conservative Party, the party of Margaret Thatcher, the prime minister who was a chief backer of the U.S. base and its nuclear-headed missiles. But when this woman began thinking about the Greenham women's peace camp, she recalled that she had developed another sort of political understanding. She had cut her hair short to make it clear to her husband and sons that she identified with the Greenham women:

"Before Greenham I didn't realize that the Americans had got their missiles here. Then I realized. What cheek! It was the fuss the Greenham Common women made that made me realize.... The men in this house [her husband and two sons] think they're butch, queers." Did she? She thought for a moment. "No." Would it have bothered her if they were butch or if they were lesbians? She thought again. "No." Women irritated her men anyway, she said, not without affection. "They never stop talking about Land Rovers and bikes, and they've not finished their dinner before they're asking for their tea."[73]

It was due largely to the Greenham Common peace camp women's activism, not just to the ending of the Cold War, that the British government decided that, when the Americans left Greenham, the land should not be given to the British military. Instead, it should revert to the local people to again become common agricultural land.[74]

Running any military base—a local military's base or a foreign military's base; a base within the country's borders or a base operated time zones away; a NATO, African Union, or United Nations peacekeeping base; a private military company's base—is a complicated operation.[75] Moreover, many institutions that are not usually labeled "military bases" can be fruitfully studied for their similarly intense interactions of place, femininity, masculinity, and militarized purpose: for instance, the World War II encampment at Oak Ridge, Tennessee, where women and men, whites and African Americans, worked and lived in racialized and gendered intimate secrecy to create the essential elements of the first atomic bomb.[76]

Every military base depends for its operation on women occupying a range of social locations, performing quite different roles. To make visible that gendered base system, one must take seriously the lives and ideas of the military base laundress, the military wife, the woman in prostitution in a disco just outside the gates, a woman who is paid to sneak on base to have sex with a male soldier, the military enlisted woman and woman officer, and the woman who has become a public critic of the base. They are not natural allies. Many of these women may disagree with the others' assessments; they may not trust each other. But they all have interesting base stories to tell. Moreover, the separations between them are among the things that sustains that base.

To analyze any base as if it were simply the sum of its budget, its equipment, its land, its chain of command, its legal basis, and its mission is to seriously underestimate all the power that is used to manage it, all the ideas that are devised to underpin it, and all the policies that are implemented to keep it running smoothly. "Smoothly" is a measure of success in the eyes of the commanders and their uniformed and civilian superiors, as well as in the eyes of any local civilians—mayors, police officers, business operators, employees—who see that base as good for their own security and well-being. "Smoothly" does not automatically translate into gender equality or women's empowerment. "Smoothly" usually serves to perpetuate patriarchal international relations.

Hundreds of military bases run smoothly. Their operations are greased by daily humdrum. They do not make headlines. The unheadlined bases are as worthy of feminist-informed gendered analysis as the bases that become suddenly visible because of a scandal. International politics are composed of more than just crises and scandals. International politics can be humdrum, with power flowing unnoted and uncontested. Humdrum is political. Humdrum is gendered.

CHAPTER FIVE

Diplomatic and Undiplomatic Wives

Madeline Albright, Condoleezza Rice, Hillary Clinton. Three influential U.S. secretaries of state. Their appointments to one of the contemporary world's most powerful diplomatic posts would seem to put to rest the patriarchal notion that international diplomacy is naturally—and rightly—a men's game.

And in fact, these three women's rise to diplomatic influence has had gendered consequences. Some male heads of government began, especially during Hillary Clinton's term as secretary of state (2009–13), to appoint women as their ambassadors to Washington. In the middle of Clinton's term at the State Department, Mozambique's ambassador to the United States, Amelia Matos Sumbana, explained, "Hillary Clinton is so visible.... She makes it easier for presidents to pick a woman for Washington."[1]

By 2010, in fact, of the ambassadors posted to Washington, 25 were women. This was an all-time high. In context, however, it appears somewhat less transformative: these women were 25 out of a total of 182 ambassadors serving in Washington. Moreover, the 25 women were not evenly distributed geographically.

Figure 18. *(Left to right:)* Ambassador Deborah Mae Lovell of Antigua and Barbuda with Ambassador Jacinth Henry-Martin of St. Kitts and Nevis at the Women's Foreign Policy Group, Washington, D.C., March 2013. Photo: Women's Foreign Policy Institute.

Eleven were appointed by African governments; 4 by Caribbean governments.[2]

The first government of an Arab country to appoint a woman as its ambassador to Washington was Oman. In 2005, Hunaina Sultan Al-Mughairy, who had a masters in economics from New York University and years of experience advising her government on international trade and investment, became Oman's ambassador to the United States.

It is important, however, to keep one's gender goggles in place over the long haul. Was the "Hillary effect"—or even the Albright-Rice-Clinton effect—an historical blip or a politically sustainable transformation? Even though President Barack Obama appointed Susan Rice and Samantha Powers, two formidable foreign policy

Figure 19. Ambassador Hunaina Sultan Al-Mughairy of Oman, on the left, the first woman ambassador from an Arab state to Washington, and her spouse, in Washington, D.C., 2013. Photo: Alan Schlaifer, Elite Images, Bethesda, MD.

insiders, to senior posts soon after Hillary Clinton's resignation, his appointment of Senator John Kerry to succeed Clinton as secretary of state seemed to return the elite international club to its earlier masculinized norm. The Group of Eight's foreign ministers met in London in April 2013, soon after Kerry's appointment. Their agenda included crafting a common approach to such pressing international questions as those posed by the Syrian civil war and the nuclear buildups in Iran and North Korea. The gendered collective portrait of these eight foreign ministers produces an effect on the viewer strikingly similar to that of portraits of the

Figure 20. Group of Eight foreign ministers summit meeting in London, 2013, including, on the left, Catherine Ashton, chief of foreign affairs, European Union. Photo: Gov.uk, Open Government License v2.0.

Group of Eight's heads of government: one woman in the group photograph makes the viewer suddenly notice that all the other senior officials are men.

Nor was the masculinized profile of foreign ministers confined to the affluent countries in the Group of Eight. In 2013, at a meeting in Indonesia of the foreign ministers of the newly formed Forum for East Asia–Latin America Cooperation, only eight of the total thirty-eight foreign ministers were women.[3] A year before, the Chinese government had convened a meeting of the foreign ministers from a new regional interstate group that it had launched in 1996, the Shanghai Cooperation Organization. When these eight foreign ministers gathered, there was not even one woman present to raise the viewer's gender consciousness.

The ongoing political history of marriage plays a decisive part in opening or shutting doors to women in diplomacy. So long as women are seen—by politicians, career diplomats, media editors, and other women—first and foremost as wives, the sexist barriers will remain high and the normalization of masculinized diplomacy will remain entrenched. Of the five recently most prominent American women senior foreign-policy appointees—Albright, C. Rice, Clinton, S. Rice, and Powers—two were not married, while three, Clinton, Susan Rice, and Powers, were married during the time they served in the senior post. Their spouses had their own professional careers and were not expected to serve as appendages to their politically prominent partners.

For most women, marriage operates not only as a barrier that excludes women from foreign policy influence. It is also a tool for governments to wield. The conduct of international relations between governments has relied on women in their roles as wives. Marriage is domestic, but it is also national and international. The gendered politics of marriage inform the gendered politics of international relations.

IMPERIAL MARRIAGE DIPLOMACY

"It is a lamentable fact that almost every difficulty we have had with Indians throughout the Country may be traced to our interference with their Women or their Intrigues with the Women of the Forts in short 9 Murders out of 10 Committed on Whites by Indians have arisen through Women."[4] This statement marked a U-turn in the marriage policy of the North West Company, which, along with the Hudson's Bay Company, was Britain's principal vehicle for colonizing Canada. Until the early

1800s, the British and French fur-trading companies had encouraged marriages between their white male fur traders and local Indian women. Such marriages, officially encouraged by the North West Company's officers and unofficially sanctioned by managers of the Hudson's Bay Company, were considered strategically and politically important.

Trapper-Indian marriages became a means of cementing commercial alliances on a North American frontier that still eluded secure imperial control. Indian women were expected by British and French policy makers to lead the men of their tribes into cordial relations with the companies' men. At the same time, through marriage, European male trappers gained the chance to create a family despite the hardships of life on the northern frontier. Moreover, marriage to an Indian woman gave a white man a sense that he was superior, that he was saving a woman from the deplorable condition of savagery. This belief bolstered white men's sense of the moral rightness of their role in the lucrative international beaver-pelt trade.

Though they were treated merely as a strategic resource by the French and British trading companies and governments in the eighteenth and nineteenth centuries, the Indian women were making their own decisions. They were not passive in the face of imperial rivalries in Canada. They had their own reasons for promoting marriages with white men. Some Indian women valued the objects, such as metal kettles, that they gained through the fur trade and thus did what they could to ensure that the trade continued. Others preferred life inside the forts, where food was more plentiful than was often the case in their villages. A few native Canadian women accumulated considerable influence through liaising between their tribal communities and the trading companies.[5] Nevertheless, in 1806, when the

British marriage policy changed and officials began to encourage the trappers to seek European wives, the Indian women could do little to resist. Their control over the international politics of marriage was severely constrained. After the companies decided that their male trappers' relations with Indian women were fomenting as many hostilities as alliances, and that the costs of maintaining so many women and children outweighed these marriages' commercial advantages, the companies transformed their ideological rationale for the marriages.

Previously, the London-based officials of the fur-trading companies had judged that the dangers and hardships of Canadian fort life made the forts no place to bring a white woman, certainly not a "lady"; white women would be a costly burden and a nuisance for the company. In 1686, the Hudson's Bay Company managers adopted a resolution forbidding their men in Canada from importing white wives. A few European women managed to join their trader husbands, but only by deception. Among the most renowned was Isabel Gunn, who arrived at a fort in 1806 from the Orkney Islands, where many of the Hudson's Bay Company's men came from. She had skirted the company's ban on white women by disguising herself as a man.[6] By the middle of the nineteenth century, however, white men in the companies were praising the contributions that white women, "the delicate flowers of civilization," were making to fort life. Their graces were compared to the alleged "deficiencies" of Indian wives. In reality, white women lacked the skills that Indian women possessed to assist their fur-trading husbands. They followed their husbands to Canada out of what they imagined to be wifely loyalty and duty, but, once there, many endured boredom and isolation.[7]

In colony after colony, governments tried to fashion marriage strategies to suit their imperial political ends. There were many variables to consider—and reconsider: white men's presumed sexual needs, white women's presumed frailty, the vulnerability or security of the colonial administration, the availability and assets of local women, the threats posed by local men, and the desirability of establishing a full-fledged white community (not just forts and plantations) in the colony.

Governments never have been as effective in controlling the foreign policies of marriage as they would have liked. But they have not given up. Today many governments are being challenged by those women who for generations have been thought to be among the most compliant: diplomatic wives.

DOMESTICATING DIPLOMACY

During the 1970s and 1980s—the decades of the second wave of national and transnational women's movements—women married to Swedish, Canadian, British, and American male diplomats created new organizations and revitalized existing organizations. They demanded recognition for the contributions they made to their countries' foreign policy operations in their work as wives of male diplomats. Some of these women wanted more than recognition: they wanted jobs, pensions, alimony, even (most radically) salaries. This was at a time when women married to male soldiers also were rethinking their own roles and organizing to make demands on their governments. Diplomatic wives' organizing efforts revealed how reliant their governments were on their control of marriage in order to conduct international relations.[8]

Any government seeking to extend its influence in the world must send abroad at least some of its own citizens to represent its interests. Diplomatic influence requires foreign-service officers on-site. Governments' marriage policies have changed, but the intent of those policies remains the same: to achieve the governments' political and economic goals. A woman is thought either to enhance a male diplomat's efforts to reach his government's goals or to threaten that diplomat's ability to serve his government efficiently and effectively. Governments are not for or against marriage. They are for the sort of marriage that serves their own political ends.

Today the diplomatic wife is a fixture of international politics. It wasn't always so. The diplomatic wife was created. Beryl Smedley was the wife of a senior British diplomat. She had given up a promising government career of her own in New Zealand to marry a then-young British foreign service officer. As he rose in the ranks, so did she. In these later years, she was supposed to take on the added diplomatic responsibilities of being the wife of a British ambassador. Beryl Smedley saw her work as a diplomatic wife as a profession in itself.[9] When she and her husband retired, she decided to research the history of British diplomatic wives in order to show readers how that (unacknowledged, unpaid) profession had developed. Smedley found that the first British woman to accompany her husband as an ambassador's wife—not simply as the wife of a colonial official—was Lady Mary Wortley Montagu, who went with her husband to Constantinople in 1716. Today Montague is more famous for her lively letters and her critiques of women's second-class status than for her diplomatic significance. But in accompanying her diplomat husband on assignment to the capital of the Ottoman Empire, Lady Mary Wortley Montagu marked a turning point in the way diplomacy was conducted between governments.[10]

Her breakthrough initially went unnoticed because the men in governments had not yet realized the positive uses to which they could put their ambassadors' wives. For the next century and a half, women married to senior British diplomats only occasionally joined their husbands in foreign embassies. They, like their husbands, came from the nobility and supplied their own staff and paid their own way.[11] While many of these women were well educated and skilled reporters, little was expected of them by their governments. And it was still mainly senior male diplomats whose wives accompanied them. Men of junior rank were expected either to remain single or to leave their wives at home.[12]

By the end of the nineteenth century, however, diplomacy and hostessing had become tightly intertwined. It became harder for women married to diplomats to pursue their own interests. They were not on the official payroll, but they were on their government's minds. For many of these women, hostessing was what they had been raised to do. After 1900, the British Foreign Office began to open its ranks to men outside the nobility, although serving abroad still required one to have an independent income. This encouraged the sons of industrialists who joined the Foreign Office to look upon daughters of the aristocracy as appropriate wives.

Not all of these successors to Lady Mary Wortley Montagu were eager to serve as hostesses for their governments. "I don't like diplomacy, though I like Persia," wrote a disgruntled Vita Sackville-West in 1926. She had gone out to Teheran to join her diplomat husband, Harold Nicolson. Despite her forceful resistance to playing the dutiful wife in private or in public, by the 1920s Vita had encountered role expectations she could not avoid: "She paid calls, attended and gave luncheons and dinners[;] ... she even gave away hockey prizes."[13] Yet her heart was not in it. She was writing intense letters from Persia to her new friend, Virginia Woolf, and within a few months was heading back to England, leaving Harold to cope with diplomatic rituals on his own.

Any woman considering marriage to a man who is set upon a career in the diplomatic corps should think hard about "the itinerant life and the poor pay." This was the advice of Beryl Smedley, one of Britain's most seasoned diplomatic wives. After having served with her husband—like military wives, foreign-service wives refer to themselves as "serving" abroad—for thirty years in posts as varied as Sri Lanka, Laos, and Rhodesia, she had no regrets, but she also was aware that she was of a particular historical generation: "Most of us who married in the forties and fifties felt that we were partners in diplomacy; some of us had careers, but we had no hesitation in giving them up to work alongside our husbands."[14] Smedley learned to take satisfaction in contributing to her husband's diplomatic mission by doing volunteer work wherever they were posted, representing her adopted country by her very presence abroad, and by being her husband's "eyes and ears" at public functions. Some diplomatic wives also act as a safe sounding-board, one of the few people on whom their diplomatic husbands can try out controversial ideas. These remain key functions performed by today's diplomatic wives, even if the politics of marriage in their countries has changed.

Diplomacy runs smoothly when there is trust and confidence between officials representing governments whose interests are often conflicting. That trust and confidence has to be created in a congenial environment; it does not sprout naturally. Most men find that congenial environment outside their offices. The home—the ambassador's official residence, or the homes of lower-ranking diplomats—is seen as the place where this trust between men can best be cultivated. The home is the domain of the wife. The domestic duties of foreign-service wives include creating an atmosphere where men from different states can get to know one another "man to man."

The more that male diplomats rely on informal relationships to accomplish their political tasks, the more formal are the expectations that their wives will come to the government's aid. One male diplomat explained: "Quite frankly, it is only by meeting people socially that you get the sort of relationship that you are seeking. You'll never establish it just going to visit people in their offices.... There is a great deal of diplomatic life which is irksome.... I do find the social side of the thing tedious and so does my wife: not, I hasten to say, the concept of entertaining in itself, which is a valuable—indeed essential—part of the business.... Actually off-the-record conversations are the stuff of diplomacy.[15]

There are implications of this belief for those women pursuing their own diplomatic careers: the more that interstate politics depends on a manly sort of trust-building that, in turn, relies on feminized domestic settings, the more difficult it becomes for women as diplomats to cultivate the same sort of interstate trust. Most women diplomats do not have wives. Even if a few now do have women partners, those partners may resist becoming conventional "wives."

To be considered worthy members of the "embassy team," male diplomats have depended on their wives; for without a wife's active cooperation, a male diplomat cannot perform the essential social tasks well. The higher the male foreign-service officer climbs up the career ladder, the more time he will have to devote to these social duties, and thus the more he will rely on the participation of a wife. During the Thatcher years of the

1980s, the wife of the British ambassador to India, where Britain has one of its largest embassies, described a typical day in her life:

> On Monday morning we already had Mr. and Mrs. Norman Tebbit staying with us [Norman Tebbit was then a senior cabinet minister in the Conservative government], so the day began with a briefing meeting here for the minister with members of the high commission. Quite often when we have briefing meetings here in the house we invite the wives of our own members of staff to come and meet the wife of the visitor who is being briefed. It is very valuable for everybody and great fun for the girls [that is, the wives] to be included. In the evening we had the Director of the Washington National Gallery and his wife.... He had come to look at things to borrow, and was a great friend of friends. Then we went out to an official dinner being given for Mr. Tebbit.... So on that day there was the morning meeting, people to lunch, people to drinks, dinner out. Tuesday morning at 11 o'clock I went to call on the wife of a colleague to talk about the Delhi Flower Show, which is run by the YWCA to make money for their village projects. The Delhi Flower Show is quite old and traditionally diplomats, particularly British diplomats, have been involved in running it.[16]

Though they are all feminized, the exact expectations that foreign-service wives must try to meet vary from post to post. The expectations that the wife of a British ambassador posted to the capital of a country once part of the British empire must try to meet might be quite different from those that a woman married to the Cambodian ambassador who is posted to Indonesia must meet. Some women say that they prefer assignments to countries where their governments are not the leaders of the diplomatic community or where their governments' interests are not vital. This sort of posting gives even women married to ambassadors more leeway; they are less visible, and what others expect of them is less rigid. Such a posting may not suit their husbands, however. These men—and their female foreign-service counterparts—joined their countries' foreign services to pursue careers, and thus they need increasingly prestigious postings as they climb the foreign service ladder. Some women married to career diplomats share their husbands' ambitions and take pride in acquiring the skills required to run the American ambassador's home in Tokyo or the Brazilian ambassador's home in Washington.

The British ambassador's wife described her house in Washington as "my tool of the trade." It is used for more than just entertaining. In the 1980s, Britain's Washington embassy, with a staff of three hundred, was one of (and today remains) its largest, reflecting the closeness that British senior politicians have sought to sustain with the United States since 1945. The 1980s was the era of the Cold War rivalries, Britain's war in the Falklands, American nuclear-headed missiles based in Britain, and Greenham women peace activists camped outside one the U.S. military's bases to protest those missiles. But less noticed than international crises are the diplomatic politics of trade. Fostering commercial trade is among the duties of any ambassador and thus of his wife. One of the priorities of the British embassy in Washington is to sell British goods, especially British military equipment, to American buyers. So the ambassador's wife, supervising a domestic staff of twenty, used her home to promote sales. Her husband, the ambassador, explained to a BBC reporter: "Our houses are a part of that and one doesn't entertain simply to have a good scoff and a booze-up. One entertains because it does in fact facilitate the transaction of business. People are in a better temper when they know each other and have had a meal together."[17]

The ambassador's wife has learned her trade well if she can plan the progress from drinks to formal dinner to coffee so that a maximum amount of business can be conducted "with a minimum of artificiality."[18] Diplomats' wives have become part of an international strategy to reduce trade imbalances. By playing that part well, diplomatic wives also grease the wheels of the international arms trade.

"DON'T AGONIZE, ORGANIZE!"

Even a successful diplomatic wife may have a gnawing sense that her work is not valued. It is expected by governments, but it is not truly respected. In Beryl Smedley's small study, stuffed with books on diplomatic history and notes from her research at the British Museum, there was one file she described as summing up this gap between expectation and respect: her obituary file. She opened it with annoyance. When men who have been diplomats die, they are accorded long obituaries describing their careers, their various postings abroad, their achievements. When their wives die, they receive nothing more than a cursory death notice. That does not add up to the full partnership that diplomatic wives devoted themselves to and that governments have come to depend on in the twentieth century for the sake of smooth international relations.[19]

In the mid-1980s there were political stirrings among diplomatic wives in several countries. They realized that more and more women in their own countries—countries they supposedly were expected to represent abroad—were insisting that they be fairly paid, that they not be treated as mere dependents of or accessories to their husbands, that they be able to pursue their own careers, that they not be judged solely in terms of their domestic skills. The diplomatic wives became aware that, as diplomatic wives, institutional dependents, they were leading lives that were less and less like those of most of their countries' women. They were becoming societal relics.

On the other hand, they knew that their governments still relied on the traditional wifely roles they played, and that any radical upsetting of those roles would be met with masculinized alarm and perhaps masculinized scorn. These were women who also knew from intimate encounters how their own governments' foreign policy machinery worked. They had lived it. Thus their first strategic moves were diplomatic.

Britain's Diplomatic Service Wives Association was housed in a large room in the Foreign Office in London, a stone's throw away from Westminster. Two secretaries paid by the Foreign Office worked away at desks, art posters decorated the walls, a teakettle was steaming, and tables were cluttered with work in progress. This was 1987. Gay Murphy, a diplomatic wife finishing her term as chair of the DSWA, was in the office for one of her two days a week of unpaid organizational work. As the DSWA had adopted a more activist role, the job of chair had become increasingly demanding.[20]

"We're always about fifteen years behind," Murphy observed. She was explaining why it was not until the early 1980s that women married to men in the British diplomatic corps began to speak out on some of the subjects that had fueled Britain's women's movement in the 1970s. The reasons for this time lag included the fact that diplomatic wives are constantly moving and cut off from British society for years at a time. Although many people imagined the fourteen thousand members of foreign-service families to be from the upper classes, the social mix had been changing since the 1940s, and the isolation and bureaucratic socialization was more of an obstacle to conscious-ness-raising than class background. Furthermore, like the women married to military officers, women married to diplo-mats have to worry about how their actions will look to their husbands' superiors. If a diplomatic wife starts to be seen inside the Foreign Ministry or State Department as "not a team player," as "disloyal," will her husband miss the chance for a promotion that would make not only his life but perhaps her own more financially secure and more respected?[21]

In the early 1970s the wife of a British foreign-service officer had committed suicide. Her friends believed that she did it out of loneliness. After spending years with her husband on assign-ments overseas, when she finally came "home" she was unpre-pared for the loneliness and lack of support. Her suicide shocked the Treasury's medical officer, the official in charge of providing medical care for civil servants and foreign service personnel. He was one of the first within the government to take seriously the problems facing foreign service wives. His solution was to set up networks of women volunteers in the different parts of the coun-try, who could help returning foreign service wives readjust to life in Britain. But one diplomatic wife who had trained as a psy-chologist argued that this was only a bandage; there were deeper problems that the government had to confront. The Foreign Office agreed to employ a civilian psychologist to conduct a more thorough study. Though his report uncovered profound problems and frustrations, little action was taken to rethink the role of the diplomatic wife and thus the way the Foreign Office did its overseas business. For the rest of the decade, the DSWA itself remained chiefly concerned with social activities for its women members; its members did not yet see themselves as political lobbyists.

Nonetheless, by the early 1980s more diplomatic wives had absorbed the lessons of the wider women's movement. They were less willing to rely solely on private solutions to problems posed by the way the government chose to carry on its international relations. They were less willing to sacrifice their own career aspirations for the sake of their husbands' careers. Her experience of being posted with her husband to Washington in the early 1980s convinced Gay Murphy that a diplomatic wives association could move beyond writing self-help manuals to changing the conditions that she and her colleagues coped with. There she had a firsthand look at what American foreign-service wives were doing to push their State Department to officially acknowledge the contributions wives made to state business. They were pressing for salaries or, short of that, for enhanced family services. Under pressure from internal advocates, the Department of State had created a Family Liaison Office and a mental health program within its own departmental medical services.

The State Department's creation—and funding—of the Family Liaison Office was its tacit acknowledgment that conducting family affairs globally, often in difficult, even dangerous, environments, was not the same as running a middle-class suburban home in Maryland. At the time the office was established, however, some of the State Department's male officials ridiculed the idea of an office to address the needs that had been uncovered by diplomatic wives: "Why do we need to hold the hands of whining wives?"[22]

Today the U.S. State Department employs twenty-two psychiatrists to provide both counseling and medication prescriptions to the U.S. Foreign Service employees and their family members deployed around the globe, who together number thirty-seven thousand. Each psychiatrist is assigned to a major American embassy—for instance, in Moscow, Rome, Lima, Beijing, Mexico City—and then travels to all the American consulates and smaller embassies in that region to counsel employees and family members who are coping with the stresses and constraints of diplomatic life. Those mental health services, however, are rarely sought out equally by all the thirty-seven thousand Americans.[23] Careerists in the diplomatic corps, as in militaries, are encouraged, after all, to present themselves publicly as fully capable of handling even extreme stress on their own, as therefore not needing mental health assistance. That assistance, presumably, is for the more fragile, feminized spouses and their children. If deemed by the psychiatrist to have reached the point that they can no longer cope with the intense stresses of embassy life, spouses or children can be sent home to the United States.

As they tried to change their governments' perceptions of them, activist diplomatic wives had to break some of their own habits or, rather, some practices they had learned during their years in this gendered foreign policy role. For instance, they began to make a conscious effort not to relate to each other according to their husbands' ranks, a common practice among diplomatic wives when posted overseas. When an association volunteer said a phone call had come in from "one of the senior women," she quickly caught herself: "I'm really trying to break that habit. I meant one of the women married to a senior man."[24]

During the 1980s, British diplomatic wives who were activists began to lobby in earnest. They pressured the Treasury, the Foreign Office, and the committees of the House of Commons to stop the standard practice of superiors including a wife's performance in the periodic evaluation of her husband's performance. A wife's hostessing and volunteer work should not, they argued, be assessed in deciding whether her husband would be promoted. The Annual Confidential Report may mention a wife's health and any special language skills she has, but, thanks to the DSWA's successful political campaigning, today the report no longer may include comments on her entertaining or charity work. Of course, this political victory has had the effect of pushing further out of sight those contributions that an unpaid woman makes to her husband's professional performance.[25] However, it left diplomatic spouses somewhat freer to pursue their own jobs at home and abroad if they wished to do so. Furthermore, a diplomatic wife who wanted to take a paid job overseas was required to ask permission from the head of post, and permission "was by no means regularly given."[26] That practice too has been ended as a result of DSWA women's lobbying.

If more and more women today continue to insist upon having paid jobs of their own, who will do the entertaining? Who will create the environment in which diplomats can build manly trust, in which British arms and other goods can be sold to international customers? On a deeper level, recognizing diplomatic wives as more than mere appendages, as autonomous people with their own skills, financial aspirations, and personal identities, makes it harder to sustain the fiction that embassies are "families" or "teams," in which all the members (paid and unpaid) pitch in for the sake of achieving their government's global objectives.

To transform the roles, perceptions, and rights of diplomatic wives, women activists have discovered, they have had to transform their own marriages. As one diplomatic wife reminded listeners: "You are living with part of the bureaucracy."[27] Realigning relationships inside a marriage is political work in the eyes of feminist activists. Some marriages cannot withstand the contradictory pressures of the diplomatic life. Divorce is common in the foreign service, as it is in civilian life today. But the financial risks to the divorced (or widowed) wife of a foreign service careerist husband are especially acute, because being a diplomatic wife has routinely required that a woman-as-wife sacrifice her own paid work life and the financial cushion that that paid work life can create.

In 1986, diplomatic wives associations from the twelve countries then belonging to the European Economic Community met for the first time. They created an international political campaign to transform the gendered politics of foreign policy making. The idea was introduced by the British government, which at the time held the presidency of the EEC (now the European Union) and was intended by its male conveners to be a relatively harmless public event that would reflect well on the British government. This is a common incentive and expectation held by government officials when they call meetings to address women's issues. But once the European diplomatic wives got together, they went "off script" and launched into serious discussions; they made comparisons and formulated strategies to bring about change. The diplomatic wives associations that had been in existence longer, such as Britain's and Sweden's, were represented by assertive women who had come to feel autonomous in their own right. Newer diplomatic wives associations still were at the stage of having to earn their legitimacy and so were represented at the meeting by "senior women"; those women were more politically cautious.

There were three hot topics at the 1986 international diplomatic spouses meeting: the lack of pensions, the unfair divorce rules, and the tainted public image of foreign services. Women at the gathering were especially impressed by the success of the

Swedish diplomatic wives association in winning the right of Swedish diplomatic wives to receive their own pensions. Divorce raised multiple issues because laws governing alimony settlements reflected so clearly just how much—or how little—a government valued the unpaid work done for years by a diplomatic wife. The women whose husbands divorced them after they had sacrificed their own earning power and had invested years of unpaid service in promoting their husband's careers were left impoverished in their old age. They were angry not at the "other woman" but at their own patriarchal governments. When the women from the twelve countries compared their respective conditions, they discovered that the Swedish and the Danish wives associations had been most successful in lobbying their governments to ensure alimony fairness. In Sweden and Denmark a man in the foreign service who divorced his wife was required to divide a portion of his pension among his former and current wives according to the number of years each woman had served as a partner in diplomatic postings.[28]

Because they saw themselves as doing daily battle with their own governments' bureaucracies in order to gain mundane services, financial security, and respect, diplomatic wives from the European countries voiced concern and even resentment at the public's seeming lack of respect for their foreign services. On the one hand, activist diplomatic wives had developed a new appreciation of how inadequate their foreign services' responses were to women's real needs. Even if they spoke in discreet tones, they were critics, savvy critics. On the other hand, nevertheless, their husbands' careers still depended on their wifely skills and on the marital partnership. This realization, in turn, drew them into a quasi-familial relationship with their government's foreign service. Consequently, European women married to

foreign-service officers defended the foreign service as an institution when it was being criticized—or when diplomats' influence was overshadowed by that of the military—even if they felt
exploited by it.

Two decades later, the European Union's diplomatic wives
looked back on these formative years as "turbulent." They tal-
lied up the advances made. Especially, they noted, government
officials today hesitated, at least in public, before they slipped
into the old assumption that a woman married to a foreign service officer would simply trail along with her husband and
uncomplainingly contribute her time and skills to embassy
affairs. Nowadays, there was an understanding that many
women wanted their own paid careers; thus any unpaid contributions that a spouse made (and the spouse still was assumed to
be female) was publicly referred to as "voluntary." But under-
neath the pseudofeminist public facade of official acceptance of
gender changes that had gone on in their societies, the EU
observers noted, the marital realities of what it means for a
woman to be married to a European male diplomat, a man who
must serve for years abroad, had not dramatically changed over
twenty years. The myth of feminized "voluntary" work was
alive and well, according to one diplomatic wife: "There is a
certain disingenuousness to this position—as long as it can be
said that it is the spouse's choice to contribute, however great
that contribution might be, it can then be freed of any contrac-
tual taint and the issue of pay can be ducked."[29]

WAGES FOR DIPLOMATIC HOUSEWORK

For thirty years women active in the Associates of the American
Foreign Service Worldwide have lobbied the State Department

and the congressional Foreign Affairs Committee to improve the conditions under which wives, husbands, and the children of U.S. Foreign Service officers live in Washington and abroad. While its members have learned the lessons of political discretion integral to diplomacy, the AAFSW's activist women have useful resources with which to press their case. Not least of these are their own social skills. Many American foreign-service wives feel at home in Washington, a city with a long-established and large African American community but in which the power elite remains overwhelmingly white. They have become experienced in taking the political pulse of the capital as one political party replaces another in the White House and Congress. Many American foreign service wives have class backgrounds similar to those of many of the still largely male (83 percent) members of Congress whom they lobby. "They entertain these guys in their homes," one feminist observed as she described their political advantage. She was comparing foreign service wives' resources with those of American military wives, who have also become more vocal in demanding that the government stop taking for granted the unpaid labor of women, but who do not possess this social advantage. This military wives advocate explained that while leaders of the military wives groups are usually wives of senior officers, they nonetheless were less likely to be familiar with the white upper-class milieu in Washington than are most foreign service wives.[30]

Foreign service wives have said that they learned most about lobbying through watching the CIA wives in action. Until the 1970s the Central Intelligence Agency prohibited its officers' wives from meeting together in groups of more than three. Despite the prohibition, CIA wives started to share concerns and to speak out about the special hardship imposed on women married to secret intelligence officers serving overseas. Both they and their children suffered: "Who's the spy?" was a favorite game among diplomatic children. CIA wives called meetings, created a formal (carefully guarded) mailing list and pushed for an agency office mandated to deal specifically with the problems encountered by CIA families. Faced with women no longer willing to remain dutifully silent, CIA male administrators decided to be accommodating rather than risk attracting public attention.

CIA wives pressed the congressional Intelligence Committee—behind closed doors, keeping their demands inside "the intelligence community"—to adopt benefit packages that addressed their special needs. Like foreign service wives, these women generally had university educations and felt comfortable in Washington policy-making circles. When abroad, they tended to live in the same diplomatic communities as their State Department colleagues, giving them a chance to share information and strategies. In addition, however, CIA wives could go to congressional Intelligence Committee meetings and hold out the threat, if only implicitly, "Think of the stories we could tell." The very notion of an intimate, close-knit "intelligence community" may create a stifling environment for women married to CIA agents. Yet it also provided them with a lever with which to pry open the government's coffers.[31]

The first major change to send ripples through the gendered U.S. foreign-policy system came in 1971. Women pursuing careers in the State Department took a cue from the wider American women's movement and called for an end to the government's policy of compelling a woman in the foreign service to resign if she got married. Through their newly created Women's Action Organization, these women foreign-service officers successfully pressed the State Department to put an end to the foreign-service marriage rule, a rule that the British foreign service also had adopted. This rule and the collective demand that it be withdrawn threw into stark relief diplomacy's dependence on certain sorts of marriages.

The question then being posed by many American women outside the corridors of power finally took on significance for women within government organizations: why should marriage *advance* a man's capacity to gain money, skills, and influence, but *hinder* a woman's chance to acquire the same? Increasing numbers of women who were marrying male foreign-service careerists in the 1970s had university degrees and career aspirations of their own. Yet the government—and most of their husbands—expected them to put those aside or use them only to advance their husbands' careers and the international political interests of the U.S. government. More and more diplomatic wives were refusing to accept this assumption as central to being a loyal wife and a patriotic citizen, at the same time that more single women pursuing professional careers inside the foreign service demanded that they be allowed to continue those careers if they became wives.

In 1972, the State Department, having been forced to end its marriage ban for women foreign-service careerists, was compelled to drop the other shoe. It declared that henceforth foreign service spouses were "private persons." In any patriarchal organization or society, this is a radical assertion. According to the directive, spouses—most of them wives—were no longer to be treated by the government as if they were unpaid employees. Specifically, American diplomatic wives would cease to be evaluated in the efficiency reports that mean life or death to a foreign-service official's career. The State Department's twofer system hereafter was allegedly dead: in principle, the United States government would have to conduct its foreign policy without getting a team of two for the price of one. The State Department had been compelled to admit that women had their own lives to live.[32]

The two State Department declarations of the 1970s—declaring diplomatic wives autonomous persons and declaring married women eligible to pursue foreign service careers—by themselves did not transform political practice. Such formal declarations may simply reveal the distance between official policy and daily political patriarchal reality. American women married to foreign-service men still had to travel to the countries where their husbands were posted if they wanted to sustain their marriages. They still felt they had to help their husbands perform the public and social duties that the host country, visiting American dignitaries, and businesspeople expected of them. They were still relied on to keep the children happy and healthy despite the frequent moves and unfamiliar surroundings. The second State Department declaration, itself a victory for diplomatic wives, did not change any of that.

Thus in 1984 some foreign-service wives lobbied Congress for an amendment to the pending Foreign Service Act. The amendment proposed that a foreign-service wife be paid for services rendered to her embassy. If she were no longer an unpaid handmaiden of diplomacy but a cog in the foreign-policy machine, then she should be paid for her work. The women asked Congress to pass an amendment ensuring that a spouse who agrees to carry out representational responsibilities would be paid a salary equivalent to 40 percent of the foreign service employee's—usually, the husband's—salary. The men in Congress rejected the proposed amendment.[33]

Today activists of the U.S. diplomatic spouses association—the renamed Associates of the American Foreign Service World-wide—continue to offer spouses of diplomats candid financial advice: for instance, you never know when divorce or death will end your marriage; create your own financial autonomy. Three decades after Gay Murphy, the British diplomatic wife and activist who took inspiration from her American counterparts, both British and American wives of diplomats still struggle to find ways to cope with the international political economy of diplomatic marriage. An AAFSW activist, writing under the *nom de blog* "Cyberspouse," knew that in 2012 there were diplomatic husbands (gay and straight—the first diplomatic visas for same-sex partners of U.S. Foreign Service officers had been issued in 2009) among her association's spouses, but she addressed her financial advice to wives; the reality, she explained, was that most American diplomatic spouses still were in the position of wives. In fact, virtually all the officers of the AAFSW were women. Cyberspouse went on to explain that diplomatic wives had financial problems distinct from those of their diplomatic husbands: "Many Foreign Service spouses are disappointed with their career prospects. Few of us were raised and educated to throw dinner parties for a living[,] ... and [most spouses share] the fear of total financial dependence in an uncertain world."[34]

Cyberspouse also acknowledged the anxieties that still stem from being under the control of one's husband's employer: "Departing for your first Foreign Service post as an Eligible Family Member can feel a bit like jumping off a cliff. Suddenly, you are completely subject to the whims of the Department of State, and considered to be decidedly secondary to your spouse. This can be difficult when you are used to being treated as an independent adult!"

With these persistent gendered realities in mind, Cyber-spouse offered down-to-earth advice to diplomatic wives:

- Make sure that you get that Joint Property Statement signed and notarized before you leave for the post—this gives you the rights to everything that is stored at government expense.

- Read the pamphlet *The Unthinkable Can Happen: Divorce in the Foreign Service.*

- *Foreign Service spouse* is just a small piece of who you are. It is not the entire package.... You have the Internet, your means of direct contact with the real world outside the Foreign Service bubble. Use it to create an independent financial identity for yourself!

- No Foreign Service spouse should board the plane to post without making sure she has direct access to all major savings and checking accounts.... The account to which the employee's pay is deposited should be joint, because, frankly, both the employee and the spouse are going to be earning money while overseas—one at the office, and the other everywhere else at post.

- The Cyberspouse is the financial manager in her family, and sends a status report automatically generated by Microsoft Money by email to her husband at the end of every month.... Should the Cyberspouse suffer an untimely death (or run off with her personal trainer) he would be able to access all the family accounts, investments, and insurance policies.

- ... Every spouse should also keep some money in an easily accessible checking account in her own name[,] ... money you want to get your hands on quickly in case your husband runs off with another women! Some things never change ...

- Very few Foreign Service spouses who are not officers themselves [i.e., in a dual-career State Department marriage] manage to maintain the same career momentum as their employed partners. You should, however, make the most of what you have accomplished professionally, by keeping a record of all your paid and volunteer activities and any recognition you may have received for them. Start a file.[35]

What Cyberspouse's practical guide reveals is that, while diplomatic wives have had some success in pushing their governments to realize that women in the twenty-first century have identities and aspirations that differ from those of women in the 1960s, governments' foreign policy machineries still run on the expectation that women married to their male diplomats will subordinate their own needs to those of their governments and do whatever strategizing they do to provide some economic security for themselves privately. That is, the people running foreign affairs still think they need a certain sort of patriarchal marriage to make the machinery run.

GENDER REVOLUTION IN FOGGY BOTTOM

The foreign policy politics of marriage have channeled women both as foreign service careerists and as diplomatic wives. Too often these two groups of women are talked about as if they lived on different planets—just as women as soldiers, women as wives of male soldiers, and women living as civilians around a military base are discussed as if all three groups of women were not manipulated by the same gendered institutional culture.

The story of how the ban on married women in the U.S. Foreign Service was lifted remains little known. The revolution began with lunch. During the summer of 1970, a small group of high-ranking women in the State Department (affectionately known as "Foggy Bottom," a formerly swampy section of Washington), together with their counterparts in State's "sister" agencies—the U.S. Information Agency and the U.S. Agency for International Development—began having informal lunches. Their agenda: to discuss women's issues that shaped their professional lives in the government's three foreign services. They were angered by the way reports allegedly designed to reassess the operations of the State Department completely ignored women. One of the women, Jean Joyce, remembers attending a task-force meeting chaired by a male ambassador. Not long before that, Joyce had been energized by hearing Gloria Steinem speak. She thus went to the meeting armed with figures "showing the frightful state of women's promotions." She sat in the front row.

> I got up and said, "Mr. Ambassador, has your committee looked into the question of the inequity in rate of promotion of men and women in the Foreign Service?" And he said something hastily: "Of course, we have women on the committee. We don't happen to have one here today but I think she couldn't come" ... And then he said to me in the kind of unctuous tone that I've heard often at diplomatic parties, when the wife of one ambassador by rank has to sit next to another ambassador and he makes some pleasantry and then turns to the man on the other side or across from him and starts the *real* conversation ... "I'm sure that men and women will always get on together very well, as they always have," with a great big smile, with that kind of unctuous false flattery ... as if to say, "Women, you know, need only to be charmed."
>
> I remained standing.... I stood there right in front of him and I said, "Mr. Ambassador, you have not answered my question ..." and I read the list out for all of them to hear and of course all the officials from the Office of Equal Employment and various other officials were there and it was devastating.[36]

After that, the numbers of women attending the informal lunches grew. "Our lunches began to be twenty-five, thirty-five people. And the level of indignation, of a sense of grievance, of bitterness, of anger, was immediately apparent. The thing caught fire just like that. As soon as there was a match."[37] They told each other stories of women who put off getting married until they were fifty so that they could pursue their careers and keep their retirement benefits. They told of secretaries who were "treated as drones." They described departmental "suit-ability" rating charts used to determine overseas assignments, which ranked a married man as "most stable" and an unmarried woman as "least stable." They decided to organize the Women's Action Organization in order to systematically attack policies that marginalized and exploited women in the foreign policy establishment. Fighting battles as individuals on a case-by-case basis, as they had done in the past, was neither effective nor efficient.[38]

WAO activists knew the ways of Washington. They picked their time wisely. In 1970, State Department officials were demoralized, after the Kennedy and Johnson years had brought a decline in State Department influence. Foreign-policy deci-sions were more likely to be made inside the National Security Council than in the State Department. Presidents were increas-ingly skeptical of the foreign service's ability to give them the advice and information they wanted. Special task forces were being commissioned to reassess all aspects of the State Depart-ment's operations. It was this process of examination that the women of WAO believed might permit them to raise their issues at the highest levels of the State Department. They pointedly made the feminist link between sexist attitudes and practices affecting diplomatic wives and State Department clerical work-ers, and those attitudes and practices that were marginalizing women as foreign policy careerists.

The WAO activists insisted upon a meeting with the State Department's senior management officials to press for changes in four areas:

- The State Department's policy that compelled foreign-service women and secretaries to resign when they got married.
- The policy barring a professional woman with children from an overseas assignment.
- The policy that prohibited even unmarried women professionals from being posted to any Muslim countries or to any of the Soviet-dominated eastern European countries, though women in secretarial jobs could be sent to those countries.
- The policy of treating foreign-service wives as if they were adjuncts to their husbands.[39]

The women activists of the WAO won concessions on all four points. The U.S. State Department lifted its ban on married women in 1972.

When, in 1987, sixteen years after the lifting of the ban, Phyllis Oakley was appointed deputy assistant secretary of state (the department's liaison with the Washington press corps), two questions, she recalled, were asked repeatedly by reporters: "How old was I?" and "Was I married?" Questions she thought would never have been asked of a man in her senior foreign policy position.[40] But marriage was more relevant than most reporters might have supposed. Oakley had entered the foreign service in 1957 and was forced to resign from the service after she married another foreign service officer. She suddenly became a diplomatic wife. Oakley soon afterward accompanied her husband to Sudan and then from post to post around the world. She refers to these as her "wilderness years."[41] But after the State Department was pressured into lifting its marriage ban for women foreign service careerists, Phyllis Oakley quickly reentered the foreign service. Now she was both a diplomat *and* a diplomatic wife. She and her husband became what the Family Liaison Office called a "tandem couple." In 1975, when her husband was appointed ambassador to Zaire (now the Democratic Republic of Congo), an African country of strategic importance to the United States, Oakley became the first American ambassador's wife to work as a paid professional foreign-service officer in an embassy where her husband was ambassador.[42]

Nonetheless, the Foggy Bottom revolution remained incomplete. Masculinized practices and attitudes die hard. In the late 1980s just 21.2 percent of U.S. Foreign Service officers were women; a mere 5 percent of the service's senior officers were women.[43] Moreover, race played its part: at the end of the Cold War, white men and women together constituted 89 percent of all U.S. Foreign Service employees.[44]

In April 1989, President George Bush's new secretary of state, James Baker, announced that he would comply with federal court rulings that found the State Department guilty of sexist discrimination. In deciding *Baker v. Palmer,* the court ordered the Department to revise its foreign service entrance examinations so that the questions were less biased in favor of male applicants and also to invite any women foreign-service officers to apply for appointments to better posts if the women believed their current assignments were at a level below their formal capabilities. This court ruling was the outcome of a thirteen-year-long case brought by Alison Palmer, a foreign service officer. She filed her class action lawsuit after three male U.S. ambassadors to three different African countries refused to accept her in their embassies, despite her advanced degree in African studies, because, the men said, they did not want a woman. Palmer eventually was assigned to serve as social secretary to the wife of the U.S. ambassador to Ethiopia, one of the men who had refused to have Palmer on his team. Not until 2010 was the State Department found in satisfactory compliance with the court's orders of over two decades earlier. Today, the suit still is referred to as "the Palmer case."[45]

CONCLUSION

By 2004, 18 percent of all U.S. ambassadors—appointed by the president with the Senate's approval—were women. That was 20 women and 137 men. The proportion was just a bit higher than that of women in the U.S. Congress. Many of those women ambassadors were single—divorced, widowed, or never married. But some were married. Among those who were married, some were married to men who also were diplomats.[46]

Marriage—ideas about it, practices of it, and rules to control it—is constructed out of presumptions about femininity and masculinity, presumptions that can be unstable and that can, on occasion, be challenged. That is why being a husband and being a wife have distinctly different meanings and consequences for the people treated as one or the other. The politics of husbands are not the same as the politics of wives. Many of the diplomatic wives associations have changed their names to blot out the wives. *Spouses* and *accompanying partners* have become the preferred official language in diplomatic circles. These linguistic adjustments have been made in the spirit of equality and of acknowledging broader possibilities in the contemporary worlds of marriage. But making the genderings of marriage less linguistically visible carries with it the risk of making the ongoing gendered politics of marriage harder to track and thus harder to contest.

Changing inheritance laws, child custody laws, travel laws, divorce laws, immigration laws, sexuality laws, bankruptcy laws, property laws, banking credit laws, tax laws, criminality laws, and employment laws has called for rethinking what sorts of femininities and masculinities society and its governing state require for their sustainable development and genuine security. Marriage reform campaigns—in Rwanda, the United States, Iceland, South Korea, Italy, Chile, Japan, Egypt, Tunisia, Iraq, and South Africa—have been most effective when they have been deeply informed by feminist understandings of how and why patriarchal systems work the way they do. Marriage reform efforts deprived of (or resistant to) feminist analysis are likely to leave patriarchy in place and women on shaky ground.

There are scores of international institutions today that rely on—and try to enforce—particular ideas of the preferred gendered marriage: the International Monetary Fund, the United Nations, and international humanitarian organizations such as the International Committee of the Red Cross, as well as globalized companies. The politics of each of these institutions would be more comprehensible if we had a feminist-informed analysis of their marriage policies and practices.[47] Institutions adopt ideas about, practices of, and rules for marriage that their senior officials believe serve their own institutional objectives and reinforce their own institutional culture. Those ideas, practices, and rules are passed down from one generation of officials to another. They become "the way things work around here." They are designed to put women in some places and men in other places. But they are designed to be more than divisions of labor. They are designed to ensure that particular relationships of unequal power are perpetuated.

Not taking women as diplomatic wives seriously jeopardizes one's ability to make realistic sense of how contemporary foreign affairs are conducted. Paying close attention to women who have been, or today are, married to their government's male diplomats enables one to lift the curtain on government's reliance not only on a certain kind of marriage but also on those women willing to adopt a certain kind of wifely role.

Women organizing as foreign service professionals and women organizing as foreign service wives should be examined together. The two groups of women are not always easy allies. But when their challenges to the institutional cultures of marriages are taken seriously, whole arenas of international politics that usually are kept safely in the shadows suddenly can be seen vividly.

CHAPTER SIX

Going Bananas!

*Where Are Women in the International Politics
of Bananas?*

Banana wars. Hurricanes and monsoons. Modernity. Capitalist expansion. Repressive regimes. Pesticide pollution. Workers organizing. Nationalism. Hollywood. Bananas are big, globalized business.

India produces the most bananas in the world today, but it is Ecuador that has become the world's number one banana exporter. Ranking two, three, and four are Costa Rica, Colombia, and the Philippines.

All three of the largest producing/marketing corporations in the global banana industry—Dole, Chiquita, and Del Monte— are American.[1] These top three control two-thirds of the world's banana market. Number four in the global banana rankings is Fyffes, a global food corporation based in Ireland. Among the fastest-growing global banana companies is Noboa, owned by the Ecuadoran magnate Alvero Noboa, which uses the sticker name "Bonita." Though less well known, fast-growing Noboa is today among the large plantation companies and has been sharply accused of labor abuses.[2] Together, these five companies wield influence in Washington, in the capitals of Central and Latin America, and in Geneva, headquarters of the World Trade Organization.

Among the countries whose residents consume bananas, the United States is by far the world's top banana importer. In second place are the countries of the European Union. While the banana plantation companies are perhaps more familiar to international observers than are the retail food giants, the globalizing supermarket chains have become increasingly influential players in the worldwide food industry. Bananas are the most profitable products for supermarkets to sell: for every dollar's worth of bananas sold, thirty-four cents goes to the markets, and only five cents goes to the producers (banana company managers and workers combined). As supermarkets and wholesale food chains have merged and opened outlets in more and more countries, their executives have been able to pressure the banana suppliers to keep banana prices low, allegedly for the benefit of food consumers. In 2013, the world's five largest food retailers/wholesale supermarkets were as follows:

1. Walmart (United States–owned)
2. Tesco (U.K.-owned)
3. Carrefour (French-owned)
4. Costco (United States–owned)
5. Kroger (United States–owned)[3]

Whether standing in the fresh produce section of a grocery store, deciding whether one should buy conventional or organic bananas; or slicing a banana on top of one's morning cereal; or baking banana bread for a benefit sale, one is playing one's part in the politics of the global banana. Those banana politics are gendered. Women play different roles than men in producing bananas, with different consequences. Ideas about masculinity and femininity have been wielded in the global production and marketing of bananas. Paying serious attention to women makes one a more realistic analyst of the international politics of bananas—and of tea, coffee, broccoli, and mangos.

CARMEN MIRANDA, HOLLYWOOD, AND FRUIT

Today, most people have forgotten Carmen Miranda. Or if they know her, it is because of her over-the-top imitators who now appear at drag parties or on YouTube. Carmen Miranda has become the cartoonish version of the Latin American star.

However, in her prime, Carmen Miranda broke international cultural barriers. In the 1940s, when she appeared on the American movie screen, the tempo quickened. Dressed in her deliberately outrageous costumes, her head topped by hats featuring bananas and other tropical fruits, Carmen Miranda sang and danced her way to Hollywood stardom. She was rarely cast as the romantic lead. Instead, directors made the most of her feisty comic performances. She added wit and energy to any film. But Carmen Miranda also played a part in a serious political drama: the realignment of American power in the Western Hemisphere. Her 1940s movies helped make Latin America safe for American banana companies at a time when U.S. imperialism was coming under wider regional criticism.

Between 1880 and 1930 the United States colonized or invaded Hawaii, the Philippines, Puerto Rico, the Dominican Republic, Cuba, and Nicaragua. Each was strategically valuable for its plantation crops. The British, French, and Dutch had their plantation colonies producing rubber, tea, coffee, palm oil, coconuts, tobacco, sisal, cotton, jute, rice, and of course the monarch of plantation crops, sugar. Bananas, sugar, coffee, pineapples—each had become an international commodity that some Americans were willing to kill for. But by the time Franklin Roosevelt entered office in 1933, sending in the marines was beginning to lose its political value; it was alienating too many potential regional allies. New, less direct means had to be found to guarantee the United States' control of Latin America. Popular culture would be harnessed for foreign policy ends.

Carmen Miranda was born in Lisbon in 1909 but emigrated as a child with her parents to Brazil, where her father established a wholesale fruit business. Despite her parents' hopes that their convent-educated daughter would grow up to be a respectable young woman, she secretly auditioned for and won a regular spot on a Rio de Janeiro radio station. She became a hit and soon was an attraction on the local nightclub circuit. By 1939, Carmen Miranda had recorded over three hundred singles, appeared in four Brazilian films, and was identified by her compatriots as a national institution. At this point in her career, Broadway theatrical producer Lee Shubert saw Carmen Miranda perform and offered her a contract to move north. When she stepped off the boat in New York on May 4, 1939, Shubert had the press corps already primed to greet his new "Brazilian bombshell." With her outrageous headgear and limited but flamboyant (and often deliberately flawed) English (she also spoke French and Spanish, as well as Portuguese), she was on her way to being turned into the 1940s American stereotype of the Latin American woman. In response to reporters' questions, Miranda replied, "Money, money, money … hot dog. I say yes, no, and I say money, money, money and I say turkey sandwich and I say grape juice."[4]

Carmen Miranda was a European Brazilian. But she took her musical inspiration from Brazil's African heritage. Her fruit-laden hats were inspired by those worn by Afro-Brazilian market women in Bahia, the northeastern state of Brazil. She not only sang songs derived from Afro-Brazilian culture but also chose Black Brazilian men as her band members. Miranda's new American producers wanted her to leave her Black band musicians behind in Brazil. But she insisted that they come with her to the United States. That is, Miranda was willing to play the silly Latin American woman on stage and screen, but she had serious ideas of her own.[5]

When Carmen Miranda arrived in New York in the summer of 1939, the world's fair was attracting throngs to the Sunken Meadow fairgrounds just outside the city. Nonetheless, Miranda still managed to make Shubert's show, *Streets of Paris,* a commercial success. *Life* magazine's reviewer noted, "Partly because their unusual melody and heavy accented rhythms are unlike anything ever heard in a Manhattan revue before, partly because there is not a clue to their meaning except the gay rolling of Carmen Miranda's insinuating eyes, these songs, and Miranda herself, are the outstanding hit of the show."[6]

In 1940, Hollywood studio directors were getting on board the Latin America bandwagon. Men like Darryl Zanuck, head of Twentieth Century Fox, had long cultivated friendships with politicians in Washington. It was one way to overcome the barriers of anti-Semitism confronting many of the film industry's moguls. Thus when President Franklin Roosevelt launched his Latin American "Good Neighbor Policy," the men who ran Hollywood were willing to help the government's campaign to replace a militaristic, imperial approach to United States–Latin America diplomacy with a more "cooperative" strategy. Roosevelt and his

Figure 21. Carmen Miranda in an undated Hollywood publicity photograph.

advisers were convinced that gunboat diplomacy was arousing too much opposition among precisely those Latin American governments that American businessmen would have to cultivate if the United States were to pull itself out of the Depression. Tourism and investment were promoted in glossy brochures. Pan American Airways flew holiday-makers to Havana and Managua. Construction of the Pan-American Highway was begun. Nicaragua's Anastasio Somoza, on his way to creating a repressive regime, was invited to New York's world's fair in 1939 to celebrate regional democracy and progress. Latin American movie stars replaced the marines as the guarantors of regional harmony.[7]

Darryl Zanuck enticed Carmen Miranda away from Broadway to be his studio's contribution to the Good Neighbor Policy. She appeared in the 1940 film *Down Argentine Way,* starring Betty Grable and Don Ameche. Singing "South American Way," Miranda made the song a hit. She popularized platform shoes. Her film career soared during World War II, when Washington officials believed that it was diplomatically vital to keep Latin American regimes friendly to the United States and out of the enemies' Axis alliance. Propaganda and censorship agencies urged the entertainment industry to promote Latin actors and popularize Latin music.[8]

Perhaps Miranda's most lavish film was Busby Berkeley's *The Gang's All Here* (1943), whose set was adorned with giant bananas and strawberries. She mastered English but was careful to maintain in her performances a heavily accented pronunciation, which suggested feminine naïveté. This naïveté, combined with the studios' insistence that she not be cast in the roles of romantic leads, meant that the cinematic Miranda presented a very specific and narrow portrayal of Latin American femininity. For many Americans, she became a guide to Latin culture. While Hollywood's

Latin American male actors stereotypically played loyal but none-too-bright sidekicks, like Donald Duck's parrot pal, José Carioca, Miranda personified a culture full of zest and charm, unclouded by intense emotion or political ambivalence. Like the bananas she wore on her head, Miranda was exotic yet mildly amusing.[9]

"Carmen Miranda is the chief export of Brazil. Next comes coffee." So recalls Uruguayan historian Eduardo Galeano.[10] Many Brazilians were proud of Miranda's Hollywood success yet ambivalent about her not-quite-respectable femininity. When she died suddenly of a heart attack in 1955, her body and effects were shipped back to Rio de Janeiro, where throngs turned out to pay public tribute to her. Brazilian President Juscelino Kubitschek declared a national day of mourning. Today, Carmen Miranda is memorialized in Rio with a museum devoted to her life and cultural contributions.

"I'M CHIQUITA BANANA AND I'VE COME TO SAY"

The banana has a history, a gendered history. Bananas have their origins in India and were carried westward by traders. By the fifteenth century they had become a basic food for Africans living along the coast of what is now Gambia, Sierra Leone, and Liberia. Portuguese traders transplanted bananas to the Canary Islands. When Portuguese and Spanish slave-traders began raiding the coast for Africans to serve as forced labor on colonial estates, they chose bananas as the food to ship with them; it was local and cheap. These were red bananas, a variety still popular in the West Indies and Africa.[11]

The yellow banana so familiar today to consumers in Europe, Japan, the Persian Gulf, and North America—the Cavendish—

is one of sixty-seven varieties of banana. The Cavendish is the industrialized banana, designed for global trade and maximized profit. It was not developed as a distinct variety until the nineteenth century. The Cavendish was imagined to be food fit not for slaves but for the palates of the wealthy. The first record of bunches of bananas being brought to New York from Havana is from 1804. But it was when the yellow banana was served as an exotic delicacy in the homes of affluent Bostonians in 1875 that it took off as an international commodity. In 1876 the banana was featured at the United States Centennial Exhibition in Philadelphia. The yellow banana symbolized America's new global reach.[12] The banana was becoming a sign of modernity, specifically of modern prosperity.

Notions of masculinity and femininity have been used to shape the international political economy of the banana. Banana plantations were developed in Central America, Latin America, the Caribbean, Africa, and the Philippines as a result of alliances between men of different but complementary interests: businessmen and male officials of the importing countries, on the one hand, and male large-landowners and government officials of the exporting countries, on the other. To clear the land and harvest the bananas, these male banana industrializers decided they needed a male workforce, one sustained at a distance by women as prostitutes, mothers, and wives.

However, company executives' manly pride was invested not so much in their extensive plantations as in the sophisticated equipment and technology they developed to transport the fragile tropical fruit to far-away markets: railroads, wire services, and fleets of refrigerator ships. Company officials still take special satisfaction in describing their giant cold-storage ships circling the globe, directed by a sophisticated international communications network, all to ensure that the bananas leaving Costa Rica or the Philippines by the green tonnage will arrive in New York or Liverpool or Doha undamaged and unspoiled, ready for the ripening factory.[13]

The companies envisaged their customers to be women: mothers and housewives concerned about their families' nutrition and looking for a reliable product. The most successful way of bonding housewives' loyalty to a particular company was to create a fantasized market woman.

The United Fruit Company—it later changed its name to United Brands, then to Chiquita Brands Corporation—became the largest commercial grower and marketer of bananas in the first half of 1900s. It made its own contribution to the American government's Good Neighbor Policy. In 1943, the company opened a Middle American Information Bureau to encourage "mutual knowledge and mutual understanding." The bureau wrote and distributed materials emphasizing the value that Central American products such as hardwoods, coffee, spices, and fruits contributed to the U.S. war effort. It targeted schoolchildren and housewives: those who ate bananas and those who bought them. *Nicaragua in Story and Pictures* was a company-designed school text celebrating the progress brought to Nicaragua by foreign-financed railroads and imported tractors. "Fifty Questions on Middle America for North American Women" and "Middle America and a Woman's World" explained to the North American housewife, United Fruit's chief customer, how the war in Asia was affecting her family budget: the Japanese invasion of British-ruled Malaya, it explained, made imported foods from Nicaragua and Costa Rica all the more important to her own wartime security.[14]

United Fruit's biggest contribution to American culture during these decades, however, was "Chiquita Banana." In 1944, when Carmen Miranda was packing movie houses and American troops were landing on Asian and European beaches, United Fruit's advertising executives created a half-banana, half-woman cartoon character. Chiquita Banana would soon rival Donald Duck. Dressed as a Miranda-esque market woman, this feminized banana sang her calypso song from coast to coast. Chiquita Banana helped to establish a twentieth-century art form, the singing commercial. Across the country, Chiquita could be heard on radio stations singing the praises of the banana 376 times daily.

Americans who are now in their sixties still can give a rendition of her memorable song:

> I'm Chiquita Banana
> And I've come to say
> Bananas have to ripen
> In a certain way.
> When they are fleck'd with brown
> And have a golden hue
> Bananas taste the best
> And are the best for you.
> You can put them in a salad
> You can put them in a pie-aye
> Any way you want to eat them
> It's impossible to beat them.
> But bananas like the climate
> Of the very, very tropical equator.
> So you should never put bananas
> In the refrigerator. No no no no![15]

United Fruit sales strategists set out in the 1940s to do the seemingly impossible—to create among American housewives a

Figure 22. The United Brands Company's recording for children of
the "Chiquita Banana" song. Original music by Len Mackensie, 1945;
updated commercial lyrics, 1975, copyright Maxwell-Wirges, 1945.

brand-name loyalty for a generic fruit. They wanted women to
think "Chiquita" when they went to the grocery store to buy
bananas. Franklin Roosevelt's Good Neighbor Policy and Carmen Miranda's Hollywood success had set the stage; animated
cartoons and the commercial jingle did the rest. Between the
woman consumer and the fruit, there now was only a corporation
with the friendly face of a bouncy Latin American market
woman. Seventy-five years later the United Fruit Company has

become Chiquita Brands. Today the company brings American consumers not only bananas but also melons, mangos, and papayas. An updated cartoon version of Chiquita still appears on its blue-and-yellow fruit stickers and on its corporate web page.[16] She is no longer a half-woman, half-banana character. She has become a full woman, slender and appealing.

Today, virtually every affluent country imports bananas from mainly poor, largely agrarian countries. Each consumer society gets its bananas from a large agribusiness corporation that either has its own large plantations or controls the marketing system through which small growers sell their fruit. Since United Fruit's advertising coup in 1944, its competitors have followed suit, designing stickers for their own bananas. In Europe, North America, the Middle East, or Japan, a shopper can look for the sticker with a corporate logo and, usually, the country of origin. In London and Dublin, one can look for Fyffes. In Detroit or Toronto, a shopper would be more likely to find Dole-, Chiquita-, Del Monte–, or Bonita-stickered bananas. In Tokyo, Sumitomo's bananas will be more visible.

Bananas, however, are not grown or exported evenly throughout the world's tropical regions. Latin America, where American food corporations are dominant, accounts for a stunning 82 percent of the world's total banana exports. By contrast, African countries together export only 4 percent of the world's total, while the Caribbean's banana exports amount to a mere 0.3 percent of all the world's exported bananas.[17]

Within regions, particular countries have become banana powerhouses. For instance, Ecuador, the world's largest, single, banana-exporting country, produces 43 percent of all the Latin American exported bananas, while Costa Rica, Colombia, and Guatemala, also major players in the global banana trade, produce 15 percent, 15 percent, and 13 percent, respectively, of the total Latin American exports. In the Caribbean, it is the small Windward Islands—Saint Lucia, Saint Vincent, and the Grenadines—that are the region's principal banana exporters. Among African countries, the former French colonies of Cameroon, Senegal, and Côte d'Ivoire have become that region's main banana exporters. In Asia, the Philippines has been that region's principal banana exporter for decades, attracting agribusiness investment from large Japanese and American corporations.[18]

One more twist: a country's banana exports might appear puny on the world stage yet still be crucial for its own government's balance of payments and its own farmers', agricultural workers', and local market vendors' economic well-being. Thus, while the West African country Côte d'Ivoire is a minor banana player, the local banana business supports twelve thousand of the country's rural and city workers, including women fruit sellers in Abidjan's main market. Market women such as Isabelle Lou Kouhelou, moreover, think internationally about their bananas. They worry about World Trade Organization rulings that have opened up global markets even further to the big American corporations selling Latin American bananas. Isabelle Lou Kouhelou also calculates that she could sell more local Côte d'Ivoire bananas in neighboring African countries if only her own government's officials would invest more in road and rail development.[19]

WOMEN IN BANANA REPUBLICS

A great deal has been written about countries derisively labeled "banana republics." The term was coined in 1935 to describe countries whose land and soul were in the clutches of a foreign company supported by the repressive politics of their own governments.[20] That is, a country becomes a banana republic as a result of a particular blending of exploitive foreign capital, local corruption, and authoritarian rule. The national sovereignty of a banana republic becomes so thoroughly compromised that it becomes the butt of jokes, not the object of respect. It has a government, but that government is staffed by people who line their own pockets by doing the bidding of the overseas corporation and its political allies. Because it is impossible for such compromised rulers to win the support of their own citizens, many of whom are exploited on the corporation's plantations, the government depends on guns and jails, not ballots and national pride.

The quintessential banana republics were those Central American countries that came to be dominated by the United Fruit Company's monoculture, the U.S. Marines, and their handpicked dictators. Their regimes have been backed by American presidents, mocked by Woody Allen, and overthrown by nationalist guerrillas. From the 1930s to the 1980s, banana republics were in their prime.

These corrupted political systems, and the international relationships that underpinned them, have been discussed as if women scarcely existed. Conventional commentators have portrayed the principal actors on all sides as men, and as if their being male were insignificant. This has left unexamined the ways in which their shared, though rival, masculinity allowed agribusiness entrepreneurs to form alliances with men in their own diplomatic corps, and with men in Nicaraguan, Guatemalan, or Honduran society. Enjoying Cuban cigars together after dinner while wives and mistresses powder their noses has been the stuff of smug cartoons but not of gendered political curiosity. Similarly, a banana republic's militarized ethos has been taken for granted without an investigation of how militarism feeds on masculinist values to sustain it. Most marines, diplomats, corporate managers, and military dictators may have been male, but they, like corrupted and corrupting men in contemporary societies, have needed the feminine "other" to maintain their self-assurance.

One of the conditions that pushed women off the banana-republic stage has been the presumed masculinization of the banana plantation. Global banana-company executives imagined that most of the jobs on their large plantations could be done only by men. Banana plantations were carved out of wooded acres. Clearing the brush required workers who could use a machete and live in rude barracks, and who, once the plantation's trees were bearing fruit, could chop down the heavy bunches of bananas and carry them to central loading areas and, from there, to the docks to be loaded by the ton onto refrigerator ships. This was "men's work."

Not all plantation work, in reality, has been masculinized. Generally, crops that call for the use of machetes—tools that can also be used as weapons—are produced with large inputs of male labor: bananas, sugar, palm oil. On the other hand, producers of crops that require a lot of weeding, tapping, and picking hire large numbers of women, who sometimes constitute a majority of the plantation workers: tea, coffee, rubber. That is, while tea, coffee, bananas, and rubber today are globalized, and are grown for export mainly on large foreign-owned or state-owned plantations, their gendered international politics are not identical.

Nor is the gendered labor formula on any single plantation fixed. Plantation managers who once relied heavily on male workers may decide to bring in more women if the men become too costly; or if their union becomes too threatening; or if the international market for the crop declines, necessitating cost-cutting measures such as hiring more part-time workers; or if new technology allows some physically demanding tasks to be done by workers with less strength. Today both sugar and rubber are being produced by plantation companies using more women workers than they did fifty years ago.[21] What has remained constant, however, is the presumption of international corporations that their position in the world market depends on manipulations of masculinity and femininity. Gender is injected into every Brooke Bond or Lipton tea leaf, every Unilever or Lonrho palm-oil nut, every bucket of Dunlop or Michelin latex, every stalk of Tate and Lyle sugarcane, and every bunch of Dole or Chiquita bananas.

Like all plantation managers, banana company executives considered race as well as gender when employing what they thought would be the most skilled, low-cost, and compliant workforce. Thus although the majority of banana workers were men, race was used to divide them. On United Brands' plantations in 1980s Costa Rica and Panama, for instance, managers recruited Amerindian men from the Guaymi and Kuna communities, as well as West Indian Black men and Hispanicized Ladino men (of mixed Amerindian and Spanish backgrounds). They placed them in different, unequally paid jobs, Ladino men at the top (below white male managers), Amerindian men at the bottom. Amerindian men were assigned menial jobs such as chopping grass and overgrown bush, thus ensuring that Ladino men's negative stereotypes of Amerindians—cholos, unskilled, uncultured natives—would be perpetuated. The stereotypes were valuable to the company because they forestalled potential alliances between Ladino, Black, and Amerindian men over common grievances. For instance, scholar Philippe Bourgois recorded these revealing explanations offered by men working on one Central American banana plantation:[22]

> MANAGER: It's easier to work with *cholos*. They're not as smart and don't speak good Spanish. They can't argue back at you even when they're right.... Hell, you can make a *cholo* do anything.
>
> LADINO FOREMAN: My workers are [not] *cholos*.... It's different here. Sure I can grab them [Ladino and Black male workers] and make them work faster; but the consequences will catch up with me tomorrow. We're not *cholos* here ... you understand?
>
> GUAYMI WORKER: They used to have up to 200 of us crammed into shacks eating boiled bananas out of empty kerosene cans.[23]

To say, therefore, that a banana plantation is masculinized is not to say that masculinity, even when combined with social class, is sufficient to forge political unity. On the other hand, the presumption that a banana plantation is a man's world does indeed affect the politics of any movement attempting to improve workers' conditions or to transform the power relationships that constitute a "banana republic."

In the 1920s, when Honduras was the hemisphere's largest banana exporter and United Fruit dominated the global banana industry, Central American banana workers began to organize and to conduct strikes to which even the U.S. government and local elites had to pay attention. The banana workers' demands reached beyond working conditions to political structures— from low pay and dangerous pesticides to political coercion and national sovereignty. These workers' protests took on strong nationalist overtones: the locally complicit regimes were as much the target of their anger as were the foreign plantation companies. But so long as banana plantation work was imagined to be men's work, and so long as the banana workers' unions were organized as if they were men's organizations, the wider nationalist cause would also be masculinized. A banana republic might fall, but patriarchy would remain in place.

For this reason, the emergence of women as activists in the two-pronged protests of the 1980s against exploitive foreign agribusinesses and corrupt local elites—in Guatemala, Honduras, Nicaragua, El Salvador, and, in a less violent form, Costa Rica—had special importance. Their activism made it clear that women had a stake in the local and international banana politics, while, at the same time, their involvement in the antiregime movements altered the meaning of *nation* and the nationalist movement's agenda.[24]

WOMEN GROW FOOD AND WASH BANANAS

The banana plantation has never been as exclusively male as popular imagery suggests. It has taken women's paid and unpaid labor to bring the golden fruit to the world's breakfast tables. Currently, an estimated 8 percent of all employees on banana plantations are women. Although they are a small percentage of all banana workers, in Latin America alone this adds up to an estimated five hundred thousand women banana workers. That 8 percent, however, is a new, lower proportion of plantation workers than just twenty years ago. It marks plantation company executives' successful efforts in reducing the numbers of women workers. Women, these banana executives have decided, are, despite their low wages, "high cost" workers.[25]

A banana plantation is closest to being an all-male enclave at its beginning, when the principal task is bulldozing and clearing the land for planting. But even at this stage women are

depended upon by the companies—and their male employees—to play their roles. As in the male-dominated mining
towns from Chile to South Africa to Indonesia, companies can
recruit men to live away from home only if someone back home
takes care of their families and maintains their land. The "feminization of agriculture"—that is, leaving small-scale farming to
women—has always been part and parcel of the masculinization of mining and banana plantations.[26] The male laborers have
to make private arrangements with wives, mothers, or sisters
that will assure them of a place to return to when their contracts expire, when they get fed up with supervisors' contemp-
tuous treatment, or when they are laid off because world prices
have plummeted. Behind every male-dominated banana plantation, consequently, stand scores of women—as wives, daughters, and mothers—performing unpaid household and farm
labor.

In the twenty-first century, the feminization of farming is
slowly being recognized as a major stumbling block to entire
societies' sustainable development. The problem is not that
women are incompetent farmers. The United National Special
Rapporteur for the Right to Food issued a report in 2013 point-
ing to the real cause for women-run small farms' low productivity—sexism: "Discrimination denies small-scale female farmers
the same access men have to fertilizer, seeds, credit, membership in cooperatives and unions, and technical assistance."[27]

The UN report charged all levels of society with perpetuat-
ing the sorts of sexist attitudes and sexist policies that hold back
women farmers' productivity: burdening women with all the
family's child care and household maintenance; stereotyping
women as unworthy of agricultural extension officers' attention;
and excluding women from agricultural-policy-making inside

the family and inside the national government.[28] At a basic level, women farmers are denied legal title to the land they farm. For instance, only 3 percent of all agricultural land in Bangladesh is owned by women; only 8 percent of all agricultural land in Egypt is owned by women. In Brazil the figure is 11 percent, in Nicaragua 16 percent, in France 15 percent, in Norway and the United States, a measly 9 percent.[29]

Banana company executives, union spokesmen, and export-driven government officials all have preferred not to take account of the farming responsibilities of the wives and mothers of their male workers outside the plantation. But unpaid women's farming is in fact part of what makes a banana plantation viable, since, without it, those companies would not be able to hire all the male workers that banana production requires.

Once the banana trees have been planted and have started to bear fruit, more women become residents and workers on the plantation itself. In the 1960s, corporate strategists introduced on-site packinghouses to maximize the advantages of their new containerized shipping process. They gendered the packinghouses by hiring women as their principal workers. The sheds where bananas were washed and packed became the banana plantation's most feminized work site.

Just as one can follow a pair of blue jeans from factory floor to retail shop, so one can follow a bunch of bananas along its global supply chain from plantation to supermarket. One can do the same sort of step-by-step global tracking along the supply chain with other now-globalized foods and plants as well: broccoli, tea, chocolate, tomatoes, mangos, flowers. At each step ideas about women and ideas about men are put to work. Typically, those gendered ideas are devised and enforced by both company and government policy-makers.[30]

Figure 23. Women workers wash bananas at cleaning troughs in Costa Rica, 2006. Photo: Terrance Klassen/Acclaim Images.

Out among the long rows of banana plants, on the company docks, aboard the company's refrigerated ships, and on the trucks at the port of destination, men do what company managers think of as "men's work." Inside the banana packinghouses, however, one finds women cutting bunches of still-green fruit from their thick stems, an operation that has to be done carefully (one might say skillfully) so that the bananas are not damaged. The women then wash the pesticides off the bananas in troughs of water that become pesticide-saturated. Women select the rejects, which can amount to up to half the bananas picked in the fields. Companies often dump rejected bananas in nearby streams, causing pollution, which kills local fish. Women weigh the bananas, attach the company's telltale sticker to each banana, and pack them for shipping. These packinghouse women are paid piece-rates, often with no overtime pay. Foremen expect them to work at high speed to meet supermarkets' demand. Their employment is precarious, since between harvests the women have little paid work.[31]

Tess was one Filipino woman who worked for TADECO, a subsidiary of United Brands/Chiquita Brands, Philippines. She was employed on a plantation on the country's southern island, Mindanao. A twenty-year war has been fought on Mindanao between government troops and indigenous Muslim groups protesting against the leasing of large tracts of land either to multinational pineapple and banana companies or to wealthy Filipino landowners, who then worked out lucrative contracts with those corporations. Tess herself is a Christian Filipina. She, like thousands of other women and men, migrated—with the government's encouragement—to Mindanao from other islands in search of work when the bottom fell out of the country's once-dominant sugar industry. She worked with other young women in the plantation's packing plant, preparing bananas to be shipped to Japan by Japanese and American import companies. She was paid approximately one dollar a day. With an additional living allowance, Tess could make about forty-five dollars a month; she sent a third of this to her family in the Visayas, her home region.

Tess used a chemical solution to wash the company's bananas. There was a large, reddish splotch on her leg where some of the chemical had spilled accidentally. At the end of a day spent standing for hours at a time, Tess went home to a bunkhouse she shared with a hundred other women, twenty-four to a room, who slept in eight sets of three-tiered bunks.[32]

Many women working in banana plantation packinghouses are heads of households and take exploitive jobs in order to support their children; other women see their employment as part of being dutiful daughters, sending a portion of their meager earnings back to parents, who may be losing their own farmland as acquisitive agribusinesses expand.[33] Neither women nor men working on any plantation—producing bananas, tea, rubber, sugar, pineapples, palm oil, or coffee for export—are simply "workers." These banana workers are also wives, husbands, daughters, sons, mothers, and fathers. Each role has its own politics. That distinctive role, that set of societal expectations, can shape how they think about their banana work. "Dutiful daughter," "responsible mother," and "loyal wife" are ideas on which the international banana industry depends.

BROTHELS AND BANANAS

Feminists have learned always to ask about prostitution. It is not that one knows what one will uncover, only that whatever one finds is likely to be revealing of the larger gender political system at work.

Bananas have long been the objects of sexual jokes and allusions. There were corporate complaints when an AIDS-prevention education campaign used a banana to demonstrate how a man should put on a condom. But the banana industry—not the banana itself—is far more seriously sexualized. Sexual harassment helps to control women working in the plantation packinghouses; prostitution has been permitted by male managers in order to control the largely male plantation workforce.

Historically, plantations have been self-contained worlds. Workers, managers, family members, and the crops they cultivate live together side by side, their interactions regulated by strict spatial hierarchies. Plantations can look like military bases. Male managers and their wives live in comfortable houses with gardens and kitchens maintained by local employees; these residents often have access to their own clubs with well-stocked bars and refreshing swimming pools. Foremen and their families have their own more modest housing compounds and certain privileges. Workers live in spartan, sex-segregated accommodations that often lack minimal sanitary facilities. Some plantations are better equipped than others. Head offices like to talk about the clinics and schools they provide. They rarely talk about the isolation or the paralyzing debts accumulated by employees at the company store. Some companies have had to provide basic necessities for workers in order to obtain land rights and tax concessions from local governments.

Caribbean critics of their countries' past dependency on neoliberal capitalist monoculture have coined the term *plantation economy:* foreign agribusiness giants have so dominated entire societies that those societies are reduced to the status of dependency and their cultures suffused with paternalism.[34] Prostitution historically has been woven into that gendered plantation dependency and paternalism.

When investigating life on Dutch-owned sisal, tea, rubber, and palm-oil plantations in early-twentieth-century colonial Indonesia, feminist historian Ann Laura Stoler asked about sexual politics.[35] She found that prostitution was integral to the way Dutch male managers recruited and controlled male workers from several different Indonesian ethnic groups. There were many more men than women on these estates. Women were hired at half the rates paid to men, not enough to meet daily necessities. Most were single Javanese women hired on contract and living far away from home. To make ends meet, many of these women provided sexual services to Chinese male workers living in the plantation barracks. Some young women were pushed into prostitution by sexual harassment by the foremen in their packing plants. White male plantation supervisors enjoyed the privilege of selecting their sexual partners from the most recent female arrivals.

Prostitution became the norm on many plantations by design, not simply by chance. Company records reveal that male managers debated the advantages and disadvantages of prostitution for their company. The debates have a familiar ring: they echo debates among male military officers about the pros and cons of facilitating prostitution around their bases. In the early twentieth century, some Dutch colonial commentators were alarmed at the high incidence of venereal disease among male plantation workers and blamed the prostitutes. Other Dutch critics noted that white male supervisors were assaulted by male Javanese workers who believed their daughters were being lured into prostitution. But the prevailing management view was that it would be too difficult to recruit male workers for plantation work if they were not provided with female sexual services. Furthermore, in the eyes of many plantation managers, prostitution was a lesser evil than homosexual relations between male workers deprived of female companionship. Finally, devoting a sizeable portion of their wages to prostitution left many male workers further in debt, making it harder for them to abandon estate work when their contracts expired.

Almost a century later, brothels had become commonplace around United Brands/Chiquita plantations in Central America. This time it is American male managers, not Dutch male managers, who are engaging in a sexual calculus. Brothels are situated just outside the banana plantation gates. While the men on these banana plantations are Amerindian, Black, and Ladino, the women working in the brothels are overwhelmingly Ladino. Information is limited, but most women servicing banana workers seem to have done other sorts of work before becoming prostitutes. Many of the women are the sole supporters of their children. Racism and sexism have been woven together in Central America's banana-plantation brothels, as is so often the case in prostitution politics. Ladino women in prostitution told one researcher that they preferred Amerindian male customers because, they said, those men were too shy to fully undress and got their intercourse over with quickly. This was not necessarily meant as a compliment to Amerindian masculinity and may have served to reinforce negative stereotypes among Ladino and Black male workers.[36]

WOMEN GROWERS AND THE "BANANA WARS"

The 1990s and the beginning of the twenty-first century was a time of "banana wars." These international conflicts were waged without guns, but they were heated. A lot was at stake because so much depends on the banana. The rivals were global banana companies. The international dispute was over this question: could the European Union continue to impose hefty import tariffs on bananas shipped to Europe from Latin America for the sake of protecting the import of bananas grown in West Africa and the Caribbean?

Several narratives were being played out in these intense international banana wars. The Caribbean bananas were chiefly from the tiny Windward Islands Saint Vincent and Saint Lucia, while the West African bananas were from Senegal, Cameroon, and Côte d'Ivoire; bananas from both regions were grown by small farmers. By contrast, most of the Latin American bananas, on which the European Union commissioners wanted to impose stiff tariffs, were grown on large plantations.

The contest seemed to pit small growers against plantation behemoths: a fruity David versus a fruity Goliath. As in any mythic tale, however, complexity lies just below the surface. Dole, then the world's largest banana company, had bought the French firm Compagnie Fruiti in 2009 to deliberately gain control of its West African smallholder-grown bananas and thus take advantage of the EU's tariff regime.[37]

A further layer of meaning and interest shaped this global trade contest: the Windward and West African growers—and the local governments that benefited from favored access to the European banana market—were former British and French colonial subjects, to which trade officials in London and Paris continued to feel some paternalistic postcolonial obligation. The Latin American banana plantations, on the other hand, were owned by major U.S.-based corporations—Dole, Chiquita, and Del Monte. Even though their bananas were Latin American, the corporations were seen by Washington officials as their own important domestic political allies.

A final layer in this war: in the current global political economy, the arena for this heavyweight banana contest was the World Trade Organization. The WTO was created by governments to negotiate settlements between competing trade-dependent governments in order to keep today's neoliberal global economic gears turning smoothly, in particular to stave off escalating trade wars.

It took twenty years to resolve the banana war. In the end, the Latin American corporations and their Washington allies won. The Geneva-based WTO officials concluded that the EU's tariffs and their rationale were protectionist. Protectionism is counter to the new global economic order. The head of the WTO, Pascal Lamy, declared the resolution a "truly historic moment." The small growers in the Caribbean and West Africa were given several years to adjust to the newly unfettered global competition for European market share, but adjust they would have to.[38] This suggests why Isabelle Lou Kouhelou, the market seller in Côte d'Ivoire, had her eye on both the WTO and her own potential neighboring markets. Market women's calculations were close to the heart of the forced "adjustment."

Beyond the market women—the local banana vendors who inspired Carmen Miranda and the creators of Chiquita Banana—are other women whose livelihoods have been tied up in the EU system of tariffs and in the Washington/Dole/Del Monte/Chiquita frontal challenge to that postcolonial system. These are the women in the Windwards and West Africa who are themselves small growers of bananas. If one holds a Fyffes Windward Island banana and a Dole Ecuador banana, one is holding two quite differently gendered bananas.

The women and men who are smallholders sell their bananas to a locally influential growers cooperative, which in turn sells them to an international banana marketing company such as Fyffes. While the small banana farmers have had more autonomy than plantation workers have, their economic fortunes have been tied to those of the growers cooperatives and to the global marketers. In recent years, even some of the major plantation companies have been finding smallholder systems attractive: by shedding their own large plantations and, instead, buying bananas from smallholders and small plantation suppliers, they can rid themselves, presumably, of the social responsibilities of hiring workers directly. In this sense, the banana companies are following in the footsteps of the global garment companies, which have tried to fine-tune contracted outsourcing.

Thus one should resist romanticizing banana smallholdings. They too are gendered. While male smallholders are likely to be married, giving them a second adult to help with farm and family work, many of the women banana farmers are single mothers. Furthermore, women farmers are less likely than male farmers to have property titles to the land they farm. For instance, on the Windward Island of Saint Lucia, the source of many Caribbean exported bananas, a mere 25 percent of all agricultural landowners are women; 75 percent are men.[39]

In addition, both the influential local grower cooperatives and the global marketing companies to which they sell their bananas are male-dominated. One telling indicator of women farmers' marginalization in the local banana politics appears on the Windward Islands Farmers Association's own website. Among the association's "major objectives," its leaders list "mainstreaming of gender-related issues in all WINFA programs." The implication is that gender mainstreaming is still out there on the association's horizon, far from achieved. To underline that yet-to-be-achieved rolling back of the farmers association's masculinized internal culture, the group later states among "WINFA's efforts": "Women are encouraged to participate actively in assemblies and exchanges."[40]

Paying attention to women in the recent "banana wars" throws light on how these intense economic conflicts were fueled by rival masculinities at every level of the globalized trade, fueled in ways that served to further marginalize women.

THE *BANANERAS:* WOMEN BANANA WORKERS ORGANIZE

Banana workers have been organizing for decades. Because banana plantations have been a site for cooperation between powerful global corporations and local elites, banana workers' unions have spearheaded nationalist movements that have simultaneously challenged foreign exploitation and their own governments' political repression.

For most of those turbulent decades, local and overseas observers did not seem to notice or care that those unions were themselves male dominated. What mattered to sympathetic labor observers was class and capital. It took a handful of women packinghouse workers to compel them, belatedly, to pay attention to women and to the politics of gender inside banana workers' unions.

They called themselves *bananeras*. These were women who worked long hours for low pay in the damp, pesticide-infused plantation packinghouses. They did not wield machetes. They were not photogenic. They did not fit the usual profile of national heroes.[41]

The first women banana workers to wonder aloud why men monopolized the leadership of their labor unions were Honduran women. Their story started in 1985. The location: La Lima, an old United Fruit (later Chiquita) plantation town. They were union members. They belonged to SITRATERCO, the Sindicato de Trabajadores de la Tela Railroad Company, named after the banana company's transportation subsidiary. SITRATERCO had been born out of a mass workers strike in 1954, in the depths of the Cold War, when workers' organizing was considered subversive. The 1950s were also a time in the gendered history of banana plantations when women's role in production was confined to that of unpaid wives of male workers. The introduction of the plantation packinghouse was still a decade away. The union ultimately won the right to negotiate with corporate management and, out of those negotiations, had secured contracts giving banana workers a modicum of employment stability that other workers on plantations hostile to unions lacked. Thirty years later, in the mid-1980s, military coups had toppled successive governments in Latin America, and women had joined antiregime guerrilla movements in Guatemala, Nicaragua, and El Salvador. In the same years, energy in the Latin American feminist movement had mounted. It was a transnational movement, out of which came analyses of and activism against militarism, nationalism, capitalism, racism, poverty, and patriarchy.[42] These were heady years. But on the plantations and inside their unions, it was hard to get women's leadership potential recognized and women workers' specific issues taken seriously.

"The men thought we were crazy." That was what women union activists said of the initial response by their male coworkers and union comrades when, in 1986, Gladys Valle and Maria Teresa Aguilar introduced a motion at the SITRATERCO meeting calling for the creation of a Women's Committee, with its own status and its own officers. The men "were laughing at us." The motion was defeated.[43]

The men's opposition and ridicule energized the women. They began meeting to talk about their experiences in the packinghouses. But soon they realized that they could not confine their issues simply to what they experienced on the job. Their responsibilities at home—as single mothers or with their male partners—were so tightly woven into their paid-work lives. Rashes caused by pesticides that seeped under their gloves, and working what Latin American feminists had named the "double day"—paid work and unpaid work—were impossible to separate. They were part of the same politics of women's lived experiences that were not being taken seriously by their male comrades.

Over the next two years, the Honduran plantation women began to seek out individual men in the union, choosing those men who seemed most approachable, who at least did not openly ridicule their ideas. At the same time, when the union leadership called strikes on the plantations, women made certain that their male coworkers saw their support and realized how crucial their support was to any union campaign to win better working conditions for everyone. In 1988, the women again introduced their resolution. This time it passed. Only 8 women could vote. But they had gained the support of 120 male voters. The union's Comite Femenil was launched.

As the *bananeras* continued meeting, trading ideas and experiences, they decided to hold training workshops. The workshop was a feminist skill-building technique that middle-class Latin American feminists had developed. A workshop brought together a dozen or more women, sometimes just for a few hours, sometimes for two days, to share fun, comradeship, and education. The women organizers realized that a principal obstacle to getting more women into union leadership roles was that women were not given the chance to develop their leadership skills. That leadership was a skill, and not just something men naturally took on, was itself part of these women's new gendered political understanding. But attending a workshop—just like taking part in a peace camp—meant taking time away from family. Someone else would have to mind the children and prepare a meal. Thus workshop attendance itself raised questions about the gendered division of labor inside the family and about male partners' distrust of "their" women when the latter were away from home.

During the 1990s, banana labor unions were buffeted from many sides. The large banana companies reduced plantation

Figure 24. On a plantation owned by Tres Hermanas, a key supplier to Chiquita, women banana workers protest the plantation owner's violations of workers' rights, including unpaid overtime and suppression of their union, SITRAINBA. Honduras, 2013. Photo: COSIBAH, March 8, 2013.

workforces; hurricane Mitch devastated Central American banana plants; and governments continued to repress labor activists. In Ecuador, the new Noboa banana company banned unions altogether. These were years of violence, unemployment, ill health, stress, and overwork. Nonetheless, through sharing their experiences, women formed friendships with women working on different plantations, some owned by Dole, others by United Fruit/United Brands/Chiquita, and still others by Del Monte. Information, strategies, and encouragement were circulated among women plantation workers across national borders, especially among women in Honduras, Costa Rica,

Guatemala, and Colombia. More women ran for low-level union offices and won. Women workers became more confident, offering these women officers a realistic sense of their "double day" lives. Knowledge was accumulated. Women started comparing the workings of machismo inside their plantations, their unions, and their homes.

By 2002, women had been elected to senior posts in the banana unions. Women on stage at annual union meetings were no longer an oddity. But the *bananeras* were still organizing workshops in order to empower the newest generation of women banana workers. The older, pioneering *bananeras* were aware that the banana companies now were deliberately avoiding hiring older women—women over thirty years old—and instead targeting younger women, some as young as seventeen.[44] One such workshop took place in Guatemala, led by older, experienced activist women, who had traveled to the session in a pickup truck across the border from Honduras. This time the topic was domestic violence. Bananas and domestic violence. Making this connection was the product of years of thinking and sharing. The workshop started as it usually did, with each young woman in the group saying what she hoped to get out of the gathering:

"I want to learn, and then show others."

"I want to learn how to defend myself from whoever tries to oppress me, whether it's my husband, my union, or my boss."[45]

Women and men employed in the global banana sector have created alliances not only across national borders and gender divisions but also between geographic regions. They have sought to bring Filipino and Latin American plantation workers together with men and women operating smallholder banana farms. To tackle issues of the global banana industry, they contended, those on the bottom rung of the industry had to globalize their own relationships. Simultaneously, with the support of new transnational groups promoting fair trade and sustainable agriculture movements in affluent countries, such as Banana Link and the Fair Food Network, workers' advocates pressured the big banana production and marketing companies to join the new World Banana Forum.[46] The forum is a gathering at which the full range of economic and social justice issues can be discussed among all the world's major banana players. The first World Banana Forum met in 2009.[47] Without women's activism, this would have been precisely the sort of international economic forum at which masculinized influence would have been normalized.

A leading proponent of the new World Banana Forum was COLSIBA, the Coordinating Body of Latin American Banana and Agro-Industrial Workers, a federation of labor unions. One of COLSIBA's members is the Honduran banana workers union to which the early *bananeras* belonged. When the World Banana Forum gathered in Guayaquil, Ecuador, in 2012, COLSIBA was represented by Iris Munguia, the first woman to be elected the federation's senior coordinator. Back in 1985, as a packinghouse worker, Munguia had been one of the original young women plantation workers who had proposed that her male-dominated union create a Women's Committee. In 2012, Munguia helped to launch the first-ever global meeting of women banana workers and women banana smallholders. Women from all over the banana-growing world came together on the eve of the World Banana Forum's official gathering to share information and strategize about the harsh labor conditions, market pressures, and double days that intertwined to shape their lives.[48]

At the World Banana Forum's meeting that followed, Iris Munguia bargained directly with Chiquita. Amid discussions of fair trade, organic agriculture, sustainability, and union organizing, Munguia brought up sexual harassment. Pushed by her, Chiquita's corporate executives agreed for the first time to take seriously the sexual harassment of women workers by male supervisors on their plantations. As Munguia explained, "This can be an example for other companies, such as Dole and Del Monte."[49] Women's ideas, too, about what constitutes a workers' issue now determined what made it onto the international economic agenda.

CONCLUSION

For the traveler sated with sugarcoated muffins and bags of chips, the bowl of fresh bananas comes as a welcome sight. In airports and train stations, the bananas usually shine like a nutritious beacon near the cash register. They are not coated with anything but their own bright yellow skins. Finally, amid all the fake food, something natural.

Those skins are a reassuring yellow, however, because their plants were sprayed with pesticides. The weary traveler can peel the banana without fear because women workers have spent hours in a damp plantation shed washing off that pesticide.

Any product that has traveled miles to be consumed far from where it was grown or assembled is the product of multilayered manipulations of ideas about manliness and femininity. Men chop, women wash. Men load ships, women take care of the children. Men lead, women loyally follow. Making sense of the past, current, and future international politics of any product calls for exercising one's feminist curiosity, for squinting one's eyes skeptically at anything that is reassuringly labeled "natural."

Students at Connecticut College, a small liberal arts college in New England, decided to learn more about what they were eating in the campus cafeteria. They chose to focus on the banana. It appeared in their dining hall in a seemingly complete form, unlike most of the foods, which came to them wholly or partially processed. They were soon hot on the trail of the globalized banana corporations. They used the findings from their months of research to persuade their campus administrators and dining hall concessionaires to switch from the corporate banana to a fair-trade-certified banana, imported into the United States by an import company that bought its bananas from Colombian smallholders who had survived years of guerrilla warfare.[50]

However, even a fair-trade-certified banana company should be investigated for its gender politics: who are pictured on the company's website as "the farmers"? Do as many women as men hold legal title to the local banana-farm land? This is just the start. Feminist-informed gender investigators will dig into the local community's decision-making processes, into the recruitment of the export company's executive personnel, into the control of money inside each smallholder's household. Did the women in these Colombian smallholder banana-growing families take part in the 2012 international meeting of women banana workers and farmers? Making the switch in the campus dining hall should be done with one's gender-focused eyes wide open.

The globalized banana is not static. Even if it still looks like the fruit that Carmen Miranda and Chiquita Banana made famous, its politics are constantly in motion. And that political motion is shaped in large part by how corporate male executives forge bonds with local male political elites. Simultaneously, those ongoing political operations are shaped by how banana-company decision-makers imagine the utility of feminized labor. That political motion is also determined by whether male workers see the value of women's unpaid work or they resist women coworkers' efforts to gain a foothold inside local and international banana labor unions.

Each of the players in today's globalized banana business deserves to be analyzed with gender-sharp tools. We will not know the full gendered story of the banana until we have gender analyses of Chiquita, Dole, Del Monte, Fyffes, and Noboa, until we have gender analyses of Walmart, Tesco, Costco, and Carrefour, until we have gender analyses of COLSIBA and the World Banana Forum, until we have gender analyses of Banana Link and the Fair Food Network, and, of course, until we have a gender analysis of the WTO.

Slipping on a banana peel may not be merely a vaudeville comic act. It may be slipping into the naive political assumption that the banana is natural.

CHAPTER SEVEN

Women's Labor is Never *Cheap*

Gendering Global Blue Jeans and Bankers

On April 24, 2013, the collapse of the Rana Plaza building killed 1,129 Bangladeshis. Most of the dead were women, all of whom had been working in the five garment factories housed in the poorly constructed building. The collapse was the deadliest disaster in the history of the garment industry, a globalized industry long plagued by disasters. What made headlines around the world, however, was less the deaths of Bangladeshi women and more the discovery that the garments they had been sewing were for global brand-name companies. And even then, the collapse of the Rana Plaza building, on the sprawling fringe of Dhaka, the capital city, might not have attracted sustained international attention had this tragedy not come only five months after another Bangladeshi garment-factory tragedy. The workers who had died when that factory burned were mostly women, and they too had been sewing clothes for popularly known brand-name corporations, such as Walmart, Gap, and Tommy Hilfiger.

Would these headlined deaths significantly alter the deeply gendered politics of the international garment industry?

THE DOOR OPENED INWARD

The factory door opened inward. That was a fire code violation. It would prove deadly.

It was November 24, 2012, when fire broke out in the Tazreen Fashions garment factory on the outskirts of Dhaka. The factory was nine stories high; the top three floors had been added illegally. The company had fifteen hundred employees and sales totaling $35 million per year. Women, who constituted 70 percent of the factory's workers, were at their sewing machines when they first smelled the smoke. Their supervisors told them not to worry, to stay at their machines.

In today's globally competitive garment industry, the men who own the factories producing jeans, bathing suits, lingerie, and basketball uniforms under contract for European and North American brand-name companies cannot risk falling behind in their production deadlines. Those deadlines are set by their global corporate clients, who want to put new fashions on store shelves more and more often, to match impatient consumers' expectations. The Bangladeshi factory owner's anxiety over meeting his global clients' tight production deadlines had trickled down to his assembly line supervisors. As the smoke seeped upward, they pushed the women to keep sewing.[1]

The fire spread. Women defied their supervisors and dashed for the exit doors. They and their male coworkers found most of the doors locked or blocked by piles of fabric. The owner later claimed that he had ordered the doors locked to prevent workers from stealing materials. Some women did find one unlocked door; it opened inward. In the smoke and confusion, scores of women were crushed against the door. Other women died when they jumped out of windows. Many met their deaths not far from where they had sewn the brand-name garments. A total of 112 workers, women and men, died in the Tazreen factory fire; hundreds more were injured.

One of the workers able to escape was Sumi Abedin. She has told of the fire, the locked doors, the blocked stairways, the confusion. A male coworker broke a window. As she jumped through it, she thought her life was ending, but that at least her parents would have her body to bury. She still wonders how she survived. When she was twenty-three, Sumi had migrated from a small rural village to the outskirts of sprawling Dhaka to seek paid work in one of the scores of garment factories sprouting all over Bangladesh. She took a job at Tazreen Fashions as a "senior" sewing machine operator, earning fifty-five dollars per month, almost twenty dollars more than the Bangladeshi garment worker's legally mandated average wage of just thirty-seven dollars per month. She tried to send part of her earnings home to her parents. For her fifty-five dollars per month, Sumi worked at Tazreen Fashions eleven hours per day, six days a week. She recalls seeing labels for Walmart, Disney, and Gap.[2]

The Tazreen Fashions fire made global headlines. It was not the first Bangladesh garment fire, however. Even before the deadly Tazreen fire, between 2006 and 2012, five hundred Bangladeshi workers had died—and many more had been injured—in other garment factory fires. Furthermore, the Tazreen tragedy would not be the last time that the deaths of Bangladeshi women garment workers would feature on the world's nightly news.

To many, it seemed as if the clock had spun backward. Women garment workers, locked in their flaming factories, jumping out of upper-story windows, meeting their deaths as a result of owners' abuses: was this March 21, 1911, all over again? That was the

Figure 25. The charred remains of burned sewing machines in the Tazreen Fashions factory in Bangladesh after the 2012 fire. Photo: Khaled Hasan/The New York Times/Redux.

date of the infamous Triangle Shirtwaist Factory fire in lower Manhattan, in which so many Jewish, Irish, and Italian young women and men had perished: 129 women; 17 men. In March 2011, on the Triangle fire's hundredth anniversary, feminist labor historians reminded us that it had taken such a deadly fire to wake up the American public to the exploitive and unsafe working conditions on which the country's garment industry was built and to compel the all-male legislatures at the time to pass the country's first meaningful labor safety laws.[3] In the past century had no lessons been learned? Why were we all still wearing clothes threaded with the exploitation of women workers?

The weeks following the 2012 Bangladesh garment factory fire produced exposés and calls for reform. We learned that in recent years Walmart, Tommy Hilfiger, Benetton, H&M, Zara,

Sears, Mango, and Gap had put another layer of agents in between themselves and the women workers: suppliers. The global companies hired local suppliers, such as Success Apparel, to hire the local factory contractors. Those factory contractors, such Tazreen Fashion's owner, were the men who, in turn, hired the sewers, pressers, and cutters. These men—the factory owners and the managers of the suppliers and contractors—had cultivated political ties to influential local Bangladeshi officials to ensure they would not be fined for safety violations and that they would be issued the questionable zoning permits. Some of the garment factory owners even held seats in the Bangladesh parliament. The profits of the global brand-name corporations depended on those local masculinized political relationships— whom they trusted, whom they bribed, whom they entertained.

As the fire's death toll mounted, some multinational company executives, worried about their global reputations, initially denied using Tazreen. They soon had to backtrack, however, when Bangladeshi labor advocates displayed their brands' labels and the documents that named them as Tazreen customers. In fact, one high-risk form of activism that Bangladesh labor advocates had resorted to was running into burning factory buildings to pull out company labels and garment orders in order to challenge what they predicted would be posttragedy denials by global company executives.[4]

In the early twenty-first century, increasing numbers of consumers had become concerned about the human rights of workers. In response, government agencies, such as the U.S. Marine Corps and U.S. Air Force, which stock their military-base stores with low-cost, outsourced apparel, and corporations such as Nike, Apple, Disney, Walmart (all United States-owned), Loblaws (Canadian), Zara and Mango (Spanish), Calvin Klein and Tommy Hilfiger (both owned by the German company PVH), H&M (Swedish), and Gap (the American company that also owns Banana Republic and Old Navy) scrambled to devise a slightly revised business formula that would allow them to do two things simultaneously: (a) continue to seek out the world's lowest-cost apparel manufacturers, and (b) assure consumers in North America and Europe that they were taking responsibility for their subcontracted employees' safety and rights. When the two goals conflicted, more often than not, the first goal trumped the second.[5]

The corporate strategy to assuage the concerns of rights-conscious consumers without jeopardizing profits has been to devise a system of workplace monitoring conducted under contract with "independent" accreditation monitors. Thus, as the ashes of the Tazreen fire still smoldered, some corporate executives claimed that their companies had hired monitors to inspect their subcontractors' far-flung factories, and that Tazreen had met the monitors' safety and fairness standards. What the executives neglected to note, however, was that those reputedly independent monitoring organizations depended financially on their corporate clients for their own incomes. Furthermore, some monitors routinely subcontracted out their safety inspection work to local monitors, over whom they exerted only minimal quality control.[6]

When told of the global brands' claims that they were committed to compliance by Tazreen and other subcontracted manufacturers with international worker-safety standards, Kalpona Akter, a Bangladeshi woman advocate of garment workers' rights, and the head of the Bangladesh Center for Worker Solidarity—who herself had begun working in a garment factory as a twelve-year-old—asked rhetorically, "In this factory, there was a pile of fabrics and yarn stored on the ground floor that caught fire. Workers couldn't evacuate through the stairs. What does this say about compliance?"[7]

Putting geographic and political distance between their own boardrooms and the factory floors where low-waged women sewed their products has been one of the core globalizing business strategies of current-era companies. Now, however, labor rights campaigners, such as those in Bangladesh, were not only running into burning buildings, but they were also forging international alliances (with groups such as the Amsterdam-based Clean Clothes Campaign and the Washington-based Workers Rights Coalition, which represented a coalition of anti-sweatshop colleges) in order to globalize corporate accountability.[8] It has not been easy.

By 2012, Bangladesh had become the world's second-largest garment exporter (China was first). When Bangladeshis had waged a war to gain their independence from Pakistan in 1971, there had been no garment factories in Bangladesh. But entrepreneurs and policy makers in the newly independent Bangladesh soon realized that the world's rapidly globalizing apparel industry provided their country with an opportunity to capitalize on a resource that the labor-intensive industry needed and that Bangladesh had in abundance: low-waged workers. By 2004, there were thirty-three hundred garment factories in Bangladesh. Together, they employed 1.7 million workers: 1,320,000 women and 380,000 men.[9] By 2012, the year of the Tazreen fire, the number of garment factories had grown to forty-five hundred, employing over 3 million Bangladeshi workers—that is, as many garment workers as the entire population of Albania. Many of the factory owners were Bangladeshi men, although overseas male entrepreneurs, too, were moving into Bangladesh's lucrative garment manufacturing sector. One of the largest factories was YoungOne, chaired by the Korean businessman Kihak Sung. YoungOne had seventeen factories in Bangladesh by 2012 and was producing outdoor apparel for global brand-name companies such as Nike and North Face.[10]

In Bangladesh, garment production was now more than Big Business; it was also Big Politics. Local businessmen sought to influence mayors, zoning boards, political parties, regulators, and parliament. Workers began to unionize. When the government, in support of the factory owners, suppressed their organizing efforts, workers called wildcat strikes. After an especially violent confrontation between striking workers and armed police, Bangladesh's prime minister, Sheikh Hasina (a woman, but head of a masculinized ruling party, the Awami League, closely allied with the male garment-industry owners), agreed to raise the country's minimum monthly wage from twenty-one dollars to thirty-seven dollars.[11] Still, at an average wage of thirty-seven dollars per month, Bangladesh remained the *cheapest* place for global apparel companies to produce their clothes. So the brand-name companies kept coming. The operations of the suppliers and the contractors kept expanding. The cost of the sewn products for the global brands and the retail prices of clothes for consumers were kept low not only by the low wages paid to Bangladeshi workers but also by both the factory owners' lack of investment in factory safety and health measures and by the global companies' lack of insistence on those safety and health measures.

The end of the quota-setting Multi-Fiber Agreement in 2005, an international agreement designed to protect garment workers' jobs in North America and Europe, made Bangladesh's garment factories all the more attractive to multinational brand companies in their constant search for low-cost contractors. When the Geneva-based World Trade Organization ruled that the MFA gave unfair advantage to developed countries, Los Angeles and New York garment workers lost thousands of jobs (many of them held by immigrant women), while the global garment companies became freer to roam the world in search of low-cost production.[12]

Then in the early years of the twenty-first century, Chinese women garment workers, who had been calling wildcat strikes, succeeded in pressing for higher wages. This development added even more luster to Bangladesh's low-cost manufacturing. And at this gendered historical moment, Tazreen Fashions' factory burst into flames.

GENDER MATTERS

It is all too easy to tell this tale of globalized garments, money, and death as if gender politics do not matter. It is all too comfortable for many commentators to narrate the story of the Tazreen factory fire—and the other factory disasters that followed soon after, not only in Bangladesh, but also in Pakistan, Cambodia, South Korea, and Mexico—as if it does not matter that the majority of the dead and injured were women. Women may be mentioned, they may be photographed and filmed, yet they are rarely interviewed by mainstream journalists about their complex experiences of being women factory workers. Similarly, observers too often craft explanations and propose reforms as if there were nothing to be gained from exploring the workings of masculinities at the senior levels of the global and national business and political elites. Men are much more likely to be interviewed by journalists, but their experiences of developing masculinized business and political relationships are left uninvestigated.

This ease of ungendered telling and this comfort in crafting ungendered explanations are risky.

To rely simply on critiques of profit-maximizing, individualistic, lightly regulated, cost-suppressing global capitalist business practices and the worldview that drives them—called by commentators the "neoliberal economic model"—to describe and explain (and thus to prevent) future garment factory disasters is unreliable. To provide an alternative and more realistic political analysis of today's international garment industry, one must stay attentive to the appeals of the neoliberal model, and one must become a lot more curious about the lives of diverse women and the racialized, classed ideas about women as low-waged workers. Moreover, making women-as-garment-workers visible will make men-as-men visible as factory owners, global corporate executives, civil servants, union organizers, and politicians.[13]

The majority of people trapped in the Tazreen fire—and in most garment factory disasters, which are so common today around the world—were not merely "workers." They were *women* workers. To stay incurious about these women's experiences as women leaves journalists, scholars, human rights activists, and citizens unable to reliably explain how and why women's labor is made *cheap.*

No one's labor is automatically cheap. It has to be *made* cheap. It is the deliberate manipulation of ideas about girls and women, and of notions of femininity, that empowers those who try to cheapen women's labor.

Chobi Mahmud grew up in Tangail, Bangladesh's northern district. She migrated from her family's rural village when she was a teenager. As her country's garment industry expanded, its

workforce had become more feminized. Chobi entered the globalized garment workforce at a time when feminization of Bangladesh's garment industry had progressed significantly. What
had not been available to Chobi's mother had become available
to her. In 1990, women had constituted only 28 percent of all of
Bangladesh's garment workers. By contrast, in 2002, when Chobi
was nineteen and speaking to a journalist, women's proportion
of all Bangladesh's garment workers had grown to a remarkable
85 percent.[14]

That is, there was nothing "natural" about such a high proportion of women working in the twenty-first-century Bangladesh garment factories. It had been in part the result of male factory owners' coming to the realization that they could keep
wages low—and thus keep the factories globally attractive to
the executives of Nike, North Face, Walmart, Mango, H&M,
and Tommy Hilfiger—if they began to feminize their workforces, to hire more young women from poor rural villages.

But it had taken a second change for this gendered formula to
work: more and more young women in those villages had to
change their own ideas about what they could do with their lives
and to persuade their mothers and fathers to let them leave
home. Without this effective redefinition of girlhood and feminine respectability, the global brand-name companies would not
have migrated to Bangladesh.

Chobi, like most of these young factory women, was unmarried when she took a job in an urban factory. She and her fellow
sewers started to earn wages for their work. They gained a sense
of importance as they sent money back to their parents, who, in
turn, soon realized that their daughters were more likely to send
money home from their urban jobs than were their sons. With
this realization, parents became less likely to define a daughter's

goodness in terms of her marrying a young a man of their choosing. Not only did the women factory workers put off marriage, but when they did marry they also often managed to negotiate a new division of household labor with their husbands. If they continued to work and bring home money after they married, many of Chobi's women factory friends were able to persuade their husbands to start sharing in more of the housework. According to Mashuda Shefali Khatun, head of the Dhaka-based women's advocacy group Nari Uddug Kendra (Centre for Women's Initiatives), studies revealed that men married to women with paid jobs did more hours of housework than those men married to women without paid jobs.[15]

Many Bangladeshi women garment workers became acutely aware of the unfair, even dangerous, conditions under which they sewed seams, hems, and pockets—there were unclean toilets, long hours, poor ventilation, blocked stairways. When deciding whether to risk organizing and whether to risk taking part in protests, each woman garment worker had to weigh the gendered advantages of taking and keeping her paid factory job against her growing frustration at the exploitive collusion between an array of men: the global companies, their factory owners, and the local politicians who suppressed her wages, discouraged her organizing efforts, and endangered her health. That gendered calculus was fraught.

The Tazreen fire broke out at a particular moment in gendered local and international histories. Just as New York's Triangle Shirtwaist Factory fire of 1911 happened at a particular moment in the history of women's international migration and in the history of American women's suffrage organizing, so too the Tazreen fire of 2012 happened at a particular moment in transnational women's politics and in Bangladeshi women's own organizing. One popular racialized myth that has enabled the global companies and their local allies to cheapen women's labor holds that women on the social margins in affluent countries, and women living in poor countries, are less conscious of and less in need of their rights—or that they will pursue their rights only if tutored and led by more privileged women and men.

In reality, by 2012, Bangladeshi women's political thinking and organizing had become elaborate and sophisticated. Bangladesh's women activists had named, exposed, and campaigned against local men's acid-throwing intended to disfigure women and girls. Other women activists not only had taken part in microfinance schemes but also had begun to expose how those schemes, intended to economically empower poor women, too often empowered men and left the women recipients burdened by debt. Some women also had begun to challenge Bangladesh's male-dominated political parties and religious clergy. Local feminists were supporting those Bangladeshi women who now, after decades of silence, were defying the powerful notions of nationalist pride and feminized sexualized shame to publicly tell their stories of having survived rape during the 1971 war for independence.[16]

The politics of marriage, of parenting, of daughterhood, of women's friendships, of gendered divisions of paid and unpaid labor, of women's organizing, of feminized sexuality and silence—each of these politics is gendered. That is, each is shaped by acceptance of or resistance to certain ideas about femininity and masculinity. Those ideas are *political* insofar as they not only take power to legitimize and sustain but also take power to transform or debunk.

These ideas and the interlocking gendered politics they fuel are not timeless. They can be altered, sometimes only super-ficially, other times profoundly. Each one of these deeply gendered politics has been and continues to be a pillar of the international political economy of jeans, bikinis, dresses, sweatshirts, and tank tops. Making women visible is crucial to making reliable sense of the international politics of making women's labor *cheap.*

HOW IS WOMEN'S LABOR MADE *CHEAP?*

It is commonplace to speak of "cheap women's labor." The phrase is used in public policy discussions as if cheapness were somehow inherent in women's work—especially in the work of those women pushed to the societal and international margins.

Reality is quite different: women's work is only as unrewarded or as low-paid as it is *made* to be.

Feminist investigators are always on the lookout for decisions—and the people who make and enforce those decisions. The international political economy works the way it does in part because of the decisions that have cheapened the value of women's work, making it either unpaid or low paid. These decisions are made invisible, however, when they are dismissed as being not decisions at all but merely the result of "natural" processes. Imagining anything as "natural" takes it out of the realm of politics. A lot of what goes on in international politics is left underinvestigated because it is mistakenly assumed to be natural. One of the hallmarks of unfeminist commentaries on international politics is their underestimation of power.

Organizing factory jobs, designing machinery, and enforcing factory rules to keep women productive and feminized—these were crucial strategies devised by entrepreneurs and supportive government officials to launch Europe's nineteenth-century industrial revolution. Industrialized textile production and garment-making were central to Britain's rise to global power. Male entrepreneurs in industries deliberately feminized labor in order to make it profitable and internationally competitive. Investors and officials in other countries learned the British lesson in order to compete in the emerging global political economy and to ward off foreign control. That is, lessons in feminizing industrial labor were traded across national borders. The making of the "mill girl" proved crucial in not only imperial but also anti-imperial efforts. American male textile investors, postcolonial businessmen, traveled from Boston to England's textile factories to learn the gendered industrializing formula in the early decades of the nineteenth century.[17] Japanese male entrepreneurs, backed by their government's Meiji reformers who were determined to resist Western colonization, also chose young rural women as their first industrial workers.[18] In industrializing czarist Russia, owners of new textile factories steadily increased the proportion of women workers, with government approval. A half century and a revolution later, in the 1970s, women still constituted 93 percent of all Soviet sewing-machine operators.[19]

Feminization, however, has never been as easy to sustain as mainstream historians, limited by their lack of gender curiosity, have made it appear to be. Mothers and fathers have had to be persuaded to let their daughters leave home and delay marriage. Women textile workers and garment workers themselves frequently have been hard to control, shrugging off, even laughing derisively at, their employers' lectures to them on Victorian feminine propriety.[20] Sometimes women have walked out on strike, whether or not male union leaders advised it. It has taken managers', parents', and officials' threats, coercion, enticements, and revised legal structures to bring factory women back into line.

Furthermore, industrial productivity and profit-maximizing goals have frequently contradicted prevailing cultural norms of femininity. On those occasions, government economic strategists, industrialists, technology engineers, and their media supporters have had to find ways to deny, or at least defuse, the gendered ideological awkwardness. For example, in the mid-nineteenth century the sewing machine, so central to the industrialization of garment making, set off both liberated women's cheers and sexualized patriarchal alarm.

The sewing machine initially was praised by feminists. It drew crowds when it was demonstrated at the 1851 exposition in London and at the 1855 exposition in Paris.[21] Thomas Cook's guided tourists were among the throngs who heard the sewing machine being heralded as woman's liberator. It symbolized progress: technology was a liberator. Countries whose women had access to sewing machines could congratulate themselves on their women's freedom from the sort of physical toil that characterized the benighted societies crowded at the bottom of the imperial ladder.

While women were encouraged to see the sewing machine as a liberating home appliance, male entrepreneurs were purchasing the machines in bulk for women who would work in their factories. The sewing machine allowed company owners to break down the process of making a dress or a pair of pants into discrete operations and thus impose a rationalized factory system on the seamstresses: each woman would sew only a small part of the garment—a sleeve, a tuck, a back pocket. The garment-factory owner could pay employees by the piece, rather than by the hour or by the entire finished product. This, in turn, allowed manufacturers to transform the makers of garments: they were no longer seen as skilled artisans; henceforth they could be imagined as mere interchangeable employees. This allowed male factory owners to free themselves of artisan men, who thought of their labor as worth more compensation and who were less likely to submit to supervisory control. That is, the rise of the industrialized garment and textile factories required a denigration of one form of masculinity, the masculinized artisan. Moreover, the piece-rate pay system instituted in the feminized factories increased competitiveness between women workers themselves, diluting their sense of solidarity and thus extending a factory manager's control over the entire production process.

The sewing machine, though, had its detractors. Just like the bicycle, the sewing machine, so central to the industrialization of garment making, was thought by many to jeopardize a woman's sexual purity. In French towns large numbers of women, employed by the 1860s to work sewing machines, complained of fatigue and ill health. Eugène Guibout, a Parisian male physician, reported to the Société Médicale des Hospitaux in 1866 that he believed that the extended use of the machine produced extensive vaginal discharges, sometimes hemorrhages, and extreme genital excitement, due to rubbing of the thighs during operation of the double-pedal mechanism that then powered the machines used in industrial production. The debate spilled over to Germany and Italy. Some male scientists were less alarmed than Dr. Guibout, but they, too, raised their eyebrows at the potentially masturbatory effects of the bipedal sewing machine. There was palpable relief in international medical circles when a single-pedal machine was introduced. Still, it was not until the advent of the electrically powered sewing machine in the next century that the controversy over the sewing machine's sexual consequences was laid to rest.[22]

BLUE JEANS ARE HISTORICAL:
EXPLORING YOUR GLOBAL CLOSET

Any piece of clothing has its own gendered international political history.

The story of jeans is usually told as if it were an ungendered story, full of male actors, but told without any curiosity about either masculinities or the lives of women. For instance: San Francisco wholesale goods merchant Levi Strauss and his partner, tailor Jacob Davis, invented jeans (a term derived from a cotton material first developed in Genoa, Italy) in 1873 by using tough denim cotton (a refinement of the Genoa material created by textile makers in Nîmes, France, thus "de Nîmes") and adding the now-distinctive copper rivets to reinforce the pant seams. The earliest jeans were sewn by tailors, who were considered artisans. Soon jeans became a popular clothing choice for working men in California and beyond. To meet the demand and maximize profits, denim jeans became a factory product, making Levi Strauss one of the titans of a globalizing garment industry.[23]

Alternatively, telling the more realistic, gendered, ongoing story of globalized blue jeans makes the masculinities of gold miners and artisan tailors, the femininities of women as industrial workers, and feminized respectability more visible. The gendered political story also makes men's efforts to control women's labor more central. As Levi's blue jeans moved from being an artisan product to being an industrial product, the company's sewing workforce became feminized. Commercial success came to depend less on manly artisanal skill and more on the cheapening of feminized piecework labor.

You can start your own international, gendered, blue-jeans historical research by going into your closet. Bring out all the

268 / Women's Labor is Never Cheap

blue jeans (and black jeans too) and spread them out according to their age. Are all of them, from the oldest faded pairs with threadbare knees to the new ones not yet broken in, made of 100 percent cotton? Today, China, India, the United States, Pakistan, Uzbekistan, and Brazil are the largest producers of raw cotton, prompting one to wonder about women's roles and men's roles in each of these countries' cotton cultivation.[24] Now look at the labels inside each pair of your jeans: list the countries where the jeans were sewn. Try to remember in what year you bought each pair of jeans. You are on your way to charting blue jeans' historical and international politically gendered patterns.

Levi Strauss maintained factories in the United States for longer than many large brand-name clothing companies. It also resisted outsourcing its production to contractors for longer than many of its competitors. At the same time, however, Levi's senior executives were hostile to workers joining independent unions. Before it followed other clothing companies in moving its operations abroad, the company moved its factories to the American South and Southwest, regions whose conservative state legislators made it hard for workers to form unions. By the early 1980s, El Paso, Texas, had become known locally as "the jeans capital of the world."

The majority of American workers sewing Levi's in the 1980s, using its telltale orange thread, were Latina women, women who at the time were politically marginalized in American society and voiceless in federal politics.[25] But already Latinas were being displaced by overseas workers. The company's feminized, racialized U.S. production formula proved unable to match the Levi's executives' profit expectations. By 2004, Levi's had moved all its manufacturing out of the United States—to the Philippines, China, Indonesia, and Turkey—closing its last remaining

Figure 26. Filipina sewing Levi Strauss jeans, Manila, in the 1980s. Photo by the author.

U.S. factory, in San Antonio, Texas.[26] The production location changed, the ethnicities and nationalities of its workers changed; but Levi's executives continued to prefer women as the back-bone of its manufacturing workforce.

Thus, looking at the labels stitched inside one's historicized clothes to see their country of manufacture is a useful first step in a feminist investigation of your global closet. But a label will not reveal the genders or ethnicities of those who designed, cut, sewed, pressed, packed, and marketed that pair of jeans—or

which of these workers was paid a living wage. The label, furthermore, will not spell out which national and international
masculinized alliances were forged to keep the sewers' wages
low or what each sewer thinks about her low wages. The label
also will not tell you whether the door to the factory workshop
opened inward. For all this crucial information, you will have to
dig deeper.

In the late 1970s, emerging women's movements in a host of
countries were altering many women's notions of what it meant
to be "feminine" and "respectable." American and European
women of all social classes began to wear jeans—"designer jeans"
to distinguish them from what male miners and dockworkers
wore. The most popular blue jeans were all-cotton denim.
Women consumers redefined feminine respectability at a time
when garment companies were looking further afield for labor
they could cheapen.

Between 1970 and 1986, the International Ladies Garment
Workers Union, one of the then-two major unions in the U.S.
garment industry, lost more than 200,000 members. The cause
was easy to spot: production of women's and children's clothes
in the United States had dropped by more than 50 percent. Still,
the New York metropolitan area remained home to thousands of
women and men working in garment factories: as late as 1986, the
union, with its mainly male leadership and overwhelmingly
female rank and file, had 75,400 New York members.[27]

"Deindustrialization" was a source of political anxiety, since
industrial decline meant the laying off of male factory workers in
steel and automobile towns such as Pittsburgh, Birmingham, and
Detroit—and presumably because, in the minds of many male
elected officials, it was only high male unemployment that could
create a societal crisis. By contrast, American garment workers'

earlier economic hardships and the international transforma-
tions they reflected were easier for officials to overlook because
most garment workers were women, many of them immigrant
urban or poor rural women. Furthermore, women's need for
decently paid employment still looked to these masculinized
policy makers like a societal aberration. Women losing paid
work was not, for the policy makers, a cause for political alarm.

THE BENETTON MODEL: GLOBALIZING
HOMEWORK IN THE 1980S

As Levi Strauss and other U.S. garment companies moved their
factories south and hired more rural white women and African
American and Latina women to sew their products, British companies looked to Black and Asian British women. Many of these
women were recent arrivals from the Caribbean, Pakistan, and
Bangladesh and were vulnerable to isolation in seasonal employment at low pay with minimum benefits and maximum health
hazards. Large British retailers such as Marks and Spencer,
which in the 1980s sold one-fifth of all garments bought in Britain, decided to become "manufacturers without factories." Their
managers began farming out contracts to smaller garment producers, who in turn hired workers or employed another layer of
subcontractors. Many of them hired women to sew in their own
homes. The industrial homeworker was not new, but now she
became globalized.[28]

Although the women homeworkers were paid low wages,
received few health or pension benefits, and had to cover their
own electricity bills, these new home-based working arrangements often appealed to women caring for their own young
children. Taking in sewing meant women did not have to choose

between motherhood and paid work, while the women's fathers or husbands found the work arrangement reassuring since their wives and daughters would be shielded from the harsh racist realities—and, perhaps these men imagined, the immoral temptations—of British industrial society. The sexual and racial politics of postimperial British immigration were woven into blouses destined for Marks and Spencer. One Asian British woman homeworker explained in the 1980s:

> When you live in Newham [in the East End of London], you have little choice, sister. Burning down of an Asian home does not even make news any longer.... How can I look for jobs outside my home in such a situation? I want to remain invisible, literally.
>
> Also, sister, I am a widow and I really do not know what my legal status is.... At the moment, my uncle brings machining work to my home. It works out to be 50 pence per hour, not great! But I earn and I feed my children somehow. Most of all, I do not have to deal with the fear of racist abuse in this white world.[29]

By 2010, however, Marks and Spencer had reduced its reliance on British Asian homeworkers, instead joining other large, brand-name garment retailers in moving many of its manufacturing operations to Bangladesh.

It was in the 1990s that Benetton became a fashionable, admired, and globally successful garment company. Its headquarters were in northern Italy, a region of farms and small towns whose prosperous industrial companies earned it the nickname of "the Third Italy": "[Luciano] Benetton, whose leonine curling gray-brown hair and horn-rimmed glasses are familiar to millions of Italians from endless photographs in the press, was dressed in his usual assortment of casual clothes: voluminous khaki pants, brown L.L. Bean-style oxfords, a tweed jacket, and a shirt with a button-down collar.... [He was

on his way to do something that] excited him more than anything else in life: the opening of a Benetton store in a 'remote,
almost unbelievable' part of the world. We were going that
morning to attend a Benetton opening in Prague."[30]

Benetton was admired for its stylish designs, its bold interracial advertising images, and its ability to change fashions as
rapidly as fickle consumers changed their tastes. This corporate
formula depended on *flexibility:* Benetton had to be able to
employ advanced computer technology to redesign patterns at a
moment's notice. Simultaneously, maximizing flexibility meant
Benetton's executives had to be able to call on small-scale local
sewing workshops to change their products faster than most big
companies could, all the while keeping prices low enough to
enable Benetton to stay ahead of mass retailers.

The solution: Italian family-based subcontractors hiring Italian women to work in their homes or in small, nonunionized
workshops. Although in the mid-1980s, Benetton had eight plants
of its own in northern Italy, these operations employed only two
thousand of the company's eight thousand garment workers.
Most of the Italian women who then depended on Benetton for
their livelihood did not work directly for the company. This was
one of the secrets of a successful—that is, profitable—corporate
model designed to maximize fashion flexibility. When the company conducted tours for visiting reporters, it did not take them
to the small, nonunionized shops clustered around Benetton's
impressive new plants, even though those small subcontractors
performed about 40 percent of Benetton's knitting and 60 percent of the garment assembly. If one took a tour of a garment
factory in northern Italy today, one would walk though a factory
where most of the low-paid, nonunionized sewers and cutters
were not Italian; today they are Chinese immigrants.[31]

Teenage girls, who by the 1980s had been turned into a prime consumer market, began to adopt the "Benetton look." With their apparent postnationalist "colors of the world" advertising campaign, Benetton executives set out to create a style that could dissolve national borders. Benetton was preparing Europe's adolescents for the expansion of the multinational European Union. This apparent globalizing, postnationalist consumer campaign relied on a domesticated, isolated, and feminized workforce.

By 2013, however, Benetton executives had subcontracted some of the company's production to Bangladesh, to factories whose women workers were also sewing clothes for Marks and Spencer, Zara, Walmart, and the Gap.

THE BANKER AND THE SEAMSTRESS

Nike was a pioneer in shedding its factories. When Nike's Oregon-based male executives decided to rely on subcontractor factory-owners overseas, they chose South Korea. The government was friendly. In the 1970s, South Korea's government was deeply militarized; it was also tightly bound to the United Sates by a military alliance and was hosting fifty thousand American troops on scores of U.S. bases. To the Nike executives, this Cold War arrangement made South Korea seem a good bet for investment. But then came the South Koreans' successful popular pro-democracy movement of the mid-1980s, a movement in which women as university students and as factory workers played vital political roles. When South Korea's new civilian democratic political system replaced the military regime, and both the local women's movement and labor unions became more influential, Nike's executives ended their contracts with Korean

factories and moved—with their Korean male subcontractors—
to Indonesia and elsewhere. Rural, migrant, young Indonesian
women thereafter became a crucial part of the global profit formula for Nike—and Puma, Adidas, and Reebok.[32]

By the start of the twenty-first century, garment factories had
become part of the local landscape in countries that otherwise
appeared politically dissimilar. Each pair of jeans, each blouse
or bikini, was sewn, that is, with threads of particular gendered
political hues. For instance, under apartheid, the white-domi-
nated South African government officials had encouraged foreign companies to set up shop in Bantustans, a territorial scheme
intended to bolster apartheid and the fiction of self-sustaining
Black "homelands." Companies from Hong Kong, Taiwan, and
Israel accepted Pretoria's invitation.[33] For their part, in 1986,
Vietnamese Communist government officials adopted a new
probusiness policy, called Doi Moi, to jump-start their country's
postwar economy. Within several decades, the resultant govern-
ment-promoted system would be described as the "generally
opaque world of Vietnamese manufacturing with layers of contractors and subcontractors" that produced clothing and sneakers for the international market.[34] Meanwhile, in Fiji, the government compensated for a long-term slump in world sugar
prices and a sharp fall in tourism revenues following a military
coup by enticing Australian and New Zealand garment companies to set up factories with a special offer intended to undercut
Fiji's Asian neighbors. Fijian officials hoped that Fijian women's
sewing could paper over the problems caused by a weakened
plantation economy, interethnic strife, and militarization.[35]

The international politics of garments stretched from the
women at their sewing machines stitching the tricky pant-
leg seam of a pair of blue jeans, to the men in boardrooms and

ministerial offices drafting memos on loans and investments. Bankers, both in private banks and in international banking agencies such as the World Bank and the International Monetary Fund, have been prime movers in the globalization of the garment industry and its deliberate reliance on low-paid feminized workforces. Bankers, however, do not talk with, much less bargain with, women sewing-machine operators. Bankers deal with corporate executives and with government officials, especially those men who dominate their countries' finance ministries.

These dealings take place behind closed doors and are often tense, and they also are usually masculinized. We know all too little about how the workings of diverse masculinities shape these important financial dealings. We do know that the outcomes not only determine women's lives but also depend on controlling women's lives. Bankers have tied their government and company loans to their borrowers' ability to promote internationally competitive garment exports. It has been a loan condition that has proved hard to meet without government officials and manufacturing executives taking deliberate steps to suppress the costs of manufacturing labor—that is, women's labor

Lending and stitching—the two activities have become globally interdependent. Each has become a process reliant on bolstering gendered assumptions and gendered relationships: while the floors of the exporting garment factories remain feminized, the boardrooms of international lenders remain masculinized.[36]

Risk taking has been at the core of the masculinized conception of banking. Just as travel to "exotic" regions was once imagined to be a risky and therefore peculiarly masculine form of adventure, so today manly risk-taking is thought by many financiers to be integral to the globalized financial industry and to manly banking. The value assigned to risk taking, furthermore, has become even greater since governments eagerly deregulated banking in the 1990s and the beginning of the twenty-first century. Widespread banking deregulation made a distinctly American, masculinized style of banking more popular in Britain, Ireland, Iceland, Spain, Greece, and Japan. This transnational masculinized banking style also helped sustain cooperative relations between otherwise fiercely competitive male bankers. It is a shared masculinized risk-taking style that makes their "world." It also has helped keep women, allegedly more risk averse than "manly men," on the margins of this "ceaselessly competitive" financial world.

Thousands of women today do work in global banking. They provide banking's crucial support services; but only occasionally do women gain promotions to the still-masculinized senior policy positions. In the United States, for instance, women constitute a mere 16 percent of all banking executives. Among those women trying to gain senior promotions into banks' higher echelons, where long hours and constant travel are unquestioned requisites for proving one's corporate commitment, the stubborn conventional politics of marriage and the politics of motherhood reinforce the masculinized character of the executive suites.[37]

The banking industry's masculinized structure and culture would persist up to and even after the disastrous financial crash of 2008. By the later phases of the global financial crash, more women were making careers in the financial industry, some rising to middle management. Nonetheless, by 2013, no woman yet had served as head of one of the European Union's Central Banks, as president of the World Bank, as secretary of the U.S.

Treasury, or as chancellor of the exchequer in Britain. Only in 2011 was the first woman—Christine Lagarde—chosen to head the International Monetary Fund. Only in 2014 was the first woman—Janet Yellen—appointed to the powerful post of chair of the U.S. Federal Reserve. And each of these breakthroughs was in large measure a response to concerted political pressure. By themselves, they are not proof that the patriarchal conventions of global banking have been radically subverted.[38]

The masculinization of international banking has been politically costly. It has destabilized governments, distorted public priorities, undermined inclusive democracy, and widened the gaps between rich and poor. Many European and developing countries carry huge international debts and are scarcely able to keep up with the astronomical interest payments owed to their foreign creditors, much less to repay the principal. But Japanese, British, German, American, and other large lenders and their governments fear that global default would topple the international political economy that has been so carefully constructed in the years since World War II. So lenders and their allies press debtor governments make good on their mammoth debts. The most popular package of loan conditions—"structural adjustment"—combines cuts in a debtor government's expenditures on "nonproductive" public services (transport and food subsidies, health services, and education) with the expansion of exports: locally mined raw materials, locally grown plantation crops, or locally manufactured goods. Among the latter are garments. Unless they remain globally competitive in the export of garments, many of these indebted governments cannot pay off their international debts.

The centerpiece of the bankers' export strategy has been the export-processing zone. Indebted governments were encouraged by economists to set aside territory specifically for factories producing goods for the international market. Governments were to entice overseas companies to move their factories to these zones by offering to provide them with electricity, ports, and runways, as well as low-cost workers, and by offering tax holidays and police protection. Most attractive of all has been the governments' promise to provide "cheap labor." It should not be surprising that in most export-processing zones—in Sri Lanka, the Philippines, El Salvador, Nicaragua, and Panama—at least 70 percent of the workers are women.

The risk-taking globalized banker needs the conscientious seamstress to hold his world together. The local patriarchal politician and his financial advisors need the seamstress to keep the banker pacified. If the seamstress rebels, radically reimagining what it means to be a female citizen who sews for a living, her country may turn up on the bankers' list of "poor investments."

PATRIARCHY IS NOT OLD-FASHIONED

Garment-company managers have continued to rely on four patriarchal assumptions to help them keep women's wages low in their factories. First, they have defined sewing as something that girls and women do "naturally" or "traditionally." An operation that a person does "naturally" is not a "skill," because a skill is something one has to be trained to do, for which one should then be rewarded. In reality, many a schoolgirl has struggled through her home economics class trying in vain to make the required skirt or apron. One garment-factory manager explained that he preferred to hire young Filipino women who did *not* know how to sew, so that "we don't have to undo the bad habits they've learned."[39] But the myth of women as "natural" sewers persists and is used by factory managers to deflate women garment workers' actual skills, thereby reducing their wages. Women sewing machinists have gone out on strike to force company executives to categorize their jobs as "skilled" jobs.[40]

Second, women's labor can be made and kept *cheap* by reserving allegedly skilled jobs for men. Women, the "natural" sewers, are assigned to the sewing machines; men are hired by managers to be the cutters and the pressers and to run specialized equipment, such as the zipper inserter. Workers who cut and press fabric and install zippers are paid more than those who sew. The managerial argument that running specialized machinery and pressing require the physical strength that only men have and skills that only men can learn ignores the technological options available and the physical demands made on women by housework and farming, while conveniently also overlooking the fact that some men are weaker and slower learners than some women.

Third, factory owners and managers justify paying women workers less than men, and less than a living wage, by imagining that women are merely secondary wage earners in their families. They prefer to ignore (most of the time) the reality that the rural parents of their young female employees have come to depend on the money that those young women, as "dutiful daughters," send home. Simultaneously, however, managers strategically manipulate the daughterly expectations when they try to persuade the women not to jeopardize their jobs by going out on strike. Executives of global apparel corporations take comfort in the outdated assumption that men—as fathers and husbands—are still the breadwinners. In the 1990s, feminists working inside, and lobbying from outside, powerful international agencies persuaded their economists and development experts to see that their "men-as-breadwinners" assumption was out of touch with economic reality.[41] The assumption that men are breadwinners had been a boon to generations of garment-factory managers. Still today it is an erroneous assumption that allows managers to rationalize paying their women workers *as if* those women were being financially supported at home by a man.

In reality, divorce, abandonment, recession, AIDS, war, and separation have caused marked increases in the numbers of women who are the chief income earners—often the sole income earners—for their households. They support not only their own children but also the children of relatives, as well as elderly or impoverished parents. In 2006, outside of western Europe and North America, women were the heads of 25 percent or more of all households in Vietnam, Hong Kong, Lesotho, Namibia, Zimbabwe, Kenya, Burundi, Tanzania, Brazil, Peru, Venezuela, Colombia, El Salvador, Costa Rica, Nicaragua, Haiti, and Dominican Republic, to name only a few.[42]

Factory owners' and global clients' fourth self-serving claim is that the single woman at her machine, working eleven hours a day, six days a week, is not a "serious" member of the labor force because she intends to work only until she finds a husband and "settles down," thereafter to be supported by him. Consequently, so the modern managerial ideology of marriage goes, the single woman employee does not need to be paid as if she were a career worker: when she is sewing a collar for Gap or a back pocket for Levi's, she is just going through "a phase." When male labor union leaders also share this same vision—that women's chief and lasting vocation is to be a good wife—the prospects for women's collective action grow even dimmer.

Thus keeping women's labor cheap requires patriarchal power. Cheapening women's labor requires alliances, vigilance, and daily effort. That effort is an integral part of what is called today's "international political economy." Factory managers alone cannot keep women's labor cheap: it takes a combination of willing allies—fathers and husbands, media producers, local and national officials, police forces, global executives, labor activists—holding and promoting patriarchal ideas. That is, the profits and tax revenues earned by businesses and governments rely on the perpetuation of certain ideas about skills, marriage, dutiful daughters, child care, feminine respectability, and fashion. The politics of the global garment industry are sustained by these patriarchal ideas, which maintain gendered relationships inside homes, within communities, and in and between governments, as well as on the factory floor.

To make feminist sense of the international politics of bankers and blue jeans—and dresses, sneakers, sweatshirts, and football uniforms—requires investigating a wide range of interlocking gendered mind-sets and multiple political sites, as well as finding out who gains what from the perpetuation of those particular beliefs.

LIGHT INDUSTRY, HEAVY INDUSTRY: WHERE ARE THE WOMEN? WHERE ARE THE MEN?

The people who run the firms most dependent on human labor to produce their products are the ones most eager to pay as little as possible for human labor. The more a firm can minimize that dependence on human labor, the less preoccupied its managers will be with cutting labor costs. Nowadays the kinds of industries that are most labor-intensive are called "light industries." Those that are least labor-intensive are called "heavy industries." Light industries and heavy industries also differ in their respective mixes of human labor and capital equipment—furnaces, turbines, computers, robots, looms, sewing machines—each needs to turn out a profitable product.

Because it is more labor-intensive and less reliant on large infusions of capital, a light industry is also less likely to be concentrated in the hands of just a few owners: there are many more players in any light-industry market than in any heavy-industry market. This makes light industries more decentralized and more globally intensely competitive. That has made the gendered international politics of garments different from, say, the gendered international politics of steel.

The intensity of the global competition within a light industry heightens owners' and managers' determination to keep labor costs as low as possible. Cutting labor costs is seen as one of the chief strategies for beating one's rivals. The globalized garment industry's decentralization—especially when the global "supply chain" includes layers of suppliers and subcontractors—makes it hard for labor advocates to monitor company abuses and for even a committed government to effectively implement worker safety laws. It is much easier to hide an illegal garment factory than to conceal an illegal automobile plant. U.S. Supreme Court justice Sonia Sotomayor, the first Latina appointed to the country's highest court, recently recalled her childhood visits in the 1950s to her Aunt Aurora's garment-sewing workplace in the Bronx neighborhood of New York City. Young Sonia was puzzled to see that, even on summer days when the workshop was "steaming hot, dark, and airless," the windows "were painted black and the door shut tight." She asked innocently why her aunt and her

Puerto Rican female workmates did not complain, but she was told not to be curious, that it was just the way it had to be. That is, her aunt and her fellow employees were low-waged sewers employed in an illegal, off-the-books factory.[43]

"Light industries" are those that have been the most feminized, while "heavy industries" have been those most masculinized. This distinction does not mean that no men work in garment factories—they do, as cutters, zipper-machine operators, pressers, packers, and supervisors. Nor does it mean that no women work in heavy industries such as automobile manufacture or shipbuilding. They do. Rather, to describe light industries as "feminized" is to say that the management prefers to hire women for the majority of its workers, and that patriarchal assumptions about conventional femininity shape labor-management relations. Likewise, to say that heavy industries are "masculinized" is to say that managers presume that most of the industry's jobs are allegedly best done by men, and that patriarchal presumptions about manliness shape the dominant culture in its labor-management relations. Thus, one can do a gender-smart feminist analysis of the international automobile, steel, and shipbuilding industries, just as one can conduct a gender-smart feminist investigation of the global garment, toy, or electronics industry. Here are some of today's industries commonly thought of as falling under one of the two main categories:

Light Industries	*Heavy Industries*
Textiles	Steel
Garments	Aluminum
Food processing	Automobiles (including armored vehicles)
Cigarettes	Chemicals and petrochemicals

Toys	Machinery manufacture
Shoes	Mining
Electronics	Petrochemicals
Data entry	Aircraft and aerospace
(e.g., insurance, airline reservations)	
Small weapons	Shipbuilding
(e.g., pistols, rifles, grenade launchers)	

Beyond merely comparing light and heavy industries, we need to chart the political relationships between them. Those political relationships are gendered and determine how much influence women and men each have in their countries' affairs. Brazil has both heavy and light industries today; so does India, China, the United States, Britain, Canada, South Africa, Sweden, Japan, Russia, France, Poland, and South Korea. *If* women are popularly seen mainly as mothers, as temporary or part-time employees, and as unskilled workers, and *if* women do not have influence inside the unions that allegedly represent them—or if they have no unions at all—and *if* women are not considered serious allies or opponents by men in government ministries or political parties, *then* it will be especially difficult for women working in a light industry to hold their own in the political arena. Put another way, the influence that nonelite men who work in the mining, shipbuilding, aerospace, automobile, steel, or petrochemical industries can collectively bring to bear on their countries' political systems not only privileges heavy industry but also privileges masculinity. And this masculinized political influence undercuts women workers bunched together in light industry.

Graduating from garments to steel supposedly elevates a country's global status. Developing a country's own heavy—masculinized—industry bestows seriousness on that country and its officials: the country is imagined to have "arrived": its officials can join the Big Boys. They can seek entrance into the Group of Twenty and the even more exclusive Group of Eight. Officials of governments in South Korea and Mexico, and more recently in Brazil, Russia, India, China, and South Africa—known as the five BRICS countries—all of which have developed masculinized heavy industries, express pride in their elevated international status. Simultaneously, their counterparts in "mature" countries such as the United States, Britain, Japan, and France worry that they are losing their grip on their own masculinized elite global stature because of the relative declines of their steel, shipbuilding, aircraft, and automobile industries.

When political commentators accord the concerns of their countries' steel, aircraft, or automobile companies the seriousness reserved for issues of "national security," they are further entrenching the marginalization of women's paid work and the masculinization of international politics.

These are general gendered patterns. They are significant. They have national and international causes and consequences. Still, each garment factory, and all the men who own them and all the women and men who work inside them, exist in particular times and places. No garment factories and no women sewing machinists float above the ground, outside of history. We, each of us, live in history, and we think and act in particular times and places. Conducting a feminist investigation of any garment factory requires us to take into account these general patterns and the particulars of time and place. Abstraction is never sufficient.

SOUTH KOREA: WHO PAYS THE PRICE FOR
BECOMING A "TIGER"?

In 1982, as South Korean government officials were promoting their country for selection as the site of the 1988 Olympics, some commentators were talking about the "two Koreas." They did not mean North and South. They were referring to the South Korea of large, capitalized heavy industries and the South Korea of smaller garment, sneaker, and electronics assembly plants.

Korean women had begun working in factories as early as 1910.[44] But in 1970 a military ruler, Chung Hee Park, and his masculinist militarized regime launched a deliberate campaign to persuade mothers and fathers that letting their daughters leave home, delay marriage, and work in South Korea's export factories was not only good for their families but also good for the nation.[45] By the 1980s, women made up an estimated two-thirds of workers in the "second" South Korea. They were working more hours per week than their male counterparts, doing more housework, and being paid on average one-third less.

Women producing clothes, electronics, and shoes enabled South Korean businessmen to accumulate enough capital to launch their own heavy-industry companies, to become recognized globally as an emergent economic "tiger." That is, it took the cheapening of women's light-industry labor to fund the country's more prestigious heavy industry—and its elite's confidence in making a successful bid to host the Olympics.

It was a factory fire that underscored the cost of this particular national development strategy. In March 1988, as stairway doors remained locked and exits blocked by piles of just-finished sweaters, a fire tore through the Green Hill Textile Company. Its small factory was squeezed between a billiard parlor, a restaurant, and a church in a dormitory community outside Seoul. In its ashes were charred sewing machines, smoke-blackened piles of timber and cinder, and the meager keepsakes of women who had worked and died there: a snapshot of a young girl smiling in a field of red flowers, a magazine clipping about a popular singer, a letter from a young man in the army. Twenty-two young women died.[46]

Lee Pung Won, Green Hill's forty-four-year-old factory owner, a subcontractor for Japanese and European electronics corporations, was considered a good employer, one who treated his workers "more like a family." Most of his employees were young single Korean women who had come from the countryside to the city in the hope of finding a waged job. They were paid approximately $1.75 per hour by Lee Pung Won, who expected them to work fifty-seven hours a week. In this, their lives were similar to those of other Korean women working in nearby factories producing shoes and televisions for export. When the factory received a big order from one of its global clients, as often happened also in the seasonal garment trade, Lee Pung Won expected the women to work even longer hours. The global corporate client did not care how its deadline was met.[47]

Many South Korean women factory workers went on strike in the 1980s, joining with middle-class prodemocracy university students. Together, they brought down the authoritarian military government (a government that was a close military ally of the United States); this was the very regime that had so enthusiastically sought to transform the nationalist idea of the "dutiful daughter." The factory women knew they were jeopardizing both heir jobs and their reputations as respectable, marriageable young women by taking part in this rebellious prodemocracy action.[48] Today, twenty-five years after the Green Hill Textile fire and the military regime's fall, South Korea's women's movement has gained significant political influence by bringing together middle-class women activists and factory-women activists to press for a gender-fair form of democratization. They have pushed through the legislature reforms to undo some of the most patriarchal impacts of family law and labor law.

But the influence of the South Korean women's movement recently has been jeopardized by the decline of the country's light industries (many Korean male entrepreneurs moved their subcontracting factories to Indonesia, Vietnam, Bangladesh, and China after the fall of South Korea's military regime), as well as by recession-fueled nationalist efforts to bolster patriarchal family roles, and by the reemergence of a popular preoccupation with the country's militarized national security. The 2013 election of South Korea's first woman president, Park Geun-hye, leader of a conservative party and daughter of the country's last military ruler, has done little to empower Korean feminists or the country's women factory workers.[49]

MEXICO: AN EARTHQUAKE WAS ONLY THE BEGINNING

At 7:19 on the morning of September 19, 1985, Mexico City experienced one of North America's worst earthquakes. It left thousands of people homeless, modern office buildings cracked and useless, and Mexico's long-ruling Institutionalized Revolutionary Party, popularly called "the PRI," badly shaken. For the seamstresses who worked in the factories clustered in the neighborhood of San Antonio Abad, the earthquake marked a political and personal turning point. It destroyed an estimated eight hundred small garment factories in Mexico City that morning, killing over a thousand garment workers and leaving another forty thousand without jobs.[50]

Women who were just arriving for work as the quake shook Mexico City stood looking at the rubble that an hour before had been their source of livelihood. It was a Thursday, payday. Many of them were single mothers. Standing outside, their first thoughts, though, were of the women who had started work at 7 A.M. and were now trapped inside the flattened buildings. Their factory managers usually kept the factory windows closed and doors locked to stop women from taking work breaks or stealing materials, so few of the workers inside had had any chance of escaping. Some buildings held up to fifty different garment companies, several per floor. The floors and cement pillars on which they rested could hardly have been expected to hold the weight of heavy, industrial sewing machines and tons of fabric, though no government inspector had complained. Most companies were small subcontractors that sold to international company clients. Though not as well-known as the more visible maquiladoras strung along the U.S.-Mexican border, these Mexico City firms were part of the Mexican government's policy of using not just offshore oil but also tourism and light-industry exports to pay off its spiraling international debt. By 1986, foreign-owned and joint-venture factories such as those in the crowded San Antonio Abad neighborhood had displaced tourism as the country's second-largest source of foreign exchange.[51]

When women tried to climb over the debris to rescue their coworkers trapped inside, hastily mobilized government soldiers pushed them back. Cranes and soldiers, following company owners' instructions, began to pull away piles of fallen cement so that the factories' machinery could be retrieved. Employees still standing in the sun on the other side of the ropes watched with mounting indignation as their bosses and the government's soldiers rescued sewing machines before women workers.

In the past, Mexican factory women who had tried to organize were fired, while other women eschewed unions for fear of jeopardizing the paychecks on which their families relied. Even those women activists willing to risk being fired had had to face resentful male partners who did not understand why the women stayed after work to attend meetings. Then, too, left-wing opposition parties had paid scant attention to women working in small sweatshops; these male unionists courted the politically more influential male oil workers. Mexican feminists were active, but they were mostly middle-class women who scarcely understood the priorities of poor women with only primary-school educations.

Now, standing outside the collapsed factory buildings, growing angry at what they were witnessing, women began to talk and to act. Some women spontaneously moved to block the trucks that were about to carry off the owners' precious machines. Other women confronted the owners to demand their paychecks. When the male owners shrugged, women began to shout: "Compensation! Compensation!" Several dozen women decided that they would stay at the site overnight to prevent the army trucks from moving and the owners from leaving. Staying overnight meant neglecting male partners and children who expected them at home.

At about this time, middle-class women from feminist groups in Mexico City arrived at the sites of collapsed buildings to offer assistance. Afterward, looking back, some garment workers remembered that the feminists seemed to be urging the women workers to organize a union. But the garment workers calculated

Figure 27. Mexican garment worker, in 1985, sewing a banner that reads, "We Demand the Right to Unionize." Photo: Marco A. Cruz/ Imagenlatina.

that if they did form an independent union, one not affiliated to the ruling PRI's powerful labor federation, maybe the government would retaliate, further alienating their bosses, who then would never give them the cash they were due. And what about their *compañeros*, their male partners? Would they feel threatened if women began to take their working conditions so seriously? The feminists stepped back and instead donated typewriters and used their contacts with the city's media to publicize the women workers' demands.

The Mexican garment workers did decide to launch their own union, keeping it independent of all political parties and naming it the September 19th Garment Workers Union. The activists set up child-care centers, held the first-ever public discussions about domestic violence, and tried to persuade their male partners that it was not sexual disloyalty for the women to devote some of their time to the union. By 1987, the union had gained workers' support and official recognition in twelve factories. It was difficult, however, to be of assistance to women in factories as far away as Juarez in the north or the Yucatan in the south. Bus fares were expensive. Debate over exactly what their political independence meant during Mexico's first competitive presidential election campaign, in 1988, caused strains inside the fragile union. And while the government appeared accommodating during the period when journalists featured the garment workers' story, once the journalists went home and public attention was distracted the government reforged its alliance with the garment companies and withdrew official certification of the union. Teenage male thugs were sent to the factories to throw stones at women activists. Some *compañeros* prohibited their wives and companions from taking part in activities that carried such physical risks.

The September 19th union did not survive the 1994 passage of the North American Free Trade Agreement—the neoliberal treaty between the governments of Mexico, the United States, and Canada. NAFTA not only made U.S.–based corporate access to Mexican labor and consumers easier, but it also confronted Mexican farmers with massive U.S. imports of corn and beans, driving many of them off their farms to seek jobs in Mexico's already-crowded light-industrial maquiladoras or across the border as immigrant agricultural and domestic workers.[52]

The Mexican women's movement today remains politically active, mobilizing support for reproductive rights and to stop violence against women. The alliance between middle-class women activists and working-class women, still fragile, needs constant nurturing. Mexico's political parties have become competitive, though one of the strongest parties to challenge the once-dominant PRI was the National Action Party, "the PAN," a probusiness party. Mexico's senior male government officials have become less concerned about the feminized politics of garments and more preoccupied with the masculinized politics of drug cartels and oil exports.

CHINA: WOMEN ON THE MOVE

Looking at a social atlas of today's China, one is struck by the dramatic differences, many of them gendered, between the country's coastal and interior provinces. Since Chairman Deng Xiaoping's 1970 launch of China's distinctive, Communist Party–controlled, capitalist, foreign-investment-driven industrialization, the economic gaps have widened between the coast and the interior.[53] Alongside these geographic inequalities are the growing gaps between the cities and countryside, and between the superrich and everyone else.[54]

By 2005, the southern coastal province of Guangdong alone had become the *world's* third-largest garment-exporter.[55] Chinese young women by the thousands migrated from poor rural villages to coastal cities and sent money home to their impoverished rural parents. If not for the money they sent home, the gap between city dwellers and rural Chinese would have been even wider. It was young women, too, who filled the majority of jobs in China's fast-growing light industries: electronics, textiles, sneakers, and garments. This post-1970 generation of young women became literate, left home, delayed marriage, sent money home to struggling rural parents, and in the process, elevated the value that parents accorded to their daughters.[56]

Earlier generations of Chinese women had demanded to be seen as more than just daughters, wives, mothers, and mothers-in-law. Most of those women had come from the cities. Since the early twentieth century, Chinese women had been writers, reformers, and campaigners for voting rights; thousands had joined popular movements that challenged the dynastic monarchies and resisted European, American, and Japanese imperial intrusions and military occupations. Rural as well as urban women had contributed to the Chinese Communist Party's 1949 revolutionary victory over exploitive landlords and their political allies.[57]

Nonetheless, in the most recent era—from the late 1970s through the first decade of the twenty-first century—those young women who had migrated from the countryside to work in the export factories had seemed, at least superficially, to fit a model of the feminized Chinese factory worker. This model was comfortably shared by masculinized networks of four sets of players: Chinese growth-driven government officials, their enriching local allies, the local Taiwanese subcontractors, and the executives of foreign brand-name corporations. According to this model, the women workers were numerous and thus replaceable; they were hardworking and unorganized; they were intent upon saving enough money to go back to their home villages to marry; and when they married, they were glad to give up seniority to make way for their younger sisters to fill their places on the assembly lines.

These young women, in fact, had ambitions, made assessments and calculations, and had worries and disappointments. But even if they acknowledged women workers' strategizing abilities, Chinese and foreign male elites were reassured to note—as they forged masculinized bonds over sumptuous banquets and liquor-fueled karaoke—that these young women factory workers had embraced neoliberal capitalism's individualism: they had privatized their discontents, calling radio advice lines, exchanging ideas with friends, and fine-tuning their personal workplace strategies.[58] And the mantra of these women was: "The only person you can trust is yourself."[59]

It turns out, however, that Chinese women are not "naturally" pliant or self-absorbed. They have gradually reassessed their rights as Chinese citizens and developed capacities to act collectively. They have begun to make their complaints about abusive working conditions public, embarrassing Nike, Levi's, Apple, and other global brands whose products are manufactured in the factories owned by contractors, such as the Taiwanese manufacturing giant Foxconn.[60] They are aware of their environments, which have been grim. One journalist described the contrast between Apple's American headquarters and the factory zone in the industrializing hub of Zhengzhou, where thousands of women and men assemble products for Apple: "Unlike Apple's modernistic new campus in Cupertino, California, which will be surrounded by apricot trees, the Zhengzhou factory has all the charm of a penal colony."[61]

The Chinese Internet microblog site Sina Weibo and smartphones have enabled more Chinese women and men to share information about the extraordinary wealth of Chinese elites and the corrupt masculinized practices of those business and political male elites (taking mistresses, driving BMWs, playing golf at exclusive clubs). As a result, the idea of simply working hard for the sake of oneself and the abstract nation began to lose its legitimacy among young factory women.[62]

When Chinese factory women began to make collective demands and to stage walkouts, it was at a time when the consequence of the Beijing government's one-child policy was making it harder to simply treat young women workers as endlessly replaceable. These women workers' newfound sense of collective leverage also came at a time when more consumers in Europe, North America, and Japan were conscious of—and disturbed by—who was making their clothes and their electronic devices and under what dangerous and exploitive conditions.

To keep their restless women workers on the job and to lessen the anxieties of their global reputation-sensitive corporate clients, China's factory managers have been forced to address at least some of the workers' complaints and to raise the factory women's salaries.[63] Together, by 2010, these two moves made China less competitive in the global capitalists' continuing race to find cheapened labor. It was becoming clear that the Chinese factory woman who was marriage-focused, dutiful, compliant, and self-absorbed was never "natural"; she was a product of decisions and of a historically gendered set of conditions. Decisions

Figure 28. Garment factory workers ride to work in trucks in Phnom Penh, Cambodia, 2010. Photo: Will Baxter.

can prove to be shortsighted; and gender conditions can be transformed.

By 2010, China-based garment subcontractors and their brand-name global corporate clients began to do once more what they had done for decades. They looked for new countries in which to locate their electronics, sneaker, and garment factories, countries whose government officials wielded authoritarian power and were eager to offer their women's cheapened labor to international exporters; whose local entrepreneurs were eager to become the newest class of suppliers and subcontractors; and whose young women were seemingly politically naive, just looking for alternatives to village life, early marriage, unpaid farm work, and unpaid housework. Bangladesh looked promising. So did Cambodia. By early 2014, Cambodia was losing its allure for corporate executives, as hundreds of Cambodian garment workers took to the streets to protest not only their low monthly wages (on average eighty dollars per month) but also the authoritarian regime of Prime Minister Hun Sen, which enforced those low wages.[64]

CONCLUSION

The IMF, WTO, and NAFTA matter. The neoliberal economic model and the structural adjustment formula intended to promote that model both matter. Levi Strauss, Chung Hee Park, Deng Xiaoping, and Sheikh Hasina all matter. Political parties such as the PRI, the Awami League, and the Communist Party matter. Walmart, Nike, Tommy Hilfiger, H&M, Marks and Spencer, Mango, North Face, Zara, Benetton, and Gap matter. Bankers matter. The scores of lesser-known suppliers, subcontractors, safety monitors, and retailers all matter. Mothers, fathers, and husbands matter. Labor unions matter. Consumers—those preoccupied with ever-changing fashion and artificially low prices, as well as those concerned about workers' lives—matter, too. Each plays her, his, or its own part in the story of how our clothes have become globalized—at what true cost and to whose benefit.

Each is gendered.

That is, each—the WTO, Walmart, contractors, bankers, political parties, parents, consumers, labor unions—is shaped by how ideas about masculinity and femininity are used in their daily practices. Together, most of these interlocking genderings promote the powerful notion that women are the most "natural" industrial sewers of globalized clothes. Together, they *make* women workers' labor *cheap*.

If we ignore—remain incurious about—the daily workings of masculinities and femininities within and between these groups of actors, we will fail to provide a reliable explanation of how the garment industry has propped up governments and become profitably global for some and globally exploitive for others.

Making women visible will keep us alert to the multilayered politics of gender. Cultivating an alert gender curiosity means taking seriously the too-short life of Shaheena Akhtar.

Five garment factories rented space inside Rana Plaza, an eight-story building constructed haphazardly by the politically connected entrepreneur Sohel Rana. Shaheena had left an impoverished Bangladeshi rural village and come to Savar, this industrial suburb of Dhaka, to work in one of Rana Plaza's garment factories as a sewer of globally branded clothes.[65] By the age of thirty-two, she had become a single mother—of her son, Robin—after escaping an abusive husband. Shaheena had worked in the factory up until just hours before giving birth to Robin and had returned to her factory sewing machine two months later. As a gesture of her new autonomy, she had adopted a new surname, Akhtar. For a low-paid woman garment worker, autonomy took the form of choosing her own name and sharing two small rooms with her son and five other people. Together, the roommates were able to pay the monthly rent of fifty-six dollars.

Factory pay was low; money came only if she went to work. When women workers noticed the cracks opening up in Rana Plaza's walls, Shaheena's friends urged her not to go to work the next day, April 24. But despite the alarming cracks, the owners of the factories in Rana Plaza insisted upon opening their businesses for work. They had foreign corporate deadlines to meet. Shaheena told her friends that she had to go. If she did not appear at work she would not be able to pay her monthly twenty-five-dollar share for the slightly larger apartment that the seven of them were hoping to move into together. Her sister Jesmine recalled Shaheena explaining on April 23: "If I don't go to work tomorrow, I'll be absent, and I will not get paid for the day.... They may delay my month's wages. I need to buy milk for my son."[66]

During the morning shift on April 24, 2013, the building started to buckle. Shaheena and others did not have time to escape before it pancaked on top of them. The Rana Plaza collapse was a mere five months after the deadly Tazreen factory fire. A total of 1,127 Bangladeshi women and men would die under the broken beams and crumbled cement of what had been Rana Plaza. Among the global companies who were compelled to admit that their clothes were being sewn by Shaheena and her coworkers in this unsafe building were Cato Fashions, Loblaws, Mango, Children's Place, JCPenney, and Walmart.[67]

In the wake of the back-to-back Bangladesh factory disasters, global companies scrambled to meet and take joint action. Torn between protecting their global reputations in the eyes of consumers and sustaining their global profits, the executives could not agree on what to do. As Bangladeshi rescuers were still trying to dig bodies out from the Rana Plaza rubble, H&M, the Swedish retailer; Carrefour, the large French retailer; Marks and Spencer, Britain's best-known department store; Zara and Mango, the Spanish global retailers; and several German retailers under pressure from the German government, all signed an agreement, the Accord on Fire and Building Safety in Bangladesh. It formally committed each company that signed the accord to support both tougher safety inspections and Bangladeshi workers' right to organize independent unions.[68]

In the United States, however, executives of Walmart, Target, and Gap, as well as officials in federal agencies with employees whose uniforms are made in Bangladesh factories, and which stock military-base stores with apparel made in those factories, dragged their heels. U.S. Labor Department officials wanted American companies to take responsibility for effective reforms. Their colleagues across town in the State Department worried that putting pressure on Bangladeshi officials would jeopardize their bilateral antiterrorism alliance. The Labor Department and their labor advocate allies won this round. In June 2013, the Obama administration announced it would suspend Bangladesh's trade privileges until the country's policy makers demonstrated a genuine commitment to improving safety conditions for Bangladeshi garment workers.[69]

For their part, Bangladeshi politicians promised they would hire more factory inspectors and stop suppressing local labor unions. Parliament passed a new law guaranteeing the right of workers to organize and barring the Ministry of Labor and Employment from its usual practice of giving factory owners the names of those workers who voted for establishing a union in their factory. But labor advocates feared that, despite the new law, the collusion between officials and politically influential factory owners would continue, and that factory owners would continue to fire those employees who supported a union. The garment-factory-owners association, known as BGMEA, was used to having a decisive say over all government regulations of its industry. Bangladesh's parliament was tilted toward business, with 60 percent of its seats held by business executives; garment factory owners alone held 10 percent of the total number of legislative seats.[70]

Furthermore, Bangladeshi officials continued to avoid holding any of the male factory owners accountable; only occasionally were their subordinates, the factory managers, arrested for neglecting unsafe conditions that had allowed fires to start and that had killed dozens of workers.[71] Rarely, too, was any factory owner charged with environmental crimes, despite the gallons of toxic dyes they poured into neighborhood streams, turning them bright blue.[72] Moreover, the government hired too few qualified inspectors to inspect the thousands of garment factories. Those inspectors were called upon to conduct their inspections quickly and were hindered by confusing lines of authority.[73]

Disney executives, for their part, announced that they would pull their contracted apparel production out of Bangladesh. Bangladeshi labor activists, such as Kalpona Akter, and their international allies asked Disney and the other global companies not to run away to another country offering *cheap* labor but, instead, to stay and be part of authentic reform.[74]

The pledges of reform were not new. Government officials, local businessmen, and global brand-name companies' executives each had made such reassuring promises before—in Bangladesh, Mexico, Pakistan, Indonesia, Cambodia, China, Nicaragua, Guatemala, and South Korea. The question remained whether, after the media's and consumers' restless attention was diverted elsewhere, the implementation of these newest pledges would be monitored over the long-term. In five years, would conditions genuinely have improved for the women whose cheapened labor was still at the core of the international politics of garments?

And what of Chobi, Sumi, and Shaheena's surviving sister? What about the Bangladeshi woman who survived but now wakes up screaming at night thinking she is still trapped under cement beams? What about the woman who lost her daughter and the young woman who lost both her legs?[75] What about all these women's counterparts working in garment factories around the globe?

For all the news coverage, expressions of outrage, and gestures of political contrition, there was little talk about what sort of organizing would mean the most to the women actually sewing these globalized clothes, generating these company profits, and ensuring the government revenues. There was talk of fire codes, corporate reputations, monetary donations, and profit margins, but there was little serious talk of the complex lives being crafted by today's women garment workers. And there was no discussion of the workings of those masculinities that continue to make women's labor *cheap*.

As the ashes cooled and the rubble was cleared, gender politics was left unexplored.

CHAPTER EIGHT

Scrubbing the Globalized Tub

Domestic Servants in World Politics

A woman working on a Honduran banana plantation and a woman working in a Bangladeshi garment factory both think about housework. Each not only has her own housework to do at the end of her long, paid workday—she is living the "double day"—but she also calculates the relative advantages of quitting her current low-waged, dangerous job to do someone else's housework, becoming a domestic worker. Would she be less exposed to toxic chemicals? She wonders if she would have less sexual harassment to cope with. Would she have a better chance of joining a labor union? Each woman weighs the pluses and minuses of different sorts of precarious, low-paying feminized work.

At the same time, in other countries, a woman who was once a hairdresser in Baghdad or another who was a civil servant in Sarajevo may conclude that becoming a paid domestic worker is the only employment option available after war has shredded her society's social fabric and destroyed her former job. For a woman who already has immigrated to a new country, pursuing work as a live-in maid in someone else's home may seem the only job choice available as she tries to learn a new language, find shelter, gain legal status, and support her children.

In the twenty-first century, domestic workers constitute one of the globalized economy's major employment categories. There are 53 million domestic workers, male and female, in the world today. The overwhelming majority—83 percent—are women.[1] Thousands of women migrate internationally to clean other people's homes. Some of these women are forced or tricked into overseas domestic work. Violence, debt, and deception have been woven into domestic workers' lives. Domestic workers have become contested territory between governments. At the same time, domestic-worker activists are building transnational alliances to demand that their rights as workers and as women be recognized. "Globalized domestic work"—it is not an oxymoron.

Think about Theresa M. Dantes.[2] She is a Filipina who, when she was twenty-nine, decided that she could best support her family in Quezon City by signing a contract with a Philippines labor contractor, agreeing to travel to the Persian Gulf state of Qatar to work as a maid. Qatar is a small country ruled by an ambitious, modernizing monarchy, one that hosts a U.S. military base and wields political influence throughout the region. Enriched by its oil and natural gas, Qatar has the world's highest per capital income. Only 13 percent of Qatar's residents are Qataris. The remaining 87 percent are immigrant workers, tightly controlled immigrant workers. They are Pakistanis, Indians, Nepalis, Egyptians, and Filipinos, and they are building skyscrapers for global banks and football stadiums for the 2022 World Cup; staffing hospitals, hotels, museums, and government offices; and cleaning the private homes of Qataris.

Theresa Dantes was following millions of Filipinas who had gone abroad to find work. In 2011, there were 1.03 million women from the Philippines working abroad.³ Qatar already hosted a Filipino community of a hundred thousand migrant workers; most of the men worked as construction workers and hotel staff, and most of the women as cleaners in hotels and private homes. Filipino migrants living in Qatar were severely limited in their ability to organize, but they had created their own Facebook page. Theresa knew that women who had gone to the Persian Gulf—Saudi Arabia, the United Arab Emirates, and Qatar—to work as domestic workers and hotel housekeepers were sending money ("remittances") home to support their families. These women used Facebook, texting, and Skype to stay in touch and take part in their children's lives (a Filipina working in Canada reported, "My son says that even when I'm away, I still nag").⁴ So she did not think she was taking a big risk when she signed the labor contract. It assured her a $400 monthly salary, plus room and board provided by her employer. With this written assurance, Theresa boarded the plane to Doha, Qatar's fast-growing capital.

The reality that awaited Theresa caught her by surprise. Her employer said he would pay her only $250 per month for her live-in domestic work. She felt she had to accept the lower-than-contracted wages because her Filipino family back home, like so many Filipino families, was counting on her remittances. Her employer, the adult Qatari male in the household, fed her only a single meal a day, and that was a meal of leftovers: "If no leftovers, I didn't eat."⁵ The exploitation went further. Theresa was expected to work seven days a week, with no time off, and to clean not only her employer's house but also the houses of his sister and mother-in-law. After eight months, Theresa had had enough. She told her employer she wanted to quit. He just laughed. Under Qatar's migrant labor laws, Theresa could not quit her job unless her employer agreed. He refused. At this point she decided to escape. There were no support groups to whom she could appeal, but she knew that the Philippine government, reliant for its economic development on the remittances sent home by its citizens working overseas, had established an Overseas Labor Office in Doha. That is where Theresa took refuge. She found fifty-six other Filipinas already taking refuge there.[6]

Now think about Rosa (not her real name). Doreen Mattingly, a feminist researcher, met Rosa while doing research in San Diego on how Mexican women working as domestic workers in California's middle-class households created their own networks that enabled them not only to earn incomes but also to care for their own children. By 2011, Latinas made up 59 percent of all women working as domestic workers in American metropolitan areas.[7] This was a time, too, when Latinos constituted 16 percent of the U.S. population, when Latino political organizations—including those advocating domestic workers' rights—had multiplied, and when the "Latino vote" had become decisive in American electoral outcomes. Federal immigration reform bills, which could make Rosa's legal status less uncertain, however, were stuck in the congressional partisan logjam.[8]

Here is a typical day in Rosa's gendered transnational life: "Five days a week, Rosa boards a city bus that will take her to a distant wealthy neighborhood where she makes her living cleaning houses. Rosa is an undocumented migrant from Mexico.... The $40 she earns each day helps to feed her three children and pay rent on her family's small apartment." On alternate Tuesdays, Rosa cleans the house of Laurie, a white woman who works as a pharmacist. Even though Laurie is part of a two-parent household, she would not be able to pursue her pharmacy career without Rosa's paid assistance. Rosa arrives at Laurie's house as the family is finishing breakfast and preparing to leave for school and work. Laurie has a moment to speak to Rosa about the chores for the day and about meeting the children when they return home from school in the afternoon. "Rosa works hard and fast, trying to finish in time to catch the afternoon bus that will get her home in time for dinner." While Rosa is cleaning other people's houses and minding their children, her own youngest child is being cared for by Rosa's mother. Rosa helped bring her mother to San Diego from Mexico to care for her child so that she herself could earn an income. Her mother, too, is without legal status in the United States.[9]

International politics shape the lives of Theresa and Rosa. But feminist analysts do not stop at impacts. Feminist investigators look at causes. International politics is shaped *by* Theresa and Rosa and by the labor contractors, border patrol agents, immigration officials, and legislators who seek to control them, as well as by the women and men who employ them. Since the late 1990s, domestic workers have created local grassroots groups, and they, in turn, have begun to build transnational alliances to criticize the dominant neoliberal model of capitalist development and to advocate domestic workers' labor rights, basic human rights, and women's rights. But the challenges facing domestic-worker activists are formidable.

When thinking about the politics of domestic work, it may seem superfluous to ask, "Where are the women?" After all, whether the work is paid or unpaid, scrubbing the tub and minding the children are widely deemed to be "women's work." But it requires myriad actors in international politics to sustain such assumptions about what is women's work. This sustaining is not easy to achieve when so many women who used to have to choose between low-paid agricultural work and low-paid domestic work are now sought by corporations to provide cheapened labor for their globalizing garment and electronics factories. It is made difficult, too, by the increase in women in many countries seeking an education and changing their notions of what it means financially to be a wife and mother while, simultaneously, most men continue to eschew housework on the grounds that it is "unmanly." Thus the gendered international politics of domestic work is dynamic; it does not stand still. Theresa and Rosa are players in ongoing gendered international political history. So are the women and men who hire them.

MAIDS, GOVERNESSES, AND THE EMPIRE'S RESPECTABLE WOMEN

"The colonies which promote emigration from the United Kingdom by means of their public funds are New South Wales, Victoria, South Australia, Tasmania, *some* of the provinces of New Zealand, the Cape of Good Hope, and Natal.... In *all*, the persons assisted must belong strictly to the labouring classes."[10] Nineteenth-century British feminist Maria Rye quoted this passage from Her Majesty's Emigration Commissioners in disgust. How could Britain's unmarried middle-class women hope to take advantage of employment opportunities in the colonies if their government offered assistance only to those women who would go out as domestic servants?

Maria Rye belonged to a circle of nineteenth-century activist British women calling themselves the Langham Place Group, who sought to open up paid work to middle-class single women.

In mid-Victorian Britain, women outnumbered men. There were not enough men to allow all eligible women to get married—the conventional patriarchal solution to women's financial worries. Moreover, as the women of Langham Place had pointed out in articles and parliamentary petitions, women's economic security in marriage always had been more myth than reality. There also were not enough governess positions to support the thousands of single middle-class "surplus" women who needed the sort of work that was both respectable and economically viable. So, in 1861, Maria Rye helped launch the Female Middle Class Emigration Society: *respectable* paid work in the homes of white colonial settlers. These reformers would further the government's imperial aims at the same time that the government addressed unmarried British women's pressing economic needs.

Maria Rye did not intend for middle-class white women to work as mere domestic servants; that would jeopardize their social status and underuse their considerable skills. The activists of the Female Middle Class Emigration Society wanted middle-class women to emigrate as nannies, governesses, and shop managers. The empire needed respectable, skilled nannies to elevate the white settler communities in the colonies.

In actual numbers, the Society made only a small dent in the economic problems faced by nineteenth-century British single women. In 1861, its first year of activity, it managed to place just fourteen women in paid positions in the colonies: twelve in Australia and two in Natal in South Africa. The following year it was a bit more successful: twenty women were sent to Australia, six to Natal, seven to Vancouver Island in Canada, three to New Zealand, and one to India. Although Maria Rye herself developed a fondness for Canada after reading Susannah Moody's autobiographical account of being a pioneer on the Canadian frontier, Australia became the favored destination for British governesses because of the gold rush and growing white settlement. India and Africa were far down on the list of colonies considered promising for respectable white single working women.[11]

Middle-class single women stood in Manchester or Kent and looked out at an empire of tea plantations, gold mines, and trading ports, an empire organized to keep women dependent yet make their skills and reproductive capacities useful to that empire. It was a world in which more privileged women had as much stake in maintaining differences of class and race between themselves and other women as in maintaining their feminine distinctiveness from men. Thus while women who sought assistance from the Female Middle Class Emigration Society knew that they would have to learn how to cook and wash if they were to be acceptable applicants for the colonial emigration schemes, they also recognized that one of the few valued assets a middle-class single woman possessed was her feminine respectability. This is what they had to sell. They would rather have stayed in Britain than go out to the colonies as domestic servants, a position that would surely cost them that prized respectability; but given the lack of waged work and the slim chances for marital security, staying in Britain did not seem feasible to many women.

Consolidating an empire, nonetheless, required domestic servants as well as nannies. Scores of Indian, Malaysian, Aborigine, Maori, Native Canadian, and African women worked as servants in the homes of white settlers. The paternalistic relationship between the white mistress on a tea or sugar plantation and her local servants frequently was held up as an example of what the colonizing mission was all about. Under South Africa's white-imposed apartheid system of the late twentieth century,

Black South African women developed a theory of internal colonialism by analyzing the paternalistic relations between Black maids and white "madams."[12] Many colonialists, on the other hand, either felt more comfortable hiring working-class women of their own racial groups, or found that the demand for servants outran the supply of local women willing to work in colonialists' homes. In Canada at the turn of the twentieth century, the federal government bent its immigration rules to allow local agencies to import young working-class white girls from Britain to work as maids. When that pool proved insufficient, Canadians turned to young Finnish women. Some feminists urged poor British women take up colonial domestic service. An impoverished young British white woman, they reasoned, was better off emigrating than being unwittingly drawn into a life of crime at home. If she emigrated to the colonies under the care of an appropriate chaperone, these advocates reasoned, she could be assured of placement in the sort of household that would nurture her future respectability.[13]

British women ranked the regions of the empire where they could find paid domestic work. Australia, with its growing white settler population and its suppressed and marginalized Aboriginal population, ranked high. New Zealand sounded appealing, though it was a newer colony and its Maori people were still a cause for some anxiety among whites. Canada's colonial administrators were still refining their policies to encourage middle-class women emigrants.[14] Britain's rule in India had just been shaken by the 1857 Mutiny, and the white colonial community in need of governesses remained small. Colonial societies of Africa ranked at the bottom of the British single middle-class women's hierarchical list, though for some it still had the attraction of providing "adventure."[15]

THE GENDERED HISTORY OF THE
"DOUBLE DAY"

By 2010, the International Labor Organization estimated that 43.6 million women in the world worked in private homes as paid domestic workers. Among men, 8.9 million worked as domestic workers. This was a jump up from 28.8 million women (and 5.9 million men) working as domestic workers just fifteen years earlier, in 1995.[16]

Furthermore, job patterns differed by geographic region because every region's gendered political economy is distinct, and the ways in which gendered globalizing pressures play themselves out in each region are distinct. Thus, over the period 1995 to 2010, the region that experienced the most dramatic increase in women—local and immigrant—pursuing (or being forced into) paid domestic work was Latin America and the Caribbean: in 1995, 9.6 million women from this region were working as domestic workers; fifteen years later, the number had almost doubled, to 18 million women. The increase was impressive in the Middle East as well: in 1995, there were 745,000 women—local and immigrant— working as domestic workers; by 2010, that number had risen to 1.3 million women.[17]

These findings were published in the first worldwide report commissioned by the International Labor Organization to focus specifically on domestic workers—where they were from, where they worked, what their rights were, and what abuses they endured while cleaning other people's homes. Earlier ILO reports had lumped domestic workers together with other migrant workers. Women working as domestic workers did indeed share many of the problems experienced by other migrant workers, but a failure to consider the distinctive problems that arose from being employed in private homes as feminized workers disguised the particular gender politics that shaped the lives of those women. The report itself, *Domestic Workers across the World,* thus was a political landmark.[18] The study was the result of women domestic workers' own international organizing directed at international agencies that, until now, had not treated domestic workers as "real workers." Studies do not "just happen." Collecting gender-disaggregated data and analyzing its implications can inform future political action; and that data collecting and analyzing can be the result of organized political lobbying.

In 1936, attendees at an international conference held in Geneva had concluded, even while lacking worldwide data, that paid domestic workers were among the world's most vulnerable workers. In 2013, the ILO researchers concluded that—seventy-seven years, multiple wars, and many social reforms and treaties later—domestic workers still were among the world's workers most likely to be exploited. Their labor could be exploited, their rights ignored, their bodies trafficked.[19] That continuity is not a product of timelessness. That continuity is a product of the politics of sustainability—the politics of sustaining sexist labor systems.

Feminized housework, paid and unpaid, is often portrayed as timeless. It is not. The feminization of any sort of work is a process that goes on in political history, in gendered international political history.

Family homes have been designed and redesigned according to which ideology of housework and feminine respectability has ruled the day during any particular era. Should the kitchen be in the basement, out of sight of the family, or next to the family dining room for the housewife's convenience? Should there be a wood-paneled study for the man of the house? Should a house be built with a top floor with small servants' quarters or with just a single room off the kitchen for the use of the daily maid? How much closet space should be set aside for the vacuum cleaner and brooms? Are the washing machine and dryer placed for the convenience of the double-day housewife? Each answer involves a gendered architectural decision, a decision derived not only from current household realities but also from values assigned to paid and unpaid gendered housework—and the debate isn't over.[20]

The double day—worked by women who are responsible for both paid work and unpaid work—has been familiar to factory and farming women since women were found to be useful to those seeking to maximize productivity and since women have sought incomes of their own. The double day is a much newer experience for most middle-class women, however. In the early 1900s, middle-class women of their country's dominant racial and ethnic groups were told by conservatives and reformers alike that, for middle-class women, women with educations, women whose chief political resource was their feminized "respectability," being a competent modern housewife was a respectable—even scientific—full-time job, albeit unpaid. They should not rely on servants to care for husbands and children; they should apply their own energies, brainpower, and skills to performing everyday household tasks, though perhaps helped by a twice-a-week female paid cleaner.

After the 1970s, more and more middle-class women in scores of countries were inspired in part by their women's movements to seek paid jobs of their own outside the home. "Domestic science" lost its allure. Their motivations were varied: to fulfill professional aspirations, to avoid marriage, to support themselves and their children after a divorce or a husband's death, or to bolster their two-adult household's finances. As these motivations moved women to seek paid work outside the home, the double day was experienced by more middle-class women. The difference was that middle-class women were more likely than women working in factories and on plantations to have options for coping with their double day.

For many educated, twenty-first-century women, becoming "superwoman" has not been an ideal to aspire to; it has been a sentence. The expectation that a "working woman"—that is, a woman with a paid job—requires superhuman strength is fertilized by masculinized inaction: the women's employers, governments, or husbands have refused to take steps to reduce the stresses imposed on women by the double day—for instance, refusing to alter office cultures that reward employees who work late into the evening, refusing to fund public child care, and only begrudgingly sharing in housework (currently, on an average day 20 percent of American men do housework, compared to 48 percent of American women; in Britain, men do seven hours of housework a week, while women do eighteen hours). Under these gendered sociopolitical conditions, women wanting and needing to work for pay have had to look for private solutions.[21] These conditions were especially taxing for the growing numbers of women, in countries as different as Nicaragua and the United States, who were single mothers with young children. Thus, for the 8.6 million American women in 2011 who both had children and were their families' sole income earners, devising a strategy for coping with the double day was a necessity.[22]

Middle-class women have adopted a variety of private strategies for lessening the burdens of their double days: some have settled for part-time jobs; others have accepted the off-track equivalent status of "associate" in law firms, even when that has meant abandoning hopes of ever becoming a law firm partner. Some of these same women have also put off having children as long as possible, until they felt they had a toehold in their careers; once they have had children, some have sunk more and more of their wages into expensive private nurseries. Over the last three decades still other middle-class women have opted for an old alternative, though now in a new political setting: they hired other women to do their housework and mind their children.

Today's patterns are the latest in an ongoing history of gendered patterns designed to sustain what each generation has imagined was the optimal social order. For centuries women had employed other women to perform household tasks. The early and mid-nineteenth century's Industrial Revolution helped create a demand in western Europe and North America for domestic servants by nurturing the notion of the respectable middle-class woman who protected her own feminine purity from manual labor and yet stayed at home to provide a refuge for her hardworking husband. The histories of working-class Irish, African American, and Japanese American women all have been shaped by the domestic jobs created by this prefeminist Victorian ideology.[23]

Over a hundred years later, feminists in the 1980s and 1990s, by contrast, pointedly critiqued both feminized housework *and* the exploitation of working-class women. Thus, hiring domestic servants to resolve the "superwoman" dilemma appeared politically suspect. Wasn't "feminist domestic employer" a contradiction? A young journalist living in a large London apartment explained how she avoided being upset by living this contradiction: yes, she did resort to hiring another woman to clean because it improved her marriage by lessening the squabbles she and her doctor husband had been having over who was going to do which household chores. But at the same time, she decided to think of her relationship with the woman who cleaned her home as not strictly economic: "I suppose when I was an idealistic socialist student I thought I'd never, never have people to do things for me. But I never look on it as a sort of employee-employer situation."[24]

Nonetheless, hiring other women to do the family's housework has become an eagerly sought status symbol in newly modernizing countries. For generations, having servants had been a symbol of upper-class privilege. Nowadays, however, hiring a servant has come to be recognized as a sign of being modern as opposed to "traditional." To modernize, a country had to show that its women had economic opportunities; even local working-class women had better things to do with their skills than using them to clean their fellow citizens' homes. For instance, only ten years ago Chilean middle-class households hired Chilean working-class women to clean their homes. Today, those working-class women and their daughters have a wider range of economic opportunities and do not have to work as maids. Instead, a Chilean homeowner now is more likely to hire an immigrant woman to do the cleaning, a woman who has immigrated to Chile from Peru, Colombia, or Haiti.[25]

Furthermore, importing women to clean the country's growing number of middle-class homes has become evidence that one's country has an expanding middle class. That, in turn, is seen as proof that the country is well along the road to modernization. Evidence that Malaysia, Chile, Qatar, and Lebanon have become modern societies is the thousands of women each country imports to clean citizens' homes.

Government officials from the sending countries have become addicted to the remittances that their women domestic workers send home. That economic addiction makes them reluctant to insist on defending the rights of their citizens working abroad. And the government officials of the importing countries have, for their part, developed a stake in demonstrating their countries' modernity. This becomes a political incentive for their investing public resources in maintaining the flow of immigrant domestic workers while controlling the women who enter the country to take those jobs.

Together, these differing sets of needs and aspirations can build a bilateral dependency between states that export and import women domestic workers; but they also can put a strain on the political relationships between the sending country and the receiving country. Indonesia's officials have criticized Malaysian officials for their efforts to deport its women migrant domestic workers. The Philippines government has publicly chastised Hong Kong officials for denying residency status to Filipinas who have lived and worked as domestic workers in Hong Kong for decades. The Sri Lankan government has protested the Saudi government's execution, without a fair trial, of a young Sri Lankan domestic worker questionably charged with murdering her employer's child.[26] These exporting countries' official criticisms, however, stop well short of effectively advocating the rights of the women abroad who send needed money home.

SOLIDARITY IS NEVER AUTOMATIC

The relationships today between a woman employer and woman employee in domestic work are complicated by racialized and

Figure 29. One of two hundred thousand foreign domestic workers in Lebanon, a Filipino domestic worker cleans her employers' bathroom, 2010. Photo: Matthew Cassel.

classed stereotypes and inequities. They are exacerbated by middle-class women's occasional political ambivalence about the power they exercise and even their status as employers. Politically active domestic workers have not always found feminists in the host countries to be reliable allies. Local feminist groups in countries importing maids either from overseas or from the poor rural regions of their own countries have frequently been led by women from precisely the social class that is hiring domestic workers. Combined with the differences of language and race that often accompany the domestic politics of paid housework, these barriers have proved hard to surmount. Moreover, some politically active women have had trouble seeing a domestic servant as a "worker." She may not capture activists' imaginations the way a garment worker or a woman in prostitution has.

The domestic worker's experiences of exploitation are not as readily obvious; or perhaps those experiences are more embarrassing for the middle-class feminist to acknowledge. Moreover, a domestic worker's collective bonds with other domestic workers are harder to recognize because each woman works alone. To the otherwise progressive woman employer, according to one domestic-worker activist, a domestic worker may seem to be "her possession, her object, her diminutive pet, or all these things."[27] Mary Castro, leader of a Brazilian domestic-workers' association, asked rhetorically, "Anyway, how can we trust the feminists when, as employers, they treat us so badly?"[28]

The relationships between women as employers and women as domestic workers are further complicated by the women's different locations in their country's political structure: most of the employers do not have to worry about and maneuver within their government's constantly changing immigration laws. Thousands of women now working as domestic servants are recent immigrants—traveling from Ethiopia to Italy; from the Philippines to Japan, Israel, Lebanon, Qatar, or Singapore; from Mexico, Brazil, and Poland to the United States; from Jamaica to Canada; from Indonesia to Malaysia; from China to South Korea; from Ecuador to Spain; from Sri Lanka to Saudi Arabia; from Thailand to Jordan; from Morocco to France; from Peru to Chile. Their status as new immigrants—often without legal documentation—makes their employment lives all the more precarious. They are subject not only to the whims of their private employers but also to the ornate regulations of their home governments and their host governments.

Each government has its own reasons for controlling—or deliberately overlooking—the international trade in domestic service. Government policies thus have made even more complex the already awkward mix of intimacy and power that always has shaped relations between women doing domestic work and their female employers.[29]

In addition to differences between countries' immigration policies that help shape the relationships between employers and domestic workers, and between domestic workers themselves, are the differences in countries' rules governing political organizing. Working as an immigrant housemaid in Qatar or Saudi Arabia, for example, is far more confining than doing the same job in Hong Kong. In Hong Kong, though local officials are carefully monitored by authorities in Beijing, officials tolerate considerable social-movement organizing and activism, far more than do the Persian Gulf monarchies. The Singapore government likewise exerts tighter control over workers' organizing than do governments within the European Union. Women working as domestic workers today are aware of these differences. Women migrating to take domestic-worker jobs strategize to find work, if they can, not only in those countries where the pay is better but also where governments allow immigrant domestic workers to organize.[30]

If these obstacles to solidarity among women were not daunting enough, there has developed a hierarchy of respectability and autonomy among different sorts of domestic workers. Where they are on the pyramid affects how they see their work, their potential political allies, and their best organizing strategy. At the top of the pyramid are the professional nannies; in Europe and North America, many are white, though frequently they are from abroad. If they come to the job with formal qualifications and organizational support, they expect their employers to treat them as independent adults. In the upper levels of the pyramid are young foreign women who come into the country on temporary visas to work as au pairs. They, too, are usually white, but they see their work as a short-term job; it does not define their social status, but is, rather, a way to travel and learn another language before moving on to more serious (higher status) commitments. These young women are frequently treated as "daughters" by their European or North American employers.

Somewhat below the top of this domestic worker hierarchy of respectability and autonomy are women who are hired to provide elder care. If they live in their employer's home and are on call twenty-four hours per day, their autonomy is limited. But if they work in teams and rotate in and out of the job in any twenty-four-hour period, and thus are not be required to live in the employer's home, they can carve out substantial independence for themselves. Whether they live in or out, domestic elder-care workers are expected to have the skills (and physical strength) required to tend to the bathing, feeding, and personal hygiene needs of an often quite disabled older person. They are frequently also the main social companion of the person in their care. This can be emotionally satisfying or emotionally draining. The demand for immigrant women to provide home-based elder care—and as nurses and nurses' aides to work in nursing homes for the elderly—is mushrooming as the percentage of elderly people spirals upward in affluent countries, not only in Europe and North America, but also in countries such as Singapore and Japan.[31]

Then there are women, such as Rosa, who do not live in their employers' homes but are hired to do daily cleaning and frequently child care as well. They are not thought of by either governments or employers as professionals, no matter how extensive their experience and skills; they are presumed to be "maids," and their feminized, domesticated manual work defines their social status. More often than not, these less respected domestic workers are women of color or from less privileged ethnic communities within their employers' country or from abroad. Without either the credentials of the professional nanny or the amateur aura of the au pair, and lacking the racialized advantage of many nannies and au pairs, these women are more susceptible to economic exploitation, sexual harassment by men in the household, and perhaps even deportation by the host government. On the other hand, if they do not live in their employers' home, they may cultivate a minimal level of personal autonomy and be able to care for their own children.

The domestic workers most likely to be treated with the least respect and to be most vulnerable to abuse are those who, like Theresa, are hired to live full time in their employer's home. They are likely to be socially cut off from other domestic workers and from people in their ethnic or national community. They also have to leave behind their own families in order to take these live-in jobs. And they are the workers most likely to be on call at all times of day and night. These are the domestic workers who are most dependent on their employers, who supply them with shelter, even if inadequate (many live-in domestic workers are expected to sleep in the bedroom of the family's children), and food, even if leftovers. Because live-in immigrant domestic workers' ability to stay in the country depends on their employment (employers often take possession of the worker's passport and visa), often the best that a live-in worker can hope for from her employer is condescending paternalism.[32]

A subset of live-in domestic workers are those who have been trafficked into forced labor. Today, women and girls who work as live-in domestic workers are second only to women and girls trafficked for forced prostitution in being subjected to criminal international human trafficking. To be trafficked is to be brought across either internal regional or international borders against one's will or under false pretenses, then compelled to work for little or no pay, to be deprived of all physical autonomy, and to be forbidden to leave the job.

The latest International Labor Organization research calculates that 20.9 million persons—women, men, girls, and boys—are victims of what is legally known as "forced labor." The ILO researchers call this figure "a conservative estimate." Women and girls are a majority (55 percent) of all the persons in forced labor—labor they did not enter into willingly and cannot leave of their own free will.[33] Of the total of all persons in forced labor, 44 percent are forcibly moved away from their hometown to work. Recruiting a woman coercively or under false pretenses to travel from one region to another or abroad to work as a maid, compelling her to work long hours under abusive conditions, and denying her time off and the freedom to seek her own social relationships is to traffic that woman into forced labor.

It takes many actors to traffic a woman into forced domestic labor: recruiters, transporters, and ultimately employers. Keeping the domestic worker inside, cut off from her own chosen social connections enables an employer to hide his enslavement of the domestic worker. It is one reason why prosecution of the perpetrators of forced labor and trafficking is relatively rare.[34]

Then there is a newer, sixth, group of women who are doing paid domestic work—women who are employees of contract cleaners. The client/homeowner who hires the company to clean her or his private home does not have an employer-employee relationship directly with the women, who come every week or two to vacuum and scrub. Barbara Ehrenreich, an American feminist journalist, spent a year working in four low-paid feminized jobs in order to understand what modern job exploitation felt like.

Among the jobs she chose was that of cleaner for a housecleaning company. Ehrenreich was struck by how disdainfully the woman homeowner treated her and her workmates when they came to clean her house on a hot day. The homeowner did not bother to learn the housecleaners' names and expressed surprise when one of them politely asked for a glass of water. Even paternalism did not seem to cross this woman employer's mind.[35]

Women working as nannies, au pairs, domestic elder-care workers, daily domestic servants, live-in domestic workers, and employees of cleaning companies share many challenges. Most are not paid a living wage. Many are recent immigrants and face a labyrinth of immigration rules that can bewilder even women with confidence and a formal education. Most of these domestic workers are of a different racial, ethnic, or nationality group than their employers. Working in someone else's home raises for all of these women common issues of political invisibility, intimacy, and possible harassment. All six groups of women are commonly treated as less than "serious workers" by most men who lead trade unions, labor ministries, legislatures, and international agencies. Finally, all six groups of women are more likely than most workers to have other, more privileged, women as their employers.

Despite these shared experiences and issues, nannies, au pairs, elder-care domestic workers, daily domestic servants, live-in domestic workers, and women working for home-cleaning companies have found it challenging to build political bridges between one another within countries and across national boundaries.

DOMESTIC WORKERS ORGANIZE

Padmini Palliyaguruge had been an elementary school teacher in Sri Lanka. She also had been an activist in local women's organizations. After taking part in a strike to better the conditions of low-paid teachers, she found herself locked out of employment. Her husband and two children depended on her wages, and her husband had never been sympathetic to her activism. Desperate for work, Padmini Palliyaguruge decided that she had no choice but to sign up with one of the 450 Sri Lankan agencies recruiting Sri Lankan women to work as domestic servants in Saudi Arabia. This was the early 1980s. The Gulf states' escalating oil revenues were being translated into a demand for migrant women to clean local homes.

A woman working as a domestic servant in the Middle East at the time received a wage thirty times higher than in Sri Lanka. Even with agency fees of five hundred to a thousand dollars, and despite the fact that male recruiters had a reputation for abusing women, the opportunity seemed to Padmini worth taking.[36]

In 1984, an estimated eighteen thousand Sri Lankan women migrated to take paid jobs overseas, most on short-term, one- or two-year, contracts. This was the first time in the country's history that Sri Lankan women outnumbered Sri Lankan men in foreign employment. Of the two hundred thousand Sri Lankans in 1987 working on contract in the Middle East, 70 percent were women working as maids. Most of them were married. Most came from the country's politically dominant Singhalese ethnic community. The earnings sent home by the country's women working abroad turned foreign remittances into Sri Lanka's second-largest foreign-exchange earner, after its tea exports.[37]

Once in Saudi Arabia, Padmini, like other Sri Lankan maids, had to provide her employer with around-the-clock service. She worked seven days a week, often for more than eighteen hours a day. She describes the conditions: "Women have no access to leisure or recreation. Uprooted from their cultural environment and left for themselves in an unknown world under very trying working-conditions, they experience psychological traumas. Medical facilities are almost absent. The woman can be compelled to do any kind of work, and many of the women are severely abused physically and sexually."[38]

Speaking to a group, Padmini showed her listeners photographs of women who had returned to Sri Lanka from their jobs in the Middle East catatonic or in wheelchairs. They were victims of abuse or physical assault by irate employers who had been impatient with their inability to operate electrical appliances, angered by their unwillingness to work endless hours, or angered by their resistance to sexual advances. Despite their harsh experiences, some Sri Lankan women who were still physically able, and who were faced with their own family's financial hardships, returned to the recruiting agency, paid the fee, and signed up for another tour of cleaning, cooking, and child care abroad. And thus the flow of remittances to Sri Lanka continued, allowing the government to continue paying the interest it owed on its outstanding foreign loans.[39] Oil revenues, international debt, development strategies, dutiful wives and daughters, feminized labor, household labor, and global inequalities—they all had to be considered together, Padmini told her listeners.

Padmini Palliyaguruge was describing exploitive working conditions in Nairobi in 1985. Her listeners were women who had come from all over the world to take part in the final international gathering of the ten-year-long United Nations Decade for Women. It was a gathering that helped to make domestic work an international political issue and to show that domestic workers were among the world's newest international political actors.

Padmini Palliyaguruge spoke in Nairobi not as a victim but as an organizer, representing Sri Lanka's Progressive Women's Front. She was one of the participants in a nongovernmental panel intended to make the special problems of migrant women workers visible to other feminist and women's rights activists. Her copanelists were women from Peru, the Philippines, Japan, and Algeria, all of whom had been migrant workers or migrant-worker defenders. They all described a common experience of having been met with indifference when they had tried to get local male trade union leaders engaged with domestic workers' issues. The panelists recalled, too, how difficult it was, even among internationally conscious feminists, to keep migrant women's political issues on organizational agendas. They seemed to slip out of sight so easily. Thus organizing a separate panel at Nairobi's UN conference was a deliberate effort to make their conditions visible not only to governments but also to other politically conscious women. The activists also designed the session at Nairobi to give women domestic-worker organizers from several countries the chance to exchange analyses and strategies with each other.

In the 1980s, 1990s, and the beginning of the twenty-first century, efforts by domestic workers to organize multiplied—in Singapore, Hong Kong, the United States, Japan, Sri Lanka, Brazil, Canada, and Italy. Simultaneously, they reached out to other labor, immigration, and women's rights activists. Most domestic workers' organizations remained small. The activists were limited by the isolating character of domestic work itself, by the nationality, ethnic, and language differences among women working as domestic workers, by immigrant domestic workers' fear of deportation, by the time-constraints imposed by employers, by women's ongoing double-day responsibilities, by the political timidity of their home-country governments, and finally, by host-country governments' active discouragement of grassroots political organizing. Often the only collective organizing took the form of supplying immediate counseling and practical aid, not changing public policy; those services usually were provided by religious institutions such as the Catholic Church or by other domestic workers who volunteered on their precious days off.[40]

One of the lessons that domestic-worker advocates have fashioned out of these challenging recent experiences is that their issues will be more understandable to the public and to officials if they are framed as issues of human rights, women's rights, labor rights, civil rights, or immigrant rights, or as some combination of these.[41] A Peruvian maid in Chile is no longer just a maid; she is a worker. A Latina without documents who cleans houses in San Diego is not just a cleaner; she is an immigrant. A Filipina woman whose Qatari employer prohibits her from leaving the employer's home is not just an abused woman; she is a person being denied her human rights. A domestic worker in Italy whose issues are ignored by politicians and union organizers is not just a marginalized worker; she is a woman being subjected to sexist silencing.

This wider, multidimensional framing of their issues and demands has garnered new allies for domestic-worker activists. Supporters working on these broadly defined issues began to take domestic workers' conditions seriously, recognizing them as significant to their own broader cause. For women whose chief challenge has been to overcome the reality that their work itself separates them from each other, and that they perform their labor in what are imagined to be private spaces, this alliance-building strategy has been crucial to gaining public visibility, political legitimacy, strategic leverage, and transnational linkages.

Still, widening their political lens for the sake of being seen and taken seriously comes with risks. Such a framing has to be done in a way that does not dilute domestic workers' own specific issues. And the alliance-building that comes out of this wider framing has to be structured so that domestic workers do not get subsumed under more visible causes or more masculinized organizational leadership.

Indonesian, Filipina, Nepali, and Thai domestic workers in Hong Kong decided to take advantage of the media attention showered on the territory during anti–World Trade Organization protests in 2005 to make visible their own issues.[42] They chose these days of protest to launch their own demonstrations precisely so that other critics of the WTO's neoliberal capitalist model of development would recognize the issues of immigrant domestic-worker women as part and parcel of that wider global critique. They organized what they called the "Consulate Hopping Protest," the highlight of which was the "Hall of Shame Awards." The domestic workers hired buses to take them first to the Nepalese consulate—where they protested the king's autocratic rule—then to the Indonesian consulate, where they declared the Indonesian government "Rookie of the Year" for its successful exporting of cheapened labor. The buses then carried the domestic workers to the Malaysian consulate, where they declared the Malaysian prime minister the "Sultan of Crackdown" for his suppression of democracy.

Their consulate hopping was not over yet. As the tour continued, more and more people—other immigrants as well as Hong Kong citizens—joined in; more journalists began to cover their rolling demonstration. The domestic workers next piled onto their buses and headed for the Philippines consulate, where they conferred their "Milkmaid Award" on the president in recognition of her "milking" Filipina domestic workers for the remittances that kept the Philippines economy afloat. Their fifth stop was the Thai consulate, at which they bestowed the "Absentee Government Award" on the government of Thailand for its notable neglect of its country's migrant workers. The protestors' final stop on their consulate-hopping tour was Hong Kong's own government offices. There they gave the territory's chief executive their "Edward Scissorhands Award," a giant pair of cardboard scissors with which to cut wages and social services. With their awards conferred, the domestic workers headed to Victoria Park so that they could join a protest by South Korean farmers who had come to Hong Kong to protest the damage done by WTO trade policies to small farmers' economies.

With their imaginative tour, the domestic-worker activists revealed the complex web of local and international complicities that produce today's exploitation of domestic workers.

Today, at a time when a majority of domestic workers in the United States are recent immigrants, and when labor unions are politically weakened, women organizing as domestic workers in the United States have decided to weave together an agenda of workers' rights, immigrant rights, and women's rights. Depriving domestic workers of all three sets of rights, activists argue, has made their lives precarious while, at the same time, denying them recognition as workers. The current primary target of American domestic workers: state legislatures. Elected representatives in state legislatures repeatedly have passed laws that have exempted domestic workers from labor protection laws and from minimum wage laws. Legislators in New York, California, Massachusetts, and nineteen other states have passed laws that extend the minimum hourly wage ($7.25 per hour) to live-in caregivers. However, members of twenty-eight state legislatures have refused. Among those twenty-eight are Idaho, Indiana, Oregon, North Carolina, Texas, Florida, and New Hampshire.[43]

To overturn these exemptions and to extend labor fairness requirements beyond merely minimum-wage coverage, U.S.-based domestic workers' advocacy groups such as the National Domestic Workers Alliance have had to confront head-on the myths underlying these legal exemptions. These include, first, the myth that domestic workers are somehow fundamentally different from, say, auto workers, software engineers, or retail workers, and, second, the myth that a house or apartment where a women is hired to clean, cook, mind children, or care for the elderly is not a workplace.[44]

The NDWA activists have made alliances with local domestic worker groups, immigrant rights groups, Latino organizations, labor organizations, and African American civil rights groups. They have lobbied legislators and cultivated the media, as well as collaborated with professional researchers to demonstrate the problems that need to be fixed by employers and by public policy makers. But conducting a survey of domestic workers requires subtle research strategies, because the people to be surveyed are separated in their workplaces, and their employers are often nearby. The researchers cannot just wait at the factory gates or outside the entrance to the software company's office building. Thus NDWA surveyors "went to parks, transportation hubs, churches, and shopping centers to ask nannies, housecleaners, and elder caregivers about working conditions in private households."[45] Employing this strategy in fourteen cities across the country, the NDWA and its allied academic researchers surveyed 2,086 domestic workers in places where they could express their ideas candidly.

Among their findings: domestic workers' low pay caused "acute financial hardships," as reflected in the 40 percent of domestic workers surveyed who reported that they had "paid some of their other bills [after mortgage or rent] late" during the previous year, and in the 20 percent who during the previous month had gone without food at home "because there was no money to buy any."[46] Only 2 percent of the domestic workers surveyed received either retirement or pension benefits from their primary employer; and since so many employers paid their domestic workers under the table, most would have no access to Social Security benefits when they reached their elder years. Furthermore, 65 percent of domestic workers surveyed had no health insurance, despite the fact that the work they performed in other people's homes came with physical costs: 38 percent of the workers had "suffered from work-related wrist, shoulder, elbow or hip pain in the past 12 months"; 29 percent of the home-based caregivers had "suffered a back injury in the prior 12 months."[47] On top of these workplace risks, many new immigrant women working as domestic workers expressed fear that if they voiced any complaint about their working conditions, they would face reprisals in the form of reports to U.S. immigration officials.[48]

These findings came two years after a major political breakthrough for women working as domestic workers in New York state: in 2010 the New York state legislature passed the first statewide "Domestic Workers' Bill of Rights." Although the NDWA's report revealed the ongoing work issues facing domestic workers nationally, passage of the New York bill of rights was a cause for new hope. It was the result of six years of campaigning led by two New York state organizations, the New York Domestic Workers Justice Coalition and Domestic Workers United.[49] The bill covered the estimated two hundred thousand women and men who worked as domestic workers in the greater New York City area, as well as the thousands more who worked inside private homes on Long Island and in upper New York State. Among the rights that the New York law established were (1) the right to one twenty-four-hour period of "rest" per week, (2) the right to be paid time-and-a-half overtime for any work beyond forty hours per week (with a notable exception: live-in domestic workers would be owed overtime only after they had done forty-four hours of work in a week), and (3) the right of a domestic worker to file legal charges with state authorities for sexual or racial harassment experienced while on the job.[50]

The NDWA, together with its local New York partners, pledged to push the California state legislature to pass a similar comprehensive domestic workers' bill of rights. Meanwhile, Congress would be pressed by these advocacy groups to end so many states' practices of treating domestic workers as if they were not genuine workers, and employers as if they were not genuine employers. These American efforts—their successes and their failures—would have an impact on the international politics of domestic work.

From the local domestic-worker-organized campaigns in Hong Kong, the United States, Sri Lanka, the Philippines, and elsewhere, and from the early seeds planted by women activists at the UN conference Nairobi in 1985, has grown a transnational, feminist-informed domestic workers organization, the International Domestic Workers' Network.[51] The multinational group of women activists who have energized the IDWN set their sights on Geneva, headquarters of the International Labor Organization. Their goal: to persuade the government representatives to the ILO to establish an international convention that would spell out the labor rights that should be guaranteed—by governments and by the ILO—to women and men working in the full range of domestic-worker occupations.

Organizing transnationally in a way that brought pressure to bear on a kind of interstate politics that can seem remote was a daunting prospect. How many domestic workers had ever heard of the ILO? Who could afford to fly to Geneva? The language of high-level interstate diplomacy was formal, abstract, and often deliberately obscure. Moreover, since most university-educated people around the world would be hard-pressed to name a single ILO convention, it appeared unlikely that mobilizing domestic workers' scant resources to push for a new ILO convention was worth the extraordinary investment it would take to achieve this goal.

In the face of these formidable challenges, a group of women domestic workers decided to do just that. After several years of cross-national conversations, they held their first global meeting in Amsterdam in 2006. They decided to organize as a network, a form that would allow for and encourage ongoing grassroots organizing in the places where domestic workers were working and in the places they called home. They committed themselves to avoiding secrecy and hierarchy and, instead, to cultivating transparency and democratic accountability.[52] Furthermore, these early IDWN activists—from the Philippines, Sri Lanka, Brazil, Mexico, Nepal, and other countries that promoted the export of domestic labor—decided that it made organizational sense to embed their fledgling International Domestic Workers' Network within a supportive, already-existing international labor union. They chose the International Union of Food, Agricultural, Hotel,

Restaurant, Catering, Tobacco and Allied Workers' Associations, commonly referred to as the IUF. In addition, because these activists saw their campaigning as part of the larger international women's advocacy, they accepted the offer of assistance from the transnational group Women in Informal Employment: Globalizing and Organizing. Its projects were designed to economically empower women in the informal sector (e.g., as street vendors, waste pickers, and recyclers) and stretched from Peru and Brazil to South Africa and India.[53]

Associating from the start with the IUF and WIEGO gave the transnational domestic-worker activists resources such as information about, and training in, making an impact on the workings of international agencies such as UN Women and the ILO. It also gave domestic workers more visibility, as the IUF and WIEGO could use their established media and Web networks to spread the word about what the domestic workers were trying to achieve and why it mattered to people who themselves were not domestic workers.

The launchers of the IDWN were explicit about their understanding of the consequences of racism in domestic work, especially when the workers were migrants subjected to xenophobia or when the women doing paid domestic work came from locally disempowered ethnic or racial groups. They crafted a political analysis of domestic work and domestic workers that also was explicit about gender. They made the analytical link between the gendered politics of unpaid domestic work and the politics of paid domestic work: "Domestic work fundamentally involves power relationships," they declared. Furthermore, "it is never free of a gender perspective: in all societies domestic work remains seen as 'women's work'; nowhere do men do an equal share of work in the home." They made the connection between women doing paid domestic work and women hiring domestic workers: "It is when women get jobs outside the home that— rather than men of the household doing more of the caring work—other women (or children) are brought in to do it."[54]

Over the next five years, these IDWN activists built a community and found the time and the resources to train themselves in the often arcane technical politics of the ILO. They then developed strategies for persuading government representatives to the ILO of the urgency to pass an international convention for domestic workers' rights.[55]

On June 16, 2011, the International Labor Conference of the International Labor Organization adopted Convention 189, the world's first international treaty to address the rights of domestic workers. The new convention recognized domestic workers as laborers who were due labor rights. It committed those governments that would ratify the convention to guaranteeing "decent work for domestic workers." Any government that signed and ratified Convention 189 would be obligated to reform its own national laws so that they met the conditions of the convention. These labor rights included

- the right to organize;
- the right to a minimum wage;
- the right to a weekly "rest period" of no less than twenty-four hours (during which time a live-in worker would not be required to stay in her employer's residence);
- the right to formal and transparent employer-employee work agreements; and, especially important for migrant workers,
- the right to maintain possession of her identity papers and her passport.[56]

Figure 30. Activists of the International Domestic Workers' Network lobbying for the passage of ILO Convention 189, Geneva, 2011. Photo: Institute of Policy Studies.

The adoption of ILO Convention 189 was historic. As recently as 2000, one could scarcely imagine that women working as cleaners and caregivers in millions of private homes around the globe could persuade diplomats and international civil servants (many of whom themselves hired domestic workers for their own homes) to do something that these officials had hardly had the words for, much less the incentive to do: to declare that women cleaning their household tubs had rights that deserved formal international recognition.

The positive impact of Convention 189 on domestic workers' lives would now depend on legislators and executive officials in each country ratifying it. The first government to ratify 189 was Uruguay, which did so one year after its adoption, in 2012. The governments of the Philippines, Bahrain, Thailand, Spain, Singapore, Argentina, South Africa, Costa Rica, Italy, Germany, and Brazil each ratified Convention 189 by June 2013. Ratification required domestic-worker activists to mobilize and lobby legislators in each of these countries. Behind each of these twelve ratifications is a gendered political story. But what about the governments that have not yet ratified 189? Will ILO Convention 189 ever be debated in the British House of Commons? Will the provisions of Convention 189 ever come to a vote on the floor of the U.S. Senate?

CONCLUSION

In affluent countries, oil-rich countries, and newly industrializing countries, a common formula has developed for making and keeping domestic workers' labor cheap:

- Treat domestic work as stereotypically women's work.
- Channel women from marginalized regional, racial, and ethnic groups into domestic work.
- Keep middle-class women and working-class women politically separated, even when mutually dependent.
- If they are immigrant women, make sure domestic workers' visa and citizenship status remains precarious.
- Ensure that home governments are so nervous about their reliance on domestic workers' remittances that they shy away from challenging host governments' abusive policies toward migrant domestic workers.
- Exempt domestic workers from existing host-country minimum-wage and labor rights legislation.
- Treat domestic workers' work sites as private spheres.
- Resist legally categorizing as employers the women and men who employ domestic workers.
- Treat women in domestic work as impossible to organize or not worth organizing.

- Imagine that a domestic worker has no children and parents of her own to support.

- Imagine that a woman doing paid domestic work in someone else's home is "just like family."

It turns out that none of these eleven pillars of domestic worker exploitation can stand on its own. Each pillar has to be perpetually propped up. The proppers are employers, journalists, editors, labor organizers, immigration officials, public prosecutors, state civil servants, development experts, foreign policy experts, elected politicians, and international agency officials. Women domestic workers who, against all odds, have become grassroots and transnational activists are today making each of these pillars wobble.

CHAPTER NINE

Conclusion

The Personal Is International

The International Is Personal

Theresa Dantes escaped her abusive employer in Qatar and returned home to Manila. At this point, one can imagine what Theresa might have done next. Perhaps she joined a Filipina domestic workers' group that persuaded her country's government to ratify the International Labor Organization's Convention 189 on domestic workers' rights—though she and her fellow domestic workers do not trust their government to enforce all of the convention's commitments. Officials will have to be monitored and pressured by domestic workers to ensure that Filipinas going abroad to clean other people's homes are treated as full-fledged workers, fairly, and with respect.

Imagining the future, we might picture Theresa deciding to invite women from around the world who have experienced international politics firsthand to come to Manila for a workshop. Through Facebook, Skype, and occasional meetings at women's forums and UN gatherings, these women have begun to realize that their political campaigns overlap because their internationalized experiences as women overlap. Theresa thinks that holding a three-day workshop might provide the most valuable setting for a genuine exchange of ideas. She may have heard from other Filipinas working on Dole's banana plantation in the Philippines that workshops provide spaces where women can get to know each other informally, speak openly, compare experiences, and build their own collective understandings of the gendered, inequitable world and of their capacity to change that world.

The first to arrive is Iris Munguia, who flies in from Honduras. Iris has become prominent in the international politics of bananas, but she remains connected to the *bananeras,* the women who worked long hours beside her in the banana plantation's damp, pesticide-filled cleaning sheds. Landing in Manila soon after her, on a flight from Dhaka, is Chobi Mahmud. This is her first trip outside Bangladesh. In the wake of the deadly garment factory fires and building collapse, international nongovernmental organizations have been talking directly to the surviving women, like Chobi. They have paid Chobi's airfare to Manila so she could share her experiences with women from other countries. For Lucky Chhetri, it takes several plane changes to travel from Katmandu to Manila. But she and her entrepreneurial sisters are used to making things happen. If one can learn to scale the Himalayas, one can get to the Philippines.

Fortunately, Ray Acheson was still in New York when Theresa's unexpected invitation arrived. She was across the street from UN headquarters, strategizing with other feminists—from the Women's International League for Peace and Freedom and the International Action Network on Small Arms Women's Network—about how to make sure that the historic gender-violence provision in the new international Arms Trade Treaty would be implemented. They already were hearing rumors of a concerted backlash. Ray had gotten to know several Filipinas active in UN Women, but she never thought she would meet them in their home country. Much closer is Takazato Suzuyo. Flights between Naha and Manila are frequent because so many Filipinas come to Okinawa to work in entertainment businesses around the American military bases there. Some of the Filipinas have told Takazato that they had trained in Manila to be singers, assured that they would be hired as legitimate entertainers when they came to Okinawa. Instead, they told her, upon arrival they had been forced by their bosses to provide sexual services to American military men.[1] Theresa had heard through her new friends in the domestic workers' group that women who were immigrants, as she had been in Qatar, now did their cleaning and child care work without having to live in their employers' homes. These women's experiences of international domestic work seemed to have been quite different from hers. So she invited Rosa to take part. Rosa perhaps had become active in the growing California domestic workers' movement, but she surprised Theresa by suggesting that one of Rosa's middle-class employers, Laurie, come too. Rosa explained that, while she and Laurie lived different political lives, this white American woman also might have experiences of living the "double day" to contribute. Rosa and Laurie arrive together on a flight from San Diego.

There were myriad nationalist movements from which Theresa might have chosen a woman participant. She decided to invite from Marie-Aimée Hélie-Lucas. Although she grew up in Algeria and, as a young woman, fought in the Algerian nationalist movement against French colonialists, Marie-Aimée had felt that she had to go into exile in order to pursue her feminist goals. Her fellow members in Women Living Under Muslim Laws urged her to accept Theresa's invitation.

Before she sent out her workshop invitations, Theresa had talked to local domestic-worker activists about whether to invite a woman married to a diplomat. It seemed as though such a woman's experiences would be too distant from those of a banana worker and the mountain guide. But one of Theresa's new activist friends had cleaned the house of a diplomat and his family stationed in Manila and said the wife seemed frustrated at not being able to pursue her own career as a biologist and was dissatisfied with the constant rounds of social events she was expected to attend. So in the end, Theresa invited Yoko, the wife of the Japanese embassy's first political officer. She asked that only her first name be used so as not to make any waves for her husband, who was on the verge of being promoted to ambassador. Yoko had been posted in Manila for two years and already had raised diplomatic eyebrows when she had invited a group of local Filipina feminists to her home for tea and conversation.

One might imagine that Theresa was a bit nervous when everyone finally was gathered, but she could see that some of the other women were, too, and that put her at ease. She welcomed her nine guests, Iris, Chobi, Lucky, Ray, Takazato, Rosa, Laurie, Marie-Aimée, and Yoko. It did not take much prompting for most of the women to start talking. They began by asking each other about their families. That is always the place to start. Were they raising children on their own? Were they caring for elderly parents? They passed around photos and their smartphones, showing pictures of their children, friends, and extended family members to each other. Then the conversation became more political. Was there a male partner or father who had been reluctant to "allow" them to come to Manila? Who was caring for the children and doing the housework while they were away? Could they afford to lose five days of pay, even low pay?

As they become more relaxed, they start trading stories, especially stories about what people had said upon hearing that the women were invited to take part in a feminist workshop. Many of their male friends, and even some of their female coworkers, were puzzled; some of the men actually laughed. The least understanding called feminists rude, sexist names. But sharing their stories helped take the sting out of these recent memories. It also led the women to talk candidly about how sexism works, how ridicule can be silencing, and how hard it is sometimes for a woman to find her voice when the topic is deemed to be "politics" or "international policy."

One might imagine these ten women talking knowingly about things that affected their sense of genuine security—for instance, governments' immigration policies, the lack of publicly funded child care, the subtleties of racism, stereotypes that place some women on pedestals and others in the gutter, militarism's nurturing of fear and distorted notions of security, corporations' escalating production demands, and unaccountable labor contractors. Together, these women have a wealth of information about global brands, remittances, international debt, nationalist agendas, military bases, development slogans, human trafficking, and environmental hazards, all garnered from their everyday experiences. Yet these topics are not the ones they start with. They start with their most personal relationships, but not because they are naive, parochial, or apolitical. They start there because they know that the one who does the unpaid housework and the feminized caring is integral to the production of blue jeans and bananas, to the promotion of tourism, to the mobilization of nationalist movements, and to the operation of militaries and diplomacy. They know, too, that the way power operates within families is crucial to how power operates in their communities, in their social movements, in their political parties, in their governments, and within international agencies and alliances.

One of the simplest and most disturbing feminist insights crafted in recent decades is that "the personal is political." It is a profound theoretical statement that can be transferred to a T-shirt or bumper sticker. Asserting that "the personal is political" is disturbing, intentionally disturbing, because it means that relationships we once imagined were (and many of our friends and colleagues still prefer to think are) private or merely social are in fact infused with power. Furthermore, those allegedly private, personal relationships are infused with power that is unequal and backed up by public authority.

But the assertion that "the personal is political" is like a palindrome, one of those phrases that can be read backward as well as forward. Read as "the political is personal," the assertion suggests that politics is not shaped merely by what happens in legislative debates, voting booths, political party strategy sessions, court rooms, or war rooms. While men who dominate public life in so many countries have told women to stay in the proverbial kitchen (not travel to workshops in Manila, not organize, not theorize), those same men have used their myriad forms of public power to construct private relationships in ways that have bolstered their own masculinized political control. Without these deliberate gendered maneuvers, men's hold over political life might be far less secure.

Without these gendered maneuvers, moreover, most men's seeming "expertise" in politics would look less impressive. A 2013 cross-national survey of citizens' political knowledge found that in virtually every one of the ten countries studied, "women know less about politics than men regardless of how advanced a country is in terms of gender equality."[2] The authors of the study speculated that this gender gap in political information might be due to the fact that few women play prominent roles in news journalism and elite political life, which discourages many women viewers and readers from seeing how current news accounts are relevant to themselves. While this possible explanation for the country-by-country political information gaps appears feasible, a British feminist journalist analyzing the same ten-country study offered an additional explanation: perhaps the researchers' definitions and measures of what counts as "politics" were too narrow.[3] Perhaps what many women do pay attention to, and do store information about, is encompassed by a broader, some might say more realistic, map of politics—for instance, the availability of affordable child care, the condition of public parks, the accessibility of public transport, the readiness of police to treat a woman with respect when she brings a rape charge, the government's willingness to use sexualized pictures of local women to lure foreign tourists, and the impunity with which employers abuse women on the job. That is, perhaps if the map of what is counted as political were redrawn by feminist-informed cartographers, the gap between women's and men's political knowledge would shrink dramatically.

Explaining why any country has the kind of politics it does should motivate us to be curious about how public life is constructed out of struggles to define masculinity and femininity. Accepting that the "political is personal" prompts one to investigate the politics of marriage, the cheapening of women's labor, ideologies of masculinity, sexually transmitted diseases, and homophobia—not as marginal issues but as matters central to the state. Doing this kind of research becomes just as serious as studying military weaponry or taxation policy. In fact, insofar as the political *is* personal, the latter categories cannot be fully understood without taking into account the former.

To make sense of international politics, we have to read power backward and forward. Power relations between countries and their governments involve more than troop maneuvers and diplomatic emails. Read forward, "the personal is international" insofar as ideas about what it means to be a "respectable" woman or an "honorable" man have been shaped by colonizing policies, international trade strategies, and military doctrines. Today it has almost become a cliché to say that the world is shrinking, that state boundaries are porous: think of KFC opening in Shanghai, sushi eaten in Santiago, Cézannes hanging on walls in Doha, a Korean pop star drawing crowds in New York, and Russian weaponry propping up a Syrian autocrat. We frequently persist, nonetheless, in discussing personal power relationships as if they were contained by sovereign states. We frequently consider violence against women without investigating how the global trade in Internet pornography operates, or how companies offering sex tours and mail-order brides conduct their business across national borders. Similarly, we try to explain how women learn to be "feminine" without unraveling the legacies left by colonial officials who used Victorian ideals of feminine domesticity to sustain their empires; or we try to trace what shapes children's ideas about femininity and masculinity without looking at governments' foreign investment policies that encourage the global advertising campaigns of such giants as McCann Erickson, BBDO, or Saatchi and Saatchi.

Becoming aware that personal relationships have been internationalized, however, may make one only feel guilty for not having paid enough attention to international affairs. "You should know more about the IMF," "Don't switch channels when experts start talking about climate change," "Find out where Guam is." While useful, this new international attentiveness by itself is not sufficient. It leaves untouched our conventional presumptions about just what "international politics" is and where it takes place. Coming to realize that the "personal is international" expands the politically attentive audience, but it fails to transform our understandings of what is happening on the multiple stages of international politics.

The implications of a feminist understanding of international politics are thrown into sharper relief when one reads "the personal is international" the other way around: *the international is personal.* This calls for a radical new imagining of what it takes for governments to ally with each other, to compete with and wage war against each other.

"The international is personal" implies that governments depend on certain kinds of allegedly private relationships in order to conduct their foreign affairs. Governments need more than tax revenues and spy agencies; they also need wives who are willing to provide their diplomatic husbands with unpaid services so those men can develop trusting relationships with other diplomatic husbands. They need not only military hardware but also a steady supply of women's sexual services, as well as military wives' gratitude, to convince their male soldiers that they are manly. To operate in the international arena, governments seek other governments' recognition of their sovereignty; but they also depend on ideas about masculinized dignity and feminized sacrifice to sustain that sense of autonomous nationhood.

Thus the international politics of debt, investment, colonization, decolonization, national security, diplomacy, trade, and military occupation are far more complicated than most conventional experts would have us believe. This may appear paradoxical. Many people, and especially women, are taught that international politics are too complex, too remote, and too tough for the so-called feminine mind to comprehend. If a Hillary Clinton, Angela Merkel, Ellen Johnson Sirleaf, Michelle Bachelet, or Christine Lagarde enters, it is presumably because she has learned to "think like a man."

Conventional analyses stop short of investigating an entire area of international relations, an area that feminist-informed researchers in the still-expanding field of gender and international relations are pioneers in exploring: how states depend on particular artificial constructions of the domestic and private spheres to achieve their political goals. If we take seriously the politics of domestic servants, of women living on or near a military base, or of women who sew Gap and Zara apparel, we discover that international politics are more complicated than nonfeminist analysts imagine.

This is worth saying again: explanations of international politics that are devoid of feminist questioning are too-simple explanations. Such nonfeminist explanations shy away from complexity. They underestimate power.

A feminist investigatory approach exposes a remarkable assortment of the kinds of power it takes to make the complex international political system work the way it currently does. Admittedly, conventional analysts of interstate relations do talk a lot about power. In fact, they put power at the center of their commentaries. These are the sorts of commentaries that are presumed to be most naturally comprehended by manly men; women, especially those women presumed to be conventionally feminine, allegedly do not have an innate taste for either wielding or understanding power. However, feminist-informed explorations of agribusiness plantation prostitution, foreign service corps sexism, and repeated attempts to tame outspoken nationalist women all reveal that, in reality, it takes much *more* power to construct and perpetuate international political relations than we have been led to believe. One result of feminists' insight is that they do not erect false barriers between the fields of "security studies" and "international political economy." Feminists realize that the actual workings of gendered politics routinely blur these artificial fields of investigation.

This is why the ten politically savvy women who might come together for Theresa's imagined Manila workshop start with their domestic lives. It has taken power to deprive women of land titles and pressure them to leave home to work as domestic workers abroad or to stay on banana plantations. It has taken power to keep women marginalized in their countries' diplomatic corps and out of the upper reaches of central banks and finance ministries. It has taken power to exclude women from labor bargaining. It has taken power to keep questions of inequity between local men and women off the agendas of many nationalist movements in industrialized as well as developing societies. It has taken power to keep diverse women in their separate places for the sake of the smooth running of any military base. It has taken power to ensure that UN treaties do not recognize the rights of sexual minorities. It has taken power to ensure that the UN treaties that do take account of violence against women are not implemented. It has taken power to construct popular cultures—through films, advertising, school curricula, television, books, music, fashion, the Internet—that reinforce, rather than subvert, globally gendered hierarchies.

"The international is personal," combined with a sustained feminist curiosity about women's lives and the workings of masculinities, provides a guide to making sense of the WTO, the ILO, the IMF, the Group of Eight, the Group of Twenty, the World Bank, the EU Commission, the Vatican, the Qatar emirate, the Chinese Politboro, the UN Security Council, the International Crimes Court, the African Union, and the Arab League. "The international is personal" is a starting point for making sense of Gap, Apple, Disney, Foxconn, Chiquita Banana, Deutsche Bank, and H&M, as well as the International Committee of the Red Cross, CARE, OXFAM, and Human Rights Watch. To make realistic sense of international politics, we need thorough, feminist-informed gender analyses of each of these organizations—and more.

One can do a feminist-informed gender analysis of anything. And each will make us smarter about how this world works, or fails to work.

Taking seriously the assertion that "the international is personal" means that women—in all their diversity—must be made visible, analytically visible, in our investigations of every one of these organizations, and in the relationships between these organizations. If it is true that cooperative as well as hostile relations between governments, corporations, and international organizations rely on constructions of women as symbols, women as providers of emotional support, women as both unpaid and low-paid workers, women as voters, and women as token participants, then it does not make sense to continue analyzing international politics as if women were a mere afterthought. It does not make sense to collect ungendered data on refugees, private security personnel, earthquake victims, militia members, corporate executives, factory owners, journalists, or peace negotiators. It does not make sense to treat women as if they made eye-catching photo images but do not need to be interviewed.

International policy-making circles may at times look like men's clubs, but international politics as a whole has required women to behave in certain ways. When enough women have refused to behave in those prescribed ways, relations between governments and between governments and corporations have had to change.

That is, women are not just the objects of power, not merely passive puppets or unthinking victims. As we have seen, women of different classes and different ethnic groups have made their own calculations in order to cope with or benefit from the current struggles between states. These calculations result in whole countries becoming related to one another, often in hierarchical terms. In search of adventure, the physical and intellectual excitement typically reserved for men, some affluent women have helped turn other women into exotic landscapes. In pursuit of meaningful paid careers, some women have settled in their governments' colonies or hired women from former colonies. Out of a desire to appear fashionable and bolster their sometimes shaky self-confidence, many women have become the prime consumers of products made by women working for low wages in dangerous factories. And in an effort to measure the progress they have made toward emancipation in their own societies, some women have helped legitimize international global pyramids of "civilization" and "modernity."

Therefore, when asking "Where are the women?"—and following up with "How did they get there?" "Who benefits from their being there?" and "What do they themselves think about being there?"—one should be prepared for complex answers.

Acting out of a new awareness that women, especially in poorer countries, need to be made visible—and audible—on the international stage, one can risk painting over the important dif-

ferences between women. The widening economic class differences between Chinese, for instance, are alarming even Beijing's
male political elite. Those gaping inequalities are sharpening
the differences between rural and urban women, between
women married to politically connected businessmen and
women working on the assembly lines in those men's factories.
Noting inequalities among women is not just a comparative
statement—for instance, noting that urban girls are more likely
to reach secondary school than rural girls, or that affluent women
are more likely to have access to the Internet than working-class
women do. It is a comparative statement with relational consequences. Women's diverse experiences of social class—as well as
of race and ethnicity—can translate into often surprising differences in understandings of femininity, in marital economics, in
relationships with particular men, and in encounters with the
state. In the United States, China, India, Turkey, South Africa,
Vietnam, Mexico, Brazil, Malaysia, Iraq, and Egypt, these widening material and political inequalities between affluent
women, middle-class women, urban poor women, and rural poor
women, especially when exacerbated by racism and ethnocen-
trism, present daunting challenges for any women who are working to create and sustain a vibrant national or transnational
women's movement.

Creating transnational women's banana workers' groups,
launching the International Domestic Workers' Network, building a transnational alliance to lobby for a gender-conscious
arms-trade treaty, organizing a transnational network of women
living near overseas American military bases, creating unions
for women garment workers, sustaining a transnational network
of feminists living under patriarchal religious laws, building a
UN-focused alliance that can take on the "unholy alliance"—

not one of these efforts has been easy. And every day there are those who act to defend their local or global stake in having diverse women lose trust in each other, withdraw support from each other. One might make a list of those patriarchal stakeholders, those people who have come to rely on women's fragmentation. Not all the people on the list will be corporate moguls and political autocrats.

Male officials who make foreign policy might prefer to think of themselves as dealing with high finance or military strategy, but in reality they have self-consciously designed immigration, tourism, labor, foreign service, cultural, and military-base policies in order to divide and control women. They rarely admit it, but they have acted as though their government's or organization's place in world affairs has hinged on how women behaved.

Uncovering these efforts has exposed men *as men*. International politics have relied not only on the manipulation of femininity's multiple meanings but also on the manipulation of ideas about masculinities. Ideas about adventure, modernity, civilization, progress, expertise, rationality, stability, growth, risk, trust, and security have been legitimized by certain kinds of masculinized values, systems, and behavior. That is one of the reasons that each of these ideas has become so potent.

Frequently, male government officials and company executives seek to control women in order to optimize their influence over other men: men as husbands, voters, migrant workers, soldiers, diplomats, intelligence operatives, plantation and factory managers, editors, and bankers. Thus, understanding the international workings of masculinity is important to making feminist sense of international politics. Men's sense of their own manhood has derived from their perceptions both of other men's masculinity and of the femininities of women of different races and social classes. Thus a caveat: one cannot make adequate sense of the international politics of masculinity by avoiding paying close attention to women and femininity. Ideas about masculinities—the full array of masculinities—have been crafted out of ideas about, myths about, and uncertainties about femininities and about actual women. To conduct a reliable investigation of masculinity, one must take women seriously.

Climate change, capitalist globalization, the new arms race, and widening gaps between rich and poor—it is tempting to plunge into the discussion of any of these contemporary issues without bothering to ask, "Where are the women?" In fact, the more urgent the issue—"New York will soon be under water!" "China's military build up is going to set off a world war!"—the more reasonable it seems to *not* ask "Where are the women?" In patriarchal hands, "urgency" is the enemy of feminist investigation.

The previous chapters suggest, however, that these urgent issues demand a gendered analysis precisely because they are urgent, because they call for the fullest, most realistic understandings. As feminist environmental researchers and activists already are revealing, the causes of climate change, for example, and not just its effects, can be realistically tracked only if one exposes the workings of ideas about manliness and femininity and the relations between women and men, each fostered by the deliberate uses of political power. So too can the causes of the new arms race, exploitive globalization, and the widening gaps between rich and poor.

Theresa, Chobi, Takazato, Iris, and the other workshop participants are now, we can imagine, deep into their discussions. The deeper they dig, the more candid they become with each other. They have tried to create an atmosphere of trust, one that encourages each woman to be honest about her worries and puzzles. Together, they are on a journey to understand how banana plantations work, how garment subcontractors perceive women seamstresses, whose security a military base protects, and why women and men who employ domestic workers do not see them as real workers.

Every time the conversation slips into abstractions, one of the women pulls it back to women's complex everyday realities. This is what making feminist sense of international politics sounds like.

NOTES

CHAPTER 1. GENDER MAKES THE WORLD GO ROUND

1. For suggestive clues on what taking seriously women as secretaries would reveal about the Iran-Contra affair, see Barbara Gamarekian, "Consequences of Fawn Hall," *New York Times,* February 28, 1987; Mary Sit, "Hall Tells Secretaries: 'Stand by Your Boss,'" *Boston Globe,* September 30, 1988. For a feminist political analysis of the surprising roles that women as secretaries played in the otherwise masculinized Israeli-Palestinian peace negotiations, see Sarai Aharoni, "Gender and Peace Work: An Unofficial History of Israeli-Palestinian Peace Negotiations," *Politics and Gender* 7, no. 3 (2011): 391–416. For a feminist study of women as secretaries, based on interviews with five hundred Australian secretaries, see Rosemary Pringle, *Secretaries Talk: Sexuality, Power and Work* (London: Verso Books, 1988). An eye-opening study revealing how differently working-class and middle-class Israeli women have interpreted their work as conscript secretaries in the Israeli Defense Force is: Edna Lomsky-Feder and Orna Sasson-Levy, "Serving the Army as Secretaries," *British Journal of Sociology* (2014, forthcoming).

2. I am deeply indebted to feminist scholar Gyoung Sun Jang for opening my eyes to the still barely acknowledged history of diverse

women's work inside the League of Nations. Her fascinating dissertation is: Gyoung Sun Jang, "The Sexual Politics of the Interwar Era
Global Governance: Historicizing the Women's Transnational Movements with(in) the League of Nations, 1919–1940" (PhD diss., Women's
Studies, Clark University, Worcester, MA, 2009).

3. Hillary Clinton is the U.S. lawyer who has served as First Lady
(that is, the wife of the male president), been elected U.S. senator from
New York, and been appointed U.S. secretary of state; Mary Robinson
is the Irish lawyer who has been elected president of Ireland, served as
the United Nations high commissioner for human rights, and served as
the U.N. secretary general's special envoy for the Great Lakes Region
of Africa; Ellen Johnson Sirleaf is the Liberian economist who has been
a World Bank economist, elected president of Liberia, and awarded a
Nobel Peace Prize; Shirin Ebadi is the Iranian lawyer who, for her work
defending Iranians' human rights, was awarded the Nobel Peace Prize;
Angela Merkel is leader of Germany's Christian Democratic Party and
the German chancellor (head of government); Christine Lagarde has
been France's minister of finance and is the first woman ever appointed
managing director of the International Monetary Fund.

4. Two books that bring together thoughtful reflections on how to
conduct investigations of women's experiences of international politics and the workings of masculinities and femininities in their often
tension-filled lives are: Dyan Mazurana, Karen Jacobson, and Lacey
A. Gale, eds., *Research Methods in Conflict Settings: A View from Below*
(New York: Cambridge University Press, 2013); Brooke Ackerly, Maria
Stern, and Jacqui True, eds., *Feminist Methodologies in International Relations* (New York: Cambridge University Press, 2006).

5. These figures come from a study by the independent monitoring group Media Matters for America, which examined evening programs during the month of April 2013 broadcast on CNN, Fox News,
and MSNBC. Rob Savillo and Oliver Willis, "Report: Diversity
on Evening Cable News in 13 Charts," Media Matters for America,
May 13, 2013, http://mediamatters.org/research/2013/05/13/report-
diversity-on-evening-cable-news-in-13-ch/194012. The British group
Women in Journalism revealed a similarly masculinized pattern
when, in 2012, they surveyed the front-page stories in nine of Brit-

ain's national newspapers. They found that, of the nine papers, only one (*Daily Express*, a tabloid) gave 50 percent of its front-page stories to women journalists. On the front pages of the well-known and influential *Times*—sometimes referred to as "the Times of London"—male journalists had 82 percent of the bylines, while women journalists had a mere 18 percent. This same study found that of all those quoted or mentioned by name in the lead stories of Britain's nine national papers, 84 percent were men. Jane Martinson, Kira Cochrane, Sue Ryan, Tracy Corrigan, Fiona Bawdon, "Seen but Not Heard: How Women Make Front Page News," Women in Journalism, October 15, 2012, www.womeninjournalism.co.uk/wp-content/uploads/2012/10/Seen_but_not_heard.pdf. For more data on the likelihood of men rather than women being chosen by television news producers to appear as experts on their shows, see Cynthia Enloe and Joni Seager, "Media," *The Real State of America Atlas: Mapping the Myths and Truths of the United States* (New York: Penguin Books, 2011), 40–41.

6. For a description of the three Ukrainian young women who launched Femen, noted for its bold feminist protest uses of feminine nudity, see David M. Herszenhorn, "Ukraine's Feminist Shock Troops," *International Herald Tribune*, June 1–2, 2013. For a report on physical assaults on Femen activists, see David M. Herszenhorn, "Feminists Ask Protection after Attack in Ukraine," *New York Times*, August 19, 2013.

7. See Catia Cecilia Confortini, *Intelligent Compassion: Feminist Critical Methodology in the Women's International League for Peace and Freedom* (Oxford: Oxford University Press, 2012).

8. Learn more about each of these transnational feminist groups by going to their respective websites: Women Living Under Muslim Laws, www.wluml.org; International Network of Women in Black, www.womeninblack.org; Women's Global Network for Reproductive Rights, www.wgnrr.org; International Women's Health Coalition, http://iwhc.org; Our Bodies Ourselves Global Network, www.ourbodiesourselves.org; Equality Now, www.equalitynow.org; International Action Network on Small Arms Women's Network, www.iansa-women.org; Women's Initiatives for Gender Justice, www.iccwomen.org; International Domestic Workers Network, www.idwn

.org; International Gay and Lesbian Human Rights Commission, www.iglhrc.org; Women's International League for Peace and Freedom, www.peacewomen.org; NGO Working Group on Women, Peace and Security, www.womenpeacesecurity.org; and Women in Conflict Zones Network, www.yorku.ca/wicznet. For an exploration of how feminist groups become globalized and with what consequences, see Mary Hawksworth, *Globalization and Feminist Activism* (Lanham, MD: Rowman and Littlefield, 2006).

9. Among the outpouring of feminist-informed academic explorations that has helped create and enliven the academic field of gender and international relations are: J. Ann Tickner, *Gendering World Politics* (New York: Columbia University Press, 2001); J. Ann Tickner and Laura Sjoberg, eds., *Feminism and International Relations* (London: Routledge, 2011); Christine Sylvester, *Feminist International Relations: An Unfinished Journey* (Cambridge: Cambridge University Press, 2001); V. Spike Peterson and Anne Sisson Runyan, *Global Gender Issues in the New Millennium* (Boulder, CO: Westview Press, 2010); Jan Jindy Pettman, *Worlding Women: Feminist International Politics* (London: Routledge, 1996); Laura Shepherd, *Gender, Violence and Security* (London: Zed Books, 2008); Shirin Rai, *The Gender Politics of Development* (London: Zed Books, 2008); Elisabeth Prugl and Mary Meyer, eds., *Gender and Global Governance* (Boston: Rowman and Littlefield, 1999); Laura Sjoberg, ed., *Gender and International Security: Feminist Perspectives* (London: Routledge, 2010); Annick T. R. Wibben, *Feminist Security Studies* (London: Routledge, 2011); Marianne Marchand and Anne Sisson Runyan, eds., *Gender and Global Restructuring* (London: Routledge, 2000); Carol Cohn, ed., *Women and Wars* (Cambridge: Polity Press, 2013); Marysia Zalewski, *Feminist International Relations* (London: Routledge, 2013); Joyce Kauffman and Kristen Williams, *Women, the State and War: A Comparative Perspective on Citizenship and Nationalism* (Lantham, MD: Lexington Books, 2007); Cynthia Weber, *International Relations Theory* (London: Routledge, 2014); Laura Sjoberg, *Gender and International Relations* (New York: Routledge, 2009); Laura Shepherd, ed., *Gender Matters in Global Politics* (New York: Routledge, 2014); Cynthia Weber, *Queer International Relations* (Oxford: Oxford University Press, 2014). The academic journal that has been created to provide an interdisciplinary

space for feminist-informed studies of international politics is the *International Feminist Journal of Politics*. Among *IFJP*'s contributors and editors are many of these same authors, but also many scholars from dozens of countries who more recently have entered and shaped the field of gender and international relations.

10. For comparative data on women and men in U.S. print, television, radio, and Internet news outlets, see Diana Mitsu Klos, *The Women's Media Center: The Status of Women in the U.S. Media 2013*, Women's Media Center, 2013, www.womensmediacenter.com/pages/statistics. The Women's Media Center conducts regular research on the treatment of women in the media, as well as on the conditions of women as professional media producers, editors, and reporters. The Center was founded by Gloria Steinem, Robin Morgan, and Jane Fonda. For British gender monitoring of news media, see Women in Journalism, http://womeninjournalism.co.uk.

11. Women's eNews, http://womensenews.org/.

12. Copies of these lively publications from the late 1800s to the present, as well as the records of the influential feminist bookstores, such as New Words of Cambridge, Massachusetts, are collected and available to the public at several women's history libraries and via their online sites: the Schlesinger Library on the History of Women in America, Radcliffe Institute, Harvard University; the Sophia Smith Collection, Smith College, Northampton, MA; the Women's Library (formerly the Fawcett Library), London School of Economics; the Lesbian Herstory Archives, Brooklyn; the Lesbian Archives, Amsterdam.

13. When the Center for Women's Global Leadership brought together activists and scholars to create a strategy for pressing the UN to take explicit account of women in its post-2015 development goals, one of the topics they put on their agenda was making media aware of the expertise of feminist economists: *Towards the Realization of Women's Rights and Gender Equality: Post 2015 Sustainable Development* (New Brunswick, NJ: Center for Women's Global Leadership, Rutgers University, 2013), www.cwgl.rutgers.edu.

14. See Nell Irvin Painter, *Sojourner Truth: A Life, a Symbol* (New York: W.W. Norton, 1996); Margaret Washington, *Sojourner Truth's America* (Urbana: University of Illinois Press, 2009).

15. Claire Midgley, *Women against Slavery: The British Campaigns, 1780–1870* (London: Routledge, 1992).

16. A exciting new biography of the mid-nineteenth-century American writer, editor, and women's rights advocate Margaret Fuller reveals how she came to make the connection between the enslavement of Africans in the United States and the slavery-like conditions experienced by white married women. Megan Marshall, *Margaret Fuller: A New American Life* (Boston: Houghton Mifflin Harcourt, 2013).

17. See, for example, Margot Badran, *Feminists, Islam and Nation: Gender and the Making of Modern Egypt* (Princeton: Princeton University Press, 1995); Bonnie S. Anderson, *Joyous Greetings: The First International Women's Movement, 1830–1860* (Oxford: Oxford University Press, 2000); Caroline Daley and Melanie Nolan, eds., *Suffrage and Beyond: International Feminist Perspectives* (New York: New York University Press, 1994). For a huge online database (already 150,000 pages and still growing) of documents and reports on women's international organizing from the mid-nineteenth century to the present, see Kathryn Sklar and Thomas Dublin, eds., *Women and Social Movements, International, 1840 to Present* (Alexandria, VA: Alexander Street Press, n.d.), http://alexanderstreet .com/products/women-and-social-movements-international.

18. This account is based on conversations and email exchanges by the author between March and July 2013 with Ray Acheson, Maria Butler, Madeleine Rees, and Abigail Ruane, all of the Women's International League for Peace and Freedom (New York and Geneva offices), and Sarah Taylor of the NGO Working Group on Women, Peace and Security, based in New York. Each played a key role in the multiyear, transnational feminist activist campaign to insure that gender-based violence was specifically and effectively addressed in the historic 2013 Arms Trade Treaty. Written sources for this narrative include: WILPF, IANSA Women's Network, Amnesty International, and Religions for Peace, "A United Call to Explicitly Include Gender-Based Violence in the Criteria," June 2012, www.wilpfinternational.org; International Action Network on Small Arms Women's Network, "About the IANSA Women's Network": www.iansa-women .org/about.html, accessed May 10, 2013; IANSA Women's Network, "IANSA Women Continue to Push for a Strong ATT That Will

Prevent Gender-Based Violence": www.iansa-women.org/node/819, accessed May 10, 2013; Women's International League for Peace and Freedom, "Make It Binding: Include Gender-Based Violence in the ATT," PeaceWomen, April 2013; www.peacewomen.org/pages/att; Ray Acheson, "A Tale of Two Treaties," *Arms Trade Monitor*, no. 6.9 (March 27, 2013), http://reachingcriticalwill.org/images/documents /Disarmament-for a/att/monitor/ATTMonitor6.9.pdf; Rebecca Gerome (IANSA Women's Network) and Maria Butler (WILPF's Peace-Women), "A Step Back? 'Gender-Based Violence' vs. 'Violence against Women and Children,'" *ATT Monitor*, no. 5.11 (March 2013), www .peacewomen.org/assets/file/ATT/att_and_gbv.pdf; Ray Acheson, Maria Butler, and Sofia Tuvestad, "Preventing Armed Gender-Based Violence: A Binding Requirement in the New Draft ATT Text," WILPF, March 28, 2013, http://peacewomen.org/assets/file/article_ gvb_march28_final.pdf; Ray Acheson and Beatrice Fihn, "The Failure of Consensus," *Arms Trade Treaty Monitor: The Blog*, April 1, 2013, http:// attmonitor.blogspot.com/2013/04/the_failure_of_consensus_html; Robert Zuber, "Distance Runner," *Arms Trade Treaty Monitor: The Blog*, April 1, 2013, http://attmonitor.blogspot.com/2013/04/distance-run-ner.html; Katherine Prizeman, "Looking to the Future of the ATT: Shifting Attention to Implementation," *Arms Trade Treaty Monitor: The Blog*, April 2, 2013, http://attmonitor.blogspot.com/2013/04/looking-to-future-of-att-shifting.html; Ray Acheson, "The ATT: A Start to Challenging the Status Quo," April 2, 2013, http://attmonitor.blogspot. com/2013/04/the-att-start-to-challenging-status-quo.html;   Maria Butler, editorial, *PeaceWomen Enews*, April 2013, www.peacewomen.org.

19. United Nations General Assembly, *Final United Nations Confer-ence on the Arms Trade Treaty, Draft Decision, Submitted by the President of the Final Conference: The Arms Trade Treaty* (New York: United Nations, March 27, 2013), 6. To take effect internationally, the Arms Trade Treaty will have to be both signed and ratified by at least fifty govern-ments. The U.S. government, as of the end of 2013, had only signed the ATT, without even a date scheduled for its ratification to be debated and voted upon by the U.S. Senate. Prospects for the ATT's adoption by the U.S. government are deemed slim, owing to the political influ-ence wielded in American politics by the pro-gun lobby, led by the

National Rifle Association. "Editorial: Containing the Conventional Arms Trade," *New York Times,* October 1, 2013. On the other hand, several recent international treaties (e.g., the treaty banning land mines and the treaty establishing the International Crimes Court) have garnered sufficient numbers of government ratifications to go into effect without ratification by the United States.

20. A rare effort to chart and compare murders of women (as distinct from women's wartime deaths) around the world is: Joni Seager, "Murder," *Penguin Atlas of Women in the World* (New York: Penguin Books, 2009), 30–31.

21. There is a growing body of provocative studies that track the evolutions of, and contests between, masculinities within particular countries, many of them conducted by gender-curious ethnographers. See, for instance, John Osburg, *Anxious Wealth: Money and Morality among China's New Rich* (Stanford, CA: Stanford University Press, 2013); Robin Le Blanc, *The Art of the Gut: Manhood, Power, and Ethics in Japanese Politics* (Berkeley: University of California Press, 2010); Daniel Conway, *Masculinities, Militarisation and the End Conscription Campaign: War Resistance in Apartheid South Africa* (Manchester: Manchester University Press, 2012). Among the innovative cross-national studies of diverse masculinities, their interactions, and their political implications are: Marysia Zalewski and Jane Parpart, eds., *The "Man" Question in International Relations* (Boulder, CO: Westview Press, 1998); Jane Parpart and Marysia Zalewski, eds., *Rethinking the Man Question: Sex, Gender and Violence in International Relations* (London: Zed Books, 2008); Paul Kirby and Marsh Henry, eds., "Rethinking Masculinity and Practices of Violence in Conflict Settings," special issue, *International Feminist Journal of Politics* 14, no. 4 (2012); Paul Higate, ed., *Military Masculinities: Identity and the Sate* (Westport, CT: Praeger, 2003); Paul Amar, "Middle East Masculinity Studies," *Journal of Middle East Women's Studies* 7, no. 3 (Fall 2011): 36–71; Terrell Carver, "Being a Man," *Government and Opposition* 41, no. 3 (2006): 477–95.

22. Sandra Harding, a pioneering theorist in the feminist studies of science, has written extensively on how rational thinking has been presumed to be a hallmark of masculinity. See, for instance, Sandra Harding, *The Science Question in Feminism* (Ithaca, NY: Cornell Univer-

sity Press, 1986); Sandra Harding, *Sciences from Below: Feminisms, Postcolonialities and Modernities* (Durham, NC: Duke University Press, 2008).

23. Carol Cohn, "Sex and Death in the Rational World of Defense Intellectuals," *Signs* 12, no. 4 (1987): 687–718; Carol Cohn with Felicity Hill and Sara Ruddick, *The Relevance of Gender in Eliminating Weapons of Mass Destruction* (Stockholm: Weapons of Mass Destruction Commission, 2005).

CHAPTER 2. "LADY TRAVELERS," BEAUTY QUEENS, STEWARDESSES, AND CHAMBERMAIDS

1. "China Becomes World's Biggest Source of Tourists, Academy Says," *Bloomberg News,* April 25, 2013, www.bloomberg.com/news/2013–04–25/china-becomes-world-s-biggest-source-of-tourists-academy-says.html. As a tourist destination, China was, by 2013, ranked number 3 in the world, after France and the United States. Associated Press, "World Briefing: China: Foreign Tourism Falls, and Smog May Be One Reason," *New York Times,* August 14, 2013. France has become the favorite overseas destination for Chinese tourists, with 1.4 million Chinese tourists visiting France in 2012 alone. Dan Levin, " Wooing, and Also Resenting, Chinese Tourists," *New York Times*, September 17, 2013.

2. Dan Smith, *The State of the World Atlas,* 9th ed. (London: New Internationalist; New York: Penguin Books, 2013), 52–53.

3. UN Women and UN World Tourism Organization, *Global Report on Women in Tourism 2010* (New York: UN Women and UN World Tourism Organization, 2011). See also Thomas Baum, "International Perspectives on Women and Work in Hotels, Catering and Tourism" (Gender Working Paper 1/2013, International Labor Organization, Geneva, 2013). Baum estimates tourism's contribution to global GDP as having reached 9 percent by 2012 (p. 8).

4. "Tourism a Vehicle for Gender Equality and Women's Empowerment," UN Women, March 11, 2011, www.unwomen.org/2011/03/tourism-a-vehicle-for-gender-equality-and-womens-empowerment.

5. Ibid.

6. For a thorough discussion of how gender conventions shape women's travel—and how that in turn shapes women's limited access to rights and opportunities—see Mona Domosh and Joni Seager, *Putting Women in Place: Feminist Geographers Make Sense of the World* (New York: Guilford, 2001).

7. Joni Seager, "In Their Place," *The Penguin Atlas of Women in the World,* 4th ed. (New York: Penguin Books, 2009), 18–19.

8. U.K. Department of Transport, *National Travel Survey 2010: Driving License Holding and Vehicle Availability* (London: Department for Transport, 2010), www.gov.uk/government/uploads/system/uploads/attachment_data/file/8933/nts2010–02.pdf.

9. From Richard Montague's *The Life and Adventures of Mrs. Christian Davies,* 1740, quoted in Julie Wheelwright, "Amazons and Military Maids," *Women's Studies International Forum* 10, no. 5 (1987): 491. See also Julie Wheelwright, *Amazons and Military Maids* (London: Pandora Press, 1989).

10. Vita Sackville-West, October 5, 1920, quoted in Nigel Nicolson, *Portrait of a Marriage* (New York: Atheneum, 1973), 109–11. Some Muslim women at this time dressed as men in order to escape the confines of class and gender. On the eve of World War I, Turkish women in the Organization for the Rights of Women launched a campaign to gain for women the right to travel without male consent. One stunt undertaken to make their point was a flight in 1913 by Belkis Sekvet, the first Turkish woman to pilot an airplane; she wore men's clothes and meant to demonstrate that women were as brave, and thus as able to travel, as their male counterparts. See Sarah Graham-Brown, *Images of Women: The Portrayal of Women in Photography of the Middle East, 1860–1950* (New York: Columbia University Press, 1988), 142–43.

11. Lisa Wenner with Peggy Perri, "Pack Up Your Sorrows: The Oral History of an Army Nurse in Vietnam" (typescript, Smith College, Northampton, MA, 1986), 15–16.

12. Mildred Cable and Francesca French, quoted in Mary Morris, with Larry O'Connor, eds., *The Illustrated Virago Book of Women Travellers* (London: Virago Press, 1996), 133.

13. Mary Seacole, a Black Caribbean woman, is an important exception to the otherwise white Victorian lady travelers. For an

account of her adventures in the Crimea and Europe, see Ziggi Alexander and Audrey Dewjee, eds., *Wonderful Adventures of Mrs. Seacole in Many Lands* (Bristol, U.K.: Falling Wall Press, 1984). Two useful guides to the abundant literature written by lady travelers, much of it now in new editions, are: Jane Robinson, ed., *A Bibliography of Women Travellers* (Oxford: Oxford University Press, 1989); Marion Tinling, ed., *Woman into the Unknown: A Source Book on Women Explorers and Travelers* (Westport, CT: Greenwood Press, 1989).

14. Katherine Frank, *A Voyager Out* (New York: Houghton Mifflin, 1986). For a more critical assessment of Mary Kingsley, see Deborah Birkett, "The Invalid at Home, the Samson Abroad," *Women's Review* (London), no. 6 (1987): 18–19. Also Deborah Birkett, "West Africa's Mary Kingsley," *History Today* (May 1987).

15. *Ladies in the Field: The Museum's Unsung Explorers,* exhibition at the American Museum of Natural History, New York, December 1986. The papers and diaries of Delia Akeley, Dina Brodsky, Sally Clark, Mrs. Bogoras, and Yvette Borup Andrew are available in the museum's Rare Book Department.

16. Robert W. Rydell, *All the World's a Fair: Visions of Empire at the World Expositions, 1876–1916* (Chicago: University of Chicago Press, 1984), 2.

17. Ibid., 118.

18. Jeanne Madeline Weimann, *The Fair Women* (Chicago: Academy Press, 1981). On the 1876 Centennial Exhibition, see William D. Andrews and Deborah C. Andrews, "Technology and the Housewife in Nineteenth Century America," *Women's Studies* 2 (1974): 323–24.

19. Louis Turner and John Ash, *The Golden Hordes: International Tourism and the Pleasure Periphery* (New York: St. Martin's Press, 1976), 20–21.

20. Maxine Feifer, *Tourism in History: From Imperial Rome to the Present* (New York: Stern and Day, 1986), 10–11. For more on later European travel, especially by male aristocrats in the seventeenth and eighteenth centuries, see John Tower, "The Grand Tour: A Key Phase in the History of Tourism," *Annals of Tourism Research* 12 (1985): 297–333; Judith Adler, "Youth on the Road: Reflections on the History of Tramping," *Annals of Tourism Research* 12 (1985): 337–50; Susan L. Blake, "A Woman's Trek: What Difference Does Gender Make?" in *Western*

Women and Imperialism, ed. Margaret Strobel and Nupur Chaudhuri (Bloomington: Indiana University Press, 1992).

21. The principal source of information on Thomas Cook Tours is the Thomas Cook Archives. They have been digitalized and are available online as part of the United Kingdom's National Register of Archives, www.nationalarchives.gov.uk/nra/onlinelists/GB2065 ARCHIVES.pdf. The archives hold the collections of Cook's *Excursionist,* launched in 1855, and *Travellers' Gazette,* which made its debut in 1905.

22. "How Four Ladies Visited the Rhine," *Cook's Excursionist and Cheap Trip Advertiser,* August 20, 1855, 2. In Boston, abolitionist and anti-war campaigner Julia Ward Howe helped launch the Women's Rest Tour Association in 1891. Its upper-class members, eager to travel abroad without male companions, created a file of practical information about places to stay in Europe suitable for respectable women. Today the association and its files exist as the Travel International Exchange; see William A. Davis, "Travel Exchange Is Still Marching On," *Boston Globe,* November 15, 1987.

23. "About Thomas Cook," Thomas Cook, www.thomascook.com, accessed January 7, 2014.

24. Peter Stalker, "Going Places: Westerners Invade Paradise," *New Internationalist,* December 1984, excerpted in *Utne Reader,* July–August 1987, 104.

25. Orlando Crowcroft, "Tourism in Egypt: Hope Amid a Slow Recovery," CNN, May 23, 2013, www.cnn.com/2013/05/23/travel/egypt-tourism.

26. David D. Kirkpatrick, "Egypt: Last Place on Tourism List," *New York Times,* March 14, 2013; Jennifer Blanke and Thea Chiesa, eds., *The Travel and Tourism Competitiveness Report 2013* (Geneva: World Economic Forum, 2013), www.weforum.org/issues/travel-and-tourism-competitiveness. The report's writers assessed 140 countries' tourism industries not only in terms of safety for tourists but also in terms of services, effective planning, and infrastructure. Based on these combined criteria, the World Economic Forum ranked the world's top ten countries for tourism, in descending order, as Switzerland, Germany, Austria, Spain, United Kingdom, United States, France, Canada, Sweden, Singapore. After Singapore, the next three non-Western countries

in the World Economic Forum's tourism rankings were South Korea (twenty-fifth), Barbados (twenty-seventh), and United Arab Emirates (twenty-eighth). For an exploration of the complex international cultural politics of Western tourists in Egypt, see Elisa Wynne-Hughes, "The International Contact Zones in Cairo" (PhD diss., Department of Politics, University of Bristol, U.K., 2013).

27. For a study of the role of Egyptian women's campaign against sexual harassment in Egypt's Arab Spring, see Cynthia Enloe, *Seriously! Investigating Crashes and Crises as If Women Mattered* (Berkeley: University of California Press, 2013).

28. Sohaila Abdulali, "I Was Wounded; My Honor Wasn't," op-ed, *New York Times,* January 8, 2013. The essay appeared in the *New York Times* online on January 7, 2013, www.nytimes.com/2013/01/08/opinion /after-being-raped-i-was-wounded-my-honor-wasnt.html.

29. See, for instance, Swapna Majumdar, "India's Rape Furor Catalyzes New Alliances," Women's eNews, January 14, 2013, http:// womensenews.org/story/rape/130112/indias-rape-furor-catalyzes-new-alliance; Jim Yardley, "Urging Action, Report on Brutal Rape Condemns India's Treatment of Women," *New York Times,* January 23, 2013; "Full Text of Justice Verma's Report (PDF)," *The Hindu,* January 23, 2013, www.thehindu.com/news/resources/full-text-of-justice-vermas-report-pdf/article4339457.ece.

30. Maseeh Rahman, "India Tourist Visits Down 25% Following Fatal Delhi Gang Rape," *The Guardian,* March 31, 2013, www.guardian .co.uk/world/2013/mar/31/india-tourist-visits-down-delhi-gang-rape.

31. Neha Thirani Bagri and Heather Timmons, "India Scrambles to Reassure Tourists Shaken by Recent Attacks on Women," *New York Times,* June 11, 2013.

32. Ibid.

33. "The Miss World History," Miss World, http://missworld.com /History, accessed June 20, 2013; Maurn Judkis, "Miss World Pageant," *Washington Post,* August 17, 2012, www.washingtonpost.com/blogs /arts-post/post/miss-world-pageant-what-in-the-world-is-it.

34. Colleen Ballerino Cohen, Richard Wilke, and Beverly J. Stoeltje, eds., *Beauty Queens on the Global Stage* (New York: Psychology Press, 1996); Colleen Ballerino Cohen, *Take Me to My Paradise: Tourism*

and Nationalism in the British Virgin Islands (New Brunswick, NJ: Rutgers University Press, 2012).

35. A valuable analysis of the complex debates surrounding India's participation in global beauty contests is: Rupal Oza, *Making of Neoliberal India: Nationalism, Gender and the Paradoxes of Globalization* (New York: Routledge, 2006). Another provocative exploration of contemporary femininities and Indian nationalist media is: Purnima Mankekar, *Screening India, Viewing Politics: An Ethnography of Television, Womanhood and Nation in Postcolonial India* (Durham, NC: Duke University Press, 1999). Regarding the debate among overseas South Sudanese over whether a Miss South Sudan would fortify or undermine a South Sudanese nationalist spirit, see Caroline Faria, "Gender and Nation-Building in Diasporic Discourse," *International Feminist Journal of Politics* 12, no. 2 (June 2010): 222–43. Caroline Faria has also investigated men's roles in South Sudanese women's beauty pageants: "Staging a New South Sudan in the U.S.A.: Men, Masculinities and Nationalist Performance at a Diasporic Beauty Pageant," *Gender, Place and Culture* 19, no. 36 (October 2011): 1– 20.

36. For a world map showing which countries' women have won the most international beauty queen contests, see Seager, *Penguin Atlas of Women in the World*, 52–53.

37. Janet Elise Johnson, Thorgerdur Einarsdottir, Gyda Margart Petursdottir, "A Feminist Theory of Corruption: Lessons from Iceland," *Politics and Gender* 9, no. 2 (June 2013): 189.

38. Annadis Rudolfsdottir, "Blonde Ambition: The Rise and Decline of the Miss Iceland Beauty Contest" (lecture presented at the Gender Institute, transcript of a lecture given at the London School of Economics, November 1998).

39. A Miss Iceland brochure quoted in ibid.

40. I am grateful to Annadis Rudolfsdottir, a faculty member and feminist at the University of Iceland—and one of the self-nominated Miss Iceland candidates—for sharing this account. Email correspondence with the author, June 2013. See also "MP Signs Up for Miss Iceland Beauty Contest," *News of Iceland,* June 14, 2013, www.newsoficeland.com/home/entertainment-leisure/other /item/1696-mp-signs-up-for-miss-iceland-beauty-contest.

41. Jo Stanley, "Women at Sea," *Spare Rib*, September 1987, 26–27. See also Henriette Louise, *Sailors in Skirts* (London: Regency Press, 1980); John Maxtone Graham, *Liners to the Sun* (London: Macmillan, 1985). For reports on the booming cruise-ship industry, see *New York Times*, September 28, 1987 and August 28, 1988. I am indebted to David G. Enloe for his research on ocean-liner crews. The most recent feminist-informed study of the racialized gendered divisions of labor used by large cruise ship companies is: Christine B.N. Chin, *Cruising in the Global Economy: Profits, Pleasure and Work at Sea* (London: Ashgate, 2008). See also Christine B.N. Chin, "Labour Flexibilization at Sea," *International Feminist Journal of Politics* 10, no. 1 (2008): 1–18. For demographics and revenues of the global cruise industry (in which Carnival and Royal Caribbean are the two largest companies), see the Cruise Lines International Association's annual survey: www.cruising.org.

42. Kelli Gant, "Women in Aviation," The Ninety-Nines, www.ninety-nines.org/index.cfm/women_in_aviation_article.htm, accessed June 13, 2013.

43. Kathleen M. Barry, *Femininity in Flight: A History of Flight Attendants* (Durham, NC: Duke University Press, 2007), 18–23.

44. This fascinating story, based on interviews by Christine Yano with scores of Japanese American women flight attendants who formerly worked for Pan Am, is told in Christine R. Yano, *Airborne Dreams: "Nisei" Stewardesses and Pan American World Airways* (Durham, NC: Duke University Press, 2011).

45. Air Lanka advertisement, *Far Eastern Economic Review*, May 1, 1986. See also Jane Clarke and Amanda Hood, "Hostess with the Mostest," *Spare Rib*, October 1986, 15–17.

46. Barry, *Femininity in Flight*, 174–209. See also Victoria Vantoch, *The Jet Sex: Airline Stewardesses and the Making of an American Icon* (Philadelphia: University of Pennsylvania Press, 2013).

47. Barbara Vanderhei, quoted by Joe Sharkey in "Stewardesses Blazed a Trail in Feminism," *New York Times*, June 4, 2013.

48. A collection of studies on West Indian Caribbean masculinities—diverse by ethnicity, class, and country—and West Indian women's responses to them, is: Rhoda Reddock, ed., *Interrogating Caribbean Masculinities* (Kingston, Jamaica: University of West Indies Press, 2004).

49. Tom Barry, Beth Wood, and Deb Preusch, *The Other Side of Paradise* (New York: Grove Press, 1984), 85. See also E. Philip English, *The Great Escape: An Examination of North-South Tourism* (Ottawa: North-South Institute, 1986).

50. Jan H. Mejer, "Capitalist Stages, State Formation and Ethnicity in Hawaii," *National Journal of Sociology* 1, no. 2 (Fall 1987):199; Phyllis Andors, "Women and Work in Shenshen," *Bulletin of Concerned Asian Scholars* 20, no. 3 (1988): 27.

51. Veronica M. Fenix, "Beyond 8 to 5: Women Workers Speak Out," in *Kamalayaan: Feminist Writings in the Philippines,* ed. Pennie S. Azarcon (Quezon City, Philippines: Pilipina, 1987), 37. For more on the effects of tourism on women's economic status during this era, see Janice Monk and Charles Alexander, "Free Port Fallout: Gender, Employment and Migration on Margarita Island," *Annals of Tourism Research* 13 (1986): 393–413; Shireen Samarasuriya, *Who Needs Tourism? Employment for Women in the Holiday Industry of Sudugama, Sri Lanka* (Colombo, Sri Lanka: Women and Development, 1982).

52. These data come from two UN reports: Thomas Baum, *International Perspectives on Women and Work in Hotels, Catering and Tourism* (Geneva: Bureau for Gender Equality and Sectoral Activities Department, International Labour Organization, 2013); UN Women and UN World Tourism Organization, *Global Report on Women in Tourism 2010: Preliminary Findings* (New York: UN Women; Madrid: UN World Tourism Organization, 2011).

53. Baum, *International Perspectives on Women and Work in Hotels, Catering and Tourism,* 2013.

54. Aldo Salvador and Ana Garcia Pando, "Empowering Women through Entrepreneurship in the Galapagos Islands Ecuador," in UN Women and UN World Tourism Organization, *Global Report on Women in Tourism 2010,* p. ix.

55. Kristie Drucza, "Three Pioneering Nepali Sisters," in UN Women and World Tourism Organization, *Global Report on Women in Tourism 2010,* p. viii. The Three Sisters Adventure and Trekking Company's website is www.3sistersadventures.com.

56. I am indebted to Lois Wasserspring, professor of political science at Wellesley College, for her many insights into the difficulties facing

craftswomen dealing with their own government and with tourism middlemen. Her fifteen years of studying highly regarded Mexican women ceramics artists in rural Oaxaca, women whose works have become well-known among discerning tourists and gallery owners, has revealed the ways in which even successful, celebrated craftswomen remain impoverished. See her *Growing Up Poor and Female in Rural Mexico* (forthcoming).

57. Thomas Fuller, "Thais Cast a Wide Net for Diverse Tourists," *New York Times,* August 4, 2013.

58. An especially valuable ethnography of Thai young women working in urban garment factories in the 1990s is: Mary Beth Mills, *Thai Women in the Global Labor Force* (New Brunswick, NJ: Rutgers University Press, 2002). An innovative comparison of militarized tourism in two places where U.S. military bases are prominent, is: Vernadette Vicuna Gonzalez, *Securing Paradise: Tourism and Militarism in Hawaii and the Philippines* (Durham, NC: Duke University Press, 2013.

59. The population figures come from a Malaysian journalist, Halinah Todd, in her article "Military Prostitution: Assault on Women," *The Mobilizer* (Mobilization for Survival) (Summer 1987): 8. The figures on business establishments, and the quotation of a women working in one of these establishments, come from Pasuk Phongpaichit, "Bangkok Masseuses: Tourism—Selling Southeast Asia," *Southeast Asian Chronicle,* no. 78 (April 1981): 15–16. Among the new studies of the early-twentieth-century anti-sex-trafficking international movements is: Stephanie A. Limoncelli, *The Politics of Trafficking: The First International Movement to Combat the Sexual Exploitation of Women* (Stanford, CA: Stanford University Press, 2010).

60. According to South Korean feminist Mi Kyung Lee, in the 1980s the South Korean military government made the service industry, and within it the sexualized entertainment industry, one of the major props of its entire development program. The low pay that women in the industry received compelled them to enter the prostitution subsidiary of that industry: Mi Kyung Lee, speaking at the International Trafficking in Women Conference, New York City, October 22, 1988. For a report of the entire conference, see "The First US Conference on Trafficking in Women Internationally," *Off Our Backs,* December 1988, 1–5. An earlier conference to organize women against prostitution is

described in Kathleen Barry, Charlotte Bunch, and Shirley Castley, eds., *International Feminism: Networking against Female Sexual Slavery* (New York: International Women's Tribune Center, 1984).

61. For a detailed account of how contemporary elite Chinese businessmen use hotels and other entertainment venues to build bonds of mutual obligation with other businessmen and with government officials, and of how the sexual services of diverse Chinese women are made central to that male-bonding process, see John Osburg, *Anxious Wealth: Money and Morality among China's New Rich* (Stanford, CA: Stanford University Press, 2013).

62. A particularly careful investigation of these questions is: Denise Brennan, *What's Love Got to Do with It? Transnational Desires and Sex Tourism in the Dominican Republic* (Durham, NC: Duke University Press, 2004). One of the most infamous cases of men creating a sex trafficking ring designed to provide commercialized sex to off-duty international male police and male soldiers occurred in the late 1990s in Bosnia. Postwar Bosnia was then under joint supervision of the United Nations and NATO. The men who were eventually exposed as sex traffickers were American white male police officers contracted by the U.S. company DynCorp. The young women they trafficked were from states of the former Soviet Union. Their customers in postwar Bosnia at the bars and discos that became brothels were men from several countries on assignment as contracted police and NATO military peacekeepers in postwar Bosnia. The sex trafficking was revealed by an American woman police officer working in Bosnia, Kathryn Bolkovac. She was fired by DynCorp when she tried to bring the sex-trafficking ring to light. Her principal supporter within the otherwise hostile UN bureaucracy was Madeleine Rees, then the Special Representative for Bosnia for the High Commissioner for Human Rights. The UN High Commissioner for Human Rights at the time, who in turn backed Madeleine Rees, was former president of Ireland Mary Robinson. Kathryn Bolkovac, with Cari Lynn, *The Whistleblower: Sex Trafficking, Military Contractors and One Woman's Fight for Justice* (New York: Palgrave Macmillan, 2011). For a joint interview with Kathryn Bolkovac and Madeleine Rees, see Elisabeth Prugl and Hayley Thompson, "The Whistleblower: An Interview with Kathryn Bolko-

vac and Madeleine Rees," *International Feminist Journal of Politics* 15, no. 1 (2013): 102–9.

63. See, for instance, Phillip Martin, *Trafficking Stories from Boston to Bangkok,* an eight-part series in print and radio broadcast on trafficking of women and men, girls and boys, from East Asia to New York and Boston, cosponsored by WGBH Boston Public Radio and the Schuster Institute for Investigative Journalism, Brandeis University, January 2013, www.schusterinstituteinvestigations.org/#!trafficking-boston-to-bangkok/c1y6t. A fascinating study of migrant women working in prostitution in the capital of Malaysia, Kuala Lumpur, is: Christine B.N. Chin, *Cosmopolitan Sex Workers: Women and Migration in a Global City* (Oxford: Oxford University Press, 2013).

64. Seager, *The Penguin Atlas of Women in the World,* 56–57.

65. Ibid., 56.

66. See, for instance, Wenona Giles, "Women Forced to Flee: Refugees and Internally Displaced Persons," in *Women and Wars,* ed. Carol Cohn (Cambridge, UK: Polity Press, 2013), 80–101.

67. U.S. Department of State, *Trafficking in Persons Report 2013* (Washington, DC: U.S. Department of State, June 19, 2013), http://www.state .gov/j/tip/rls/tiprpt/2013/.

68. "Combating Child Sex Tourism," United Nations Human Rights, April 10, 2013, www.ohchr.org/EN/NewsEvents/Pages/Child-SexTourism.aspx.

69. One of the most active transnational feminist NGOs working to track and prevent sex trafficking is Equality Now (www.equalitynow .org), whose global director is the Pakistani feminist Yasmeen Hassan. The agency whose mission includes charting and promoting state-level prevention of human trafficking, of which sex trafficking is a major part, is the International Organization for Migration, the IOM (www.iom.int).

CHAPTER 3. NATIONALISM AND MASCULINITY

1. For a map of the current U.S. empire, see Cynthia Enloe and Joni Seager, *The Real State of America: Mapping the Myths and Truths of the*

United States (New York: Penguin Books, 2011), 18–19. See also Stephen Burman, *The State of the American Empire* (Berkeley: University of California Press, 2007).

2. For a map of the spread of Coca-Cola, Walmart, Starbucks, the global film, and Barbie dolls, see Enloe and Seager, *The Real State of Americas*, 102–3.

3. Among the most influential studies exposing the uneasy—often tense—relationships between women and nationalism is: Nira Yuval-Davis and Floya Anthias, *Woman, Nation, State* (London: Macmillan, 1990). See also Sita Ranchod-Nilsson and Mary Ann Tetreault, eds., *Women, States, and Nationalism* (London: Routledge, 2000); Jenny White, *Muslim Nationalism and the New Turks* (Princeton, NJ: Princeton University Press, 2013).

4. The North African colonial postcards are displayed and analyzed in Malek Alloula, *The Colonial Harem* (Minneapolis: University of Minnesota Press, 1986), with a helpful introduction by Barbara Harlow.

5. Rana Kabbani, *Europe's Myths of the Orient* (Bloomington: Indiana University Press, 1986; reprint, London: Pandora Press, 1988). See also Sarah Graham-Brown, *Images of Women in Photography of the Middle East, 1860–1950* (New York: Columbia University Press, 1988); Edward Said, "Orientalism Reconsidered," *Race and Class* 27, no. 2 (1985).

6. Sylvia Van Kirk, *Many Tender Ties: Women in Fur-Trade Society, 1670–1870* (Winnipeg: Watson and Dwyer, 1980; reprint, Norman: University of Oklahoma Press, 1983); Jennifer S.H. Brown, *Strangers in Blood: Fur Trade Company Families in Indian Country* (Vancouver: University of British Columbia Press, 1980).

7. Mona Etiene and Eleanor Leacock, eds., *Women and Colonization* (New York: Praeger, 1980); Esther Boserup, *Women's Role in Economic Development* (New York: St. Martin's Press, 1970); E. Frances White, *Sierra Leone's Settler Women Traders: Women on the Afro-European Frontier* (Ann Arbor: University of Michigan Press, 1987).

8. I am greatly indebted to Insook Kwon, the South Korean feminist scholar, for introducing me to the lives of—and risks taken by—these early Korean New Women and to the debates that continue to swirl around them: Insook Kwon, "The 'New Women's Movement' in

1920s Korea: Rethinking the Relationship between Imperialism and Women," in "Feminisms and Internationalism," ed. Mrinalini Sinha, Donna J. Guy, and Angela Woollacott, special issue, *Gender and History* 10, no. 3 (November 1998): 381–405. Insook Kwon continues her exploration of this contested gendered political territory in "Feminists Navigating the Shoals of Nationalism and Collaboration: The Post-Colonial Korean Debate over How to Remember Kim Hwallan," *Frontiers* 27, no. 1 (2006): 39–66. See also Ruri Ito, "The 'Modern Girl' Question in the Periphery of Empire: Colonial Modernity and Mobility among Okinawan Women in the 1920s and 1930s," in *The Modern Girl around the World: Consumption, Modernity, and Globalization*, ed. Alys Eve Weinbaum et al. (Durham, NC: Duke University Press, 2008), 240–62. For another investigation of local women trying to navigate the traps and opportunities of Japanese occupation, see Norman Smith, *Resisting Manchukuo: Chinese Women Writers and the Japanese Occupation* (Vancouver: University of British Columbia Press, 2007).

9. Two of the most sophisticated feminist explorations of current Korean nationalism are: Elaine H. Kim and Chungmoo Choi, eds., *Dangerous Women: Gender and Korean Nationalism* (New York: Routledge, 1998); Katherine H. S. Moon, *Protesting America: Democracy and the U.S.-Korea Alliance* (Berkeley: University of California Press, 2012).

10. Marie-Aimée Hélie-Lucas, "The Role of Women during the Algerian Struggle and After: Nationalism as a Concept and a Practice Towards Both the Power of the Army and the Militarization of the People," in *Women and the Military System*, ed. Eva Isaksson (London: Wheatsheaf; New York: St. Martin's Press, 1988), 186. See also Marie-Aimée Hélie-Lucas, "Against Nationalism: The Betrayal of Algerian Women" *Trouble and Strife*, no. 11 (Summer 1987): 27–31. A revealing novel by an Algerian feminist is: Fettouma Touati, *Desperate Spring* (London: Women's Press, 1987). See also Peter R. Knauss, *The Persistence of Patriarchy: Class, Gender and Ideology in Twentieth Century Algeria* (New York: Praeger, 1987).

11. Hélie-Lucas, "Role of Women during the Algerian Struggle and After," 176.

12. Women Living Under Muslim Laws, www.wluml.org.

13. I have tried to chart this marriage trend and Iraqis' interpretations of it in *Nimo's War, Emma's War: Making Feminist Sense of the Iraq War* (Berkeley: University of California Press, 2010). See also Nadje Al-Ali, *Iraqi Women* (London: Zed Books, 2007); Nadje Al-Ali and Nicola Pratt, *What Kind of Liberation? Women and the Occupation of Iraq* (Berkeley: University of California Press, 2010); Deborah Amos, *Eclipse of the Sunnis* (New York: Public Affairs, 2010). Regarding the international politics of ethnic intermarriage, see Joyce Kauffman and Kristen Williams, *Women at War, Women Building Peace* (Boulder, CO: Kumarian Press, 2004).

14. These excerpts are from an undated typescript written by Pattie (Paxton) Hewitt, held by the Schlesinger Library on the History of Women in America, Radcliffe Institute, Harvard University.

15. Kathleen Barry, *Susan B. Anthony: A Biography of a Singular Feminist* (New York: New York University Press, 1988), 327–28. Anne Summers's history of British women military nurses suggests some similar contradictions that existed among feminist suffragists on the subject of British imperialism, since proving women's value to the empire was a tempting strategy to use in persuading antisuffrage male officials. *Angels and Citizens: British Women as Military Nurses, 1854–1914* (London: Routledge and Kegan Paul, 1988), 182–83.

16. Among the feminist histories of women's varied roles in German, American, Soviet, and British imperial enterprises are: Clare Midgley, ed., *Gender and Imperialism* (Manchester, U.K.: Manchester University Press, 1998); Lora Wildenthal, *German Women for Empire, 1884–1945* (Durham, NC: Duke University Press, 2001); Laura Briggs, *Reproducing Empire: Race, Sex, Science, and U.S. Imperialism in Puerto Rico* (Berkeley: University of California Press, 2002).

17. American and European women's varied and complex roles in their government's colonizing efforts are analyzed in Margaret Strobel and Nupur Chaudhuri, eds., "Western Women and Imperialism," special issue, *Women's Studies International Forum* 13, no. 2 (1990); Helen Callaway, *Gender, Culture and Empire: European Women in Colonial Nigeria* (London: Macmillan; Chicago: University of Illinois Press, 1987); Jane Hunter, *The Gospel of Gentility: American Women Missionaries in Turn of the Century China* (New Haven, CT: Yale University Press,

1984); Elisabeth Croll, *Wise Daughters from Foreign Lands: The Writings of European Women on China* (London: Pandora Press, 1989); Claudia Knapman, *White Women in Fiji* (London: Unwin Hyman, 1989); Margaret Strobel, "Gender and Race in the Nineteenth and Twentieth Century British Empire," in *Becoming Visible: Women in European History,* ed. Renate Bridenthal and Claudia Koonz, rev. ed. (Boston: Houghton Mifflin, 1987); Margaret Strobel, *European Women and the Second British Empire* (Bloomington: Indiana University Press, 1991); Patricia R. Hill, *The World Their Household: The American Women's Foreign Mission Movement and Cultural Transformation, 1870–1920* (Ann Arbor: University of Michigan Press, 1988); Helen M. Bannan, "Womanhood on the Reservation: Field Matrons in the United States Indian Service" (working paper no. 18, Southwest Institute for Research on Women, University of Arizona, Tucson, 1984); Luis Martin, *Daughters of the Conquistadors: Women of the Viceroy of Peru* (Albuquerque: University of New Mexico Press, 1983); Susan Bailey, *Women and the British Empire: An Annotated Guide to Sources* (New York: Garland, 1987); Margaret Macmillan, *Women of the Raj* (London: Thames and Hudson, 1988); Joanna Trollope, *Britannia's Daughters: Women of the British Empire* (London: Hutchinson, 1983).

18. James Mills, *History of India,* quoted by Mrinalini Sinha, "Gender and Imperialism: Colonial Policy and the Ideology of Moral Imperialism in Late Nineteenth Century Bengal," in *Changing Men: New Directions in Research on Men and Masculinity,* ed. Michael S. Kimmel (Newbury Park, CA: Sage, 1987), 218.

19. Sinha, "Gender and Imperialism," 218–19.

20. Joanna Liddle and Rama Joshi, "Gender and Imperialism in British India," in "Review of Women's Studies [in India]," supplement, *Economic and Political Weekly* (New Delhi), 20, no. 43 (October 26, 1985): WS72–WS78. See also Joanna Liddle and Rama Joshi, *Daughters of Independence: Gender, Caste and Class in India* (New Delhi: Kali for Women; London: Zed Books, 1986); Kumkum Sangari and Sudesh Vaid, eds., *Recasting Women: Essays in Colonial History* (New Delhi: Kali for Women, 1988); Dagmar Engles, "The Limits of Gender Ideology: Bengali Women, the Colonial State and the Private Sphere, 1890–1930," *Women's Studies International Forum* 12, no. 4 (1989).

21. Robert Baden-Powell, *Rovering to Success* (London: Herbert Jenkins, 1922), 120.

22. Ibid., 109–10. See also Michael Rosenthal, *The Character Factory: Baden-Powell's Boy Scouts and the Imperatives of Empire* (New York: Pantheon, 1986); Raphael Samuel, "Patriotic Fantasy," *New Statesman,* July 18, 1986, 20–22; Simon Schama, *The Embarrassment of Riches: An Interpretation of Dutch Culture* (New York: Knopf, 1987). I am indebted to Patrick Miller for his insights into the American debates at the turn of the century over masculinity and imperialism; his dissertation is: "College Sports and American Culture" (Department of History, Rutgers University, New Brunswick, 1988). For new critical thinking on masculinity and the state, see Robert W. Connell, *Gender and Power* (Stanford, CA: Stanford University Press, 1988).

23. I am grateful to Ayse Gul Altinay, a friend and a professor of cultural studies at Istanbul's Sabanci University, for having long conversations with me about the politics of women's attire in contemporary Turkey. See Ayse Gul Altinay, *The Myth of the Military-Nation: Militarism, Gender, and Education in Turkey* (London: Palgrave and Macmillan, 2004).

24. A town-by-town history of implementing Ataturk's modernist ban on men's wearing of the red fez—and many Turkish men's resistance to the ban—is: Jeremy Seal, *A Fez of the Heart* (New York: Harcourt, 1995).

25. I am especially grateful to Turkish feminist and anthropologist Ayse Gul Altinay for sharing her eyewitness accounts of the Taksim Square demonstrations and the government's violent responses. Email correspondence with the author, June–August 2013.

26. Altinay, *Myth of the Military-Nation,* 2004; Margot Badran, *Feminists, Islam and Nation: Gender and the Making of Modern Egypt* (Princeton, NJ: Princeton University Press, 1995); Douglas Northrop, *Veiled Empire: Gender and Power in Stalinist Central Asia* (Ithaca, NY: Cornell University Press, 2004); Hélie-Lucas, "Role of Women during the Algerian Struggle and After"; Cynthia Nelson, "Akram Khater, 'al-Harakah al-Nisa'eyya: The Women's Movement and Political Participation in Modern Egypt," *Women's Studies International Forum* 11, no. 5 (1988); Selma Botman, "The Experience of Women in the Egyptian

Communist Movement, 1939–1954," *Women's Studies International Forum* 11, no. 2 (1988); Graham-Brown, *Images of Women in Photography of the Middle East;* Margot Badran, "Dual Liberation: Feminism and Nationalism in Egypt, 1870–1925," *Feminist Issues* 8, no. 1 (Spring 1988); Huda Shaarawi, *Harem Years: The Memories of an Egyptian Feminist* (London: Virago, 1986); Mervat Hatem, "The Politics of Sexuality and Gender in Segregated Patriarchal Systems: The Case of Eighteenth and Nineteenth Century Egypt," *Feminist Studies* 12, no. 2 (Summer 1986); Elizabeth Sanasarian, *The Women's Rights Movement in Iran* (New York: Praeger, 1983).

27. I have tried to explore these discussions among today's Egyptian feminists in *Seriously! Investigating Crashes and Crises as If Women Mattered* (Berkeley: University of California Press, 2013).

28. Mervat Hatem, "Through Each Other's Eyes: Egyptian, Levantine-Egyptian and European Women's Images of Themselves and of Each Other, 1862–1920," *Women's Studies International Forum* 12, no. 2 (March 1989).

29. For further discussion of these tensions, see Yuval-Davis and Anthias, *Woman, Nation, State;* Floya Anthias, Nira Yuval-Davis, and Harriet Cain, *Resistance and Control: Racism and "The Community"* (London: Routledge, 1989).

30. "A Letter from the Women's Study Circle of Jaffna," *Women's Studies International Forum* 12, no. 1 (1989). This point was confirmed by Anita Nesiah, a Sri Lankan feminist, in her lecture at Clark University, Worcester, MA, November 7, 1988.

31. Malathi de Alwis, Julie Mertus, and Tazreena Sajjed, "Women and Peace Processes," in *Women and Wars,* ed. Carol Cohn (Cambridge, U.K.: Polity Press, 2013), 169–93. See also "Team 1325 Sri Lanka," International Civil Society Action Network, www.icanpeacework.org/team-1325-sri-lanka, accessed June 17, 2013.

32. "Philippine Women Say Repression Is Worsening," *Listen Real Loud* (American Friends Service Committee, Philadelphia), 9, no. 1 (1988): 7.

33. See, for instance, Sandra McEvoy, "Loyalist Women Paramilitaries in Northern Ireland," in *Gender in International Security,* ed. Laura Sjoberg (New York: Routledge, 2009); Vina A. Lanzona, *Amazons of the*

Huk Rebellion: Gender, Sex, and Revolution in the Philippines (Madison: University of Wisconsin Press, 2009).

34. See, for instance, "Nicaragua: Working Women in a Women's Brigade," *Off Our Backs* (June 1988): 12–13; Ailbhe Smyth, guest ed., "Feminism in Ireland," special issue, *Women's Studies International Forum* 11, no. 4 (1988); Eileen Fairweather, Roissin McDonough, and Melanie McFaryean, *Only the Rivers Run Free—Northern Ireland: The Women's War* (London: Pluto Press, 1984); Ailbhe Smyth, Pauline Jackson, Caroline McCamley, and Ann Speed, "States of Emergence," *Trouble and Strife*, no. 14 (Autumn 1988): 46–52; Clio Collective, *Quebec Women: A History* (Toronto: Women's Press, 1987); Stephanie Urdang, *And Still They Dance: Women, War and the Struggle for Change in Mozambique* (New York: Monthly Review Press, 1989).

35. Henry Kamm, "Afghan Peace Could Herald War of Sexes," *New York Times,* December 12, 1988.

36. Afghan Women's Network, *UN SCR 1325 Implementation in Afghanistan* (Kabul: Afghan Women's Network, 2011). UN Security Council Resolution 1325 was passed in October 2000, requiring all UN member states and all UN agencies to meaningfully include women as formal participants in any peace negotiations and in all planning for postwar national reconciliation and national rebuilding projects.

37. Curtis Wilkie, "Roles Change for Palestinian Women," *Boston Globe,* May 17, 1988.

38. Ellen Cantarow, "Palestinian Women Resisting Occupation," *Sojourner* (April 1988): 19. See also Beata Lipman, *Israel—the Embattled Land: Jewish and Palestinian Women Talk about Their Lives* (London: Pandora Press, 1988); Hamida Kazi, "Palestinian Women and the National Liberation Movement," in *Women in the Middle East,* ed. Mageda Salman (London: Zed Books, 1987). See also Rhoda Ann Kanaaneh and Isis Nusair, eds., *Displaced at Home: Ethnicity and Gender among Palestinians in Israel* (Albany: SUNY Press, 2010); Ellen Freishmann, *The Nation and Its "New" Women: The Palestinian Women's Movement, 1920–1948* (Berkeley: University of California Press, 2003); Simona Sharoni, *Gender and the Israeli-Palestinian Conflict* (Syracuse, NY: Syracuse University Press, 1994).

39. Hue-Tam Ho-Tai, lecture, Clark University, Worcester, MA, October 25, 1987. See also Tai's gender-curious studies of the

Vietnamese revolution: *Radicalism and the Origins of the Vietnamese Revolution* (Cambridge, MA: Harvard University Press, 1992); *Passion, Betrayal, and Revolution in Colonial Saigon: The Memoirs of Bao Luong* (Berkeley: University of California Press, 2010).

40. David Marr, *Vietnamese Tradition on Trial, 1920–1945* (Berkeley: University of California Press, 1981); Kumari Jayawardena, *Feminism and Nationalism in the Third World* (London: Zed Books; New Delhi, Kali for Women, 1986), 196–212.

41. I am grateful to Christine White of Cornell University for introducing me to two accounts of Vietnamese women who fought as guerrillas in the nationalist movement: Nguyen Thi Dinh, *No Other Road to Take*, trans. Mai V. Elliott, data paper no. 102 (Ithaca, NY: Southeast Asia Program, Cornell University, June 1976); Phan Thi Nhu Bang, *Ta Thi Kieu: An Heroic Girl of Bentre* (Ho Chi Minh City: Liberation Editions, 1966).

42. Sophie Quinn Judge, "Vietnamese Women: Neglected Promises," *Indochinese Issues*, no. 42 (December 1983). See also Christine White, "On Promissory Notes," and "Vietnamese Socialism and the Politics of Gender Relations," both in *Promissory Notes: Women in the Transition to Socialism*, ed. Sonia Kraks, Rayna Rapp, Marilyn Young (New York: Monthly Review Press, 1989).

43. One of the most active, current women's studies faculty groups is at Hoa Sen University in Ho Chi Minh City. Its Gender and Society Research Center publishes an online newsletter in Vietnamese, French, and English: *Gender and Society Newsletter* (www.hoasen.edu.vn).

44. Jayawardena, *Feminism and Nationalism in the Third World*, 1.

45. Conversations with Sri Lankan feminists Anita Nesiah and Kumari Jayawadena, Cambridge, MA, March 1988. South Asian lesbians in the United States published a newsletter that grappled with some of these same issues: *Anamika* (Brooklyn, NY). In *Anamika* 1, no. 2 (March 1986), a Sri Lankan lesbian described Sri Lankan society as tolerant and/or ambivalent toward homosexuality, permitting a substantial degree of intimacy between women. But the pressure for a woman to marry was great, and the only women living as lesbians that this author knew were upper-class women living in the capital, Colombo. Jamaican feminists in the 1980s, too, were taunted with

charges of "lesbian." Sistren, with Honor Ford Smith, *Lionheart Gal* (London: Women's Press, 1986), xxvi. Irish lesbians' relationships to nationalism are discussed in *Out for Ourselves: The Lives of Irish Lesbians and Gay Men* (Dublin: Dublin Lesbian and Gay Men's Collective and Women's Community Press, 1986). Also helpful: Carmen, Shaila, Pratibha, "Becoming Visible: Black Lesbians Discuss Feminism," special issue, *Feminist Review,* no. 17 (Autumn 1984). On experiences by Serbia's Women in Black of being taunted by nationalists during the Yugoslav war, see Cynthia Cockburn, *From Where We Stand* (London: Zed Books, 2007).

46. E. Frances White, "Africa on My Mind" (lecture, Clark University, Worcester, MA, March 31, 1988). See also Ayesha Mei-Tje Imam, "The Presentation of African Women in Historical Writing," in *Retrieving Women's History,* ed. S. Jay Kleinberg (Oxford: Berg, 1988).

47. Yasmin Saikia, *Women, War, and the Making of Bangladesh: Remembering 1971* (Durham, NC: Duke University Press, 2011).

48. Sistren, with Honor Ford Smith, *Lionheart Gal,* xxiii.

49. Delia Aguilar, "On the Women's Movement Today," *Midweek* (Manila), November 9, 1988.

CHAPTER 4. BASE WOMEN

1. I am indebted to Fijian feminist researcher Teresia Teaiwa, director of Pacific Studies at Victoria University, New Zealand, for alerting me to the practice of private defense-contracting companies recruiting Fijian woman as laundry workers for U.S. military bases in Iraq. See also Teresia Teaiwa, ed., "Militarism and Gender in the Western Pacific," special issue, *Asia Pacific Viewpoint* 52, no. 1 (2011): 1–55.

2. Among the multinational comparative studies of U.S. overseas military bases and local residents' reactions to them are: Joseph Gerson and Bruce Bichard, eds., *The Sun Never Sets* (Boston: South End Press, 1991); John Lindsay-Poland, ed., "Closing Bases: Supporting Communities," special issue, *Fellowship* (magazine of the Fellowship of Reconciliation), 71, nos. 1–3 (Winter 2007); Catherine Lutz, ed., *The Bases of Empire: The Global Struggle against Military Posts* (London: Pluto Press, 2009).

3. Perhaps the most influential American analyst to argue that the worldwide reach of U.S. military bases qualifies the United States to be defined as an "empire" is the late Chalmers Johnson. See his trilogy: *Sorrows of Empire* (2004), *Blowback* (2004), and *Nemesis* (2006), all published in New York by Metropolitan Books.

4. To begin an investigation of the gendered militarization of Guam, read Keith Camacho, *Cultures of Commemoration: The Politics of War, Memory, and History in the Mariana Islands* (Honolulu: University of Hawai'i Press, 2013); Setsu Shigematsu and Keith Camacho, eds., *Militarized Currents: Toward a Decolonized Future in Asia and the Pacific* (Minneapolis: University of Minnesota Press, 2010); Catherine Lutz, "Introduction: Bases, Empire, and Global Response," in Lutz, *Bases of Empire,* 1–44.

5. See, for instance, David Cronin, "France's Power Games in Africa," *New Europe,* January 21, 2013, www.neueurope.eu/article/frances-power-games-in-africa; Nick Hopkins, "UK to Withdraw 11,000 Troops from Germany by 2016," *The Guardian,* March 4, 2013, www.guardian.co.uk/2013/mar/05/uk-withdrawal-troops-germany-2016; Dan Smith, *The State of War and Peace Atlas* (New York: Penguin, 1997).

6. "Camp Le Monier/Lemonier/Lemonnier, Djibouti (CLDJ)," GlobalSecurity.org, October 26, 2012, www.globalsecurity.org/military/facility/camp-lemonier.htm.

7. Nick Turse, "The Increasing US Shadow Wars in Africa," *Mother Jones,* July 12, 2012, www.motherjones.com/politics/2012/07/us-shadow-wars-africa; Eric Schmitt, "In a First, the U.S. Army Houses an Antiterror Strategy for Africa, in Kansas," *New York Times,* October 10, 2013. For an analysis of how the Defense Department has reorganized and expanded its bases in Italy for the sake of bolstering its operations in Africa, see David Vine, "The Italian Job: How the Pentagon Is Using Your Tax Dollars to Turn Italy into a Launching Pad for the Wars of Today and Tomorrow," TomDispatch.com, October 3, 2013, www.tomdispatch.com/blog/175755/.

8. Eric Schmitt, "Drones in Niger Reflect New U.S. Tack on Terrorism," *New York Times,* July 11, 2013; Eric Schmitt and Scott Sayre, "U.S. Troops at Drone Base in West Africa," *New York Times,* February 23, 2013.

9. A detailed ethnographic study of what the U.S. military base takeover of their land has meant for the displaced local people of Diego Garcia is: David Vine, *Island of Shame: The Secret History of the U.S. Military Base on Diego Garcia* (Princeton, NJ: Princeton University Press, 2009). David Vine has continued his anthropological investigation of U.S. military bases in a new cross-national study: *Base Nation* (forthcoming).

10. A provocative study of the history of how so many American civilians in the Plains States came to support the placement of underground, nuclear-headed missile bases in their communities is: Gretchen Heefner, *The Missile Next Door: The Minuteman in the American Heartland* (Cambridge, MA: Harvard University Press, 2012).

11. The most historically rich and ethnographically subtle study of a single military base is anthropologist Catherine Lutz's detailed account—in all of its evolving racial, gender, and class complexity—of the U.S. Army base, Fort Bragg, located in Fayetteville, North Carolina: *Homefront: A Military City and the American Twentieth Century* (Boston: Beacon Press, 2002).

12. "Camp Le Monier/Lemonier/Lemonnier, Djibouti (CLDJ)."

13. An ethnographic study of the perceptions of the civilian residents of Manta, Ecuador, regarding the U.S. base in their city is: Erin Fitz-Henry, "Distant, Allies, Proximate Enemies: Rethinking the Scales of the Anti-Base Movement in Ecuador," *American Ethnologist* 38, no. 2 (May 2011): 323–37. See also Luis Angel Saavedra, "The Manta Base: A U.S. Military Fort in Ecuador," *Fellowship* 73, no. 1–3 (Winter 2007): 20–21; John Lindsey-Poland, "U.S. Military Bases in Latin America and the Caribbean," in Lutz, *Bases of Empire*, 71–95; Joshua Partlow, "Ecuador Giving U.S. Air Base the Boot," *Washington Post*, September 4, 2008, www.washingtonpost.com/wp-dyn/content /article/2008/09/03/AR2008090303289.html.

14. Feminist environmental researcher Joni Seager has charted the course of American civilian housewives' protests against base runoff and resultant pollution of their civilian communities' water supplies, as well as the condescending sexist attitudes of U.S. military base commanders that their protests exposed: *Earth Follies: Feminism, Politics and the Environment* (New York: Routledge, 1993).

15. Duncan Campbell, *The Unsinkable Aircraft Carrier: American Military Power in Britain* (London: Paladin Books, 1986).

16. Ibid., 16.

17. The following account draws on Graham Smith, *When Jim Crow Met John Bull: Black American Soldiers in World War II Britain* (London: I. B. Tauris, 1987; reprint, New York: St. Martin's Press, 1988). Also see Mary Penick Motley, ed., *The Invincible Soldier: The Experience of the Black Soldier, World War II* (Detroit: Wayne State University Press, 1987).

18. On racial policies in a dozen different armed forces, see Cynthia H. Enloe, *Ethnic Soldiers: State Security in Divided Societies* (London: Penguin, 1980).

19. Philippa Levine is the feminist historian who has conducted the most thorough cross-national investigations of British imperial militarized prostitution policies: *Prostitution, Race and Politics: Policing Venereal Disease in the British Empire* (New York: Routledge, 2003).

20. Smith, *When Jim Crow Met John Bull*, 188.

21. Ibid., 192–93. For a history of the African American women who served in the U.S. Army's groundbreaking 6888th Central Postal Directory Battalion, the only unit of African American women deployed overseas during World War II, see Brenda L. Moore, *To Serve My Country, to Serve My Race* (New York: New York University Press, 1996).

22. Ben Bousquet and Colin Douglas, *West Indian Women at War: British Racism in World War II* (London: Lawrence and Wishart, 1991). The authors' mothers were among the West Indian women who had served in the British military during World War II.

23. Smith, *When Jim Crow Met John Bull*, 186.

24. Ibid., 200.

25. John Costello, *Virtue under Fire: How World War II Changed Our Social and Sexual Attitudes* (Boston: Little, Brown, 1985), 254. On British women who married Canadian soldiers, see Joyce Hibbert, *War Brides* (Toronto: New American Library of Canada, 1980).

26. Smith, *When Jim Crow Met John Bull*, 206.

27. Susan Zeiger, *Entangling Alliances: Foreign War Brides and American Soldiers in the Twentieth Century* (New York: New York University Press, 2010); Maria Hohn and Seungsook Moon, eds., *Over There: Living with*

the U.S. Military Empire from World War Two to the Present (Durham, NC: Duke University Press, 2010).

28. Norman Lewis, "Essex," *Granta,* no. 23 (Spring 1988): 112.

29. Mark L. Gillem, *America Town: Building the Outposts of Empire* (Minneapolis: University of Minnesota Press, 2007).

30. Betty Friedman, *The Feminine Mystique* (New York: Dell, 1964).

31. On the long-running debates among male strategists over the uses of military wives—and women's responses to those debates—see Myna Trustram, *Women of the Regiment: Marriage and the Victorian Army* (Cambridge: Cambridge University Press, 1984); Cynthia Enloe, *Maneuvers: The International Politics of Militarizing Women's Lives* (Berkeley: University of California Press, 2000). For an analysis of the lives and thoughts of women married to men who migrate to Britain as overseas recruits in today's British military, see Vron Ware, *Military Migrants: Fighting for Your Country* (London: Palgrave Macmillan, 2012). For an ethnography of British women married to British soldiers and stationed in Germany on British bases while their husbands were deployed in Afghanistan during 2011 and 2012, see Alexandra Hyde, "Insecure Sovereignties: The Transnational Subjectivities of Military Wives on a British Army Base Overseas" (paper presented at the Gender Institute, London School of Economics, June 13, 2013). See also Deborah Harrison and Lucy LaLiberte, *No Life Like It: Military Wives in Canada* (Toronto: Lorimer, 1994); Mona Macmillan, "Campfollower: A Note on Wives in the Armed Forces," in *The Incorporated Wife,* ed. Hilary Callan and Shirley Ardener (London: Croom Helm, 1984); Rosemary McKechnie, "Living with Images of a Fighting Elite: Women and the Foreign Legion," in *Images of Women in Peace and War* (London: Macmillan, 1987; reprint, Madison, University of Wisconsin Press, 1988), 122–47; Ximena Bunster, "Watch Out for the Little Nazi Man That All of Us Have Inside: The Mobilization and Demobilization of Women in Militarized Chile," *Women's Studies International Forum* 11, no. 5 (1988): 21–27.

32. U.S. Department of Defense, *Demographics 2010: Profile of the Military Community* (Washington, DC, 2010), www.ncdsv.org/images/DOD_DemographicsProfileOfTheMilitaryCommunity_2010.pdf.

33. Rachel L. Swarns, "Military Rules Leave Gay Spouses Out in the Cold," *New York Times,* January 20, 2013. One of the organizations

pressing the Defense Department to recognize the rights of civilian men and women in same-sex marriages with U.S. military personnel is the Servicemembers Legal Defense Network (www.outserve-sldn.org), headquartered in Washington, D.C. In August 2013, the U.S. Defense Department officially extended spousal benefits to gay and lesbian married military couples, though only to those married in one of the thirteen states where gay marriage has been made legal. Emmarie Huetteman, "Gay Spouses of Members of Military Get Benefits," *New York Times,* August 15, 2013.

34. Donna Alvah, *Unofficial Ambassadors: American Military Families Overseas and the Cold War, 1946–1965* (New York: New York University Press, 2007).

35. A revealing collective portrait of the seven women married to the first generation of American male astronauts, most of whom lived their adult lives as military wives, is: Lily Koppel, *The Astronaut Wives Club* (New York: Grand Central, 2013).

36. My own attempt to explore the experiences and ideas of women married to U.S. male soldiers during 2003 to 2010, the years of the U.S.-led war in Iraq is: *Nimo's War, Emma's War: Making Feminist Sense of the Iraq War* (Berkeley: University of California Press, 2010). On American military daughters' experiences living on U.S. military bases during the 1960s and 1970s, see Mary Wertsch, *Military Brats: Legacies of Childhood Inside the Fortress* (St. Louis: Brightwell, 2011).

37. This story of military wives' political organizing is told at greater length in Enloe, *Maneuvers.* I am indebted to Carolyn Becraft for sharing her political experiences and analyses with me.

38. For a fuller account of the militarized politics of domestic violence, see Enloe, *Maneuvers;* Enloe, *Nimo's War, Emma's War.*

39. A new ethnographic, gender-explicit study of one large U.S. base and the community around it (Fort Carson and Colorado Springs, Colorado), which confronts the costs of PTSD and traumatic brain injury, is: Jean Scandlyn and Sarah Hautzinger, *Beyond Post-Traumatic Stress: Homefront Struggles with the Wars on Terror* (San Francisco: Left Coast Press, 2013). See also Enloe, *Nimo's War, Emma's War, 2010.*

40. David Vine, "The Lily-Pad Strategy: How the Pentagon Is Quietly Transforming Its Overseas Base Empire and Creating a

Dangerous New Way of War," TomDispatch.com, July 15, 2012, www.tomdispatch.com/archive/175568.

41. To start a comparison of militarized masculinities in contemporary militaries, on Britain, see Ware, *Military Migrants;* Victoria Basham, *War, Identity and the Liberal State: Everyday Experiences of the Geopolitical in the Armed Forces* (London: Taylor and Francis, 2013); Claire Duncanson, "Narratives of Military Masculinity in Peacekeeping Operations," *International Feminist Journal of Politics* 11, no. 1 (March 2009): 63–80. On Sweden, see Annica Kronsell, *Gender, Sex and the Postnational Defense: Militarism and Peacekeeping* (London: Oxford University Press, 2012). On Canada, see Sandra Whitworth, *Men, Militarism and UN Peacekeeping* (Boulder, CO: Lynne Rienner, 2004). On Japan, see Sabine Frustuck, *Uneasy Warriors: Gender, Memory, and Popular Culture in the Japanese Army* (Berkeley: University of California Press, 2007). On Russia, see Maya Eichler, *Militarizing Men: Gender, Conscription, and War in Post-Soviet Russia* (Stanford, CA: Stanford University Press, 2012). On Turkey, see Nadire Mater, *Voices from the Front: Turkish Soldiers on the War with the Kurdish Guerrillas* (London: Palgrave Macmillan, 2005); Ozgur Heval Cinar and Coskun Usterci, eds., *Conscientious Objection: Resisting Militarized Society* (London: Zed Books, 2009). On South Korea, see Insook Kwon, "Sexual Violence among Men in the Military in South Korea," *Journal of Interpersonal Violence* 22, no. 8 (August 2007): 1024–42. On the United States, see Aaron Belkin, *Bring Me Men: Military Masculinity and the Benign Façade of American Empire, 1899–2012* (New York: Colombia University Press, 2012). On masculinities in private defense contractor's forces, see Paul Higate, "Cowboys and Professionals: The Politics of Identity Work in the Private and Military Security Company," *Millennium Journal of International Studies* 40, no. 2 (2012): 321–41.

42. These data come from Lory Manning, *Women in the Military: Where We Stand,* 8th ed. (Washington, DC: Women's Research and Education Institute, February 2013). The Women's Research and Education Institute (www.wrei.org), a nonpartisan organization, has been producing this valuable report every three years since the 1990s. The institute's Women and the Military project has monitored and advocated on behalf of women in the U.S. military, collecting data, train-

ing interns, testifying before Congress, and creating networks between U.S. women in the military and women in militaries of other countries, as well as with women in fire departments and police departments. The institute's Women and the Military project was closed in late 2013.

43. These data come from ibid.

44. An innovative comparison of American military women's lobbying against the Pentagon's patriarchal norms and rules with American nuns' challenges to the U.S. Catholic Church's institutional sexism is: Mary Fainsod Katzenstein, *Faithful and Fearless: Moving Feminist Protest inside the Church and Military* (Princeton, NJ: Princeton University Press, 1999).

45. A documentary film that featured the sexual assault experiences of five American military women—each serving in a different branch—attracted broad public and official attention when it was nominated for an Academy Award: Kirby Dick, dir., *The Invisible War,* 2012, 97 min., http://kirbydick.com/invisiblewar.html.

46. Among the women's advocacy groups that led the campaign to make intramilitary sexual violence a public issue was the Service Women's Action Network (www.servicewomen.org). Two articles by feminists on the issue that explicitly made the analytical connection between military men's violence against women inside the U.S. military and their violence against women living around U.S. military bases are: Lucinda Marshall, "Sexual Violence in the Ranks and the Gendered Impact of Militarism," Feminist Peace Network, 2013, www.feministpeacenetwork.org/2013/06/09/sexual-violence-in-the-ranks-and-the-gendered-impact-of-militarism; Annie Isabel Fukishima and Gwyn Kirk, "Military Sexual Violence: From Frontline to Fenceline," *Foreign Policy in Focus* (Institute for Policy Studies, Washington, DC), June 17, 2013, www.fpif.org/articles/military_sexual_violence_from_frontline_to_fenceline.

47. U.S. Department of Defense, *Department of Defense Annual Report on Sexual Assault in the Military, Fiscal Year 2012* (Washington, DC: Department of Defense, May 2013), http://sapr.mil/media/pdf/reports/FY12_DoD_SAPRO_Annual_Report_on_Sexual_Assault-Volume-ONE.pdf. See also James Dao, "When Victims of Military Sex Assaults Are Men," *New York Times,* June 24, 2013.

48. Jennifer Steinhauer, "Veterans Testify on Rapes and Scant Hope of Justice," *New York Times,* March 14, 2013.

49. One of the few studies of prostitution around an American military base on the U.S. mainland is the historically attentive ethnography of Fort Bragg, in Fayetteville, North Carolina, by Catherine Lutz, *Homefront.*

50. The most detailed historical account of the British government's imperial prostitution policies is: Philippa Levine, *Prostitution, Race and Politics: Policing Venereal Disease in the British Empire* (New York: Routledge, 2003).

51. For accounts of the British Anti-Contagious Diseases Acts Campaign, see ibid. Also see Judith R. Walkowitz, *Prostitution and Victorian Society* (Cambridge: Cambridge University Press, 1982).

52. One can read copies of *The Dawn* at the Women's Library, housed at the London School of Economics, as well as gain access to some of them online at www.lse.ac.uk/library/newsandinformation/womenslibraryatLSE/Accessing-the-Womens-Library-@-LSE-collections.aspx.

53. Joanna Liddle and Rama Joshi, "Gender and Imperialism in British India," in "Review of Women's Studies [in India]," supplement, *Economic and Political Weekly* (New Delhi), 20, no. 43 (October 26, 1985): WS–74. See also Kenneth Ballhatchet, *Race and Sex and Class under the Raj* (London: Weidenfeld and Nicolson, 1980).

54. *The Dawn,* no. 1 (May 1888): 5. For a feminist interpretation of Josephine Butler's attitudes toward imperialism, see Antoinette Burton, "The White Woman's Burden: British Feminists and 'the Indian Woman,' 1865–1915," in Margaret Strobel and Nupur Chaudhuri, eds., "Western Women and Imperialism," special issue, *Women's Studies International Forum* 13, no. 2 (1990).

55. *The Dawn,* no. 27 (May 1895): 1–2.

56. On military prostitution debates in the United States during the decades leading up to the 1990s, see Allan Brandt, *No Magic Bullet* (Oxford: Oxford University Press, 1987); Katherine Bushnell, *Plain Words to Plain People,* an undated, World War I pamphlet, Schlesinger Library on the History of Women in America, Radcliffe Institute, Harvard University; Enloe, *Maneuvers.* The Canadian debate about

soldiers' sexuality during World War II is discussed in Ruth Roach Pierson, *"They're Still Women after All": The Second World War and Canadian Womanhood* (Toronto: McClelland and Stewart, 1986).

57. In 2013, the issue of the Japanese imperial military's "comfort women" made headlines again, when the conservative mayor of Osaka, Japan's second-largest city, claimed, "When soldiers are risking their lives by running through storms of bullets, and you want to give these emotionally charged soldiers a rest somewhere, it's clear that you need a comfort women system." The mayor, Toru Hashimoto, went on to argue that a prostitution system servicing the U.S. military bases today in Okinawa, the object of Okinawan feminists' protests, was justified by the experience of the imperial army's "comfort women" system during World War II. In a sign of how much Japanese popular opinion has come to disparage that World War II system, the mayor's statement was greeted with an outpouring of dissent from ordinary Japanese and Japanese elites: Hiroko Tabuchi, "Women Sent to Brothels Aided Japan, Mayor Says," *New York Times,* May 14, 2013; Mari Yamaguchi, "Osaka Mayor Defends 'Comfort Women' Remark," *Boston Globe,* May 17, 2013.

58. The research on the lives of Asian women forced during World War II into becoming sex slaves for the Japanese imperial army's "Comfort Station" prostitution system is growing annually. To start, see Yuki Tanaka, *Japan's Comfort Women: Sexual Slavery and Prostitution during World War II and the U.S. Occupation* (New York: Routledge, 2001). A Japanese feminist group has created a small museum in Tokyo, the Women's Active Museum on War and Peace, dedicated to making visible the lives and the ideas of those women throughout Asia who survived the imperial army's "comfort women" system: www.wam-peace .org.

59. See Beth Bailey and David Farber, *The First Strange Place: The Alchemy of Race and Sex in World War II Hawaii* (New York: Free Press, 1992); John Willoughby, "The Sexual Behavior of American G.I.s during the Early Years of the Occupation of Germany, " *Journal of Military History,* no. 62 (January 1998): 155–74; Na Young Lee, "The Construction of Military Prostitution in South Korea during the U.S. Military Rule, 1945–1948," *Feminist Studies* 33, no. 3 (Fall 2007): 453–81.

60. Mary Louise Roberts, *What Soldiers Do: Sex and the American GI in World War II France* (Chicago: Chicago University Press, 2013).

61. One of the most thorough investigations of the U.S. military prostitution system during the Cold War era is: Katherine Moon, *Sex among Allies: Military Prostitution in U.S.-Korea Relations* (New York: Columbia University Press, 1997). For a continuing exploration of whether the U.S. military bases have been one of the crucial factors fueling post–Cold War gendered nationalism among South Koreans, see Katherine Moon, *Protesting America: Democracy and the U.S.-Korea Alliance* (Berkeley: University of California Press, 2013).

62. For information about Okinawa Women Act Against Military Violence, see Women for Genuine Security, www.genuinesecurity.org/partners/okinawa.html. For more on these Okinawan feminists' antimilitarist thinking and actions, see Enloe, *Maneuvers*; Cynthia Cockburn, *Antimilitarism: Political and Gender Dynamics of Peace Movements* (London: Palgrave, 2012). For an eye-opening account of how U.S. foreign policy makers during the Cold War era enlisted both American women married to American soldiers stationed in Okinawa and American women professors of home economics (especially at Michigan State University and the University of Hawaii) to build friendly relationships with Okinawan women, with the goal of providing popular support for the U.S. military bases in Okinawa, see Mire Koikari, *Making Homes, Building Bases: Women, Militarism, and the Cold War Transnationalism in the U.S. Occupation of Okinawa* (forthcoming).

63. Jessie Anglum, unpublished diary, 1901–2, Schlesinger Library on the History of Women in America, Radcliffe Institute, Harvard University.

64. Gabriela: Alliance of Filipino Women, www.gabrielaph.com; Women for Genuine Security, www.genuinesecurity.org. I am indebted to Suzuyo Takazato, one of the core leaders of the Okinawa Women Act Against Military Violence, which has documented and critiqued the negative effects of the U.S. military bases on local women. She has taught me about the complex interactions between nationalism and feminism in an antibases movement, as well as about the multiple forms of feminist activism it has taken over the last two decades to make women's voices heard in the intense debate over the

workings of and future of the American bases on Okinawa. A mainland Japanese feminist organization that has sought to support Okinawan women's antibases activism is the Asia-Japan Women's Resource Center. See, for instance, their study "Women in Okinawa: Resisting Colonialism and Militarism," special issue, *Voices from Japan*, no. 27 (March 2013). For the Center's ongoing work, see www.ajwrc.org.

65. Alexander R. Magno, "Cornucopia or Curse: The Internal Debate on the US Bases in the Philippines," *Kasarinlan* (Third World Studies Program, University of the Philippines, Quezon City), 3, no. 3 (1988): 9–12; Pilar Ramos-Jimenez and Elena Chiong-Javier, *Social Benefits and Costs: People's Perceptions of the U.S. Military Bases in the Philippines* (Manila: Research Center, De La Salle University, 1987), 9–10; *Philippine Resource Center Monitor*, no. 3 (August 12, 1988).

66. Christopher M. Lapinig, "The Forgotten Amerasians," op-ed, *New York Times*, May 28, 2013.

67. See, especially, Sandra Sturdevant and Brenda Stoltzfus, *Let the Good Times Roll: Prostitution and the U.S. Military in Asia* (New York: New Press, 1992).

68. Floyd Whaley, "U.S. Seeks Expanded Role for Military in Philippines," *New York Times*, July 13, 2013.

69. The most detailed account of the U.S. military's prostitution system around its bases in South Korea when Korean women were the majority of women in prostitution is: Moon, *Sex among Allies*. A documentary film exploring the twenty-first-century dynamics of prostitution and sex trafficking on and around U.S. military bases in South Korea is: David Goodman, dir., *"Singers" in the Band: Prostitution, Global Sex Trafficking and the U.S. Military*, forthcoming.

70. Country-by-country accounts of antibases movements can be found in Lutz, *Bases of Empire*; John Lindsey-Poland, "Closing Bases."

71. See Gwyn Kirk and Alice Cook, *Greenham Women Everywhere* (London: Pluto Press, 1983); Jill Liddington, *Road to Greenham Common: Feminism and Anti-Militarism in Britain since 1820* (Syracuse, NY: Syracuse University Press, 1989). For a fascinating analysis of an unlikely antibases movement that developed in an area that allegedly is solidly conservative and pro-military—the American Great Plains states—see Gretchen Heefner, *Missile Next Door*.

72. Quoted in Anna Coote and Beatrix Campbell, *Sweet Freedom: The Struggle for Women's Liberation,* 2nd ed. (Oxford: Basil Blackwood, 1987), 49.

73. Beatrix Campbell, *The Iron Ladies: Why Do Women Vote Tory?* (London: Virago, 1987), 126.

74. Jean Stead, "The Greenham Common Peace Camp and Its Legacy," *The Guardian,* September 5, 2006, www.guardian.co.uk /uk/2006/sep/05/greenham5. See also Beeban Kidron, "Common People," *The Guardian,* September 3, 2013.

75. Since the late 1990s, there has been a stream of reports of sexual abuse around international peacekeeping bases in countries whose women and men have been made particularly vulnerable by years of local armed conflict. One of the most detailed accounts of sexual abuse involving UN and NATO peacekeeping male personnel and American police contractors in postwar Bosnia is: Kathryn Bolkovac, with Cari Lynn, *The Whistleblower: Sex Trafficking, Military Contractors, and One Woman's Fight for Justice* (New York: Palgrave Macmillan, 2011). The film based on the Bolkovac book is: Larysa Kondracki, dir., *The Whistleblower,* 2011, 112 min.

76. Denise Kiernan, *The Girls of Atomic City: The Untold Story of the Women Who Helped Win World War II* (New York: Simon and Schuster, 2013). See also Hugh Gusterson, *Nuclear Rites: A Weapons Laboratory at the End of the Cold War* (Berkeley: University of California Press, 1998); Gretchen Heefner, *Missile Next Door.*

CHAPTER 5. DIPLOMATIC AND UNDIPLO-
MATIC WIVES

1. Quoted in Mary Jordan, "'Hillary Effect' Cited for Increase in Female Ambassadors to U.S.," *Washington Post,* January 2010, http:// articles.washingtonpost.com/2010–01–11/news/36825656_1_ambassador-meera-shankar-hillary-clinton.

2. Ibid.

3. "MFA Press Statement," Ministry of Foreign Affairs, Singapore, June 14, 2013, www.mfa.gov.sg.

4. Governor Sir George Simpson, quoted by Sylvia Van Kirk, *Many Tender Ties: Women in Fur-Trade Society, 1670–1870* (Winnipeg: Watson and Dwyer, 1980; reprint, Norman: University of Oklahoma Press, 1983), 93.

5. Ibid., 75–84.

6. Julie Wheelwright, *Amazons and Military Maids: Women Who Dressed as Men in Pursuit of Life, Liberty and Happiness* (London: Pandora Press, 1989).

7. Van Kirk, *Many Tender Ties*, 192–94, Also see Clio Collective, *Quebec Women: A History* (Toronto: Women's Press, 1987), 40–46.

8. Cynthia Enloe, *Does Khaki Become You? The Militarization of Women's Lives* (London: Pandora Press, 1988).

9. Ann Corbett, "Beryl Smedley Obituary," *The Guardian*, August 4, 2011, www.guardian.co.uk/theguardian/2011/aug/04/beryl-smedley-obituary.

10. Beryl Smedley, *Partners in Diplomacy* (London: Harley Press, 1990).

11. Ibid.

12. For a fascinating, fresh account of how Abigail Adams used her commercial acumen to keep her household solvent during the American Revolution, while her husband, John, was in Paris and London, acting as the insurgent colonies' emissary, with insufficient pay, see Woody Holton, *Abigail Adams* (New York: Free Press, 2009).

13. Victoria Glendinning, *Vita: A Biography of Vita Sackville-West* (New York: Quill, 1983), 157.

14. Beryl Smedley, interview with the author, Byfleet, England, February 2, 1987.

15. Statements by Sir John Nicholas, Britain's ambassador to Sri Lanka, and David Gore-Booth, Britain's ambassador to the United Nations, quoted in Simon Jenkins and Ann Sloman, *With Respect, Ambassador: An Inquiry into the Foreign Office* (London: BBC, 1985), 63.

16. Lady Wade-Gery, quoted in ibid., 64–65.

17. Sir Oliver Wright, quoted in ibid., 79.

18. Jenkins and Sloman, *With Respect*.

19. Beryl Smedley's own obituary in 2011 ran in the London daily newspaper *The Guardian*. It was two paragraphs long and was written

by her niece: Ann Corbett, "Beryl Smedley Obituary," *The Guardian,* August 4, 2011.

20. Much of the following information is derived from an interview with Gay Murphy, then chair of the Diplomatic Service Wives Association, London, January 30, 1987. Additional information comes from the association's occasional publication, *Diplomatic Service Wives Association,* 1985–88.

21. U.S. State Department personnel, interviews with the author, June 2013.

22. A critic quoted by Susan Parsons, Family Liaison Officer, U.S. State Department, interview with the author, Washington, DC, May 4, 1987.

23. Eve Bender, "Mission Goes Global for State Department Psychiatrists," *Psychiatric News,* July 1, 2011, http://psychiatricnews.psychiatryonline.org/newsarticle.aspx?articleid = 115820.

24. Gay Murphy, interview with the author.

25. Diplomatic Service Wives Association publication (Autumn 1986): 28.

26. Ibid., 20.

27. Gay Murphy, interview with the author.

28. Ibid.

29. Annabel Hendry, "From Parallel to Dual Careers: Diplomatic Spouses," in *Modern Diplomacy,* ed. J. Kurbalija, Diplo website, 1998, www.diplomacy.edu/resources/general/parallel-dual-careers-diplomatic-spouses.

30. Interview by the author with a Washington-based advocate for women in the military and military wives, name withheld for confidentiality, April 3, 1987.

31. Interviews by the author with Washington-based activists working on issues relating to the rights of women married to government employees, Washington, April 3, 1987, and May 6, 1987.

32. Barbara Gamarekian, "Foreign Service Wives' Goal: Pay," *New York Times,* April 10, 1984.

33. Ibid.

34. Kelly Bembry Midura, writing as Cyberspouse, "Financial Security and the Foreign Service Spouse," Associates of the Ameri-

can Foreign Service Worldwide, 2012, www.aafsw.org/articles-advice /family-life-in-the-foreign-service/financial-security-and-the-fs-spouse. A list of the AAFSW's officers is found at www.aafsw.org.

35. Ibid.

36. Jean Joyce, interviewed by Valerie Kreutzer, Women's Action Organization Oral History Project, typescript, n.d., p. 10, Schlesinger Library on the History of Women in America, Radcliffe Institute, Harvard University.

37. Ibid., 14.

38. Jean Joyce, interviewed by Barbara Good and Nira Long, Women's Action Organization Oral History Project.

39. Ibid.

40. Elizabeth Cotton, *Morning Edition,* National Public Radio, April 22, 1987.

41. Phyllis Oakley, quoted by John Goshko, "Tackling a White Male Bastion," *Washington Post,* April 29, 1987.

42. Cotton, *Morning Edition.*

43. Ibid. A year later President Reagan appointed Robert Oakley, Phyllis Oakley's husband, as acting ambassador to Pakistan on the understanding that "a job would be found in Pakistan for Mrs. Oakley." David Binder, "Washington Talk: Briefing," *New York Times,* August 22, 1988.

44. Figures for September 1987, derived from data supplied to the author by the Equal Opportunity Office of the U.S. Department of State in June 1988. See also Equal Opportunities Office, U.S. Department of State, *1987 Annual Report to Congress* (Washington, DC, September 1987).

45. "Under Pressure, State Department Moves to End Its Sex Discrimination," *New York Times,* April 21, 1989; "The 'Palmer Effect' on the U.S. Foreign Service," *DiploPundit,* January 12, 2010, http://diplopundit.net/2010/01/12/the-palmer-effect-on-the-us-foregin-service.

46. Julia Chang Bloch, "Women and Diplomacy," *Ambassadors Review* (Fall 2004): 93, http://s3.amazonaws.com/caa-production/attachments/287/93–100_Bloch.pdf?1366918904. Julia Chang Bloch was the U.S. ambassador to Nepal from 1989 to 1993.

47. I am grateful to Prisca Benelli, of the Fletcher School of Law and Diplomacy, for her insights into the politics of women as wives

whose partners work for international humanitarian organizations. See also Rosalind Eyben, "Fellow Travellers in Development," *Third World* 33, no. 8 (2012): 1405–21.

CHAPTER 6. GOING BANANAS!

1. These trade figures are for 2009. Edward Evans and Fredy Ballen, "Banana Market," University of Florida, IFAS Extension, Electronic Data Information Source, 2009, http://edis.ifas.ufl.edu /fe901.

2. "Grupo Noboa S.A., Guayaquil, Ecuador," Banana Link, 2010, www.bananalink.org.uk/grupo-noboa-sa-guayaquil-ecuador. Banana Link is an independent labor rights and sustainable fair trade advocacy organization, based in Norwich, U.K., that monitors the global banana and pineapple industries.

3. "Top 25 Global Food Retailers 2013," *Supermarket News,* 2013, www.supermarketnews.com/top-25-global-food-retailers-2013. See also "The Truth on Your Table: Facts about Women Workers in the Banana Industry," STITCH: Supporting Women Workers in the US and Central America," 2006, http://stitchonline.org/archives/Stitch-BananaFactSheet.pdf. STITCH is an independent women-workers' advocacy organization based in Washington, D.C.

4. James Robert Parish, *The Fox Girls* (New Rochelle, NY: Arlington House, 1972), 499–528.

5. The Brazilian filmmaker Helena Solberg has created a documentary film (in English and Portuguese) about Carmen Miranda's complicated career and how it has been interpreted by both Brazilians and Americans. Helena Solberg, dir., *Carmen Miranda: Bananas Is My Business,* International Cinema, 1994, 91 min.

6. Parish, *Fox Girls,* 504.

7. George Black, *The Good Neighbor: How the United States Wrote the History of Central America and the Caribbean* (New York: Pantheon, 1988), 68–71. See also Neal Gabler, *An Empire of Their Own: How the Jews Invented Hollywood* (New York: Crown, 1988).

8. For more on Hollywood studios' roles in World War II, see, for instance, Thomas Patrick Doherty, *Projections of War: Hollywood,*

American Culture, and World War II, rev. ed. (New York: Columbia University Press, 1999).

9. For more on the ways in which American films served to create and reinforce stereotypes of Latin American women, see Lester Friedman, ed., *Unspeakable Images: Ethnicity and the American Cinema* (Champaign: University of Illinois Press, 1991).

10. Eduardo Galeano, *Century of the Wind* (New York: Pantheon, 1988), 131. For Galeano's description of Hollywood's Latin American male stereotype in the 1940s, see p. 122.

11. Virginia Scott Jenkins, *Bananas: The American History* (Washington, DC: Smithsonian Institution Press, 2000).

12. Claire Shaver Houghton, *Green Immigrants: The Plants That Transformed America* (New York: Harcourt Brace Jovanovich, 1978), 30–35. Also see *People Like Bananas* (Boston: United Fruit Company, 1968).

13. *People Like Bananas.* In the 1980s, Chiquita Brands, then a subsidiary of United Brands (formerly United Fruit), published a newsletter, *Chiquita Quarterly,* which made regular mention of the company's shipping fleet, then world's largest refrigerated shipping fleet at 12 per cent of the world's total in the 1980s.

14. Black, *Good Neighbor,* 77–78. For a critical assessment of American banana companies' political role in Central America, see Stephen Schlesinger, *Bitter Fruit: The Untold Story of the American Coup in Guatemala* (New York: Doubleday, 1982).

15. I am grateful to Beth C. Schwartz of United Brands for providing the original lyrics of the Chiquita Banana song.

16. Chiquita website, www.chiquita.com.

17. Trade and Market Division, FAO, *Banana Statistics, 2011* (Rome: Food and Agriculture Organization, 2011), www.fao.org/docrep/meeting /022/AM480T.pdf.

18. Ibid.

19. Salif D. Cheickna, "Cote d'Ivoire: Banana Producers Turn to Regional Markets," *Inter Press Service,* January 25, 2010, www.ipsnews .net/2010/01/cote-divoire-banana-producers-turn-to-regional-markets.

20. Jenkins, *Bananas,* 20.

21. Books and articles analyzing the gendered dynamics of plantation agriculture include Piya Chatterjee, *A Time for Tea: Women, Labor,*

and Post-colonial Politics on an Indian Plantation (Durham, NC: Duke University Press, 2001); Shobhita Jain and Rhoda Reddock, eds., *Women Plantation Workers* (Oxford: Berg, 1998); Angela Davis, "Reflections on the Black Women's Role in the Community of Slaves," *Black Scholar,* no. 3 (December, 1971); Rhoda Reddock, "Women and the Slave Plantation Economy in the Caribbean," in *Retrieving Women's History,* ed. S. Jay Kleinberg (Oxford: Berg, 1988), 105–32; Jacqueline Jones, *Labor of Love, Labor of Sorrow: Black Women, Work and the Family from Slavery to the Present* (New York: Vintage, 1986); Elizabeth Fox-Genovese, *Within the Plantation Household: Black and White Women of the Old South* (Chapel Hill, NC: University of North Carolina, 1988); Ronald Takaki, *Pau Hana: Plantation Life and Labor in Hawaii* (Honolulu: University of Hawaii Press, 1983); Belinda Coote, *The Hunger Crop: Poverty and the Sugar Industry* (Oxford: Oxfam, 1987); Shaista Shameen, "Gender, Class and Race Dynamics: Indian Women in Sugar Production in Fiji," in "Women and Work in the Pacific," special issue, *Journal of Pacific Studies*13 (1987): 10–35; Sidney Mintz, *Worker in the Cane: A Puerto Rican Life History* (New Haven, CT: Yale University Press, 1960); Laurel Herbener Lessen, *The Re-division of Labor: Women and Economic Choice in Four Guatemalan Communities* (Albany: SUNY Press, 1984); Ravinda K. Jain, *South Indians on the Plantation Frontier in Malaya* (New Haven, CT: Yale University Press, 1970); Ann Laura Stoler, *Capitalism and Confrontation in Sumatra's Plantation Belt, 1870–1979* (New Haven, CT: Yale University Press, 1985); Rachel Kurian, *Women Workers in the Sri Lanka Plantation Belt* (Geneva: International Labor Organization, 1982); Rachel Kurian, *Ethnicity, Patriarchy and Labor Control: Tamil Women in Plantation Production* (The Hague: Institute of Social Sciences, 1986); Dan Jones, *Tea and Justice: British Tea Companies and the Tea Workers of Bangladesh* (London: Bangladesh International Action Group, 1986); Stella Hillier and Lynne Gerlach, *Whose Paradise? Tea and the Plantation Tamils in Sri Lanka* (London: Minority Rights Group, 1987).

22. Philippe Bourgois, *Ethnic Diversity on a Corporate Plantation* (Cambridge, MA: Cultural Survival, 1986).

23. Ibid., 10–11. See also Trevor W. Purcell, *Banana Fallout: Class, Color, and Culture among West Indians in Costa Rica* (Los Angeles: Center for Afro-American Studies, University of California, 1993).

24. For more on women's varied roles in the 1980s Central American rebellions and nationalist movements, see Karen Kampwirth, *Women and Guerrilla Movements: Nicaragua, El Salvador, Chiapas, Cuba* (University Park: Pennsylvania State University Press, 2002); Karen Kampwirth, *Feminism and the Legacy of Revolution: Nicaragua, El Salvador, Chiapas* (Athens: Ohio University Press, 2004).

25. "First Ever Global Meeting of Women Banana Workers!" Banana Link, 2013, www.bananalink.org.uk/first-ever-global-meeting-women-banana-workers.

26. On the feminization of agriculture and its developmental consequences, see Esther Boserup, *Women's Roles in Economic Development* (London: George Allen and Unwin, 1970); Barbara Rogers, *The Domestication of Women: Discrimination in Developing Societies* (London: Kogan Page, 1980). For a perceptive examination of the gender and ethnic hierarchies that support a multinational mining company's operations in Indonesia, see Kathryn M. Robinson, *Stepchildren of Progress* (Albany: State University of New York Press, 1986).

27. Olivier De Schutter, United Nations Special Rapporteur on the right to food, "The Feminization of Farming," *New York Times*, March 4, 2013.

28. Olivier De Schutter, *Gender and the Right to Food: Executive Summary*, (Geneva: United Nations High Commission for Human Rights, February 2013), www.ohchr.org/Documents/Issues/Food/20130304_gender_execsummary_en.pdf.

29. Joni Seager, *The Penguin Atlas of Women in the World* (New York: Penguin Books, 2009), 86–87.

30. One can start one's own global, gender-supply-chain tracking of agricultural products with these studies: Deborah Barndt, ed., *Women Working the NAFTA Food Chain: Women, Food and Globalization* (Toronto: Second Story Press, 1999); Edward F. Fischer and Peter Benson, *Broccoli and Desire: Global Connections and Maya Struggles in Postwar Guatemala* (Stanford, CA: Stanford University Press, 2006); Emma Robertson, *Chocolate, Women and Empire* (Manchester, U.K.: Manchester University Press, 2009); Orla Ryan, *Chocolate Nations: Living and Dying for Cocoa in West Africa* (London: Zed Press, 2012); Catherine Ziegler, *Favored Flowers: Culture and Economy in a Global System* (Durham, NC:

Duke University Press, 2007); Heidi Tinsman, *Buying into the Regime: Gender and Consumption in Cold War Chile and the United States* (Durham, NC: Duke University Press, 2013).

31. STITCH: Supporting Women Workers in the US and Central America, "The Truth on Your Table: Facts about Women in the Banana Industry," 2006, http://stitchonline.org/archives/Stitch BananaFactSheet.pdf. See also Elizabeth U. Eviota, "The Articulation of Gender and Class in the Philippines," in *Women's Work,* ed. Eleanor Leacock, Helen I. Safa, and contributors (South Hadley, MA: Bergin and Garvey, 1986), 199; Philippe Bourgois, correspondence with the author, October 2, 1986. On women working in the food-processing business, see Lourdes Arizpe and Josephina Aranda, "Women Workers in the Strawberry Agribusiness in Mexico," in Leacock and Safa, *Women's Work,* 174–93; Vicki Ruiz, *Cannery Women, Cannery Lives* (Albuquerque: University of New Mexico Press, 1987); Patricia Zavella, *Women's Work and Chicano Families* (Ithaca, NY: Cornell University Press, 1987).

32. Mary Soledad Perpinan, "Women and Transnational Corporations: The Philippines Experience," in *The Philippines Reader,* ed. Daniel Schirmer and Stephen R. Shalom (Boston: South End Press, 1987), 243.

33. Lorenzo Cotula, *The Great African Land Grab: Agricultural Investments in the Global Food System* (London: Zed Books, 2013).

34. Clive Thomas, *Plantations, Peasants and the State* (Los Angeles: Center for Afro-American Studies, UCLA, 1984).

35. Stoler, *Capitalism and Confrontation in Sumatra's Plantation Belt,* 30–34.

36. Philippe Bourgois, correspondence with the author, October 2, 1986.

37. Banana Link et al., *Dole: Behind the Smoke Screen* (Norwich, U.K.: Banana Link, 2009), www.bananalink.uk.org/bananalink/sites/bananalink.neontribe.co.uk/files/documents/Companies/NewDolereport7Oct09.Eng.pdf.

38. "Banana War Ends after 20 Years," *BBC News,* November 8, 2012, www.bbc.co.uk/news/business-20263308.

39. Seager, *Penguin Atlas of Women in the World,* 86–87.

40. "Windward Islands Farmers Association (WINFA)," Caribbean Agribusiness, www.agricarib.org/windward-islands-farmers-association, accessed July 2, 2013.

41. This history of the women banana workers' organizing relies on the wonderful firsthand interviews with these women union activists conducted by Dana Frank, a specialist in Honduras politics at the University of California, Santa Cruz. Frank, *Bananeras: Women Transforming the Banana Unions of Latin America* (Boston: South End Press, 2005).

42. For explorations of this formative era in Latin American feminist thinking and activism, see Jane Jaquette, *The Women's Movement in Latin America* (Boulder, CO: Westview Press, 1994); Sonia Alvarez, Evelina Dagnino, and Arturo Escobar, eds., *Cultures of Politics, Politics of Culture: Re-Visioning Latin America Social Movements* (Boulder, CO: Westview Press, 1998); Nikki Craska and Maxine Molyneux, eds., *Gender and Politics of Rights and Democracy in Latin America* (London: Palgrave, 2002).

43. Women union activists quoted by Frank, *Bananeras,* 25.

44. STITCH, "The Truth on Your Table: Facts about Women Workers in the Banana Industry."

45. Women workers quoted by Frank, *Bananeras,* 4.

46. Banana Link, www.bananalink.org; Fair Food Network, www.fairfoodnetwork.org.

47. World Banana Forum, www.fao/wfb/en.

48. "First Ever Global Meeting of Women Banana Workers!"

49. "Voices from the Field," *Fair Food International,* February 18, 2013, www.fairfood.org/2013/02/voices-from-the-field.

50. Katherine Sartiano, "Going Bananas over Chiquita," *College Voice* (Connecticut College, New London), October 3, 2011.

CHAPTER 7. WOMEN'S LABOR IS NEVER *CHEAP*

1. This description of the Tazreen Fashions garment factory fire of November 24, 2012, in Bangladesh and its aftermath is based on the following reports: Vikas Bajaj, "Fire Ravages Bangladesh Factory, *International Herald Tribune,* November 26, 2012; Julfikar Ali Manik and

Jim Yardley, "Garment Workers Stage Angry Protest after Bangladesh Fire," *New York Times,* November 27, 2012; Steven Greenhouse, "Documents Indicate Walmart Blocked Safety Push in Bangladesh," *New York Times,* December 6, 2012; Associated Press, "Factory in Bangladesh Lost Fire Clearance before Blaze," *New York Times,* December 8, 2012; "Fire Safety in Garment Factories," editorial, *New York Times,* December 10, 2012; Steven Greenhouse, "2nd Supplier for Walmart at Factory That Burned," *New York Times,* December, 11, 2012; Julfikar Ali Manik and Jim Yardley, "Bangladesh Finds Gross Negligence in Factory Fire," *New York Times,* December, 18, 2012; Amy Goodman, "Survivor of Bangladesh's Tazreen Factory Fire Urges U.S. Retailers to Stop Blocking Worker Safety," an interview with Sumi Abedin, Democracy Now, April 25, 2013, www.democracynow.org/2013/14/25 /survivor_of_bangladeshs_tazreen_factory_fire.

2. Goodman, "Survivor of Bangladesh's Tazreen Factory Fire ..."

3. See, for instance, the Remember the Triangle Fire Coalition website created by feminist historians and devoted to the history—and lessons—of the 1911 Triangle Shirtwaist fire: www.rememberthetrianglefire.org; see also two documentary films describing the Triangle fire: Jamila Wignot, dir., *Triangle Fire,* American Experience, PBS, 2011; and Daphne Pinkerton, dir., *Triangle,* HBO, 2011.

4. Greenhouse, "Documents Indicate Walmart Blocked Safety Push in Bangladesh"; Priyanka Borpujari, "Deadly Savings," *Boston Globe,* January 2, 2013.

5. Lynda Yanz, "Gap Pulls Out of Bangladesh Fire Safety Program," *Maquila Solidarity Update* 17, no. 3 (December 2012): 1–8, Maquila Solidarity Network, http://en.maquilasolidarity.org/sites/maquilasolidarity.org/files/MSN-Update-Dec-2012.pdf. For a detailed account of how U.S. federal agencies, including the Defense Department, have used garment factory subcontractors in Bangladesh, Haiti, Pakistan, Mexico, and the Dominican Republic to produce low-cost apparel for federal nonmilitary uniformed personnel and clothing sold by U.S. military base stores, see Ian Urbina, "Buying Overseas Clothing, U.S. Flouts Its Own Advice," *New York Times,* December 23, 2013. For a valuable report on how the Spanish global retailer Mango has used new distribution technology located in Spain, plus pressure on Bangladesh

factories to meet ever-shorter production deadlines, in order to provide new styles on a fast turnaround schedule for Mango shops around the world, see Jim Yardley, "Clothing Brands Sidestep Blame for Safety Lapses," *New York Times,* December 31, 2013.

6. I am indebted to Jeff Ballinger, a transnational labor advocate and close observer of global companies' uses of workplace monitors, for his years of tutoring me in the flaws in these company-serving systems.

7. Kalpona Akter, quoted in Manik and Yardley, "Garment Workers Stage Angry Protest after Bangladesh Fire." For more on the labor-advocacy work of Kalpona Akter, see James North, "Bangladeshi Garment Workers Fight Back," *The Nation,* November 15, 2013, www.thenation.com/article/177181/bangladeshi-garment-workers-fight-back.

8. Clean Clothes Campaign, www.cleanclothes.org; Workers Rights Consortium, www.workersrights.org.

9. National Garments Workers Federation, *Activity Reports, 1999–2004,* Dhaka, 2004, www.nadir.org/initiativ/agp/s26/banglad/.

10. "YoungOne Workers in Bangladesh Clash with Police, Killing 4," *Korea Times,* December 13, 2010, http://koreatimes.co.kr/www/news/nation/2010/12/113_77916.html.

11. Jim Yardley, "Fighting for Bangladesh Labor, and Ending Up in Pauper's Grave," *New York Times,* September 10, 2012.

12. For more on the politics of garment trade agreements and on the impacts of those agreements on garment workers in the United States and developing countries, see Ethel Brooks, *Unraveling the Garment Industry* (Minneapolis: University of Minnesota Press, 2007); Edna Bonacich and Richard Appelbaum, *Behind the Label: Inequality in the Los Angeles Apparel Industry* (Berkeley: University of California Press, 2000); Elizabeth L. Cline, *Overdressed: The Shockingly High Cost of Cheap Fashion* (New York: Penguin, 2012); Ellen Israel Rosen, *Making Sweatshops: The Globalization of the U.S. Apparel Industry* (Berkeley: University of California Press, 2002); Robert Ross, *Slaves to Fashion: Poverty and Abuse in the New Sweatshops* (Ann Arbor: University of Michigan Press, 2004).

13. An especially provocative exploration of the sort of manliness that has been cultivated as particularly effective in the world of contemporary neoliberal capitalist business is: Charlotte Hooper, *Manly*

States: Masculinities, International Relations and Gender Politics (New York: Columbia University Press, 2001).

14. This interview was conducted by Swapna Majumdar, "Bangladesh Garment Workers Have Taste of Freedom," Women's eNews, July 15, 2002, http://womensenews.org/story/labor/020715/bangladesh-garment-workers-have-taste-of-freedom. The gender-disaggregated employment data cited here were collected by researchers at the Bangladesh Institute of Development Studies in Dhaka.

15. Ibid.

16. For more on the current politics of Bangladeshi women's organizing—and on how and when this organizing challenges the international stereotypes of Bangladeshi women—see Elora Halim Chowdhury, *Transnationalism Reversed: Women Organizing against Gendered Violence in Bangladesh* (Albany, NY: SUNY Press, 2011); Elora Shehabuddin, *Reshaping the Holy: Democracy, Development and Muslim Women in Bangladesh* (New York: Columbia University Press, 2008); Lamia Karim, *Microfinance and Its Discontents: Women in Debt in Bangladesh* (Minneapolis: University of Minnesota Press, 2011); Yasmin Saika, *Women, War and the Making of Bangladesh: Remembering 1971* (Durham, NC: Duke University Press, 2011).

17. Judy Lown, *Women and Industrialization: Gender at Work in Nineteenth-Century England* (Minneapolis: University of Minnesota Press, 1990).

18. Mikiso Hane, *Peasants, Rebels and Outcasts: The Underside of Modern Japan* (New York: Pantheon, 1982).

19. Maggie McAndrew and Jo Peers, *The New Soviet Women: Model or Myth?* International Reports on Women, no. 3 (London: Change, 1981), 26. Women also constituted 99 percent of Soviet typists and secretaries and 98 percent of nurses.

20. Lown, *Women and Industrialization.*

21. Karen Offen, "'Powered by a Woman's Foot'—a Documentary Introduction to the Sexual Politics of the Sewing Machine in Nineteenth Century France," *Women's Studies International Forum* 11, no. 2 (1988): 93. For more on the global history of the Singer sewing machine, see Mona Domosh, *American Commodities in an Age of Empire* (New York: Routledge, 2006).

22. Offen, "Powered by a Woman's Foot."

23. James Sullivan, *Jeans: A Cultural History of an American Icon* (New York: Gotham Books, 2007).

24. Data on the international comparative rankings of national cotton producers, cotton exporters, and cotton importers are collected by the National Cotton Council of America, an industry trade association. See www.cotton.org/econ/cropinfo/cropdata/rankings.cfm, accessed March 28, 2013. For a report on the politics of cotton in one authoritarian state, see Mansur Mirovalev and Andrew E. Kramer, "In Uzbekistan, the Practice of Forced Labor Lives on during the Cotton Harvest," *New York Times,* December 18, 2013.

25. Patricia Marin and Cecilia Rodriguez, "Working on Racism: Centero Obrero, El Paso," in *Of Common Cloth: Women in the Global Textile Industry,* ed. Wendy Chapkis and Cynthia Enloe (Amsterdam: Transnational Institute, 1983), 81–85.

26. Cline, *Overdressed,* 54. A documentary film about Levi's factories in the Philippines, Turkey, and Indonesia is Marie France Collard, dir., *Working Women of the World,* produced by Icarus Films, 2002, 53 min., www.icarusfilms.com/new2002/www.html.

27. Alexander Reid, "In Hard Times, Garment Union Places Hopes in New Leadership," *New York Times,* June 3, 1986.

28. Liz Bisset and Ursula Huws, *Sweated Labour: Homeworking in Britain Today* (London: Low Pay Unit, 1984); Amy Gamerman, "Homeworkers: Bottom of the Rag Trade Heap," *New Statesman,* May 3, 1988.

29. Asian British woman interviewed by Swasti Mitter and quoted in *Common Fate, Common Bond* (London: Pluto Press, 1986), 130. Additional early-feminist studies of immigrant factory women in Britain include Sallie Westwood, *All the Live Long Day* (London: Pluto Press, 1984); Barbro Hoel, "Company Clothing Sweatshops, Asian Female Labor and Collective Organization," in *Women, Work and the Labor Market,* ed. Jackie West (London: Routledge and Kegan Paul, 1982); Sally Westwood and Parminder Bhachu, eds., *Enterprising Women: Ethnicity, Economy and Gender* (London: Routledge, 1988); Annie Phizacklea, *One Way Ticket: Migration and Female Labor* (New York: Routledge and Kegan Paul, 1983). Descriptions of the homework system are included in Wendy Chapkis and Cynthia Enloe, *Of Common Cloth: Women in*

the Global Textile Industry (Amsterdam: Transnational Institute, 1983). Homeworkers in Mexico are described subtly in Lourdes Beneria and Martha Roldan, *The Crossroads of Class and Gender: Industrial Homework, Subcontracting and Household Dynamics in Mexico City* (Chicago: University of Chicago Press, 1987). See also Alison Lever, "Capital, Gender and Skill: Women Homeworkers in Rural Spain," *Feminist Review*, no. 30 (Autumn 1988): 3–24; Laura C. Johnson, *The Seam Allowance: Industrial Home Sewing in Canada* (Toronto: Women's Press, 1982); Joan McGrath, "Home Is Where the Work Is," *In These Times*, October 14, 1987, 12–13.

30. Andrea Lee, "Profiles: Being Everywhere," *New Yorker Magazine*, November 10, 1986, 53.

31. Ibid. I was first alerted to the "Benetton model" by Swasti Mitter. For a report on the currently increasing use of Chinese immigrants as workers in Italian garment factories, see Elisabetta Povoledo, "Deadly Factory Fire Bares Racial Tensions in Italy," *New York Times*, December 8, 2013.

32. For more on Nike's relationships first to Korean and then to Indonesian factory women, see Cynthia Enloe, *The Curious Feminist* (Berkeley: University of California Press, 2004).

33. I am indebted to Ann Seidman, an expert on foreign investment in South Africa, for this information. Interview with the author, Clark University, Worcester, MA, April 21, 1988.

34. Thomas Fuller, "Vietnam Accused of Abusing Drug Addicts," *New York Times*, September 8, 2011. See also Murray Hiebert, "Hanoi Courts Capitalist Investment," *Indochina Issues*, no. 67 (July 1986): 3–4. For a rather uncritical look at current government-approved labor organizing in Vietnam, see Kent Wong and An Le, *Organizing on Separate Shores: Vietnamese and Vietnamese Union Organizers* (Los Angeles: UCLA Center for Labor Research and Education, 2009).

35. Anthony B. Van Fossen, "Two Military Coups in Fiji," *Bulletin of Concerned Asian Scholars* 19 (November 4, 1988): 29; *Far Eastern Economic Review* (March 3, 1988): 49.

36. For an investigation of the politics of masculinities inside the globalized banking industry, see Cynthia Enloe, *Seriously! Investigating Crashes and Crises as If Women Mattered* (Berkeley: University of California Press, 2013).

37. Ibid. For a report on how some married women with children are pursuing their careers at senior levels in American banks by privatizing their solutions, becoming reliant on their stay-at-home unpaid husbands, thus leaving their banks' own internal masculinized cultures unchanged, see Jodi Kantor and Jessica Silver-Greenberg, "Wall Street Mothers, Stay-Home Fathers," *New York Times,* December 8, 2013.

38. Lynn Ashburner, "Women Inside the Counting House: Women in Finance," in *Women and Work,* ed. Angela Coyle and Jane Skinner (London: Macmillan; New York: New York University Press, 1988), 130–51. Also Penny Pox, "Sisters in the City," *Observer,* May 24, 1987. On women as American stockbrokers, see Nancy Nichols, "Up Against the Wall Street," *Ms. Magazine,* November 1988, 66–69. For current data on women and banking, see Counting Women In, *Sex and Power 2013: Who Runs Britain?* (London: Counting Women In, 2013), www.scribd. com/doc/177808034/Sex-and-Power-2013-FINALv2-PDF; Yvonne Roberts, "Revealed: Shocking Absence of Women from Public Life," *The Observer,* February 24, 2013; Jill Treanor, "The Women Changing the Face of the Bank of England with Focus on Financial Stability," *The Guardian,* February 28, 2013.

39. Interview by the author with a Levi's factory manager, Manila, March 1980. See also Noeleen Heyzer, *Daughters in Industry: Work, Skills, and Consciousness of Women Workers in Asia* (Kuala Lumpur, Malaysia: Women's Program, Asian and Pacific Development Centre, 1988).

40. The most famous women's labor strike over the issue of whether stitching is a *skilled* job was in Britain, in June 1968, when 187 women sewing machinists working at the Ford Company's automobile factory in Dagenham, England—stitching seats for cars and vans—walked out to demand that Ford executives refine their job description, from "unskilled" to "skilled." "Unskilled" workers were paid less than "skilled" workers. Most of the employees in "skilled" jobs in the plant were men. Though the women strikers at Dagenham Ford paved the way for Britain's historic Equal Pay Act, the company did not change the category of their work until forced by a second women's strike in 1984. Simon Godfrey, "Women Who Took on Ford in Equal Pay Fight," *The Guardian,* June 7, 2013. Among the British femi-

nist journalists who covered the Ford women's strike at the time and who continued to track its impacts is Beatrix Campbell, http://beatrixcampbell.co.uk/media.

41. For an early feminist critique of this bureaucratic practice, see Barbara Rogers, *The Domestication of Women: Discrimination in Developing Societies* (London: Kogan Page, 1980). For a graphic display of women's country-by-country rates of marriage and of status as heads-of-household, see Joni Seager, *The Penguin Atlas of Women in the World*, 4th ed. (New York: Penguin, 2009), 22–25.

42. Seager, *Penguin Atlas*, 22–23.

43. Sonia Sotomayor, *My Beloved World* (New York: Alfred A. Knopf, 2013), 96.

44. Janice C.H. Kim, *To Live to Work: Factory Women in Colonial Korea, 1910–1945* (Stanford, CA: Stanford University Press, 2009).

45. A detailed account of Chung Hee Park's gender-transforming campaign is: Seung-kyung Kim, *Class Struggle or Family Struggle?: The Lives of Women Factory Workers in South Korea* (New York: Cambridge University Press, 1997).

46. Susan Chira, "Anyang Journal: Near Seoul, a Dream Turns to Ashes," *New York Times*, April 6, 1988.

47. Ibid. For more on South Korean women workers in the 1980s, see Bernard Stephens, "Defiant Tiger," *New Statesman and Society*, September 11, 1988, 18; Jim Woodward, "Korean Workers Consolidating Unions," *Labor Notes* (November 1988): 8–9.

48. Kim, *Class Struggle or Family Struggle?*

49. Ibid. See also Seungsook Moon, *Militarized Modernity and Gendered Citizenship in South Korea* (Durham, NC: Duke University Press, 2005).

50. This account was based on the following sources: talks by September 19th Garment Workers Union representatives Alicia Cervantes and Gloria Juandiego, Clark University, Worcester, MA, April 18, 1988; discussions by union representatives with a group of visiting American feminists at the union's headquarters, Mexico City, September 5, 1986; Marta Lamas, "The Women Garment Workers' Movement: Notes for a Feminist Reflection," transl. Elaine Burns, *Fem* (Mexico City), (March 1986); Rachel Kamel, "September 19th Garment Workers Fight

Government, Owners," *Listen Real Loud,* newsletter of the Women's Project, American Friends Service Committee (Philadelphia), 9, no. 1 (1988); Rebecca Ratcliffe, "Women United Across Borders," *Sojourner* (1987); *Correspondencia,* newsletter of Mujer a Mujer (Mexico City), 1987 and 1988 issues.

51. David Brooks, "The Future: Who Will Manage It?," special issue on Mexico, *NACLA: Report on the Americas* 21, no. 5 and 6 (September–December 1987): 23–24. Two excellent studies of working women in the U.S.-Mexican border factories, maquiladoras, are: Vicki L. Ruiz and Susan Tiano, eds., *Women on the US-Mexican Border: Responses to Change* (Boston: George Allen and Unwin, 1987); Patricia Fernandez-Kelly, *For We Are Sold, I and My People: Women and Industry on Mexico's Frontier* (Albany, NY: State University of New York Press, 1983).

52. See, for instance, Altha J. Cravey, *Women and Work in Mexico's Maquiladoras* (Lanham, MD: Rowman and Littlefield, 1998); Deborah Barndt, ed., *Women Working the NAFTA Food Chain: Women, Food and Globalization* (Toronto: Second Story Press, 1999).

53. A stunning, graphic, multilayered portrait of contemporary China and its regional differences is: Stephanie Hemelryk Donald and Robert Benewick, *The State of China Atlas* (Berkeley: University of California Press, 2009).

54. Ibid.

55. Chinese Ministry of Commerce, "Doing Business in Guangdong Province of China," http://english.mofcom.gov.cn/aroundchina /Guangdong.shtml, accessed January 5, 2014.

56. Anita Chan, Richard Madsen, and Jonathan Unger, *Chen Village: Revolution to Globalization* (Berkeley: University of California Press, 2009); Ellen Oxfeld, *Drink Water, but Remember the Source: Moral Discourse in a Chinese Village* (Berkeley: University of California Press, 2010).

57. See, for example, Gail Hershatter, *Women in China's Long Twentieth Century* (Berkeley: University of California Press, 2007); Paul S. Ropp, *China in World History* (London: Oxford University Press, 2010); Tani Barlow, *The Question of Women in Chinese Feminism* (Durham, NC: Duke University Press, 2004); Louise Edwards, *Gender, Politics and Democracy: Women's Suffrage in China* (Stanford, CA: Stanford University Press, 2008).

58. For an ethnographic investigation of how wealthy male Chinese entrepreneurs use banqueting and karaoke singing to create bonds of sentiment, moral obligation, and instrumental interest with other men in business and politics, see John Osburg, *Anxious Wealth: Money and Morality among China's New Rich* (Stanford, CA: Stanford University Press, 2013). For insights into the uses of karaoke clubs—and the women working there as hostesses—in forging masculinized bonds between Japanese businessmen, see Anne Allison, *Nightwork: Sexuality, Pleasure and Corporate Masculinity in a Tokyo Hostess Club* (Chicago: University of Chicago Press, 1994).

59. To hear Chinese migrant women's own voices, see Xinran Xue and Ran Xin, *The Good Women of China* (London: Vintage, 2003); Leslie T. Chang, *Factory Girls: From Village to City in a Changing China* (New York: Spiegel and Grau, 2009); Ngai Pun, *Made in China: Women Factory Workers in a Global Workplace* (Durham, NC: Duke University Press, 2005). A documentary film following the lives of two teenage Chinese women working in a blue jeans factory is: Micha X. Peled, dir., *China Blue,* Teddy Bear Films and Bullfrog Films, 2007, 88 min., www.bullfrogfilms.com.

60. A *New York Times* series investigating Taiwanese-owned Foxconn's relationships with its Chinese workers and with its major corporate clients, such as Apple and Hewlett-Packard, includes David Barboza, "After Suicides, Scrutiny of China's Grim Factories," *New York Times,* June 7, 2010; Charles Duhigg and Nick Wingfield, "Apple, in Shift, Pushes an Audit of Sites in China," *New York Times,* February 14, 2012; Steven Greenhouse, "Early Praise for Inspection at Foxconn Brings Doubt," *New York Times,* February 17, 2012; David Barboza, "Foxconn Plans to Sharply Lift Workers' Pay," *New York Times,* February 19, 2012; David Barboza and Charles Duhigg, "Pressure, Chinese and Foreign, Drives Changes at Foxconn," *New York Times,* February 20, 2012; Nick Wingfield, "New Chief Presses Factories to Improve Working Conditions," *New York Times,* April 2, 2012; David Barboza and Charles Duhigg, "China Plant Again Faces Labor Issues on iPhones," *New York Times,* September 11, 2012; David Barboza and Keith Bradsher, "Foxconn Shuts Plant in Wake of Worker Riot," *New York Times,* global ed., September 25, 2012. For background to the 2012 disputes over

Foxconn's labor conditions and Apple's responses, see Jenny Chan and Ngai Pun, "Suicide as Protest for the New Generation of Chinese Migrant Workers: Foxconn, Global Capital, and the State," *Asia-Pacific Journal,* 2010, http://japanfocus.org/-jenny-chan/3048; Vindu Goel, "Foxconn Audit Finds a Workweek Still Too Long," *New York Times,* May 17, 2013.

61. Dan Levin, "The Demanding Off-Hour Escapes of China's High-Tech Workers," *New York Times,* July 17, 2013.

62. Osburg, *Anxious Wealth.* For an insight into how the Chinese government treats women in prostitution whose clients are nonelite Chinese men, see Andrew Jacobs, "For Prostitutes Jailed in China, Forced Labor with No Resources," *New York Times,* January 1, 2014.

63. Keith Bradsher, "As China's Workers Get a Raise, Companies and Consumers Face Higher Prices," *New York Times,* June 1, 2011; Neil Gough, "Chinese Apparel Firm Addresses Falling Profits," *New York Times,* July 6, 2012; Keith Bradsher and Charles Duhigg, "Signs of Changes Taking Hold in Electronics Factories in China," *New York Times,* December 2012.

64. Keith Bradsher, "Hello, Cambodia: Wary of Events in China, Foreign Investors Head to the South," *New York Times,* April 9, 2013; Thomas Fuller and Keith Bradsher, "Deadly Collapse in Cambodia Renews Safety Concerns," *New York Times,* May 17, 2013; Gerry Mullany, "Workers Face Police Gunfire amid Unrest in Cambodia," *New York Times,* January 4, 2014. Major, but little-known, players in today's international garment industry are companies called "sourcing and logistics companies." Their agents act as matchmakers between the global brand companies and the local garment-factory owners. Their goal is to find the factories in any country that can produce clothes for the lowest cost. If a global brand ends its contracts with factories in, for instance, China, in order to move its production to Bangladesh, or ends its contracts in Bangladesh to move production to Cambodia, Venezuela, or Botswana, it is usually at the advice of, and with the help of, a sourcing company. The largest and most influential of these globalized sourcing companies is the Hong Kong–based Li and Fung. Ian Urbina and Keith Bradsher, "Linking Factories to the Malls Middleman Pushes Low Costs," *New York Times,* August 8, 2013.

65. The story of Shaheena Akhtar is told in Jim Yardley, "Last Hope in the Ruins: Bangladesh's Race to Save Shaheena," *New York Times,* May 6, 2013.

66. Shaheena Akhtar, quoted by her sister Jesmine, in ibid.

67. Coverage of the 2013 Rana Plaza collapse and its complicated, globalized aftermath includes Julfikar Ali Manik, Jim Yardley, "Building Collapse in Bangladesh Kills Scores of Garment Workers," *New York Times,* April 25, 2013; Julfikar Ali Manik, Steven Greenhouse, and Jim Yardley, "Outrage Builds after Collapse in Bangladesh," *New York Times,* April 26, 2013; Jim Yardley, "The Most Hated Bangladeshi, Toppled from a Shady Empire," *New York Times,* May 1, 2013; Steven Greenhouse, "Retailers Split on Contrition after Collapse of Factories," *New York Times,* May 1, 2013; Steven Greenhouse, "Wal-Mart Sets a Safety Plan in Bangladesh," *New York Times,* May 15, 2013; Jason Motlagh and Susie Taylor, "From the Ashes of Rana Plaza," *Ms. Magazine,* Summer 2013, 2–31; Stephanie Clifford and Steven Greenhouse, "Fast and Flawed Inspections of Factories Abroad," *New York Times,* September 2, 2013; Mehul Srivastava, "In Bangladesh, Inspections at Factories Have Not Begun," *Boston Globe,* October 25, 2013; Lucy Siegle, "Never Again?" *Observer Magazine,* November 6, 2013, 32–35; Steven Greenhouse, "U.S. Retailers Decline to Aid Factory Victims in Bangladesh," *New York Times,* November 23, 2013; Jim Yardley, "After Collapse, Bleak Struggle," *New York Times,* December 19, 2013.

68. Steven Greenhouse, "Clothiers Act to Inspect Bangladeshi Factories," *New York Times,* July 8, 2013.

69. Ian Urbina, "U.S. Conflicted on Overseas Labor Responsibility, " *International Herald Tribune,* May 31, 2013; Steven Greenhouse, "U.S. to Suspend Trade Privileges with Bangladesh," *New York Times,* June 28, 2013.

70. Steven Greenhouse, "Under Pressure, Bangladesh Adopts New Labor Law," *New York Times,* July 17, 2013; Jim Yardley "Garment Trade Wields Power in Bangladesh," *New York Times,* July 25, 2013.

71. Jim Yardley, "Justice Elusive in a Bangladesh Factory Disaster," *New York Times,* June 30, 2013.

72. Jim Yardley, "Bangladesh Pollution, Told in Colors and Smells," *New York Times,* July 15, 2013.

73. Jim Yardley, "After Disaster, Bangladesh Lags in Policing Its Maze of Factories," *New York Times,* July 3, 2013.

74. Steven Greenhouse, "Some Retailers Rethink Roles in Bangladesh," *New York Times,* May 2, 2013; Steven Greenhouse, "Factory Owners in Bangladesh Fear Apparel Firms Will Leave," *New York Times,* May 3, 2013. After the Tazreen fire, this stay-don't-run strategy was also supported by Jeff Ballinger and Scott Nova, prominent U.S.-based transnational labor rights activists and researchers working with local labor rights advocates in Bangladesh: email correspondence with author, December, 12, 2012; Steven Greenhouse and Jim Yardley, "Global Retailers Join Safety Plan for Bangladesh," *New York Times,* May 14, 2013; Liz Alderman, "After Collapse, a Breakthrough, *New York Times,* May 20, 2013; Steven Greenhouse, "U.S. Retailers See Big Risk in Safety Plan for Factories," *New York Times,* May 23, 2013; Steven Greenhouse, "$40 Million in Aid Set for Bangladesh Garment Workers," *New York Times,* December 24, 2013.

75. Jason Burke, "Alive but Alone: Survivors of Factory Disaster Stitch Together Broken Lives," *The Guardian,* June 7, 2013.

CHAPTER 8. SCRUBBING THE GLOBALIZED TUB

1. "Domestic Workers," International Labor Organization, www .ilo.org/global/topics/domestic-workers/lang--en/index.htm, accessed July 19, 2013.

2. This profile is drawn from Richard Morin, "Indentured Servitude in the Persian Gulf," *New York Times,* April 14, 2013, as well as from my observations in Doha, the capital of Qatar, December 2012. See also Ganesh Seshan, "Migrants in Qatar: A Socio-Economic Profile," *Journal of Arabian Studies* 2, no. 2 (December 2012): 157–71, http://academia .edu/2554359/Profile_of_Migrants_in_Qatar.

3. Philippine Commission on Women, "Statistics on Filipino Women and Men's Overseas Employment," Philippines Commission on Women, April 18, 2013, http://pcw.gov.ph/statistics/201304 /statistics-filipino-women-and-mens-overseas-employment.

4. Quoted by Ethel Tungohan, "Reconceptualizing Motherhood, Reconceptualizing Resistance: Migrant Domestic Workers, Interna-

tional Hyper-Maternalism, and Activism," *International Feminist Journal of Politics* 15, no. 1 (March 2013), published online in 2012, http://dx.doi.org/10.1080/14616742.2012.699781.

5. Theresa Dantes quoted by Morin, "Indentured Servitude in the Persian Gulf."

6. For more on Filipinas who go abroad to work as domestic workers, see Rhacel Salazar Parrenas, *Servants of Globalization: Women, Migration and Domestic Work* (Stanford, CA: Stanford University Press, 2001).

7. This account is based on Doreen Mattingly, "Domestic Service and International Networks of Caring," in *Women and Change at the U.S.–Mexico Border: Mobility, Labor and Activism,* ed. Doreen Mattingly and Ellen R. Hansen (Tucson: University of Arizona Press, 2006), 103–23. See also Linda Burnham and Nik Theodore, *Home Economics: The Invisible and Unregulated World of Domestic Work* (New York: National Domestic Workers Alliance, 2012), 41.

8. For more information on the diverse locations occupied by male and female Latinos in contemporary American life, see Cynthia Enloe and Joni Seager, *The Real State of America Atlas: Mapping the Myths and Truths of the United States* (New York: Penguin, 2011).

9. Mattingly, "Domestic Service and International Networks of Caring."

10. Quoted by Maria Susan Rye, in "On Assisted Emigration," reprinted in *Barbara Leigh Smith Bodichon and the Langham Place Group,* ed. Candida Ann Lacey, Women's Source Library, vol. 3 (London: Routledge and Kegan Paul, 1987), 337–38.

11. I am indebted to British researcher Sally Davis for sharing her findings on the Female Middle Class Emigration Society with me. Correspondence with the author, March 17, 1985.

12. See, for instance, Claudia Knapman, *White Women in Fiji, 1835–1850: Ruin of the Empire?* (Sydney: Unwin Hyman, 1989); Suzanne Gordon, *A Talent for Tomorrow: Life Stories of South African Servants* (Braamfontein, South Africa: Raven Press, 1985); Beata Lipman, *We Make Freedom: Women in South Africa* (London: Pandora Press, 1984); Jacklyn Cock, *Maids and Madams: Domestic Workers under Apartheid,* 2nd ed. (London: Women's Press, 1989).

13. Isa Craig, "Emigration as a Preventative Agency," reprinted in Lacey, *Barbara Leigh Smith Bodichon and the Langham Place Group*, 297. For information on Canadian recruitment of British and Finnish women as domestic servants, see Varpu Lindstrom-Best, "'I Won't Be a Slave!' Finnish Domestics in Canada," in *Looking into My Sister's Eyes*, ed. Jean Burnet (Toronto: Multicultural Historical Society of Ontario, 1986), 31–53. See also Carolyn Stedman, *Labours Lost: Domestic Service and the Making of Modern England* (Cambridge: Cambridge University Press, 2009).

14. For more on British and French emigration to Canada, see Susan Jackel, ed., *A Flannel Shirt and Liberty: British Emigrant Gentlewomen in the Canadian West, 1880–1914* (Vancouver: University of British Columbia Press, 1983); Clio Collective, *Quebec Women: A History* (Toronto: Women's Press, 1987).

15. Sally Davis, correspondence with the author, March 17, 1988.

16. International Labor Organization, *Domestic Workers across the World: Global and Regional Statistics and the Extent of Legal Protection* (Geneva: International Labor Organization, 2013), 25.

17. Ibid.

18. Ibid.

19. Ibid., 1.

20. I am grateful to feminist geographer Joni Seager for tutoring me in the gender history of housing design. See also Gwendolyn Wright, *Moralism and the Model Home* (Chicago: University of Chicago Press, 1985).

21. "Economic News Release: American Time Use Survey Summary," U.S. Department of Labor, Bureau of Labor Statistics, June 20, 2013, www.bls.gov/news.release/atus.nro.htm; Joni Seager, "Unpaid Work," *The Penguin Atlas of Women in the World* (New York: Penguin, 2009), 70–71.

22. Wendy Wang, Kim Parker, and Paul Taylor, "Breadwinner Moms," Pew Research Social and Demographic Trends, May 29, 2013, www.pewsocialtrends.org/2013/05/29/breadwinnermoms. For more on the history of African American women and Irish women in U.S. domestic work, see Danielle Taylor Phillips, "Moving with Women: Tracing Racialization, Migration, and Domestic Workers in the

Archive," *Signs* 38, no. 2 (Winter 2013); Erik S. McDuffie, *Sojourning for Freedom: Black Women, American Communism, and the Making of Black Left Feminism* (Durham, NC: Duke University Press, 2011).

23. For histories of nineteenth- and twentieth-century domestic workers, see Mary Lennon, Marie McAdam, and Jane O'Brien, *Across the Water: Irish Women's Lives in Britain* (London: Virago, 1987); Hasia R. Diner, *Erin's Daughters in America* (Baltimore: Johns Hopkins University Press, 1983); Joy Rudd, "Invisible Exports: The Emigration of Irish Women This Century," in "Feminism in Ireland," ed. Ailbhe Smyth, special issue, *Women's Studies International Forum* 11, no. 4 (1988); Evelyn Nakano Glenn, *Issei, Nisei, War Bride: Three Generations of Japanese American Women in Domestic Service* (Philadelphia: Temple University Press, 1986); Trudier Harris, *From Mammies to Militants: Domestics in Black American Literature* (Philadelphia: Temple University Press, 1982); Judith Rollins, *Between Women: Domestics and Their Employers* (Philadelphia: Temple University Press, 1985); David M. Katzman, *Seven Days a Week: Women and Domestic Service in Industrializing America* (Urbana: University of Illinois Press, 1981); Donna L. van Raaphorst, *Union Maids Not Wanted: Organizing Domestic Workers, 1870–1940* (Westport, CT: Greenwood Press, 1988).

24. John Rentoul, "It's So Difficult to Get Servants These Days," *New Statesman,* November 7, 1986, 20; Sara Rimer, "Childcare at Home: Two Women, Complex Roles," *New York Times,* December 26, 1988.

25. Ximena Bunster, Chilean anthropologist, telephone conversation with author, July 16, 2013.

26. For an investigation of how the Malaysian government and Malaysian middle-class families together have managed immigration of Filipino and Indonesian women to work as domestic workers, see Christine B.N. Chin, *In Service and Servitude: Workers and the Malaysia Modernity Project* (New York: Columbia University Press, 1998). See also Juanita Elias, "Foreign Policy and Domestic Workers: The Malaysia-Indonesia Dispute," *International Feminist Journal of Politics* 15, no. 3 (September 2013): 391–410; Christine Hauser, "Housemaid Is Beheaded in Death of Saudi Boy," *New York Times,* January 10, 2013; Keith Bradsher, "Hong Kong Court Denies Residency to Domestics," *New York Times,* March 26, 2013.

27. Linda Basch and Gail Lerner, introduction to *Migrant Women Claim Their Rights: Nairobi and After* (Geneva: World Council of Churches, July 1986), ii.

28. For more on the relationships between women working as maids and their middle-class Latin American employers, see Ximena Bunster and Elsa Chaney, *Sellers and Servants: Working Women in Lima, Peru* (South Hadley, MA: Bergin and Garvey, 1985); Elsa Chaney and Marcey Garcia Castro, eds., *Muchachas No More: Household Workers in Latin America and the Caribbean* (Philadelphia: Temple University Press, 1989). A novel that graphically describes a West Indian woman's impressions of her American domestic employers is: Paula Fox, *A Servant's Tale* (London: Penguin, 1984).

29. Among the most nuanced studies of the unequal, often awkward relationships between women as employers and women as domestic workers, are: Bunster and Chaney, *Sellers and Servants;* Cock, *Maids and Madams;* Nicole Constable, *Maid to Order in Hong Kong* (Ithaca, NY: Cornell University Press, 1997); Mary Romero, *Maid in the U.S.A.* (New York: Routledge, 2002); Pierrette Hondagneu-Sotel, *Domestica: Immigrant Workers Cleaning and Caring in the Shadows of Affluence* (Berkeley: University of California Press, 2001); Ruri Ito, "Crafting Migrant Women's Citizenship in Japan: Taking 'Family' as a Vantage Point," *International Journal of Japanese Sociology,* no. 14 (2005): 52–59.

30. Michele R. Grimaud, "Advocating for Sri Lankan Migrant Workers: Obstacles and Challenges," in "Distant Divides and Intimate Connections, Part 2," ed. Nicole Constable, special issue on cross-national comparisons of domestic workers' organizing, *Critical Asian Studies* 41, no. 1 (March 2009): 61–88. See also Naila Kabeer, Ratna Sudarshan, and Kirsty Milward, eds., *Organizing Women Workers in the Informal Economy* (London: Zed Books, 2013).

31. Megha Amrith, "Encountering Asia: Narratives of Filipino Medical Workers on Caring for Other Asians," *Critical Asian Studies* 45, no. 2 (June 2013): 231–54. Regarding domestic health care workers in the United States, see Karen Kahn, "The Value of Care," *Women's Review of Books* 30, no. 2 (March–April 2013): 24–25.

32. An excellent collection of case studies of the varying conditions experienced by women domestic workers working abroad is: "Distant

Divides and Intimate Connections, Part 1," ed. Nicole Constable, special issue on cross-national comparisons of domestic workers' organizing, *Critical Asian Studies* 40, no. 4 (December 2008).

33. International Labor Organization, "Executive Summary," in *ILO 2012 Global Estimate of Forced Labour* (Geneva: International Labor Organization, 2012), http://www.ilo.org/wcmsp5/groups/public/@ed_norm/@declaration/documents/publication/wcms_181953.pdf. For a detailed investigation of the ways in which boys are trafficked and the abusive labor for which they are used (including as workers in small garment factories in Ho Chi Minh City), see UN Vietnam, Government of Vietnam, and Millennium Development Goals Achievement Fund, *Exploratory Research—Trafficking in Boys in Viet Nam* (Hanoi: UN Vietnam, Government of Vietnam, and Millennium Development Goals Achievement Fund, 2012). Interestingly, the investigators found that many Vietnamese boys—and their parents and their neighbors—were made vulnerable in part because of the widely held belief that boys (as opposed to girls) were impervious to abuse when they dropped out of school and left home, because boys "naturally" seek adventure (xx29, 62).

34. See, for instance, Ai-jen Poo and Tiffany Williams, "House of Horrors: Labor Trafficking in Domestic Workers," *Daily Beast,* July 18, 2013, www.thedailybeast.com/witw/articles/2013/07/18/house-of-horrors-labor-trafficking-in-domestic-workers.html; International Labor Organization, *ILO 2012 Global Estimate of Forced Labour.* In a rare suit, a Peruvian woman working as a housemaid at the New Jersey residence of her employers, Peruvian diplomats stationed at the United Nations, freed herself and brought a legal charge against them: trafficking into forced labor. Kirk Semple, "Housekeeper Accuses a Peruvian Diplomat of Human Trafficking," *New York Times,* June 25, 2013. A diplomatic controversy between the Indian and U.S. governments erupted when, in 2013, an American federal prosecutor ordered the arrest of an Indian woman consular official in New York on charges of abusing her Indian housekeeper in violation of U.S. labor regulations. The arrest set off debates in India over the treatment of Indian domestic workers employed by Indian middle-class and upper-class

employers. Benjamin Weiser and Michael R. Gordon, "U.S. Prosecutor Defends Arrest of Indian Diplomat," *New York Times,* December 19, 2013; Gerry Mullany, "Indian Envoy Is Transferred to U.N. Post," *New York Times,* December 22, 2013; Ananya Bhattacharyya, "Having a Servant Is Not a Right," op-ed, *New York Times,* December 21, 2013. The organization in the United States that tracks labor and sexual trafficking state by state and seeks evidence to pursue legal prosecutions is the Polaris Project of the National Human Trafficking Resource Center, www.polarisproject.org/human-trafficking/overview.

35. Barbara Ehrenreich, *Nickel and Dimed: On (Not) Getting By in America* (New York: Metropolitan Books, 2001).

36. Padmini Palliyaguruge, "Sri Lanka House Maids and Free Trade Zone Workers," in *Migrant Women Claim Their Rights: Nairobi and After,* dossier no. 15 (Geneva: World Council of Churches, July 1986), 21–24.

37. Centre for Society and Religion, "Alone in a Strange Land," *Asian Migrant* 1, no. 1 (January–February 1988): 16. *Asian Migrant* is published by the Catholic Scalabrini Centrum, Quezon City, Philippines. See also Asoka Bandarage, "Women and Capitalist Development in Sri Lanka, 1977–1987," *Bulletin of Concerned Asian Scholars* 20, no. 2 (1988): 69–71.

38. Palliyaguruge, "Sri Lanka House Maids and Free Trade Zone Workers."

39. Ibid. See also Prema Embuldeniya, "Their Suffering Is Beyond Human Endurance: From the Report of the Committee on Migrant Workers, Sri Lanka," *Migration Today,* no. 40 (1988): 12–13. For a report on the increased threat of trafficking faced by women and girls, especially from the ethnic Tamil community, in Sri Lanka's northern postwar zones, see International Civil Society Action Network, "Elusive Peace, Pervasive Violence: Sri Lankan Women's Struggle for Security and Justice," in "What the Women Say" series, brief 8, *ICAN* (Spring 2013), www.icanpeacework.org/sri-lanka.

40. See, for instance, Elaine Salo, "Obscure Lives: Filipino Women Migrants in an Italian City" (unpublished MA thesis, Worcester, MA, International Development, Clark University, 1986); Constable, *Maid to Order in Hong Kong;* Hondagneu-Sotel, *Domestica.*

41. This was not the first time that women and men trying to reform abusive domestic-worker systems had succeeded by reframing their issue more broadly. Southeast Asia historian Rachel Leow has found that British reformers in the 1920s and 1930s who were trying to end a Malayan colonial system of virtually enslaving poor rural girls as servants in affluent homes did not make headway until they reframed their campaign as championing the "rights of the child." Rachel Leow, "Age as a Category of Gender Analysis: Servant Girls, Modern Girls, and Gender in Southeast Asia," *Journal of Asian Studies* 71, no. 4 (November 2012): 975–90.

42. This account is drawn from anthropologist Nicole Constable's participant observation: "Migrant Workers and the Many States of Protest in Hong Kong," in "Distant Divides and Intimate Connections, Part 2," ed. Nicole Constable, special issue on cross-national comparisons of domestic workers' organizing, *Critical Asian Studies* 41, no. 1 (March 2009): 143–64.

43. "Wage and Hour Division: State Minimum Wage and Overtime Coverage of Non-publicly Employed Companions," U.S. Department of Labor, www.dol.gov/whd/flsa/statemap, accessed July 20, 2013.

44. National Domestic Workers Alliance, www.domesticworkers.org.

45. National Domestic Workers Alliance, Center for Urban Economic Development, University of Illinois at Chicago, and Data Center, *Home Economics: The Invisible and Unregulated World of Domestic Work* (New York: National Domestic Workers Alliance, 2012), 14.

46. Ibid., xi.

47. Ibid., xi–xii.

48. Cynthia Hess and Jane Henrici, "Informing Policies to Build Career and Immigration Pathways for In-Home Care Workers," news release, Institute for Women's Policy Research, February 11, 2013, p. 5. For more on the Washington-based institute's research and policy advocacy to improve the working conditions of home care workers, see www.iwpr.org.

49. Ai-jen Poo and E. Tammy Kim, "Organizing to Transform Ourselves and Our Laws: The New York Domestic Workers Bill of

Rights Campaign," Sargent Shriver National Center on Poverty Law, http://povertylaw.org/communication/advocacy-stories/poo, accessed July 20, 2013.

50. "Domestic Workers' Bill of Rights," New York State Department of Labor, www.labor.ny.gov/legal/domestic-workers-bill-of-rights.shtm, accessed July 20, 2013.

51. International Domestic Workers' Network, www.idwn.org.

52. "Who We Are," International Domestic Workers' Network: www.idwn.info/content/who-we-are, accessed July 20, 2013.

53. Women in Informal Employment: Globalizing and Organizing, www.wiego.org.

54. "Learn about Domestic Workers," International Domestic Workers' Network, www.idwn.info/content/learn-about-domestic-workers, accessed July 18, 2013. A study of Latin American domestic workers' political organizing on the eve of the passage of the ILO Convention 189 is: Merike Blotfield, *Care Work and Class: Domestic Workers' Struggle for Equal Rights in Latin America* (University Park: Pennsylvania State University Press, 2013).

55. "C-189: Domestic Workers Are Workers," International Domestic Workers' Network, www.idwn.info/campaign/c189-domestic-workers-are-workers, accessed July 15, 2013.

56. "Convention No. 189: Decent Work for Domestic Workers," International Labor Organization, www.ilo.org/wcmsp5/groups/public/---asia/---ro-bangkok/documents/genericdocument/wcms_208561.pdf, accessed July 17, 2013.

CONCLUSION

1. A new documentary film—based on more than thirty years of research by the film's director in the Philippines and around U.S. bases in Asia—reveals this deceptive recruiting of Filipinas into militarized prostitution: David Goodman, dir., *"Singers" in the Band: Prostitution, Global Sex Trafficking and the U.S. Military,* forthcoming, 2014.

2. "Women Worldwide Know Less about Politics Than Men," a report on the ESRC's study *Gender Matters Globally,* authored by John

Curran, Economic and Social Research Council (London), July 3, 2013, www.esrc.ac.uk/news-and-events/press-releases/26789/Women_worldwide_know_less_about_politics_than_men.aspx.

3. Catherine Bennett, "Don't Blame Women If We Ignore What Passes for Politics," *The Observer,* July 7, 2013.

INDEX

Page references given in italics indicate illustrations or material contained in their captions.

Bosnia, 118, 378–79n62, 400n75
Boston (MA), 372n22
Bourgois, Philippe, 228
Bousquet, Ben, 390n22
Boy Scouts, 101–3, *102*
Brazil: as BRICS country, 286;
  cotton production in, 268;
  domestic worker political
  organizing in, 330–31; domestic
  workers from, 322; economic/
  political inequality in, 356;
  feminist media resources in, 20;
  gender-based violence in, 24–25;
  ILO Convention 189 ratified in,
  340; industry types in, 285, 286;
  militarized masculinity in, 150;
  Miranda and, 214–15, 218; women
  as household heads in, 281;
  women-owned farmland in, 231;
  women's activism in, 24–25;
  women's suffrage movement in,
  12
BRICS countries, 286
Bristol (England), 140
British Asian homeworkers, 272
British Empire: diplomatic wives
  in, 182–84; marriage diplomacy
  in, 178–80; masculinity in,
  100–103, *101*; Mutiny (1857), 313;
  nationalism and, 85; plantation
  crops in, 213–14; postcard
  imagery from, 89, *90*; racialized
  military prostitution system in,
  100, 157–60; reform movements
  in, 428n41; US military bases in,
  128; women as domestic servants
  in, 310–13; women as military
  nurses in, 382n15
British Foreign Office, 183, 189, 199
British military, 150, 390n22
British Museum, 188
British Parliament, 139, 157–58

Brodsky, Dina, 46
brothels, 236–37
Brown, John, 21
Burundi, 281
busboys, 68
Bush, George H. W., 207
Bush, George W., 148
Butler, Josephine, 158–60
Butler, Maria, 26, 366n18

Cable, Mildred, 44
Cairo (Egypt), 20, 104
Calvin Klein, 254–55
Cambodia, 75, 258, *298*, 298–99, 303
Cameroon, 224, 237
Campbell, Beatrix, 171–72, 414n40
Camp Lemonnier (Djibouti), 128,
  133
Camp Pendleton (CA), 147
Canada: banana trade in, 218–19;
  under British colonial rule,
  178–80, 311–12; corporate fishing
  off coasts of, 86; domestic
  worker political organizing in,
  330–31; domestic workers in, 312,
  313; feminist media innovations
  in, 19–20; foreign domestic
  workers in, 322, 330–31; free trade
  treaties of, 294; industry types
  in, 285; militarized masculinity
  in, 150; military recruitment in,
  143; nationalist movement in, 84,
  85, 111; nationalist sentiments in,
  86, 95; -owned garment stores,
  254–55; racialized military
  prostitution system of, 160;
  tourist industry in, 56, 372n26;
  women soldiers in, 151, 153
Canary Islands, 218
capitalism, 34, 259, 296, 358,
  411–12n13. *See also* globalization;
  neoliberal economic model

military prostitution system in,
162; woman as chancellor of,
362n3
Germany, East, 127
Girl Guides, 103
Girl Rising, 13
girls' education, 16
glass ceiling, the, 17
Global Action to Prevent War and
Armed Conflict, 24
"global films," 86
globalization, 86, 87, 117, 306, 358
Goa (India), 56
Good Neighbor Policy, 215–17, 220,
222
governesses, 311–12
Grable, Betty, 217
Great Britain: antibases activism,
170–72, *171*, 187; antislavery
movement in, 21–22; banana
trade in, 212; banking industry
in, 277, 278; deindustrialization
in, 286; diplomatic wives from,
186; feminist activism in, 36, 189,
191; feminist media innovations
in, 19–20; foreign military bases
of, 127; garment industry in,
271–72; ILO Convention 189
unratified in, 341; industrial
revolution in, 263–65, 318;
industry types in, 285; military
recruitment in, 143; -owned
garment stores, 301; racialized
military prostitution system of,
160–61; racism in, 158; United
States of America (Visiting
Forces) Act (1942), 139; US
military bases in, 134–40, 144;
US relations with, 187; Washington embassy of, 187; women as
tourists in, 41–42, 44–46, 52–53;
women's suffrage movement in,

12; world's fairs in, 49. *See also*
British Empire
Great Depression, 217
Greece, 277
Greenham Common (England),
134, 170–72, *171*, 187
Green Hill Textile Company fire
(South Korea; 1988), 287–88
Grenadines, 224
Group of Eight (G8), 28, *30*, 176–77,
177, 286, 354
Group of Seven (G7), 28, *29*
Group of Twenty (G20), 286, 354
Guam, 86, 126, 147, 164, 168–69
Guatemala, 223–24, 225–26, 229,
242, 245, 303
Guayaquil (Ecuador), 246–47
Guaymi people, 227
guerilla movements, 242, 387n41
Guibout, Eugène, 266
Guinea-Bissau, 79
gun lobby, 367–68n19
Gunn, Isabel, 180

H&M, 253–54, 255, 260, 299, 301, 354
Haiti, 281, 410n5
Haitian Quebecois, 88
"Hall of Shame Awards" (Hong
Kong; 2005), 332–33
Hapsburg Empire, 85
Harding, Sandra, 368–69n22
Hashimoto Toru, 397n57
Hasina, Sheikh, 257, 299
Hassan, Yasmeen, 379n69
Hatem, Mervat, 107
Havrilla, Rebekah, 155
Hawaii, 162, 164, 213
headscarves, 104–8, *105*
Hélie-Lucas, Marie-Aimée, 93–94,
345, 346–48
Henry-Martin, Jacinth, *175*
Hewlett-Packard, 418n60

reform measures in, 303; veil/
headscarf controversy in, 104–5
Indonesian women, 160, 275
industrial decline, 268–71, 286
industrial homeworkers, 271–74
industrialization, 48, 49, 111,
263–64, 294–95, 318
industries, "light" vs. "heavy,"
282–86
inequality, 356
Ingibjorg, Sigridur, 63
inheritance rights, 100
Institutionalized Revolutionary
Party (PRI; Mexico), 289,
293, 299
InterContinental Hotels Group, 81
intermarriage: Boy Scouts founded
to prevent, 101; colonialism and,
6–7; nationalism and, 95–96;
power dynamics of, 9–10; sex
tourism and, 74
International Action Network on
Small Arms Women's Network,
14, 24–25, 26, 27, 28, 344–45,
366–67n18
International Crimes Court, 354,
368n19
International Domestic Workers
Network, 14, 336–39, *340*, 356
International Gay and Lesbian
Human Rights Commission, 14
International Labor Organization,
39, 70, 314–15, 326, 336–37, 338,
339–41, *340*, 343, 354
International Ladies Garment
Workers Union, 270
International Monetary Fund, 209,
276, 278, 299, 354, 362n3
International Network of Women
in Black, 13
International Organization for
Migration, 379n69

international politics, 358–59;
banana industry and, 211–13,
247–49; conventional (nonfeminist) understandings of, 352;
diplomatic wives and, 187–88; of
domestic work, 309–10;
feminist-informed research
into, 3–8, 12–13, 348–59; of
garment industry, 250, 261–63,
268–71, 275–79; gender-incurious
commentators on, 10–11, 32–35;
imagining, 1–3; marriage and,
141, 178–81; masculinities in,
28–32; military bases and,
126–27, 133–34, 141, 168–69;
military sexual assault and, 156;
nationalism and, 111; as personal,
349–53; of prostitution, 168–69;
sex tourism in, 72–80; tourism
and, 40, 80–82; women as
needing to become informed
about, 32–36
international trade, 80
International Trafficking in
Women Conference (New York,
NY; 1988), 377n60
International Union of Food,
Agricultural, Hotel, Restaurant,
Catering, Tobacco and Allied
Workers' Association (IUF),
337–38
International War Crimes Court,
161
International Women's Health
Coalition, 13
Internet, 74, 80, 128, 297, 343
Internet pornography, 350
Intifadah, First, 113–14
investment, 351–52
Invisible War, The (documentary
film; 2012), 395n45
Iran, 25, 27, 79, 85, 104–5, 176, 362n3

Servicemembers Legal Defense
Network, 393n33
Service Women's Action Network,
395n46
Sevastopol (Ukraine), 127
sewing machine, 265–66
sexism, 390n14; in agriculture,
230–31; in foreign service corps,
353; institutional, 395n44;
stereotyping, 70–71
sex slavery, 40, 76, 160–61
sex tourism: beauty pageants and,
62; defined, 74–75; feminist-
informed research into, 350;
gay/lesbian, 72–73; gendered
alliances in, 76–77; sex trafficking and, 74, 75–80; in Thailand,
73–74
sex trafficking, 74, 75–80, 378–
79n62, 379n69
sexual assault: conventional
narrow understandings of, 16;
feminist-informed research
into, 156; at military bases, 134,
395n46, 400n75; against women
domestic workers, 329; against
women soldiers, 149, 153–56,
395n45; women's tourism and, 58
sexual harassment: at banana
plantations, 234, 247; conventional narrow understandings
of, 17; of domestic workers, 325,
336; prostitution and, 235–36;
women's tourism and, 58
sexuality, sewing machine and, 266
sexual trafficking, 427n34
sex workers, 1–2, 76. *See also*
prostitution; women in
prostitution
Shanghai Cooperation Organization, 177
Shenzhen (China), 69

Shubert, Lee, 214, 215
Sierra Leone, 218
silences, 153
Sina Weibo (Chinese microblog
site), 297
Singapore, 322, 323, 324, 330–31, 340,
372n26
Singapore Airlines, 66
single mothers, 317
Sirleaf, Ellen Johnson, 5, 352, 362n3
SITRATERCO (Sindicato de
Trabajadores de la Tela
Railroad Company), 241–43, *244*
Skype, 343
slavery, 21–22, 366n16
slave trade, 218
Slovakia, 84
Slovaks, 85
Slut Walks, 13
small businesses, women-owned,
71–72, *72*
smallholder systems, 239–40,
245–46, 248
Smedley, Beryl, 182, 184, 188,
401–2n19
Smith, John, 6
social class: at banana plantations,
228; colonialism and, 94–95;
conventional (nonfeminist)
understandings of, 32; of
diplomatic wives, 197; "double
day" and, 316–18; feminist-
informed research into, 356; of
foreign-service families, 189–90;
jeans and, 270; masculinity and,
228; military bases and, 133,
157–58; nationalism and, 119, 123;
women domestic workers and,
310–12, 313, 319, 320–27; women
garment workers and, 259; in
women's movements, 289, 291,
294, 316; women soldiers and,

United Nations Women's Conference (Beijing; 1995), 164

United Nations World Tourism Organization, 39, 70

United States: antibases activism in, 399n71; anti-sex-trafficking legislation in, 78; antislavery movement in, 21–22, 366n16; ATT unratified in, 367–68n19; banana trade in, 212, 218–19, 223; banking industry in, 278; battered women's movement in, 146; British embassy in, 187; British relations with, 187; cotton production in, 268; defense contractors from, 378n62, 388n1, 400n75; deindustrialization in, 270–71, 286; domestic military bases in, 147–48, 157, 390n10; domestic worker political organizing in, 330–31, 333–36; economic/political inequality in, 356; as empire, 85, 126, 219, 384n22, 389n3; "family reintegration" plan of, 166; feminist media innovations in, 19–20; foreign domestic workers in, 308–9, 322, 330–31, 333–36, 426–27n34; foreign military bases of, 92–93, 126–27, 134–41, 187, 274, 388n1, 389n3, 410n5; free trade treaties of, 294; garment industry in, 258, 268–71; as gay/lesbian-friendly tourist destination, 73; ILO Convention 189 unratified in, 341; imperial expansion of, 49–50; industrial revolution in, 318; industry types in, 285; jobs outsourced from, 268–71; Korean diaspora in, 93; labor trafficking in, 426–27n34;

marriage reform campaign in, 209; masculinity and imperialism in, 384n22; militarized masculinity in, 150; military recruitment in, 143; minimum wage laws in, 333–34; nationalist rhetoric in, 86; -owned garment stores, 254–55; prostitution in, 157; racialized military prostitution system of, 160, 161–62, 397n57, 399n69, 429n1; sex trafficking in, 77, 79; single mothers in, 317; tourist industry in, 369n1, 372n26; women as ambassadors to, 174–75, *175, 176*; women as bank executives in, 277; women as factory workers in, 264; women as household heads in, 317; women as tourists in, 46–47; women-owned farmland in, 231; women soldiers in, 151–56; women's suffrage movement in, 12; world's fairs in, 49–51

United States Agency for International Development, 204

United States Air Force, 133, 163–64, 167, 169, 170–72, 254–55

United States Army: 442nd Regimental Combat Team, 65; 6888th Central Postal Directory Battalion, 390n14

United States Centennial Exhibition (Philadelphia, PA; 1876), 219

United States Congress, 127, 152, 197, 200

United States Defense Department, 128, 142, 147, 152, 154, 168, 389n7, 393n33, 410n5

United States Federal Reserve, 278